D1297563

Military, State and Society in Pakistan

Also by Hasan-Askari Rizvi

PAKISTAN AND THE GEOSTRATEGIC ENVIRONMENT: A Study of Foreign Policy

THE MILITARY AND POLITICS IN PAKISTAN

INTERNAL STRIFE AND EXTERNAL INTERVENTION: India's Role in the Civil War in East Pakistan (Bangladesh)

Military, State and Society in Pakistan

Hasan-Askari Rizvi

First published in Great Britain 2000 by
MACMILLAN PRESS LTD
Houndmills, Basingstoke, Hampshire RG21 6XS and London
Companies and representatives throughout the world

A catalogue record for this book is available from the British Library.

ISBN 0–333–79388–9

First published in the United States of America 2000 by
ST. MARTIN'S PRESS, INC.,
Scholarly and Reference Division,
175 Fifth Avenue, New York, N.Y. 10010

ISBN 0–312–23193–8

Library of Congress Cataloging-in-Publication Data
Rizvi, Hasan Askari, 1945–
Military, state, and society in Pakistan / Hasan-Askari Rizvi.
p. cm.
Includes bibliographical references and index.
ISBN 0–312–23193–8 (cloth)
1. Civil–military relations—Pakistan. 2. Pakistan—Politics and government. 3.
Pakistan—Armed Forces—Political activity. I. Title.
JQ629.A38 C5865 2000
322'.5'095491—dc21

99–055831

This book is printed on paper suitable for recycling and made from fully managed and sustained
forest sources.

10 9 8 7 6 5 4 3 2 1
09 08 07 06 05 04 03 02 01 00

Printed and bound in Great Britain by
Antony Rowe Ltd, Chippenham, Wiltshire

Contents

List of Tables

Abbreviations

ADC	Aide-de-Camp
AKMC	Azad Kashmir Muslim Conference
APMSO	All Pakistan *Mohajir* Student Organization
APP	Associated Press of Pakistan
ATA	Anti-Terrorism Act, 1997
BD	Basic Democracies
BDS	Balochistan *Dehi Mahafiz*
BNP	Balochistan National Party
BSF	Border Security Force (India)
CENTO	Central Treaty Organization (formerly Baghdad Pact)
CII	Council of Islamic Ideology
C-in-C	Commander-in-Chief
CMLA	Chief Martial Law Administrator
COAS	Chief of Army Staff
COP	Combined Opposition Parties, 1964–65
CSP	Civil Service of Pakistan
CSS	Central Superior Services
DAC	Democratic Action Commitee, 1969
DCC	Defence Committee of the Cabinet
DMG	District Management Group
EBDO	Elective Bodies Disqualification Order, 1959
EBR	East Bengal Regiment
EPR	East Pakistan Rifles
ESAF	Extended Structural Adjustment Fund, IMF
FIA	Federal Investigation Agency
FSC	Federal *Shariat* Court
FSF	Federal Security Force
FWO	Frontier Works Organization
GHQ	General Headquarters
GOC	General-Officer-Commanding
IB	Intelligence Bureau
ICO	Indian Commissioned Officers
ICS	Indian Civil Service
IJI	*Islami Jamhoori Itehad* (Islamic Democratic Alliance)
IJT	*Islami Jamiat-i-Tulba*
INA	Indian National Army
IPG	Independent Parliamentary Group
IPS	Indian Political Service
ISI	Inter-Services Intelligence

JAS	*Jamaat-i-Ahle Hadith*
JCO	Junior Commissioned Officer
JCSC	Joint Chiefs of Staff Committee
JI	*Jamaat-i-Islami*
JUI	*Jamiat-ul-Ulema-i-Islam*
JUP	*Jamiat-ul-Ulema-i-Pakistan*
JWP	*Jamhoori Watan* Party
KCO	King's Commissioned Officer
KKH	Korakoram Highway
KSP	Krishak Saramak Party
KT	*Khaksar Tehrik*
LFO	Legal Framework Order, 1970
MI	Military Intelligence
MQM	*Muttahida Qaumi* Movement (formerly *Mohajir Quami* Movement)
MQM-H	*Mohajir Quami* Movement – *Haqiqi*
MRD	Movement for the Restoration of Democracy
NAP	National *Awami* Party
NCO	Non-Commissioned Officer
NDF	National Democratic Front, 1962
NDP	National Democratic Party
NLC	National Logistics Cell
NUST	National University of Science and Technology
NWFP	North West Frontier Province
OIC	Organization of Islamic Conference
OML	Official Muslim League
OPG	Official Parliamentary Group
PBF	Punjab Boundary Force
PCO	Provisional Constitutional Order, 1981
PDA	Pakistan Democratic Alliance
PDF	Pakistan Democratic Front
PDM	Pakistan Democratic Movement, 1967
PDP	Pakistan Democratic Party
PIA	Pakistan International Airlines
PIU	Produce Index Unit
PLS	Profit and Loss Sharing
PMA	Pakistan Military Academy, Kakul
PML	Pakistan Muslim League
PML-J	Pakistan Muslim League – Junejo
PML-N	Pakistan Muslim League – Nawaz Sharif
PML-P	Pakistan Muslim League – Pir Pagara
PML-Q	Pakistan Muslim League – Malik Qasim
PNA	Pakistan National Alliance
PODO	Public Offices (Disqualification) Order, 1959

POW	Prisoner of War
PPP	Pakistan People's Party
PRODA	Public and Representative Offices (Disqualification) Act, 1949
RCO	Revival of the Constitution Order, 1985
SCO	Special Communication Organization
SEATO	South East Asia Treaty Organization
SSG	Special Services Group
TI	*Tehrik-i-Istiqlal*
TJP	*Tehrik-i-Jafaria Pakistan* (formerly TNFJ)
TNFJ	*Tehrik-i-Nifaz-i-Fiqah-i-Jafaria*
UDF	United Democratic Front, 1973
UF	United Front, 1954
USMAAG	United States Military Assistance Advisory Group
VCO	Viceroy's Commissioned Officers
WAPDA	Water and Power Development Authority

Preface

The military in Pakistan is the most formidable and autonomous political actor capable of influencing the nature and direction of political change. This, however, represents a major shift in Pakistan's military heritage. For while the military was integral to British Imperial rule and served as its ultimate shield, it avoided active involvement in politics and accepted the primacy of civilian government. This changed gradually in the post-independence period as the top commanders expanded their role into the political arena. The changes in civil–military relations were manifested in different forms: an active role for the military in policy-making in collaboration with the bureaucracy, displacement of civilian government in October 1958, March 1969, July 1977 and October 1999, direct military rule, civilianization of military rule, and the military's penetration of civilian state institutions, the economy and society.

This book endeavours to study the changing patterns of civil–military relations in Pakistan with the objective of understanding its causes and dynamics, its impact on the polity and society, as well as the military itself. It also examines the methods adopted by various military regimes to extricate themselves from direct rule, the exercise of political clout by the military from the sidelines, and the problems of the civilian regimes that replaced military regimes. These issues have been studied with reference to four clusters of factors: the dynamics of the polity; the institutional strengths and organizational resources of the military; interaction across the functional boundaries between the military and civil society; and the international factors and considerations.

The long years of direct and indirect rule have enabled the military to spread out so widely into the government, the economy and society that its clout and influence no longer depend on controlling the levers of power. It is derived from its organizational strengths and its significant presence in all sectors of government and society. The military prefers to pursue its interests from the sidelines. Had the Sharif government (February 1997–October 1999) not attempted to undermine the military's autonomy, avoided interference in its internal and organizational affairs, and not attempted to divide the senior command in the way it divided the Supreme Court and replaced its Chief Justice, the top brass would not have dislodged the civil government. The October 1999 coup was an institutional response to what senior commanders perceived as a threat to the professional and corporate interests of the Army.

This study was undertaken while the author was Quaid-i-Azam Professor at the Southern Asian Institute, School of International and Public Affairs,

Columbia University, New York. The author acknowledges with thanks the cooperation and support of his colleagues Valentine Daniel, Philip Oldenburg, Leonard Gordon and Rounaq Jahan. Thanks are also due to Naveed Iqbal, MD, and Shaheryar Azhar, for their interest in the work. However, the author alone is responsible for what is written in this book.

H.A.R.

Prologue: the October 1999 Coup

The coup of 12 October 1999 put an end to Pakistan's troubled democratic experiment and brought the military back to power. This was a response to Prime Minister Nawaz Sharif's persistent disregard of the norms of civil–military relations which had developed in the post-withdrawal period since 1985 (see chapters 1 and 10) and attempts by him to divide the top commanders and control the Army by replacing Army Chief General Pervez Musharraf with a junior officer, known for his loyalty to Sharif.

The military was perturbed by the civilian government's political and economic mismanagement and especially by growing civilian disaffection in the smaller provinces. But the senior commanders would have continued to tolerate civilian government in view of the complexities of the domestic socio-political and economic landscape, and a global environment that was not conducive to military rule. The military overcame the inhibitions caused by these factors and dislodged Nawaz Sharif because the latter forced a situation on the senior commanders either to accept the dismissal of the Army Chief, who was on an official visit to Sri Lanka, or contest the decision. The new appointee, serving as Director General, ISI, at that time, did not command the confidence of the senior commanders, and his appointment meant that several senior officers would have lost their posts. When, on the afternoon of 12 October, the Principal Staff Officers at the Army Headquarters and the Corps Commander, Rawalpindi, learnt of the civilian government's decision to replace the Army Chief, they asked the government to suspend the order until the Army Chief returned. He was due to return that evening. However, Nawaz Sharif thought that Musharraf's removal could be more easily effected while he was out of the country. Nawaz Sharif ordered the state radio and television to announce the change of Army command; television coverage also showed the new Army Chief being decorated with the insignia of full general and then calling on the Prime Minister. Thereupon the senior commanders and the Corps Commander, Rawalpindi, moved troops to Islamabad and took control of the television station. Later, they cordoned off the Prime Minister's house, and asked Nawaz Sharif to withdraw his orders. When he refused, they arrested him and the new appointee to the top position in the Army. While the Army was busy taking over Islamabad, another dramatic development was taking place in Karachi. In accordance with a pre-planned scheme by the civilian government in Islamabad, the civilian and police officials in Karachi closed Karachi airport and ordered the Pakistan International Airlines flight from Colombo carrying Musharraf and about 200 passengers and crew to land somewhere outside Pakistan. When the pilot insisted on landing in Karachi due to shortage of fuel, they asked him to land at Nawabshah, 200 kilometres north of Karachi, and made arrangements for the arrest of Pervez Musharraf by the police. Meanwhile, the Corps Commander, Karachi, moved his troops and dislodged pro-Sharif police and civilian authorities from the airport, and Musharraf's aircraft landed safely. By the time he reached the Karachi Corps headquarters, his commanders were in control of Islamabad.

Nawaz Sharif had appointed Pervez Musharraf Army Chief in October 1998 on Jehangir Karamat's resignation when Nawaz Sharif took exception to Karamat's public comments on the political and economic situation in the country. Musharraf had the reputation of a thorough professional but Nawaz Sharif hoped that an Urdu-speaking 'mohajir' Army Chief presiding over a predominantly Punjabi-Pakhtun Army top command would be weak and unassertive, making it possible for Nawaz Sharif to strengthen his hold over the military. Initially, relations between the government and the military were cordial, with Musharraf describing his relationship with the political leadership as a 'partnership' between 'the massive mandate [of the civilian government] and the military'. However, he expressed concern about the state of the national economy.[1] While helping the government to overcome political and economic problems, the Army Chief reiterated on- and off-the-record statements concerning the military's well-known position that it would neither serve the partisan interests of civilian leaders nor could it be pushed around.

The discord in civil–military relations in mid-1999 can be attributed to three major factors. First, the Sharif government's personalized and whimsical governance by appointing trusted personnel or nonentities to key positions so that there was no resistance to the decisions made by Nawaz Sharif in consultation with a small group of advisers hailing from the Lahore/Islamabad area. After appointing loyalists to the posts of President and Provincial Governors and taming major state institutions, including the upper judiciary, through constitutional amendments and political manipulation, it was natural for him to consider penetrating the hard shell of the military.

Second, the political government ignored the reality of Pakistani politics that political stability depended on trouble-free interaction with the military who were interested in protecting and advancing their professional and corporate interests from the sidelines. Any attempt on the part of civilian leaders to monopolize power by upsetting the delicate balance of power in the polity was bound to create problems.

Third, encouraged by the resignation of Jehangir Karamat in October 1998, the Sharif government violated the well-known norm of civil–military relations which emphasized respect for the military's autonomy and civilian

[1] See M. Ziauddin, 'Dateline Islamabad: The Mystery Deepens'. *Dawn*, 15 November 1999.

non-interference in internal organizational matters and service affairs (see chapters 1 and 10). Nawaz Sharif began to interfere with promotions and the transfer of senior officers, including the posting of the Corps Commanders. This was resented by the top brass. Reports of the efforts of political leaders to make inroads into the military and cultivate certain commanders by playing on Punjabi ethnicity alarmed the Army high command. They felt that this would undermine army discipline and organizational coherence.

The civilian government wanted to consolidate its hold over the military for yet another reason. The opposition had embarked on popular mobilization by promoting street agitation against the government. Several opposition leaders had made direct and indirect appeals to the Army to remove the Sharif government. This raised the question of the disposition of the military in the evolving domestic political scenario. The government felt that it must have the unqualified support of the military to deal with the opposition. This could not be ensured without appointing loyalists to key posts, a strategy adopted by Nawaz Sharif to control civilian institutions. The government circles targeted the Army Chief, Pervez Musharraf, for criticism, on the grounds that he had launched the Kargil operation in Kashmir without the prior approval of the Prime Minister. This annoyed the Army because the Kargil operation was a joint decision made by the civil and military authorities but, by September 1999, the civil government had repudiated its responsibility. Meanwhile, reports began to circulate in Islamabad and Lahore that Nawaz Sharif wanted to remove the Army Chief in order to secure this flank. The senior commanders were already unhappy about Karamat's resignation; and they were not willing to let another Army Chief go down under civilian pressure for no good reason. They felt that a replay of the Karamat episode would undermine the Army's autonomy and corporate entity. The Corps Commanders decided to resist such a move.

The Army Chief confronted Nawaz Sharif in a meeting in mid-September by presenting concrete evidence of Sharif's consultations with his aides on ways to replace him with a loyal general. The civilian leadership backtracked and agreed to allow Musharraf to carry on as Chairman, Joint Chiefs of Staff Committee, as an additional charge until the end of his term as Army Chief in October 2001. This was decoy operation to pacify senior commanders, but the civilian government did not abandon its plan to oust Musharraf. Meanwhile, the Army headquarters replaced the Corps Commander, Mangla, and retired the Corps Commander, Quetta, for their alleged links with Nawaz Sharif; the latter had meetings with the Prime Minister in violation of army discipline.

Pervez Musharraf left for an official visit to Colombo, Sri Lanka, on 9 October. The civilian government decided to use his absence to remove him. This plan was finalized during Nawaz Sharif's hurriedly arranged one-day visit to the UAE on 11 October so that the MI did not get wind of the plan. Nevertheless, in the absence of the Army Chief, the Army headquarters was fully alert to such a possibility. Thus, when Nawaz Sharif decided to strike, the senior commanders jointly decided to take counter-measures to defend the Army Chief and the Army as an institution. The takeover was swift and bloodless and the civilian government crumbled instantly. The coup was widely welcomed in the country. However, it faced the problem of acceptability at the international level. The Commonwealth condemned the coup and suspended Pakistan from the organization. The European Union was equally critical of the displacement of the civilian government. The European Parliament resolution also made adverse comments on the establishment of military government. US criticism was carefully worded, but expressed a clear displeasure over the change. The Western states wanted a deadline from the military government for the return to democracy and constitutional rule. Pakistan's military rulers were not willing to give a definite date, maintaining that such a commitment could not be made without achieving some significant progress on their political agenda. International pressure was not expected to change the priorities of the military regime. It did make the military regime cautious and slow in adopting policies and taking action against the leaders of the ousted regime found involved in corruption and misuse of state resources and power. Yet another reason for delay in taking definite steps for policy implementation was that the military had no blueprint for the future when it assumed power. Therefore, the new leaders took a month or so to make up their minds about policy issues, causing some disappointment among the population who expected the military to move swiftly to tackle political and economic problems. International pressure eased somewhat over 5–6 weeks, but the West maintained a negative attitude towards the military regime. Such a negative perception was in sharp contrast to the support the new military rulers commanded within Pakistan. How long they can continue to enjoy this support is more critical to the future of the military regime than external pressures.

President Rafiq Tarar, installed by Nawaz Sharif, continued to hold office and Pervez Musharraf assumed the newly coined title of Chief Executive, whose recommendations were binding on the President. The federal and provincial governments were dismissed and the parliament and the provincial assemblies were suspended. The 1973 Constitution was also suspended, but the new government was to function as close to it as possible, subject to the overriding power of the Chief Executive. The country was not placed under martial law, although the emergency imposed by Nawaz Sharif in May 1998 remained in place. No restriction was imposed on political parties or political activities; freedom of the press was respected. No military courts were established; the regular courts continued to function, but these could not question the authority and orders of the Chief Executive. A new National Security Council and a federal cabinet headed by the Chief Executive were appointed. Governors headed provincial governments. The Punjab and NWFP had retired Lt.-Generals as Governors; in Sindh, a retired Air Marshal was appointed Governor. In the case of Balochistan, a former Chief Justice of Balochistan High Court assumed this office. Unlike the three previous military regimes in Pakistan, the new military government kept Army personnel in the background and ran the administration through civilian institutions and officials, described as the 'civil–military combine' by the military rulers. The military established monitoring cells at different levels to oversee and supervise the working of the civilian institutions.

The new military rulers have not given a date for holding elections and the return to democracy. They have set out seven major priorities and do not intend to hold elections until substantial progress has been made towards achieving these goals. These include (1) rebuilding national confidence and morale; (2) strengthening the federation, removing inter-province disharmony and restoring national cohesion; (3) reviving the economy and restoring investor confidence; (4) ensuring law and order and dispensing speedy justice; (5) depoliticising state institutions; (6) devolution of power to the grassroots level; (7) ensuring swift and across-the-board accountability. The major focus of the new military government is the recovery of bank loans from wilful defaulters, accountability of those misusing state power and resources, or those who made money through kickbacks and other illegal means, or who evaded taxes and other government dues, including non-payment of utility bills. A number of big industrialists and business people were arrested in November 1999 on the above counts. Nawaz Sharif and four officials were arrested on the charge of not allowing the PIA aircraft to land in Karachi, endangering the lives of 200 passengers and crew, including Pervez Musharraf. Several other officials and members of the Sharif family were arrested on charges of corruption, misuse of authority and related issues. The supporters of the ousted Nawaz government challenged the imposition of military rule in the Supreme Court. All this would produce a long drawn legal and constitutional battle in the civilian courts.

The military government did not face any problem in consolidating its position and thus it did not impose any harsh rules or punishments. Popular support for the military regime is conditional though on the hope of the people that the military government will take firm steps to end corruption and recover defaulted bank loans as well as provide some economic relief to the general population. If the military government achieves some of these objectives and fulfils the expectations of the people, it may not face a political challenge in the near future. If it falters or faces serious challenges to its authority due, *inter alia*, to policy management problems, or factors internal to the military or international pressures, it will not continue with the present lenient and liberal disposition.

The initial success of the military regime does not mean that it will be equally successful in resolving the basic socio-economic and political problems and set up political institutions that will function without the support of the top brass. It seems that Musharraf will resort to a carefully planned transition to democracy through constitutional and political engineering and cooption of political leaders. He may not have a grand vision for the future, but he is expected to institute changes in the constitutional arrangement to ensure checks and balances among key institutions and officials as well as create an institutional framework for the military's formal participation in decision-making. The pace of transition to democracy depends on the dynamics of domestic politics, the disposition and policy choices of the senior commanders and interaction between the military regime and the political forces. International pressures and the manipulation of foreign economic assistance have implications for the performance and longevity of the military regime. However, the domestic developments and considerations will be decisive. The senior commanders still uphold professionalism and are conscious of the complexities of the domestic socio-economic scene. They also recognize the inhospitable international environment for military rule. But they are not prepared to stand on the sidelines and let the country slide into the sort of uncertainty and anarchy that has engulfed Afghanistan. Their professional and corporate interests are closely linked to the survival and orderly functioning of the Pakistani state and society.

1
Introduction

The military's pre-eminent position in Pakistan's politics and society is the crystallization of the importance it has enjoyed from the beginning. Pakistan came into existence in extremely difficult conditions and faced serious domestic problems and external security pressures. State survival became the primary concern of the rulers of Pakistan, who equated it with an assertive federal government, strong defence posture, high defence expenditure and an emphasis on monolithic nationalism. The imperative of state security and a strong state apparatus were given precedence over the need to create participatory political institutions and processes.

The military was the major beneficiary of this approach because it was viewed as a guarantee of external security and a bulwark against internal turmoil and collapse. This gave a basis to the military for expanding its role. The shift away from the primacy of the civil formed gradually. Initially, the senior commanders became powerful actors in the decision-making process and a key determinant of the national priorities in collaboration with the senior bureaucracy. In October 1958, the military assumed direct power, establishing its dominance. Though the military maintained a partnership with the bureaucracy during the years in power (1958–62, 1969–71, 1977–85) and cultivated socio-economic groups to sustain itself, it never allowed any doubts to arise as to who was in command. The military withdrew from power twice, in June 1962 and December 1985, through planned disengagements by restructuring the political arrangements to its preferences, co-opting a section of the political elite and ensuring a continuity of major policies and key personnel in the post-withdrawal period. Once, in December 1971, military rule came to an abrupt ending after the military lost the Bangladesh war to India.

A new pattern of 'soft' or 'non-takeover' intervention has developed in the aftermath of General Zia-ul-Haq's death in August 1988. The emphasis has shifted from assuming power directly, although that option is available, to playing a more subtle, but still ubiquitous role from the sidelines. The military has an important influence over foreign, security and key domestic issues and

1

moderates confrontations among feuding politicians, parties or state institutions, if such confrontations are considered threatening to political order and stability. The military can play such a role because the long years of direct and indirect rule have enabled it to spread out so widely in the government, the economy and society at large that its clout no longer depends on controlling the levers of power. It is derived from its organizational strengths and its significant presence in all sectors of the government and the society.

The Army Chief is pivotal in the power structure, and along with the President and the Prime Minister, constitutes what is described as the Triangle of Power or the Troika – an extra-constitutional arrangement for civilian–military consensus-building on key domestic, foreign policy and security issues. They meet periodically, and the Army Chief also holds meetings separately with the Prime Minister for exchanges on political and security issues. The constitutional and political changes in 1997 have reduced the powers of the President and strengthened the position of the Prime Minister, but the Army Chief continues to be a key political player. The civilian government relies heavily on the Army for managing civilian affairs and to prevent the collapse of the polity.

Another institution that has gained salience is the Corps Commanders' meeting. Presided over by the Army Chief, this meeting includes top commanders, Principal Staff Officers at the Army Headquarters and other senior officers holding strategic appointments. Its members not only discuss security and organizational and professional matters, they also deliberate on domestic issues such as law and order and political conditions, especially when the government and the opposition are engaged in intense confrontation. These discussions are meant either to outline their concern or to develop a broad-based consensus. The implementation of the consensus decision is left to the Army Chief, which strengthens his position when he interacts with the civilian leadership. He also consults the Chiefs of the Navy and the Air Force and Chairman, Joint Chiefs of Staff Committee, in a national emergency. However, it is the Army Chief who decides the actual strategies and presents the military's perspective to the civilian government.

A civil–military hybrid is emerging. The military makes a significant input to policy-making, helps the government to run the state and enjoys sufficient autonomy in its professional and service affairs. However, it neither governs directly nor controls the civilian leaders. An overall civilian/democratic dispensation is maintained, with sufficient scope of action for the political leaders in managing the affairs of the state. The military and the civilian leaders constantly engage in interaction and bargaining on major policy issues. The balance may tilt in one direction or another, depending on the stakes of the military, the issue in question and the context of the interaction. At times, strains surface in their interaction: the top commanders publicly expressing concern on the performance of the elected government; and the political leaders engaging in veiled criticism of the senior commanders or over-reacting to their comments in order to show that the civilians are in control. How durable this 'mid-way' arrangement is and whether it offers a better alternative to direct military rule are yet to be determined.

The Ascendancy of the Military

Four clusters of factors explain the decline of the civilian institutions and processes and the ascendancy of the military in Pakistan. First, the societal factors and especially conflict or cohesion in the polity and political and economic management by the government without facing a dispute as to its moral right to govern go a long way to shape civil–military relations. Second, the internal dynamics of the military establishment and its organizational resources and attributes have to be examined carefully to understand its disposition towards the polity and the society. The military's professional and corporate interests, the socio-economic background and orientations of the officers, internal cohesion, discipline and professionalism are all important determinants. Third, the interaction and transactions across the functional boundaries between the civil and the military are significant indicators of how the two influence each other. Only a stable civil government enjoying popular support and legitimacy can restrain the military to its professional domain and deal with it from a position of strength. Fourth, external factors or international environment and especially the international connections the military develops influence its political orientations and behaviour.

Pakistan faced a serious crisis of political leadership within a couple of years after independence. Quaid-i-Azam Mohammad Ali Jinnah who led the movement for the establishment of Pakistan and had a charismatic appeal to the people, died in September 1948, only 13 months after independence. Liaquat Ali Khan, his lieutenant and first Prime Minister, partially filled the gap, but he was assassinated in October 1951. They did not have sufficient time to establish and legitimize participatory institutions and processes. This was different from the situation in India, where Jawaharlal Nehru led the country as Prime Minister until his death in May 1964. Nehru's charismatic appeal was more powerful than the institutions he created, he did not establish a personalized system and insisted on developing participatory institutions and processes. By the time he died a strong tradition had been established in India that the government should renew its mandate at regular intervals and that the electoral process should play a decisive role in political change.

The political leaders in Pakistan in the post Jinnah–Liaquat period did not possess a national stature, lacked imagination and were unable to inspire the people, let alone deal with difficult political and economic problems. Many had a feudal or semi-feudal background and were primarily motivated by their personal ambitions and parochial considerations. They could not evolve a broad-based consensus on the operational norms of the polity. Constitution-making proved to be a complex and painstakingly slow process which brought to the surface sharp divergences in the perspectives and goals of the competing interests. Two constituent assemblies wrestled for over eight years with issues like federalism and autonomy for the provinces, representation in the national legislature, the Islamic state, the national language and the electoral system. By the time the first 'permanent' constitution was framed in early 1956, politics had degenerated to such an extent that it was scarcely relevant to power management.

The Muslim League, which served as the vanguard of the freedom struggle, utterly failed to transform itself from a nationalist movement into a national party which could serve as an effective political machine for aggregating diverse interests and identities into a plural and participatory national framework. This was at variance with the Congress Party of India, which successfully transformed itself into a national party and functioned effectively as a party of consensus until Indira Gandhi began to squash it in the 1970s. It had developed roots amongst the masses in the 1920s as a result of Mahatma Gandhi's passive resistance movement and emphasis on organization. It produced several leaders of national stature who had acquired sufficient experience of collaborative political activity. The emphasis on consensus-building enabled the Congress Party either to resolve its internal conflicts, or to keep them within manageable limits. The Muslim League worked at the popular level and became a mass party only during 1940–7 and a large number of the leaders from the Muslim majority areas joined the party during this period, especially during the last 2–3 years, and thus had a limited experience of working together as a team. It relied heavily on the towering personality of Jinnah and, once the main objective, i.e. the establishment of Pakistan, was achieved, and Jinnah and Liaquat were gone, it lost momentum and there was no one to keep the party together. The Muslim League suffered from another drawback: most of its senior leaders, especially those holding cabinet positions at the federal level, came from Muslim minority provinces and lacked a popular base in the Pakistani territory, i.e. Muslim majority provinces. As they had faced problems with the leaders hailing from these provinces in the pre-independence period, distrust continued to taint their interaction in the post-independence period, which intensified organizational problems of the party and the national/federal leadership was not inclined towards holding early elections. The Muslim League could not develop mechanisms and skills to deal with internal dissension and conflicts. The political parties set up by Muslim League defectors and others did not offer a viable alternative; these suffered from similar problems. The political leaders, especially those in power, showed little, if any, respect for democratic and parliamentary principles and conventions. Such conditions were bound to compromise the ability of civilian governments to assert their leadership.

As the political forces fragmented and the political institutions declined, the bureaucratic elite gained the upper hand and dominated policy-making. The appointment of Ghulam Muhammad, a former bureaucrat belonging to Indian Audit and Accounts Service, as Governor General in October 1951, who was succeeded by another bureaucrat-cum-military man, Iskander Mirza, in August 1955, set the stage for the ascendancy of the bureaucracy, bolstered by the military from the background. They engaged in alliance-building with the feudal, industrial and commercial elite to entrench their position. This 'ruling alliance drawn mainly from the top echelons of the bureaucracy and the army' adopted 'a concerted strategy' to exploit and manipulate rivalries among the political leaders, which accentuated political fragmentation and ministerial crises.[1] When, in 1954, the political leaders attempted to take on the bureaucratic–military axis by reducing the powers of the Governor General and completed the draft of a constitution that reduced the head of state to a titular office in the British parliamentary tradition, the Governor General retaliated by dissolving the Constituent Assembly and dismissing the government. The confirmation of the dismissal by the Federal Court sealed the fate of democracy in Pakistan.[2] The bureaucratic–military elite pursued centralized and authoritarian governance, changed federal and provincial governments at will, and excluded those who questioned their political management.

The military in Pakistan maintained a professional, disciplined, cohesive and task-oriented profile with a strong *esprit de corps*. It was viewed as important to state survival from the beginning due to its role in state-building and Pakistan's acute security problems. The civilian and military leaders were equally convinced that Pakistan's troubled relations with India (a stronger military power) and Afghanistan's irredentist territorial claims presented a serious threat to national identity and territorial integrity which led them to allocate substantial portion of national resources to the military. Strong religious fervour also created support for building a strong military in order to cope with external threats, especially from India. The refugees from India, Kashmiris and those connected with the Kashmir war were equally enthusiastic about maintaining a strong defence posture. The military also benefited from Pakistan's participation in Western alliances and especially its security relations with the United States.

Traditionally, the image of the military in Pakistan has been good. It has enjoyed respect partly due to the martial traditions of the Punjab and North West Frontier Province (NWFP) and partly because of the Islamic concept of *Jihad* (holy war), *Ghazi* (victorious) and *Shaheed* (martyr). The military's strength is also a consequence of its strong ethnic and regional cohesion. The significant majority of the army officers and other ranks hail from the Punjab, NWFP and the tribal areas. These two groups (Punjabis and Pathans/Pakhtuns) have not only developed strong mutual ties but have also established links with the civilian bureaucratic elite, most of whom have a similar ethnic background. The Punjabi–Pakhtun composition of the Army has been a source of strength which has *inter alia* contributed to enhancing the military's efficacy in politics. The interaction between the civil and the military worked to the advantage of the latter. The military was integral to state-building from the beginning and it was viewed as central to state survival. This strengthened the position of the military in the polity and its senior commanders began to perceive themselves as the guarantors of state survival, a self-image that was reinforced over time as the civilian governments, overwhelmed by the problems of governance, increasingly sought the military's support for administering the state.

The military's relevance to state survival and its self-image as the guarantor of the state was in a way a carryover from the British period. The military had played an important role in extending and consolidating the East India Company's domain and subsequently served as the ultimate shield of British rule. The Army top brass were conscious of their role as the bulwark of the Raj, undertaking external defence, internal security and support to the civilian authorities, security operations against the Pathan tribesmen in the northwest, and participation in the overseas military expeditions of the empire. Within the overall framework of civilian supremacy, the military and the civilian government in British India were quite often equal partners. The civilian authority in India, being the administration of a colony, was responsible to the British government in London, as was the Indian military. The Commander-in-Chief (C-in-C), with stature and connections in the power structure in London, could apply pressure on the civilian authority in India. He commanded all three services and was second in order of precedence to the Governor General/Viceroy, and sat in his executive council and the central legislature, which undoubtedly gave him a significant role in policy-making in British India. Defence expenditure constituted the single largest item in British India's budget and more financial resources were placed at the disposal of the military than education, health care and irrigation put together.

Though Jinnah emphasized the primacy of the civilian authority, the political and security conditions were so precarious that he could hardly question the imperial legacy of assigning importance to the military. Jinnah gave much weight to the opinion of the top brass of the military on the security affairs. He reversed the decision to send troops to Kashmir in October 1947 on the persuasion of the Army authorities. In April–May 1948, the Pakistan government formally inducted its Army into the Kashmir war after the Army Chief tendered such advice. However, it was in the post-Jinnah period that the political leaders began to lose ground to the bureaucracy and the military. As political fragmentation and ministerial crises deepened, the civilian leaders could not check the ascendancy of the bureaucratic–military elite. Their heavy dependence on the military to cope with civilian–administrative problems eroded their legitimacy and strengthened the senior commanders' perception of the military's role as the guarantors of the state.

The military's importance in the polity can also be measured from the allocation of national resources for defence and security. The budgetary allocations for defence remained very high from the beginning, which reflected a shared view of the civilian and military elite to build strong defences. All governments, civilian and military, were equally supportive of making ample resources available to the military; defence expenditure was the single largest item in the national budget until the early 1990s, when debt servicing began to top the list, pushing defence expenditure to second position. Pakistan is a classic example of a country where the abundance of resources for defence and military programmes is in sharp contrast to resource-scarcity for human development.

International factors and connections, especially arms transfers, military technology and training, do influence the disposition and options of the senior commanders. In the case of Pakistan, the American connection, developed in the mid-1950s, played an important role in shaping the military's professional and political profile. Not only did this give confidence to the military to withstand India's military superiority, it also strengthened its position in the domestic context. The acquisition of modern technology and organizational skills which could also be applied to the civilian sectors, as well as better training and weapons, accentuated the already existing institutional imbalance between the professional, task-oriented and confident military and the weak and incoherent political institutions. The growing strength of the military enabled the service headquarters to enjoy greater autonomy in professional and service matters and disbursement of the defence expenditure. The military became 'too powerful' for the political leaders 'to tamper with and [it] virtually ran itself without outside interference'.[3] The military autonomy strengthened over time and the top brass resented any interference of the civilian government in what they considered to be their professional and internal service affairs. All Army Chiefs during January 1951–December 1971 (Ayub Khan, Mohammad Musa and Yahya Khan, as against eight Army Chiefs[4] in India during the same period) served for extended terms.

However, there is no evidence available to suggest that the international factors, especially American connections, were decisive to the military's decision to stage a coup in October 1958, although the US ambassador to Pakistan knew in advance of the impending change and Ayub Khan had a good rapport with US administration. The same could be said about the coups in March 1969 and July 1977, although both military regimes later enjoyed American goodwill and support. In 1971, Nixon's 'tilt' towards Pakistan bolstered Yahya Khan's military regime. The longevity of the military regime of Zia-ul-Haq was attributed mainly to the American diplomatic, military and economic support against the backdrop of Soviet military intervention in Afghanistan. Zulfikar Ali Bhutto and his party men accused the US of supporting his political adversaries in the course of street agitation against his regime in March–June 1977 as a retaliation against his 'defiance' on the nuclear issue and other foreign policy affairs. Although there was little concrete evidence to establish American involvement in Bhutto's overthrow, a number of US policy measures in the summer of 1977 amply showed American attempt to embarrass the Bhutto regime at a time when its survival was threatened by street agitation, emboldening the right-wing/Islamic opposition and the military.

In the post-Cold War environment, international considerations continue to be important because the military commanders regard security relations with the industrialized Western states as crucial to advancing their professional goals, i.e. procurement of weapons and military technology. Though the Pakistan military resisted American pressures on the nuclear programme and shared the decision with the civilian government to explode nuclear devices on 28 and 30 May 1998, the senior commanders attach importance to improving interaction with the US and want to maintain some relationship with the American military establishment. That is why Pakistan's senior commanders want to project themselves as a professional force capable of playing a stabilizing role in the polity and the region. They fully recognize that the current global agenda, with an emphasis on democratization and good governance, economic liberalization and free trade, has created an unfavourable international climate for military rule. This contributes to the military's avoidance of direct assumption of power and support to constitutionalism and democracy. However, if the domestic political situation worsens, a minimum order and stability cannot be maintained and the military's professional and corporate interests are undermined, international factors may not hold back the top commanders.

Military Regimes

The coups of October 1958, March 1969 and July 1977 dislodged the governments that at the time were facing serious crises of legitimacy, including strong challenges at the popular level. The imposition of martial law was not contested by any civilian group and the military had no problem in assuming and consolidating power. The military established its hegemony marked by its dominance of core political institutions and processes and monopolistic control over strategic policy issues.[5] This also gave rise to 'militarism', making it possible for the military directly or indirectly to exercise 'a decisive influence upon Pakistan's domestic and foreign policies'.[6] The military commanders used their dominant position to shape the political arrangements to their preferences and satisfaction. They redefined the parameters of political competition through executive orders and decrees, constitutional and legal changes, and manipulation of political forces so as to entrench themselves and promote a leadership that was prepared to engage in politics in accordance with their game plan.

The experience of Pakistan suggests that it may be easy for a professional and disciplined army to take over the reins of government. But, a successful coup and its initial accomplishments are no guarantee that it will be equally successful in resolving the basic social, economic and political problems that are the root causes of the fragility and malfunctioning of the civilian institutions and processes. Military regimes falter in creating a viable framework for political participation and infrastructure for ensuring socio-economic justice.

Ayub Khan assumed power with an agenda for socio-economic transformation and restructuring of the polity. Some of the policy measures did have a positive impact on society. The policies on economic development and industrialization with maximum encouragement to the private sector were quite successful and his regime was described as the 'showcase' of political stability and economic development in the developing world. However, his regime not only ignored the distributive aspects of economic development which accentuated inequities and disparities, but also stifled the political process by creating a strong presidential-centralized system with an emphasis on clientalism. The Ayubian system reflected the military's organizational ethos of hierarchy, order and discipline, and neglected the democratic and participatory considerations. This could not secure widespread acceptability and utterly failed to cope with the participatory and distributive pressures mounted either by those who had been excluded or by the new socio-economic forces including the professional classes, the fast-expanding labour, students, urban unemployed and rural poor whose increase was manifold as a consequence of the regime's economic policies. The Bengalis of East Pakistan were especially frustrated and felt that the power structure largely ignored their political aspirations.

Yahya Khan, who considered himself a natural heir to Ayub Khan, lacked fully articulated views on the national affairs. His strategy of accepting the main demands raised during the anti-Ayub agitation, especially reconstitution of four provinces in West Pakistan, allocation of National Assembly seats to the provinces on the basis of population, and removal of some civil servants on corruption charges, helped to win him some goodwill. He also held general elections in December 1970. However, when the Yahya regime was faced with the most thorny issue of transfer of power to the elected representatives, it failed miserably and plunged the country into one of the most unfortunate and bloody civil wars of the post-World War II period, resulting in another war with India and the break-up of Pakistan.

The limits of military rulers to create viable political institutions and processes facilitating political participation and socio-economic justice resurfaced during the martial law regime of Zia-ul-Haq. Initially, he projected himself as a reluctant ruler, but as he succeeded in consolidating his position, he expanded the goals of the coup and presided over the longest martial law in Pakistan's history (July 1977–December 1985), co-opting a section of political leaders as 'adjuncts to military supremacy'.[7] His search for legitimacy and an acceptable post-martial law political order led him to cultivate highly conservative and orthodox Islamic groups, to pursue selective Islamization with an emphasis on the punitive, regulative and extractive aspects, and to use the state apparatus to keep dissident political forces at bay. These strategies accentuated the existing social and economic cleavages and strengthened the narrowly based ethnic, religious-sectarian groups and others who managed to lay their hands on drugs money and weapons, making Pakistan's transition to democracy in the post-1988 period more problematic and uncertain.

Military Disengagement and Civilianization of Military Rule

The military's exit from power is a complex affair. Despite the promise of an early return to the barracks, most military rulers find it difficult to surrender power, not to speak of adopting an apolitical posture. Their self-styled missionary zeal, the post-coup political problems and their political ambitions impel them to expand their goals and hang on to power. However, the military rulers can neither overcome the crisis of legitimacy nor continue ruling for an indefinite period under martial law and emergency. Sooner or later, they have to think about some political framework to replace direct military rule, although they ensure that the position of the military, especially their own, is not adversely affected by such a change. In Pakistan, the military withdrew from power twice through planned disengagement (June 1962, December 1985), and once (December 1971) its rule came to an abrupt and unceremonious end.

Ayub Khan resorted to planned disengagement and a careful transition to civilianize his military rule. His strategies included a careful tailoring of the political system for the post-withdrawal period through constitutional and political engineering, co-option of a section of political elite and exclusion of the dissenting elements, the holding of non-contested referendums, local bodies elections, non-party, indirect elections at the provincial and national levels, and his own continuation as a civilian President. This process was initiated with the introduction of a new system of local bodies, Basic Democracies, in October 1959, and was completed with the inauguration of a new constitution in June 1962, establishing a highly centralized polity with a patron–client relationship between the central executive authority and the coopted political forces.

The civilianization of Zia-ul-Haq's military rule was another case of planned extrication of the military from direct exercise of power. Zia-ul-Haq did not draft a new constitution but made so many changes to the 1973 constitution that its democratic and parliamentary character was diluted, and entrenched his position as President. He was also allowed to continue as Army Chief, a position he held until his death in an air crash in August 1988 to become the longest serving Army Chief in Pakistan (March 1976–August 1988). He followed the Ayubian formula of phased civilianization of military rule: elections to the local bodies, a carefully planned referendum to ensure his continuation in power, and strictly regulated non-party elections at the national and provincial levels. The co-opted civilian leaders were installed in March 1985, but martial law was not lifted until December. Zia-ul-Haq used his enhanced constitutional powers and his position as Army Chief to assert his primacy in the post-withdrawal period.

The military withdrew from power in an unceremonious manner on one occasion, after the débâcle in the 1971 Indo-Pakistan war. The ruling Generals had to quit as street demonstration broke out against them in major urban centres and the senior Army officers also demanded Yahya Khan's removal. Had the military not lost the war, the ruling Generals would have attempted another carefully arranged retreat ensuring continuity from martial law to the post-martial law period. A draft constitution had already been prepared, but the military regime collapsed before it was announced.

The elected civilian government of Zulfikar Ali Bhutto (20 December 1971–5 July 1977) succeeded in temporarily asserting its primacy over the military. Bhutto started with three advantages: the military débâcle and the break-up of Pakistan had undermined the reputation and image of the military; the Supreme Court judgment (April 1972) delegitimizing the assumption of power by Yahya Khan strengthened the position of the civilian leadership; and Bhutto's strong popular support. He removed a number of senior officers, especially those belonging to the Army; restructured the military high command; changed the designation of the C-in-C to the Chief of Staff and reduced its tenure from four to three years. However, the military was able to regain its salience because Pakistan's perennial insecurity syndrome and Bhutto's vision of a strong and active Pakistan kept the military relevant to foreign policy. His government continued to allocate the lion's share of the national resources for defence, expanded the defence industry, and took steps for expansion and modernization of the military. Furthermore, Bhutto did not empower the political institutions and processes, diluted the democratic character of the unanimously adopted 1973 parliamentary constitution and resorted to authoritarian and patrimonial governance. His government's reliance on the military for suppressing the Baloch nationalist insurgency, alienation of the politically active groups as he suppressed dissent, and his inability to establish the ruling Pakistan People's Party (PPP) as a viable political machine weakened the civilian government. The use of troops to contain the massive street agitation in March–June 1977 made his position extremely vulnerable and enabled the military to retrieve the initiative.

Post-withdrawal Military, State and Society

The decision of the top brass under Mirza Aslam Beg (Army Chief: August 1988–August 1991, Vice Chief: March 1987–August 1988) after the death of Zia-ul-Haq in August 1988 to abide by the constitution created the conditions for holding elections and constitutional transfer of power to elected civilian leaders. Aslam Beg and his successors[8] in the exalted post of the Army Chief reaffirmed their support of constitutional and democratic rule and devoted greater attention to professional and service affairs.

Despite this withdrawal from direct management of political affairs, the military continues to be the most formidable and autonomous political actor capable of influencing the nature and direction of political change. The military's primary consideration is not direct exercise of supreme political power, but protection and advancement of its professional and corporate interests. If these interests can be protected, it would prefer to stay on the sidelines. Given the military's political experience, organizational resources and institutional strengths, the senior commanders are confident that they can protect their interests without directly assuming power. This confidence creates flexibility in their disposition towards the civilian leadership. They are prepared to negotiate their interests and even accommodate the civilian government, but what is not acceptable to them is a frontal attack on their institutional and corporate interests as they define them, or a deliberate campaign to malign the military, or unilateral decision-making by the civilian leaders on matters which directly concern them. They do not support a discredited political regime and do not allow the civilian leaders in government or in opposition to use the military's name as a prop in their power struggle. The scope for manoeuvre for the civilian leaders can thus expand if they maintain a relationship of confidence and trust with the military.

The military's disposition towards the political process is shaped by a number of considerations and interests. National security is their first major interest. The senior commanders have traditionally made a significant input into policy-making on defence and security affairs. Their role expanded during the Zia years when the military directly controlled the nuclear policy, Afghanistan and relations with India, including Kashmir. The nuclear policy has remained their preserve, even after the establishment of civilian rule. The role of the Foreign Office and civilian leaders in formulating and implementing policy on Afghanistan increased after the Soviet withdrawal from Afghanistan, but the Army and the Inter-Services Intelligence (ISI) continue to make a significant input. Similarly, the military maintains a deep interest in policy towards India and Kashmir. The military elite are not opposed in principle to Indo-Pakistan rapprochement, but they want the civilian government not to ignore what they see as New Delhi's hegemonic agenda. Strong and credible conventional defence and nuclear weapons capabilities are viewed as vital to ward off Indian pressures and to enable Pakistan to conduct its foreign and domestic policies independently. It was not therefore surprising that, after India's nuclear explosions in May 1998 and the belligerent statements of India's Cabinet members on Kashmir in the aftermath of the explosions, Pakistan's senior commanders and the civilian leaders jointly decided on a commensurate response by detonating nuclear devices. Had India not exploded its nuclear devices, the Pakistan military would have continued with the policy of nuclear ambiguity.

Weapons and equipment procurement from abroad is a second major military interest. It expects the civilian government to pursue a foreign policy that will facilitate the modernization of the military. Furthermore, the military has acquired added importance for foreign policy because of the assignment of the troops to a number of Middle Eastern and the Gulf States as well as their participation in UN peace-keeping operations.

The senior commanders jealously guard military autonomy and civilian non-interference. This includes promotions, transfers and postings in the three services and other service-related affairs. The service chiefs view their autonomy and civilian non-interference as a prerequisite for maintaining service discipline and professionalism; they want service personnel to know that linkages with the political leaders do not improve service and promotion prospects. If the political leaders are allowed to make inroads into the military and establish their lobbies, the top brass think, the military discipline, organizational coherence and institutional capacity to cope with the political environment will be compromised.

Defence expenditure is another important military interest. The military opposes any unilateral reduction in defence spending by the civilian government, although it is open to dialogue on this matter. The senior commanders resent public denunciations of defence expenditure by the political leaders or what they perceive to be a deliberate and sustained campaign to malign the military.

The improvement of service conditions and the protection of their perks and privileges are other important considerations for the military. The repeated exercise of power has enabled the officers to accumulate considerable perks and other material rewards, including lucrative civilian jobs, which they want to be protected.

The top brass expect the civilian government to ensure effective and transparent governance and socio-political stability. They therefore constantly monitor political and economic management on the part of the government, focusing on interaction between the government and the opposition, law and order, corruption and misuse of state resources by the civilian rulers. On a number of occasions, the top Army commanders have used their influence to moderate conflict among the politicians and/or forced them into a settlement when they felt that such confrontation would cause a major disruption in the polity. Their interest in these matters stems from the assumption that a polity in turmoil cannot sustain a professional military. Furthermore, the expansion of the military's role in the industrial and business sectors through its four foundations set up for the welfare of ex-service personnel (see chapter 11), has also created its stakes in the civilian government's economic and industrial policies and fiscal management.

The senior commanders are supportive of participatory governance but they expect the political leaders to give consideration to the military's sensibilities. Governance therefore involves a delicate balancing between the imperative of democracy and the interests of the military. The elections are being held regularly, civil and political liberties have expanded considerably, and the infrastructure of civil society is growing, but the political leaders have often found it quite problematic to maintain a balance between the imperatives of a participatory system and the sensitivities of the military.

The military also influences the political process through the intelligence agencies. Using intelligence services to monitor dissident political activity is nothing new in Pakistan. However, the role of the Military Intelligence (MI), the ISI and Intelligence Bureau (IB) increased during the Zia years, and this has been carried over to the post-1988 period. The military relies mainly on the MI and the ISI to pursue its political agenda (see chapter 10 for details). Intelligence-gathering has become increasingly important for senior commanders pursuing behind-the-scenes political intervention. This is also important for protecting and advancing the military's professional and corporate interests.

The military has strengthened its position in another way. The long years of military rule have enabled it to penetrate the major sectors of the state and the society, i.e. government and semi-government institutions, the private sector, industry, business, agriculture, education, communications and transportation. The different industrial projects and commercial and business undertakings launched by the four welfare foundations have also contributed to expanding the influence of the military. Different military governments appointed a large number of serving and retired officers to important civilian jobs. The post-martial law civilian governments were too weak to reverse this policy and cut back on the military's presence and influence in the civilian sectors (see chapters 9, 10 and 11 for details).

Several other factors underline the continuing importance of the military for the Pakistani state and the society. The end of the Cold War at the global level has not resulted in improving security environment in South Asia. Civil strife in Afghanistan goes on unabated with negative spillover implications for Pakistan, and nuclearization of South Asia has created a dangerous regional security environment, enhancing the military's relevance to decision-making and assigning a priority to defence and security affairs. There is a realization among the policy-makers that military security has to be coupled with societal development and human security, and that a well-rounded state viability calls for an 'equilibrium between the edifices of the state and the vital institutions of civil society',[9] the balance continues to be tilted in favour of military security.

Pakistan's domestic political and economic conditions are far from satisfactory, making it difficult for the rehabilitated civilian leaders to develop into an autonomous political entity capable of taking command of the political process. The partisan and non-judicious use of state resources and a non-transparent and poorly managed privatization of state owned industry and assets have resulted in huge misuse of state-resources and a massive increase in corruption at the official level, adversely affecting the capacity of civilian leaders to deal with the major political and economic issues on their merits and govern effectively. These problems have been accentuated by the widening ethnic, regional and religious-sectarian cleavages, and proliferation of weapons. Pakistani society is now so fractured, inundated with sophisticated weapons, brutalized by civic violence and overwhelmed by the spread of narcotics that it is no longer possible for any civilian government to operate effectively without the Army's support. The Army is more deeply involved than any time in the past (including the periods of military rule) in support activities for the civilian government: law and order assignments, relief and rescue operations after natural disasters, use of its organizational and technological resources for public welfare projects, greater induction of its personnel in government and semi-government institutions, increased reliance on Army personnel for the management of several government and semi-government corporations and services, anti-terrorist activities and containment of drug trafficking and smuggling.

The military also gains from the lack of consensus among the political leaders as to its role in the political process. The feuding political leaders have not hesitated to call upon the Army to dislodge their adversaries from power. In a situation of acute confrontation and crisis, the military can always find civilian support for its expanded role.

The military's disposition is also influenced by the changing socio-economic character of the Army officers. The Punjab and NWFP continue to supply the bulk of the officer corps and the other ranks, but the base of recruitment within these areas has expanded. Many districts, not known for making manpower available to the Army, are now sending officers and soldiers. A large number of post-1971 Army officers come from modest rural or urban middle- or lower middle-class backgrounds and have joined the service at a time when opportunities in the civilian sector are declining. Their career and materialist orientations and a desire to enjoy material rewards at an early stage of their career make them susceptible to political temptations. Any attempt to reduce their existing perks, facilities and career opportunities will be resented. The continuing ethnic imbalances in the Army are expected to evoke more controversies as the military sustains its role as a leading employer, a ladder for lucrative jobs in the civilian sectors, and controls substantial economic resources. (see chapter 11 for details).

The current power-sharing arrangement blends the authoritarian tradition with democracy. It allows the military a share in decision-making and facilitates the functioning of the electoral process and representative government. Political stability depends on a trouble-free interaction between the civilian government and the military. Any effort on the part of the civilian leaders to wrest the initiative or to monopolize power by upsetting the delicate balance of power in the polity is not expected to enhance their credibility. The military's options increase if the government's political and economic performance falters, if it faces a crisis of legitimacy aggravated by popular unrest in the cities or if the political competition turns disorderly. The military continues to be the strongest political force and it can veto Pakistan's transition to democracy. However, the growing complexities of the domestic socio-political landscape and the global context, make direct assumption of power a dubious option.

2
Civil–Military Interaction

The attainment of independence by the states of Asia and Africa after the long period of European colonial rule engendered strong expectations that an era of participatory governance would begin. The nationalist leaders had employed a liberal democratic idiom to put forward their case for independence and vowed to create political institutions and processes based on justice and fair play, tolerance and consent. As they did not appreciate the scale of the task of evolving participatory political institutions in the postcolonial societies, they faltered and adopted authoritarian approaches to political management, increasing their reliance on the state apparatus, the military being one of the state institutions availed of the opportunity to amass political clout. This manifested itself in various ways: the senior commanders began to make a significant input into policy-making, shared power with the political elite or dominated them while staying in the background, displaced the civilian governments at will, resorted to coups d'état and assumed power, and engaged in mutiny and counter-coup.

When the first series of coups occurred in the 1950s and the 1960s, a large number of scholars interpreted the rise of the military to power as a positive development. It was argued that the military would create the necessary conditions for the protection and promotion of liberal democratic institutions and that it would facilitate economic development, social change and national integration.[1] One political scientist described the ascendancy of the military as an opportunity for bringing about a 'breakthrough from the present stagnation into a genuine developmental take off'.[2] Another writer highlighted the important developmental role of the military elite.[3] However, as military commanders ruled various countries over a period of time and their policies were analysed, political analysts began to revise their opinion. Most studies published in the mid-1970s and the 1980s expressed strong reservations about the 'modernizing' and 'developmental' role of military regimes and some viewed the military as the major obstacle to the development of democracy in the developing world. They argued that military regimes did not necessarily perform better than civilian governments so far as socio-economic development was concerned, and that these could not create viable participatory political institutions. One study argued that military regimes hardly differed from non-military regimes from the perspective of 'economic performance criteria'.[4] Another study, comparing 77 developing states during 1960–70, concluded that the military was not necessarily an agent of social change.[5] Yet another writer argued that 'self-reliant development can never occur as long as militaries continue to be involved in the governing process'.[6] These writers underlined the social, political and professional constraints which adversely affected the performance of military regimes and cautioned against the implications of the military's direct involvement in governance for the future disposition of the military, the polity and society.

The State and the Political Process

The dilemmas of the leaders of ex-colonial states in evolving institutions and processes for participatory governance can be traced to the pre-colonial and colonial legacies. The pre-colonial political culture had a strong authoritarian and subject-parochial character with an overall emphasis on ascriptive status and particularistic orientations. The colonial system introduced some changes through Western education, political and socio-economic engineering, but bureaucratic control, centralization and authoritarianism were quite pronounced. Furthermore, despite colonial intervention and the rise of an urban educated class, the majority population continued to live in a world of their own, not directly exposed to the changes. The urban educated elite had limited experience of actually managing the democratic institutions and processes, although they aspired to build a modern and democratic polity with constitutionalism and rule of law, socio-economic development and a strong national identity.

Most of them did not succeed in establishing such institutions and processes; some created personalized and authoritarian rule while others were unable to transfer their popular appeal to the political institutions they had created. As their charisma faded or they disappeared from the political scene, the political institutions began to encounter the crisis of legitimacy. The rapid and simultaneous pursuance of modernization and democratization of the predominantly traditional societies is problematic. These are complex and multidimensional processes involving technological, economic, political, cultural and attitudinal innovations. Modernization means to be 'dynamic, concerned with the people, democratic and egalitarian, scientific, economically advanced, sovereign and influential'.[7] Democratization and political development call for evolving a broad consensus on the operational norms of the polity, a participatory and responsive political management, respect for dissent and emphasis on distributive justice. Popular consent, empowerment of the disadvantaged sections of the populace and an opportunity for change of government through constitutional and peaceful means are recognized as the norms of a democratic polity.[8]

Such changes threaten the traditionally dominant power elite, who either oppose the process or manipulate it in order to protect their entrenched position. Some people are ideologically opposed to such changes. Still others take time to accept the implications of modernization and change. The fact of the matter is that when traditional societies embark on modernizing their political and economic structures, much tension surfaces in the polity, especially in the early phase. The ruling elite talk of integrating tradition with carefully selected elements of modernization and emphasize a distinction between modernization and westernization, with a preference for the former. The experience suggests that such efforts often run into difficulties as it is not always possible to draw a clear distinction between the two. Even when the contents of modernization are carefully selected, the traditional values and ethos come in conflict with them and this causes stresses in the existing social and political relations.

These transitional dilemmas can be dealt with by a leadership that enjoys popular appeal and legitimacy. If charisma is allowed to fade before the political institutions and processes are firmly established, which is most often the case, the leadership cannot muster enough clout and legitimacy to tide over the transitional problems. Politics is fractionalized and degenerates into personal and group feuds, and it becomes difficult to evolve a broad-based consensus on the operational norms of the polity. The ethnic, linguistic, regional and economic cleavages which are pushed to the periphery of the political process in the last phase of the independence struggle resurface and become important symbols of identity and instruments for political mobilization. As the polity is already under political and economic stress and invariably practises non-participatory and exclusionist governance, it is unable to accommodate such identities. A conflict between state-directed nationalism and other identities adds to political incoherence. Certain sections of the population refuse to submit to the authority of the state, which they view as oppressive and illegitimate. Some demand special safeguards to protect their rights and identity. Still others ask for maximum autonomy or separation. These problems call for a patient and pluralistic approach to nation-building, emphasizing accommodation of various sources of identity through dialogue and participatory management. However, the weak, divided and insecure leadership resorts to administrative and coercive solutions which, in the long run, prove counter productive to consensus-building.[9]

These cleavages become so deep-rooted that the leadership and the political institutions, whose legitimacy is already in question, can hardly mediate. 'Social forces confront each other nakedly' and there are hardly any leaders, institutions and procedures that can mitigate conflict.[10] This undermines governmental capacity for political and economic management in an effective, judicious and participatory manner, thereby accentuating the problems of governance, which in turn causes greater disillusionment and alienation amongst the people.

The Military

The military stands out as a distinctive institution in a large number of ex-colonial and developing states as being highly organized and disciplined, more oriented to modern technology, and has an overwhelming control of instruments of coercion and violence. It is trained to identify with the state and the state-centric perspective, with an emphasis on 'centralization, hierarchy, discipline, inter-communication and *esprit de corps*'.[11] The political institutions and organizations hardly reflect these characteristics; the bureaucracy shares some of these attributes, which helps its interaction with the military.

The military more than any other state institution operates in an international context. It constantly looks towards the outside world, especially the developed and industrialized states, for technology, weaponry, equipment and training. These linkages also channel ideas and doctrines from abroad which have implications for domestic socio-political and security affairs. This enables senior commanders to evaluate their society in a comparative international context and makes them aware of their society's economic-technological deficiencies and under-development. This attribute of the military is now gradually being diluted because many other groups and sections of population, i.e. the bureaucracy, the industrial and business elites and intellectuals, are developing frequent interaction across the territorial boundaries of the state. However, the military continues to have an edge over them because it continually upgrades its equipment and strategy through a strong external input. As defence against external threat is the key function of the military, the external environment and interaction are extremely important for them. It can be described as 'one of the key mechanisms which a nation possesses of receiving, and sometimes amplifying signals from its external environment. These signals include ideals, values, skills, techniques and strategies of political changes.'[12]

A professional military represents a way of life, and its acculturation process is so thorough that it replaces the particularistic and parochial attachments of its recruits with the military ethos. Unless its personnel are exposed to intense partisan political pressures, or some groups are able to penetrate it, professional ethos and discipline shape the disposition of military personnel. The new entrants are educated, trained and disciplined through a comprehensive pre-service and in-service training. This builds professionalism, discipline and internal cohesion, which distinguishes the military from other sectors of society. The military often protects its distinctive profession-cum-way of life by maintaining a distance from the rest of the society and by taking adequate care of the personal needs of the personnel and their families.

What helps the military to maintain a professional and task-oriented profile is *inter alia* the availability of material resources to build itself. Most ex-colonial states have a precarious existence due mainly to internal political problems and external pressures. A strong military is viewed as a precondition for state security and survival. Such a security perspective enhances the importance of the military, enabling it to make substantial claims on scarce resources, and influencing domestic economic priorities and foreign policy strategies. The military deflects some criticism of security-oriented politico-economic priorities by making its organizational resources, technological know-how and managerial skills available to the government's public welfare and relief work and industrial and economic development projects.

Expansion of the Role of the Military

The question of civil–military relations became relevant after the emergence of the nation-state and the gradual growth of democracy. The military developed into an autonomous profession and the concept of professional officer corps gained ground in the nineteenth century in place of the military brought up by and catering to the needs of the feudal lords or aristocracy. As the modern polity's features, such as legal-rational authority, the military's professional and corporate entity, and role differentiation, emerged, the contours of interaction between the political leaders and the military establishment began to take shape. The European and North American experience recognized two different domains of the civil/political and the military, each with its special characteristics, disposition and demands, although they overlapped with an overall primacy of the civil/political.

It is in the light of European and North American experience that Samuel Huntington talks of the objective control model, wherein there are clear-cut boundaries between the civil and the military. The military establishment enjoys autonomy, concentrates on professional affairs, and it is prepared 'to carry out the wishes of any civilian group which secures legitimate authority within the state'. Such an ideal model may not actually exist. Even in Western countries the military acts as a pressure group for service-related affairs, i.e. budget and other related matters. Its role in policy-making may increase during an emergency or war. However, the military's role as a pressure group for its professional and corporate interests is acceptable unless the senior commanders adopt methods other than persuasion and lobbying. What is often found in a large number of states is what is described as the subjective control, when the boundaries between the civil and the military are not clearly demarcated. The civilians de-emphasize military autonomy and the military does not stay clear of politics.[13] Amos Perlmutter talks of three patterns of military organization, each with a different pattern of civil–military relations: the professional soldier, the praetorian soldier and the revolutionary soldier.[14]

Many writers explain the erosion of the classical model of civilian supremacy over the military and the rise of the military to power primarily with reference to the weaknesses and deficiencies in the socio-political domain. Others assign greater importance to the internal attributes of the military, especially its professional and corporate interests and ambitions on the part of the senior commanders. Some talk of the functional boundaries between the military establishment and the socio-economic environment. These boundaries can be integral, where sharply differentiated boundaries have stabilized; permeable when there are no clear lines between the two and they frequently step into each other's domain; and fragmented, where these are differentiated in some respects and permeated in others.[15]

A comprehensive analysis of the expansion of the role of the military calls for examining all the three sets of factors simultaneously, i.e. the nature and problems of the civil society; the military establishment and its organizational resources, attributes and corporate interests; and the interaction across the functional boundaries between the civil and the military. Such a study will be incomplete without examining another (fourth) set of variables: the international environment, within which the civil society and the military function. Given the growing interdependence in the international system, the international factors have implications for the abovementioned three sets of variables and affect the role of the military in the developing countries.

(i) The Societal Factors

Most writers view the societal factors, especially the crisis of legitimacy, as the most important cause of military intervention in politics.[16] The factors internal to the military organization are described as less significant,[17] although by no means irrelevant. The major political features of the developing state witnessing the expansion of the role of the military include a low level of social cohesion, fragmented class structure and the absence of a strong and articulate middle class, lack of common symbols for political and social mobilization, conflict between the centre and the periphery, a low level of institutionalization, weak and ineffective political parties and voluntary organizations, poor political management by the leaders and their inability to govern with consent, and an overall anxiety and uncertainty about the future – personal, group and the state.[18]

Persistent economic crises, deteriorating economic conditions, maladministration, widespread violence and insecurity contribute to the erosion of civilian political institutions and processes. When large sections of the politically active populace question the moral right of a civilian government to rule, and that government faces the problem of political efficacy, it is vulnerable to manipulation and domination by the military. Huntington argues that the inability of the political institutions to cope with increasing social mobilization causes disorder and chaos and this increases the likelihood of military intervention. In other words, if the politico-economic and social institutions and processes can cope with the participatory and distributive pressures and voluntary group activity is strong and widespread with a large number of people maintaining a stake in the continuity of a politico-economic order, the military will have less temptation to step directly into the political domain.

(ii) Internal Dynamics of the Military

The organizational resources and internal dynamics of the military establishment, and especially its control over the instruments of violence and the disposition of the officer corps, shape the military's role in a polity.[19] A highly professional officer corps steeped in the values of aloofness from politics may initially be reluctant to assume an active and direct political role. However, if the socio-political and economic crises deepen, professionalism can impel the senior commanders to step forward and assume a political role. They can develop a 'saviour' complex and embark on rectifying the perceived 'ills' of the polity, assuming that if they can run the Army in a professional and orderly manner, these skills can be employed to rectify the problems of civil society.

A cohesive and disciplined officer corps can act swiftly and decisively, which strengthens the military's ability to pursue political goals. Strong middle-class values and security-strategic considerations can contribute to military activism or assumption of power. The institutional and corporate interests often motivate the senior commanders to indulge in politicking. In several countries, the military has resorted to pressure and lobbying, threats, revolts or overthrow of the government to secure more budgetary allocations or to stall cut-backs. Similarly, terms and conditions of service have been their important consideration.

Once the military assumes power, it becomes extremely difficult for the senior commanders to abandon an active interest in politics, even after they return to the barracks. The crises and inadequacies in the civilian political process may have brought them to power but they are unable or unwilling to create viable political institutions that can function without the support of the military. The senior commanders want to ensure a continuity of the key personnel and policies to the post-military rule period. They are also interested in retaining some rewards and benefits of exercising power. Therefore, they are careful in devising the post-military rule political order and are strongly resentful if they feel that the political government is making a conscious attempt to push them to the periphery of the political system.

The politicization of the officers can adversely affect their internal cohesion and discipline, manifesting in adventurism, or they may attempt to cultivate civilian allies. The military can also suffer from factionalism if polarized

political elements and ideological groups are allowed to penetrate its personnel. A divided military may not be in a position to exert institutional pressure
on the civilian government effectively but internal squabbles increase the
unpredictability of the military's disposition towards the political process.

(iii) Transactions across the Boundaries between the Civil and the Military

The transactions and interaction between the civil and the miliary go a long
way to shape the nature and direction of civil–military relations. A weak
political government presiding over a fragmented polity finds it difficult to
assert its primacy over the military. Rather, it cultivates the top brass of the
military to strengthen its position. The greater the reliance of the civil government on the military for political management, the lesser is its ability to
exercise the political initiative. When a civil government depends heavily
on the military for dealing with the problems of the civilian sector, especially
for sustaining itself in the wake of political challenges to its legitimacy, it has
three major implications. First, the military obtains direct experience of handling the political affairs that do not fall within its professional domain. Second, the inability of the political government to perform its basic task is
exposed and the military commanders acquire firsthand knowledge of popular antagonism towards the government. Third, an impression is created in
society that the military has the capability and the will to handle a difficult
situation when the government fails. Many civilians are fascinated by the
military's work in the civilian sector as well as by its organizational efficiency
and promptness. It begins to be viewed at the popular level as a task-oriented
and helpful institution and 'something over and above the passing regimes'.[20]
The troops have to be used for civilian, especially police duties, sparingly.

At times, ambitious political leaders may like to enlist the military as their
accomplices in dislodging the civilian/elected government that is being run
by their opponents. The overriding consideration is the removal of political
adversaries from power without paying any attention to the fact that the
removal of a civilian/elected government with the help of the military does
not serve the cause of democracy. Such a state of affairs exposes the divisive-
ness and weakness of the political forces and adds to the political clout and
bargaining power of the military. The military's position is also strengthened
if the state is confronted with a serious security problem. If the state develops
an insecurity syndrome, the role and position of the military are enhanced
and the senior commanders begin to mould foreign policy to their satisfaction and leave a strong imprint on the state's international alliances as well
as its domestic priorities.

(iv) The International Dimension

The military's political profile is also influenced by developments outside
the territorial boundaries of the state and the military's international

connections. As discussed earlier, the miliary operates in the international arena more than most other state institutions. During the Cold War period, the two superpowers cultivated the militaries of a number of developing states by supplying sophisticated weaponry and by offering them training and technical know-how. The US Military Assistance Programme aimed *inter alia* at strengthening the defence forces of the developing countries in order to ensure modernization and socio-economic development as well as to enable them to act as a 'bulwark' against a Soviet/communist ideological and military onslaught.[21] This aid relationship helped the modernization of the military, gave it greater confidence and strengthened its position within the domestic context. As the senior commanders of these armed forces developed a pro-West disposition, their assumption of power was viewed as a positive development by most American political analysts, who considered them as reliable partners in the global power game.

In the post-Cold War era, the military commanders in a large number of developing countries continue to view security relations with the Western industrialized world as an important source of weapons procurement and modernization of the military, thereby serving their professional goals. International factors impinge in another manner. Industrialized states and international financial institutions offer economic and technological assistance to developing states, enabling the former to manipulate the constellation of domestic forces in the recipient states, including encouragement or discouragement to the military to act in a particular manner. The current Western global agenda with an emphasis on economic decontrol and deregulation, elimination of trade barriers and encouragement of investments is making the developing countries more dependent on global economic forces (see section on military withdrawal below). The domestic political actors, including the military, cannot be oblivious to international economic and political factors. How a coup or expanded role of the military will connect with the external environment has become more important now than was the case in the past.

The impact of these four clusters of factors on civil–military relations varies. If the civilian procedures and mechanisms for political management and governance are functioning more or less efficiently and the civilian leaders enjoy the broad-based support of the politically active populace, they will be able to regulate the transactions across the boundaries between the civil and the military as well as manage the external environmental factors. The senior commanders make their institution-related demands or seek ventilation of their grievances through the established channels and procedures, including lobbying. However, these conditions do not exist in most developing states and the political leaders face serious problems of management and legitimacy. The senior commanders find it convenient to expand their role.

This does not mean that the military should be viewed as a neutral entity that steps in only because the political leaders have 'failed' and that a political 'vacuum' exists. The military is an important and powerful political actor in the developing states with its own 'interests and stakes' and operates 'either individually or in concert with other actors in the society'.[22] The decline of the political institutions and processes gives greater freedom of action to the military.

The senior commanders may exert pressure on weak and divided leaders in order to obtain benefits and concessions for their service or may like to share decision-making power on key domestic and foreign policy issues from the sidelines. They may replace one set of civilian leaders with another, force a settlement on feuding political leaders or change the constellation of political alignments. A widely practised strategy is the direct assumption of power. They succeed because 'the public is relatively narrow and weakly organized' and these states have 'low' or 'minimal' political culture. The popular attachment to the political institutions is so fragile or non-existent that the politically relevant people hardly dispute the legitimacy of the takeover.[23]

The Military Regime

The immediate concern of the military after assuming power is the consolidation of its authority. If the takeover involves violence and bloodshed, the ruling commanders wish to suppress all sources of immediate threat, if possible. Even if the coup is peaceful and orderly, the new regime displays its power in the initial stages by keeping the troops on the streets, and occupying key government installations. However, the desire is to revert to normal functioning at the earliest so as to demonstrate that the takeover has been widely accepted in the polity. No matter how the military commanders assume power, the ultimate sanction of their rule is the coercive power at their disposal. They are therefore wary of any possible attempt to challenge their authority. The legitimacy of miliary rule remains a live and sensitive issue.

The military commanders assume power either as caretakers or they have broader objectives. As caretakers, they purport to hold the ring for a short period to enable feuding politicians to sort out their affairs. They may return to the barracks after the completion of their 'limited mission' with an implicit threat to return if the restored civilian government could not come up to their expectations. Invariably the caretaker disposition is a tactical move on the part of the coup-makers, who later expand their goals and hold on to power after they gain confidence, or the post-coup issues and problems make their disengagement impossible.

The military commanders with broader goals work towards bringing about changes in the socio-economic and political structures on the basis of their political agenda. Most military regimes invariably succeed in coping with the immediate problems, like law and order, shortage of essential commodities in the market, and inefficiency and red tape in government offices, thereby providing some temporary relief to the populace. However, the miliary regime encounters serious problems when and if an attempt is made at socio-economic transformation of the society. They tend to consider societal problems as purely technical issues which can be tackled if 'dirty' politics is checked and the 'right orders are given'[24] in unambiguous terms by the relevant authorities. They consider restrictions on political activities as a key to the success of the changes they want to bring about in the society. The military's organizational skills and functional specialization are an asset when dealing with purely military and technical affairs, but these do not give enough capacity to bring about meaningful socio-economic changes. It is not merely their orientations that hamper their efforts, the military commanders soon realize that there are no easy solutions to 'the intractable economic, social and political problems'[25] and that they cannot drastically alter the correlation of socio-economic forces without threatening their own interests.

The senior commanders also realize that they alone cannot govern the country. The bureaucracy is their natural ally and shares a number of characteristics with the military. Both are organized, hierarchical and professional. They subscribe to a nation-state oriented perspective and have a vested interest in stability and development. They may also share antipathy towards the political leaders. The military can displace the civilian government with or without the cooperation of the bureaucracy. But, it needs the expertise of the bureaucracy to run the administration. The bureaucracy also benefits from military rule. It is saved from the day-to-day interference of the political leaders in administrative matters and thus has more freedom of action provided it does not challenge the primacy of the military. The military regime may take punitive action against some civil servants in the initial stages on the pretext of rooting out corruption, inefficiency and indiscipline. However, the two institutions soon begin to accommodate each other. They realize that cooperative interaction is to their mutual advantage and this leads to a marriage of convenience between the bureaucracy and the military. Thus, there can never be a purely and exclusively military government, and the military's socio-political choices are also shaped by the orientations of the senior bureaucrats who work as junior partners and have a greater role in implementation of the policies.

Military regimes stumble in evolving viable political institutions capable of offering enduring remedies for the pre-coup political degeneration and fragmentation as well as eliciting a widespread acceptability amongst the politically relevant circles. The organizational and professional ethos and orientations of the military-bureaucratic rulers become a serious constraint on their ability to create participatory institutions and processes. As a hierarchical and authoritarian institution, the military emphasizes internal cohesion, discipline, compliance and bureaucratic rigidity. It puts a 'premium on authoritarian rather than democratic attitudes'.[26] The emphasis is on 'the criteria of rationality, efficiency and sound administration',[27] and that 'orders are to be obeyed, not discussed and debated'.[28] One writer argues on the basis of Latin American experience that 'by their institutional structure and training', the military is not 'as well equipped as civilians for the bargaining, persuasion, compromises and dialogues that are necessary for creating consensus'.[29] This has two major implications for the political style of the military rulers. First, the political institutions they create reflect military ethos, and thus provide little room for participatory political management involving free and fair electoral process, respect for dissent and consensus-building through dialogue, bargaining and accommodation. Second, their aversion to competitive and participatory political activity makes them lean heavily on the control and regulative apparatus of the state for coping with dissent, accentuating socio-political cleavages and polarization in the society.

Military Withdrawal

Military withdrawal from direct rule is a complex affair involving factors and considerations intrinsic to the military, the socio-political conditions in the concerned polity and the international environmental factors. Finer explains withdrawal with reference to the military disposition to withdraw and the societal conditions that lead the military to consider withdrawal. He also discusses motivations that impel the military to withdraw and the conditions or prerequisites without which the military is reluctant to return to barracks.[30]

The military's disposition to withdraw depends partly on whether the senior commanders continue to believe in the principle of civilian supremacy and that governance is not their primary responsibility. An officer corps with such an orientation is likely to be more favourable to withdrawal. They may also feel that their major goals have been achieved and that they should return to barracks. The possible threats of hanging on to power to the senior commanders' cohesion or accentuation of the already existing cleavages may lead the governing generals to think about withdrawal. The original group of commanders that stage the coup fade out and the new entrants to the senior echelons may not share the enthusiasm of their predecessors for ruling the country. At times, differences develop between the officers holding political office and those who stay on professional assignments. The ruling commanders endeavour to contain this problem by distributing the 'rewards' of power widely in the military so that those who stay on professional duties are placated.

The repeated military intervention in politics or exercise of power by the senior commanders over an extended period adversely affects the reputation of the military. In the pre-coup phase, the distance the military maintains from civil society contributes to its positive image as professional and cap-able of completing an assignment in a systematic and disciplined manner. Once this distance is removed and the servicemen assume power, the ills that afflict civil society penetrate the military. There are complaints of corruption, nepotism, misuse of power and arbitrary decision-making and enforcement, although the people affected are reluctant to take up these matters publicly because the legal remedies available to them under the military rule are limited, if any. This undermines the reputation of the military and adversely affects professionalism and this starts a debate within the military about the desirability of staying on in power. The officers who stay back on purely professional assignments press those in power to extric-ate themselves to save the reputation and social standing of the military. Such internal pressures undermine the ability of the military regime to govern, and, if these are totally disregarded by the ruling junta, these can cause disaffection, revolt or a counter-coup. The ruling Generals can lose the confidence to govern due to internal and external pressures of power pol-itics. They may also be exhausted by intractable economic and political crises.[31]

Societal conditions play a role in the military's decision to withdraw from power. Voluntary and non-government groups, including the labour, stu-dents, intellectuals, industrialist, and the middle class, if sufficiently power-ful and organized, can play an important role in generating societal pressure on the military. When they develop a consensus on the need to restore civilian rule and mobilize support for that, governance becomes quite ardu-ous for the military. The military government can face additional pressures due to economic failures or a breakdown of law and order. If the ruling Generals are able to deflect such pressures or keep the political forces divided, they may prolong their rule. However, this accentuates political polarization and fragmentation in the polity and the military rulers end up with worse political conditions than the ones they set out to rectify, thereby making their withdrawal more problematic.

External or international factors also have implications for the future of a military regime. A defeat in war, external military intervention or its threat, failure to obtain sufficient economic aid and military hardware, and effective economic sanctions can cut short military rule. During the Cold War era, the two superpowers propped up many military regimes if the latter were pre-pared to identify with the former's strategic interests. With the end of the superpower rivalry and the disintegration of the Soviet Union, military and authoritarian regimes are under a lot of international pressures to liberalize and democratize. Growing economic deregulation, international trade and investment, and economic interdependence, especially the expanding role of the international financial institutions, all make the developing countries vulnerable to external influences and penetration. Currently, these develop-ments are helping the democratic and participatory process in the developing world. However, there is no guarantee that these liberal political and economic trends can ensure the long-term success of democracy. The transition to an open and competitive economic and political system is marred by rampant corruption, increased civil violence, the role of money and criminal activity in politics, and growing socio-economic inequities, which can create a desire for some kind of authoritarian rule.

It is difficult to rank the factors shaping the disposition and motivation to withdraw. Much depends on the peculiar conditions and circumstances of each case. Even within one country, different military regimes come to an end differently, with the role of each factor varying. One writer has compared the military's disengagement from power with decolonization in so far as an attempt is made in both cases to 'determine conditions, inhibit and constrain the behaviour of the successor government'.[32] This comparison holds true only to the extent that the outgoing military regime often leaves a strong imprint on the successor civilian regime and the latter finds it difficult to come out of the former's shadow.

Military rule can come to an end through planned disengagement or extrication. It involves the military's ability 'to construct and implement a well defined programme' of transition to civilian rule.[33] Most professional and disciplined militaries prefer to withdraw through a carefully planned phased programme. This ensures continuity of the key personnel and major policies and protection of its interests in the post-withdrawal period. Military rule also terminates in an abrupt and unceremonious manner, often described as unplanned breakdown when the military rulers are forced to hand over power to a civilian leadership for a host of reasons.[34] The most common reasons for such a collapse include débâcle in a war, foreign intervention or its threat, internal feuds in the officer corps, a serious economic crisis, mass uprising and social revolution. Such withdrawals are common with a military low in professionalism, internal cohesion and discipline.[35] These causes can also result in the overthrow of the ruling generals by their colleagues.

The transfer of power from the military to the civil is more feasible if the personal, professional and corporate interests of the military are not threatened by such a change. Personal interests relate to the members of the ruling junta. That the successor civilian regime will not resort to revenge against them or persecute them for their policies and decisions during the period of direct military rule. If they think that the successor regime will have an anti-military disposition and disregard the interests and concerns of the military, the senior commanders will hang on to power until such threats are eliminated or they are dislodged through a counter-coup or some other abrupt development. The senior commanders can also have non-material interests, i.e. political ideology (secularism in Turkey, Islam in Pakistan). Therefore, if the ruling Generals have reservations about the loyalties and political direction of the potential successors, or they think that the civilian leaders threaten their interests, they will be reluctant to hand over power.[36]

The major professional interests of the military include material resources for modernization of the military, especially for the procurement of weapons and equipment, and enhanced opportunities for improving professional competence. The senior commanders guard service autonomy and do not like the rehabilitated civilian leaders interfering with what they consider to be their exclusive professional domain or internal organizational matters. However, they continue to make an input into civilian policy-making, especially regarding the affairs they consider relevant to their professional objectives.

The corporate interests include service conditions, perks and other material rewards and facilities. They do not want to lose all the rewards they enjoyed while they were in power. The senior echelons of the military, especially the army, become a ladder for lucrative assignments in the civilian sector. They are accommodated in government jobs and high positions in the semi-government organizations. The private sector also accommodates them in order to gain access to their connections in the military and the government. The military commanders do not want such opportunities to be denied to them after they return to the barracks.

The ruling generals adopt three major strategies to ensure that post-withdrawal political arrangements do not threaten their interests.

(i) Constitutional and Political Engineering

A carefully tailored political system is evolved either by framing a new constitution or by introducing far-reaching changes in the existing one. These arrangements reflect the military's organizational ethos of hierarchy, order and discipline. Specific provisions may be inserted in the constitutional and legal system for the military's role in policy-making.

(ii) Co-option of the Political Elite

The military rulers create 'beneficiaries' through their political and economic policies and prop up the political elite who are willing to join them and play politics within their game-plan. A dependent and adjunct leadership is brought forward, and projected as the true representatives of the people. They are given sufficient opportunities to organize themselves and penetrate the important sectors of the society. The political adversaries are neutralized or excluded from the political process by using the coercive apparatus of the state against them.

(iii) The Assumption of Civilian Role by Some of the Ruling Generals

The head of the ruling junta and some important members of the military regime continue to hold important positions after the withdrawal of military rule. The top general may or may not resign his rank but he is projected as a popular and elected leader, although he continues to lean heavily on his traditional constituency, i.e. the military.

The military 'hands back' power to the co-opted leadership under a carefully tailored political order. The scope of autonomy for the civilianized regime varies, depending on the political context and the issue area. If the civilian leadership is nothing more than an appendage to the military or a 'front' for the serving or retired generals, these arrangements can be described as authoritarian clientalism. The civilian leadership accepts 'subordination to military leadership in exchange for some share in running the state.... The military patron offers some of the resources derived from its control over the state.'[37] The scope of their autonomy can expand if they develop a relationship of trust and confidence with the military.

The civilian leaders succeeding military rule face a dilemma. On the one hand, they want to prove that they are not under the tutelage of the military and can act autonomously. On the other, they cannot afford to alienate the top commanders whose support is critical to their ability to cope with the problems of governance and especially to counter their political adversaries who question their legitimacy. The military's position is strengthened because most of these states are faced with a precarious internal and external security situation. Furthermore, ambitious political leaders do not hesitate to cultivate the military in a bid to advance their political agenda.

Military disengagement can never be complete. Its withdrawal does not mean that it has abandoned all interest in politics and that it can no longer play an active political role. If the factors that create the disposition and motivation to withdraw disappear, the military can assume a high profile in the political domain. The best safeguard against the military's return to power or its active role in the political arena is the removal of the causes which produce intervention. As these causes persist in the post-withdrawal period and viable and participatory political institutions and processes do not easily evolve, the military continues to cast a shadow over the political process. However, coups and direct assumptions of power by the military have declined in the last decade of the twentieth century and a number of countries have reverted to democracy. The military continues to play a significant role, albeit from the sidelines.

We are moving towards a new pattern of civil–military relations. The involvement of the military in politics is becoming more subtle and a 'hybrid' of the civil and the military is emerging.[38] An overall democratic dispensation is maintained with sufficient scope of action for the political leaders. The military enjoys autonomy in professional affairs and exercises influence over policy-making, but it neither directly governs nor controls the civilian rulers. The elected civilian leadership exercises reasonable power and authority to manage its affairs, but it is expected always to consider the military's sensibilities. The civilian and military leaders engage in a constant dialogue and bargaining on major policy issues. The latter enjoys some advantage over the former in view of the problems and uncertainties of the post-withdrawal political order. However, the military acknowledges the relevance of the democratic and participatory framework. How durable this 'mid-way arrangement' is and whether it offers a viable alternative to direct military rule are yet to be determined. Nevertheless, the military will continue to be a formidable and autonomous actor in the politics of the developing countries in the twenty-first century.

3
The Heritage

The Pakistan military came into existence as the security shield of an independent and sovereign state on 14/15 August 1947, when British rule was withdrawn and the South Asian subcontinent was divided into the two states of Pakistan and India. The British had built a professional military for the external defence and internal security of British India as well as for the defence of the British Empire. This was partitioned on the demand of the Muslim League and the Congress Party, which insisted that they must have troops under their command at the time of independence; without an independent military force, independence was perceived to be unreal and hollow.

The Foundations

The roots of the British Indian military go back to the first decade of the seventeenth century when the East India Company (chartered by Queen Elizabeth I on 31 December 1600) began its trading operations on the west coast of India. It was in August 1608 that the first ship, *Hector*, commanded by Captain William Hawkins anchored at Surat and sought permission to build a 'factory' – a trading post and a warehouse for storing goods. Hawkins faced hostility from the Portuguese and the Dutch and soon realized that he could not operate effectively without securing the approval of the Mughal emperor Jahangir. He decided to go to the Mughal capital, Agra, and, for his protection on way, hired 50 Indian horsemen.[1] This was the first instance of the British hiring local people for security purposes. The contact with the Mughal court was established, but it was only in 1613 that the East India Company could get permission to build a factory at Surat. It gradually expanded to other areas and established itself at St. George (Madras), Bombay and Calcutta, not merely as a trading agency but also as an administering authority after overpowering or outmanoeuvring the local rulers and the competing European powers. These main stations of the East India Company were later designated as Presidencies and shaped up as three distinct administrative centres.

The Company's Charter allowed it to maintain troops for protection against pirates and European rivals.[2] It employed guards and watchmen for its factories and establishments. These personnel were later organized as a militia after being given some military training. As the Presidency system developed, each Presidency built its own army and recruited Indians as *sepoy* or soldiers – a practice first initiated by the French in India.[3] The Company also had European troops of different nationalities, recruited mainly in England.[4] The three Presidency armies guaranteed protection and security for its property and personnel, added to the prestige and status of the Company and its European officials, and fought against local rulers and rival European powers that challenged its authority. In 1748, the Company appointed a British Army officer, Major Stringer Lawrence (1697–1775) as the commander of the garrison at St. George (Madras) and, in 1752, he was elevated to the position of Commander-in-Chief (C-in-C) of all the Company's forces. However, the armies based in Madras, Bombay and Calcutta functioned as three distinct entities.

The first contingent of the British Army (the King's troops) arrived in India in 1754 under the command of Colonel John Adlercron who soon developed differences with Major Lawrence, leading to the latter's exit from service. Thus, the Company's troops could be categorized as the King's (British) troops, the European troops, and the Indian troops. Intensive training with an emphasis on discipline and efficiency and their separation from the 'linguistically and socially fragmented' Indian society turned the Indian soldiers into a professional fighting force. Their loyalty was to their 'homogeneous military units' which they served on a 'full-time and long-term' basis with regular pay and a pension system.[5] Towards the end of the eighteenth century, the Company began to send its troops on overseas expeditions. It overcame the reluctance of many caste Hindus to serve overseas by enlisting soldiers for such expeditions on a voluntary basis.[6] Two important frontier forces were raised for the defence of specific areas. The Sindh Frontier Force was set up in 1846 for dealing mainly with Baloch tribesmen. This force was part of the Bombay Army and was controlled by the commander of that Army. In 1849, the British raised the Punjab Frontier Force for keeping order on the northwestern border. This force was initially under the control of the Foreign Department of Government of India through the Lieutenant Governor of the Punjab. In 1886, this was brought under the operational control of the C-in-C, India, as a part of the Bengal Army. Its separate character as a frontier force was maintained until 1903, when it was incorporated into the Indian Army.[7]

The Bengal Army was the largest of the three armies and it maintained its dominant position throughout its separate existence; its commander was designated as the C-in-C of the Company's armies, although his powers over the armies of Bombay and Madras were nominal. The Bengal Army covered the area from the Bay of Bengal to the borders of British India in the north and northwest, up to the border of Afghanistan after 1849. From the second half of the eighteenth century, the Bengal Army started enlisting the communities that had once served in the Muslim armies and its recruitment tilted heavily in favour of high caste Hindus, mainly from Bihar, Oudh and Agra. The Gurkhas and the Punjabis were also recruited. Caste-consciousness was quite strong in this Army. The Madras Army covered Madras, Hyderabad, the Central Provinces and, later, Burma. The Bombay Army's domain included Bombay, Sindh, Rajputana and Aden. The Madras and Bombay Armies recruitment was mainly (but not exclusively) from their Presidency areas and observed no caste or religious distinctions.[8]

These armies underwent a major organizational transformation after the British government assumed the responsibilities of the East India Company in August 1858. The major guidelines for these changes were provided by the Peel Commission (1859) and the Eden Commission (1879) which emphasized the need of maintaining a professional, disciplined and loyal army. The system of three separate armies was maintained, although the position of the C-in-C, India, was strengthened. As the troops of the Bengal Army were largely involved in the 1857 uprising, it underwent substantial organizational and manpower changes. The distinction between the British troops and the European troops was gradually done away with. The strength of the British troops was raised and they were given total control over artillery and some other branches of the Army.

The British placed greater emphasis on the preservation of distinctiveness and separateness of different castes and communities in the Army so that they could counter-balance each other.[9] No single caste or class was allowed to dominate the Army. No Indian officer (non-commissioned) of one class was permitted to command the troops of another caste or class. The local regiments were confined to their area of recruitment except in case of an emergency situation when these could be moved out.[10] For example, the Punjabi troops could be despatched to other regions, and vice versa. The Gurkhas who were recruited from Nepal were viewed as quite suitable for emergency duties. The British troops were also used for such assignments. In 1861, separate Staff Corps were instituted for the officers of each of the Presidency armies.

The separate existence of three Presidencies armies was often debated by the British administration. The Eden Commission recommended their amalgamation, but it was not until April 1895 that the three armies were merged to create the Indian Army, headed by a C-in-C. It was divided into four commands, each headed by a Lt.-General: The Madras Command included Madras and Burma (essentially the areas of the former Madras Army). The Bombay Command included the domain of the former Bombay Army. The former Bengal Army area was split into two commands: the Bengal Command and the Punjab Command. The title – the Indian Army – began to be used officially from 1 January 1903 when the three Staff Corps were abolished and the officers were designated as the officers of the Indian Army.

The origins of the Navy in British India can also be traced to the earliest days of the East India Company when it established a small fleet at Surat to protect its trade. From 1612 to 1686 it was known as the East India Company's Marine. When the Company's headquarters moved to Bombay, it was renamed the Bombay Marine. Its name was once again changed to the Indian Navy in 1830; renamed as the Bombay Marine in 1863. It was designated as His Majesty's Indian Marine in 1877, and in 1892, it was labelled as Royal Indian Marine. Its principal duties included the transportation of troops, the guarding of the convict settlements, countering of piracy, survey of coasts and harbours, visitation to light houses, and relief to distressed and wrecked vessels.[11] It played a limited role of transportation of some troops during World War I. In 1928, The Royal Indian Marine was reorganized on combatant lines as a step towards the creation of India's own naval defence. It became the Royal Indian Navy six years later with the passage of the Indian Navy (Discipline) Act in 1934. There was no Indian commissioned officer in the Royal Indian Marine until 1932.

The beginning of the Air Force was made when, in December 1915, the first detachment of the Royal Flying Corps arrived in India. It was first based at Nowshera and later at Risalpur. More squadrons were sent to India during the course of World War I; most of these were withdrawn after peace was restored. On 1 April 1933, the Royal Indian Air Force was formally established and the first squadron of Indians trained at Cranwell was set up at Karachi.[12] The Indian Navy and the Indian Air Force had their own commanding officers but the overall control was with the C-in-C, India, an army general. These two services were inadequate for the defence of India except as an appendage of the Royal Navy and the Royal Air Force respectively. Much of their expansion took place during World War II.

The Recruitment Policy

The recruitment policy for the Army underwent a major shift in the post-1858 period. The Army began to recruit more from the north and north-western regions of India at the expense of other regions, especially Bengal, Madras and Bombay. The drift towards the north and northwestern regions became pronounced in the last quarter of the nineteenth century and it emerged as the dominant feature in the first two decades of the twentieth. The Gurkhas (from Nepal), the Punjabis (Muslims, Sikhs and Hindus) and the Pathans (Pakhtuns, Pashtuns) from the North West Frontier region were preferred. The strength of the Punjabis increased steadily. In 1875, they constituted about 44 per cent of the Bengal Army and the Punjab Frontier Force, but only a quarter of the entire armed forces. In 1893, the Punjab, which also included the North Western Frontier region until 1901 when it was made a separate province, and Nepal accounted for nearly 44 per cent troops of the entire Indian armed forces. This increased to 57 per cent in 1904.[13] This resulted in under-representation of other regions and a number of castes and social classes were practically excluded from army service.

The British Army authorities were convinced that certain classes of Indians, described as the martial races, were more suitable for army service and that they made better soldiers. The Eden Commission noted in 1879 that the Punjab was the 'home of the most martial races of India' and that it was 'the nursery' of the best soldiers.[14] The martial qualities of certain groups were not the discovery of the British authorities in India. Many communities, like Marathas, Gurkhas, Muslims and Sikhs, had demon-strated their martial skills in the pre-British period. As the British expanded their hold over India, they accommodated these communities. For example, after the annexation of the Punjab, they employed soldiers of the Sikh Army. This developed into a well-established practice which tilted the balance of recruitment in favour of the classes with long tradition of military service.

Some explanations of the rise of the martial races talk of the deterioration of military spirit of certain communities over time which made them less suitable for military service. The years of peace made life easy for many communities who lost the qualities needed for a good soldier. The practice of keeping the regiments within the recruiting areas of its Presidency deprived the Madras Army of opportunity for active service, which adversely affected its quality because the Madras Presidency area was reasonably peace-ful after the British established themselves firmly in the nineteenth century. General Lord Roberts (C-in-C, 1885–93) maintained that the 'long years of peace, security and prosperity' softened the Madras Army as well as 'the ordinary Hindustani of Bengal and the Maratha of Bombay, and that they could no longer with safety be pitted against warlike races, or employed outside the limits of Southern India'.[15] The conditions were not so peaceful and easy in the northern parts, and the communities from these regions continued to exhibit warlike qualities.

Another explanation focuses on the Aryan martial traditions. Their des-cendants were viewed as a better soldier material than the original inhabit-ants of India. The British preferred the communities with Aryan background. Such a racist perspective created much prejudice against the communities with non-Aryan background. Some British explained the variations in the warlike attributes of different communities with reference to climate and ecology. It was argued that the prolonged heat of southern India and the Ganges delta was not conducive to the development of warlike qualities. The people from these areas were 'timid both by religion and habit, servile to their superiors but tyrannical to their inferiors, and quite unwarlike'. It was only in the areas with cold climate, as was the case in the north, that the people with warlike qualities could be found who made good soldiers.[16]

Another explanation maintains that the perceived Russian threat to north-western India in the last quarter of the nineteenth century shifted British attention to this region. As the Russian Tsars expanded their empire into Central Asia during 1868–81 and reached the borders of Afghanistan, the British military authorities decided to strengthen defences on the north-western fringes of the empire in order to deter any possible Russian onslaught. An offshoot of this policy was more recruitment from the areas closer to these borders.

The availability of manpower in such a large quantity from the Punjab is also explained with reference to the working of the political economy. The socio-economic conditions of the peasants in many parts of the Punjab were bad when the British entered the region which deteriorated further as these areas were brought into the fold of the colonial economy. The peasants owned small plots of land whose agricultural output was low due to poor soil fertility, erratic rainfall and scarcity of water, and shortage of finances. The option of army service offered them an opportunity to supplement the family's faltering income from agriculture. These peasant-recruits were hard-working, disciplined and willing to undertake the assigned duties with keen-ness and commitment. A large number of them came from the Salt Range and the *Potwar* (*Potohar*) regions of northern Punjab (especially the districts of Jhelum, Rawalpindi and Attock) and the adjoining region of North Wes-tern Frontier Province (NWFP) where the peasants were facing serious eco-nomic hardships.[17]

The British policy of granting agricultural land as a reward for military service also encouraged recruitment. The British Indian government began construction of a network of canals, their branches and distributories in the plains of western Punjab. This process was initiated in 1885 and continued intermittently until the end of British rule which brought large tracts of land, hitherto largely uncultivable, mostly unpopulated or inhabited by some semi-nomadic populace, under cultivation. There were nine such areas, called the Canal Colonies, where land with sufficient canal water became available. The British Indian government distributed this land mainly on political considerations, that is, to reward the people and com-munities for services to the Raj. Substantial tracts of the colony lands were allotted to ex-servicemen, both officers and other ranks, which enhanced the attraction of army service for peasants. Land grants were also made for breeding horses, camels and other animals for supply to the Army. Substan-tial allotments of land were made to the veterans of World War I.[18] These land awards made army service an attractive profession which enabled the peasants to improve their socio-economic status. No other profession guar-anteed such a high material reward in the Punjab.

The recruitment policy also reflected the distrust of the people and communities actively involved in the uprising of 1857 and a preference for those who stood aloof or helped the British to overcome the challenge.

Many classes serving in the Bengal Army were gradually eased out and new recruitment from these classes was discouraged. The Punjab, which had come under the British rule in 1849 and had not developed grievances against the British, remained unaffected by the events of 1857. Their recruitment policy was also biased against city and town dwellers and urban educated elements whom the British viewed as 'unsafe' for recruitment.

The preference for the martial races narrowed the base of recruitment. The British government could not hold on to this policy during World War I; the increased manpower requirements compelled them to open recruitment to the so-called non-martial classes and areas. However, the response of the non-martial areas was not encouraging and the traditional recruiting areas maintained their preponderance amongst the new recruits during World War I. Bengal, with a population of 45 million, provided 7,117 combatant recruits; the Punjab with a population of 20 million offered 349,689 combatant recruits. The Punjab and the United Provinces provided three-quarters of the total combatant recruits.[19] In the Punjab, one out of 28 males was mobilized; this ratio was one to 150 in the rest of India.[20] When the demobilization process was initiated after the war, the troops from non-martial areas were the first to go. During the late 1920s, the Punjab, NWFP and the Kingdom of Nepal provided approximately 84 per cent troops. Bombay and Madras furnished only 13,000 personnel. On average, the Central Province, Bihar and Orissa provided 500 personnel each; Bengal and Assam offered none at all.[21] Similar trends could be identified during World War II. Despite the expansion of the base of recruitment, the Punjab and NWFP maintained their traditional lead.

Civil–Military Relations

The British emphasized civilian supremacy over the military as the cardinal principle of military organization, but this principle operated in India in a rather peculiar manner. The ultimate control of the Indian military was with the British (civilian) government in London which operated in India through the Governor General/Viceroy who was at the apex of the administration. The C-in-C was second most powerful authority; second in order of precedence to the Governor General, entitled to use the title of His Excellency. At the operational level, the military and the civilian government in India were more often equal partners than the former being really subordinate to the latter. The civilian authority in India, being the administration of a colony, was responsible to the British government, as was the military. The Governor General was the civil and political representative of the Crown, and the C-in-C was its military representative. A C-in-C with stature and connections in the power structure in London could apply pressure on the civilian authority in India.

The Governor General and the C-in-C were appointed by the Directors of the Board of Control of the East India Company on the advice of the Crown. After 1858, these appointments became the sole prerogative of the British government through the Secretary of State for India. The Governor General-in-Council exercised control over the civilian and military affairs in India. The C-in-C was the sole military adviser to the Governor General and an ex-officio member of his Executive Council. In 1793, the position of the C-in-C was slightly changed; instead of being an ex-officio member of the Executive Council, he began to be nominated as an extra-ordinary member. Several Governor Generals/Viceroys had military background while one Governor, (Robert Clive (December 1756–February 1760, April 1765–January 1767) – and three Governor Generals – Lord Cornwallis (September 1786–October 1793 and July 1805–October 1805) the Marquis of Hastings, Lord Francis Moira (October 1813–January 1823), and Lord William Bentinck (1828–35) – functioned as C-in-Cs. (Bentinck served in this capacity only from October 1833 to September 1835.) Field Marshal Sir Archibald Wavell, C-in-C, 1941–2, 1942–3 was elevated to the post of Viceroy in 1943, a position he held until March 1947.

Under the Charter Act of 1833, a Military Member was added to the Governor General's Executive Council to enable him to obtain advice on military affairs from another source in addition to the C-in-C. This was also meant to reduce some responsibilities of the C-in-C so that he could devote more attention to his professional matters. The Military Member headed the Military Department and was responsible for the administrative work of the Army and looked after Supply and Transport, Ordnance, Military Works and the Financial Affairs, including the preparation of the military budget. All proposals and suggestions from the Army headquarters were channelled to the government through him. The C-in-C who headed the Army headquarters with operational and administrative control of the troops was assisted by Principal Staff Officers and enjoyed autonomy in the management of the internal affairs of the armed forces.

The system of dual management of the military affairs worked smoothly until Field Marshal Lord Horatio Herbert Kitchener was appointed C-in-C in 1902. He was loath to transact business with the government through the Military Member who was junior to him.[22] He pleaded unsuccessfully with Lord George Curzon (Viceroy: 1899–1905) for the abolition of the post of Military Member which embittered their relations. Both approached the British government through their connections in London in support of their perspectives. The British government opted for a compromise. The Military Member was re-designated as the Military Supply Member with reduced powers, but he continued to be a member of the Executive Council. The powers of the C-in-C were enhanced and he was made responsible directly to the Viceroy for organizational and command functions. The financial control was assigned to a new Military Finance Department under a Joint Financial Secretary (later designated as the Financial Adviser) controlled by the Senior Financial Secretary and the Finance Member of the Executive Council. Curzon felt humiliated by this change and resigned in 1905. Kitchener did not like the half-way arrangement and insisted on nominating the Supply Member. Four years later, in 1909, the post of Supply Member and the Military Supply Department were abolished altogether.[23] The C-in-C headed the Army Department and controlled the Army head-quarters; he was the sole Military Member of the Executive Council and adviser to the Viceroy on military and security affairs. This made the C-in-C the most powerful office after the Viceroy.

The C-in-C also served as a nominated member of the upper house (Council of State) of the legislature established under the Government of India Act, 1919, addressing the members on military affairs and responding to their questions and motions. The Indian legislature had no control over defence and foreign affairs and defence expenditure. The members could, however, discuss these matters and pass non-binding resolutions. The Government of India Act, 1935, proposed no change of any consequence in the organization and administration of the military and security affairs. The administration of military, defence expenditure and security and foreign policy were assigned to the Executive Council which was not answerable to the legislature in India.

When an interim government was installed in September 1946, an Indian political leader, Sardar Baldev Singh, was appointed Defence Minister for the first time who replaced the C-in-C in the Viceroy's Executive Council. A Defence Committee was also set up under his chairmanship which included *inter alia* the C-in-C, the Defence Secretary, and the Financial Adviser. However, before the implications of this change could fully materialize, the British decided to grant independence and partition India.

The Military and Imperial Rule

The Army symbolized the might of British rule and was its ultimate guarantor. The British administration, therefore, attached importance to maintaining a professional, disciplined, efficient and loyal army. Its refusal to share the control and management of the security affairs and the Army with Indian leaders was shaped by their desire to keep a firm control of the institution deemed central to the survival of the Raj.

The Army was instrumental in extending the domain of the Company and the British government by overwhelming the regular and irregular troops of the local rulers. Even after its preponderant position was firmly established, the Army regularly undertook internal security duties in order to foil any bid to challenge the British authority and to maintain peace and tranquility. The challenges to the British administration included revolts by tribal chiefs, violent raids and guerrilla activities of various disaffected elements, banditry and peasant revolts. The troops were also deployed for coping with labour unrest and strikes. The periodic outbreak of violence as a consequence of the rise of Hindu militant movements in the last decade of the nineteenth century and the agitation against the partition of Bengal (1905–11) often necessitated the deployment of regular troops. According to one estimate the troops were used for internal security duties on 46 occasions during 1860–79. Such responsibilities increased manifold towards the end of the nineteenth century; they were called out 69 times between 1899 and 1901.[24] At times, the troops were called out to assist civil administration for curbing Hindu–Muslim communal riots.

The troops were also used to contain street agitation, which became quite common as the nationalist movement gained momentum from the second decade of the twentieth century onwards. The passive resistance movements led by Gandhi during 1920–2 and 1930–3, and the Khilafat movement, 1919–24, produced violence at one time or another. The British Indian government used draconian laws and the coercive apparatus of the state to contain these movements. The most well-known instance of excessive use of force was the Jallianwala Bagh (Amritsar) incident of 13 April 1919, when the troops opened fire on a protest meeting without warning, killing 379 people.[25] Two days later, martial law was imposed in Amritsar and Lahore; and later, extended to other districts of the Punjab. This was the first martial law imposed anywhere in South Asia in the twentieth century. During World War II, the Congress refused to cooperate with the British war efforts and, in 1942, launched the famous Quit India agitation which produced much anti-British violence. The government responded with a heavy hand on the Congress; its leaders were arrested and the troops were called out to contain agitation and ensure that the government's efforts for new recruitment to the Army and resource mobilization for the war were not disrupted. The Army also extended humanitarian assistance in the event of natural disasters like floods, famine or epidemic and helped in repairing and restoring roads, railway tracks and bridges.

The external dimension of India's security pertained to the perceived Russian threat from the northwest. The British viewed the northwestern border (British India and Afghanistan) as the outer boundary of their empire, and that any débâcle on this border not only endangered the rule in India but also threatened the empire as a whole. The Simon Commission (1930) observed: 'The northwest frontier is not only the frontier of India, it is an international frontier of the first importance from the military point of view for the whole empire.'[26] The British therefore kept the Russians at bay by strengthening defensive arrangement on this border and by maintaining Afghanistan as a buffer zone. This policy was supplemented by establishing a varying degree of control on the small states on the northern border, i.e. Nepal, Bhutan and Sikkim.[27]

The British adopted various measures to strengthen the defence of this region. These included a stepped up military presence in the region, construction of new roads to improve communication and troops mobility and greater induction of manpower in the Army from this region. The Punjab Frontier Force which looked after security of this region was transferred from the Punjab government to the C-in-C in 1886. A border agreement was signed with the Afghan government in November 1893, followed by demarcation of the agreed boundary (the Durand Line) to stabilize bilateral relations. A number of developments in the twentieth century (the Russo-Japanese war, 1904–5; the Anglo Russian Convention, 1907; the Bolshevik revolution in Russia, 1917; and the treaty of friendship with Afghanistan after the Anglo-Afghan war, 1919–21) reduced the danger of Russian/Soviet advance towards India and stabilized relations with Afghanistan. However, the British never ruled out the possibility of a Soviet advance into Afghanistan and therefore maintained a strong profile on the northwestern frontier.[28] They also entertained a relatively unfounded fear that, in case of a war involving several powers, Afghanistan could become a base for hostile activities against them, or the Soviets might use their ideology to encourage the Marxist groups in India to engage in militant anti-British agitation.

An additional security concern was the perennial conflict between the British administration and the Pathan (Pakhtun) tribes settled in what was called the tribal areas on the India–Afghanistan border. The British came in a regular contact with them after the annexation of the Punjab and continued with the policy inherited from the Sikhs with some modifications. Known as the 'closed door' policy, the British firmly established their authority in the accessible areas, i.e. Peshawar, Kohat, Bannu, Hazara and Dera Ismail Khan, but did not normally venture into hills where Pathan tribes were settled. Lord Lawrence (Viceroy: 1863–8) was willing to pull back the troops to the Indus river, viewing it as a natural geographic border. However, the British kept their military pressure on the hilly tribal areas which periodically brought them in armed conflict with the tribes. Lord Lytton (Viceroy: 1876–80) resorted to some penetration of the tribal area by moving troops to some advance positions. He also engaged in the Second Afghan War, 1878–80, which proved quite costly for the British. Later, the British adopted the 'Forward policy', pushing the effective frontier from the outer limits of the settled areas towards the northwest in the direction of Afghanistan. The regular troops were stationed in various fortifications established in different parts of the tribal areas and these were linked with roads. Lord Curzon created a separate North West Frontier Province in 1901, which was divided into the settled areas of Peshawar, Kohat, Hazara, Bannu and Dera Ismail Khan; and the unsettled (tribal) area between the administrative line of the settled area and the Durand Line. The latter was placed under the direct control of the government of India, but the area enjoyed autonomy with little or no interference from the administration. The British also adopted various methods to keep the tribes pacified: financial subsidies to the tribal chiefs willing to cooperate, playing one tribe against another, blockade of an area, hostage-taking and army operations. A local militia was set up from amongst the loyal tribesmen which was equipped with better weapons. As this militia gained strength, military fortifications were reduced in the tribal area and the regular troops were based only at key strategic points for reinforcing the militia.[29]

There were 72 army expeditions against these tribes from 1850 to 1922 – an average of one expedition every year.[30] The major army encounters in the tribal areas included Chitral (1896), Malakand (1897), the Waziri tribe (1901–2, 1919 and 1937), the Mahsuds (1925), the Waziris, the Mahsuds and the Afridis (1930–1), the Mahmands (1933) and the Tori-Khael (1936–7). The regular troops were extensively used on these occasions and, in some cases, the Air Force was called out to assist the army operations.

In addition to the tri-dimensional India-based role – internal peace and order, external security and containment of the Pakhtun tribes – the Indian Army participated in foreign expeditions for advancing the British imperial cause. Though Indian troops were used outside India during the days of the East India Company, this evolved into an important feature of the military policy after the British Crown directly assumed India's administration. During 1858–1914, Indian troops were deployed in Abyssinia, Afghanistan, Burma, Persia, Singapore, the Malay peninsula, Hong Kong, Malta, Egypt, the Sudan, Uganda, East Africa, Somaliland, South Africa and China. Its formations participated in military action during World War I in Europe, the Middle East and East Africa. The story of World War II was no different, when India contributed significantly to the British war efforts by offering material support and manpower. The Army units and the Air Force took part in military operations in Europe, Africa, the Middle East and South East Asia.

The military was thus not merely central to the establishment of the British rule, its role was critical to the stability and survival of the Raj by ensuring internal order and external security. The military's overwhelming coercive power deterred many from challenging the British rule and its periodic use to crush any challenge made it clear to Indians that the British were there to stay. But for the preponderance of power and the will to use it when and if needed, the British civilian authorities would have found it extremely difficult to maintain social and political stability. Writing in 1823, John Malcolm maintained that the government in India was 'essentially military', and that the role of the civilian institutions in preserving and improving the territorial possessions depended on the 'exercise of the military power'.[31] Similar views were expressed in a recent study, which asserted that 'the Company's dominance in north India was based on its superior military power'.[32] This reality did not change after the Crown began to administer India.

The coercive power was not the only reason that explained the military's importance. It helped the British administration by evolving multifaceted pacific interaction with the civilians. The military authorities obtained sufficient data on the communities that came forward for recruitment which was made available to the state for use in pursuance of its imperial interests, i.e. an understanding of religious, caste, linguistic and cultural differences enabled them to manipulate these cleavages to keep different Indian communities apart so that a broad-based and cohesive challenge did not emerge. The recruits, trained and disciplined in military ethos, were an important support base for the imperial rule. This was very visible in the martial race areas, where soldiers returning home on leave or for settling down after retirement generally spoke highly of their 'English Sahibs', thereby generating goodwill towards the British. The families with long traditions of military service manifested much loyalty to the British rule. The military also penetrated the civil society through its British officers who interacted with the upper strata and the educated classes. Some of them were involved in sports, and literary and cultural activities, which gave them access to the local civilian elite. Mutual goodwill, generated in the course of such interaction, expanded the military's influence in the society.

Given the pivotal role of the military in the formation and sustenance of the British Indian empire, the civilian administration made sure that sufficient resources were available for the military and security related activities. The objective was to keep the troops generally satisfied. Sufficient attention was paid to issues like salary and living conditions, facilities for their families, and post-retirement benefits and rewards so that the troops did not develop serious grievances and military service maintained its attraction for the young.

The British Indian government was quite generous towards the military. The defence expenditure was the single largest item in India's budget and more financial resources were made available to the military than education, health and irrigation together. The expenditure on the military services was Rs. 306.5 million in 1914–15 which rose to Rs. 640.7 million in 1918–19 and Rs. 873.8 million in 1920–1. The postwar retrenchment brought the defence expenditure down to Rs. 517.6 million in 1931–2 which was further reduced to Rs. 454.5 million in 1936–7. From 1933–4, the British government agreed to contribute £1,500,000 every year to India's military expenditure; this was raised to £2,000,000 in April 1939. The outbreak of World War II in September 1939 led to a steep rise in defence expenditure, touching a peak of Rs. 4583.2 million (excluding the British contribution) in 1944–5. The end of the war eased the financial burden as the allocations for military services were reduced to Rs. 3,953.2 million in 1945–6, and Rs. 2096.1 million in 1946–7, though this was still higher than the pre-war expenditure of Rs.461.8 million (1938–9).[33]

Indianization of the Commissioned Ranks

No Indian was allowed to hold the King's Commissioned Officer (KCO) ranks until 1917. They could become Viceroy's Commissioned Officer

(VCO; redesignated as JCO or Junior Commissioned Officer after Pakistan and India became independent) and the highest rank in this category was that of Subedar-Major. The Viceroy Commission was normally granted by promotion from the lower ranks and the VCOs served as a link between the British officers (KCOs) and the ordinary Indian soldiers at the company level. Lord Curzon established an Imperial Cadet Corps in 1901. The sons of Indian princes and other aristocratic families could assume the officer rank in this corps, designated as having been commissioned to 'His Majesty's Native Indian Land Forces' after some training in India. However, this was different from the regular commission (KCO), which continued to be the preserve of the British. By 1909, only 76 Indians had joined the Imperial Cadet Corps, most of whom were disappointed as its role was essentially ceremonial. It was not surprising that their number had dropped to 11 by 1914.[34]

India's politically active circles demanded that the commissioned ranks of the Army should be opened to qualified Indians. The Congress leadership was very vocal in making such a demand. A similar demand was made by the Muslim League; in 1911, its London branch petitioned the British government to allow Indians to join the commissioned ranks. These demands were made in unequivocal terms after the outbreak of the World War I. The Indian leaders were of the opinion that the ideal of self-government would not be fully realized unless the commissioned ranks of the Army were opened to Indians.

The much awaited change came in August 1917, when Edwin Montagu, Secretary of State for India, in his famous statement on 'increasing association of Indians in every branch of the administration', announced the lifting of the ban on admission of Indians to the commissioned ranks. Nine Indians who had meritorious service to their credit in World War I were promoted to the commissioned ranks by the British government; they belonged to the martial races.

Ten vacancies were created in 1918 for Indian cadets at the Royal Military Academy, Sandhurst. Any Indian interested in obtaining the King's Commission had to complete the course at this institution. The Indian government carefully screened the candidates, preferring sons of the VCOs and others from the politically acceptable families, i.e. known as loyal to the Raj. The first group of Indians passed out from Sandhurst were commissioned in 1920; they were posted to the Infantry and the Cavalry.[35] A Cadet College was opened at Indore in 1918 which functioned for one year. Its 39 graduates were given temporary commission in 1919; 32 of them were later made permanent.[36] The British could also grant honorary commissions in recognition of distinguished service to those who were not eligible for substantive King's Commission due to their age or lack of educational qualifications.

The reserved places at Sandhurst were not filled in the first couple of years because the selection process was very cumbersome and the expenses of

Sandhurst were quite high for Indian parents, not to speak of the travel to England and stay there which dissuaded Indians from making use of the new opportunity. The weak academic background of Indians also contributed to the problem. The failure rate of Indian cadets in the early years was 30 per cent as compared to 3 per cent for the British cadets.[37] Many British military and civilian officials had strong reservations about the induction of Indians to the commissioned ranks, arguing that this would undermine the professional quality of the Army as the Indians lacked the excellence needed for the officer ranks. Moreover, they were perturbed by the idea of Indian officers commanding British troops.[38] The Indian KCOs were required to spend their first year with a British regiment in India, and then they were posted on a permanent basis in one of the eight units selected in 1923 for complete Indianization (known as the Eight Unit Scheme).[39] This was to restrict the impact of Indianization to these units and enable the British commanders to monitor the performance of the Indian officers.

A committee, headed by General Henry Rawlinson (C-in-C, 1920–5), appointed in 1921, recommended an increase in the pace of Indianization. In March 1922, a pre-cadet college – the Prince of Wales Royal Indian Military College – was established in Dehra Dun for preparing young men for Sandhurst. Another committee was appointed in March 1925 under the chairmanship of Lt.-General Sir Andrew Skeen, Chief of the General Staff (known as the Indian Sandhurst Committee) for reviewing the Indianization process, including the exploration of the possibilities of setting up a military college on the pattern of Sandhurst in India. The committee comprised 13 members, including Motilal Nehru (who resigned later) and Jinnah. Its sub-committee, which also included Jinnah, visited the military training institutions in England, France, Canada and the US and examined oral evidence from the official and non-official circles.[40] Its report (submitted in November 1926 and released to the press in March 1927) recommended, *inter alia* an increase in the pace of Indianization, induction of Indians to the commissioned ranks in the technical branches of the Army as well as the Air Force, abandonment of the Eight Units Scheme, and the establishment of a military college in India. The British government did not accept the last two recommendations. Instead, it increased the places reserved for Indians at Sandhurst to 25; two vacancies per year were created at the Royal Air Force College, Cranwell, to train Indians as pilots and six places were made available at Royal Military Academy, Woolwich, for training Indian officers for the artillery.

Indianization was taken up once again in the First Roundtable Conference (1930), when its sub-committee on military affairs, which also included Jinnah, demanded immediate steps for acceleration of the pace of Indianization. It also underlined the need of setting up a military training college in India on the Sandhurst model. In May 1931, the Indian government established a technical committee for working out the details of an officers' training institution. The Indian Military Academy was established at Dehra Dun in December 1932. The first batch from this Academy was commissioned as Indian Commissioned Officers (ICOs) in 1935.

Several important changes were made after the outbreak of the Second World War. The Eight Unit Scheme was done away with and all branches of the Army were opened to Indian officers. Training facilities at the Military Academy and the Military College, Dehra Dun, were expanded and new training institutions were established. The grant of a regular commission was suspended and a large number of officers were recruited on short and emergency commissions. By early 1947, out 9,500 Indians who had obtained commissions in the Army, about 500 were pre-war KCOs and ICOs.

Only nine Indians (five non-Muslims, four Muslims) reached the senior rank of Lt.-Colonel during World War II. Out of the five non-Muslim Lt.-Colonels, one was appointed acting Colonel, another a temporary Colonel, and three became acting Brigadiers. One of the acting Brigadiers was later made permanent, who along with one acting Brigadier were appointed Major Generals a few days before India achieved independence. They were K.M. Cariappa and Rajendra Sinhji. Out of four Muslim Lt.-Colonels, one was appointed temporary Colonel and one acting Brigadier. A few days before independence, the acting Brigadier (Mohammad Akbar Khan 'Rangroot') was promoted to Major General. Promotions were given on similar lines to others in the substantive ranks below that of Lieutenant Colonel. The officers recruited during the war period were in junior positions.[41]

The first Indian was commissioned as Midshipman in the executive branch of the Royal Indian Marine (later renamed as Royal Indian Navy) in September 1932. He was Muhammad Siddiq Chaudri who later became the first Pakistan C-in-C of the Pakistan Navy (1953-9). The highest rank achieved by any Indian in the Navy by the end of 1946 was that of Acting Captain. By 1947, only seven Indian naval officers had the experience ranging between 13 to 15 years. The Indian Air Force expanded rapidly during the war period, but by 1947, only eight officers had more than 10 years of service to their credit.[42]

The Military and Politics

The military and the security affairs were the exclusive preserve of the British. They kept these matters insulated from political influences by denying powers to Indian legislature over the military and the defence expenditure. No Indian held the defence portfolio in the Viceroy's Executive Council until September 1946. The preference for the martial races for recruitment also kept the Army free of the strong influence of Indian political leaders as these regions had a favourable disposition towards the British. The training and acculturation process in the Army and the separation of the troops from society strengthened their ties with the institution which placed much premium on discipline, professionalism and loyalty to the established British authority.

The Congress and the Muslim League adopted similar positions on security and military affairs. They argued that the British policy of associating Indians with governance would be meaningless unless they were given control of defence, foreign policy and defence expenditure. The central legislature set up under the Government of India Act, 1919, passed several non-binding resolutions demanding acceleration of Indianization. establishment of an officers' training institution in India, and the grant of powers to the legislature on security affairs and defence expenditure. These issues were also raised in the Nehru Report (1928) and the Roundtable Conferences (1930–2).

The British were haunted by the fear that any loosening of the grip on these matters could undermine India's security and jeopardize the interests of the empire. The Esher Committee (1919–20) maintained that the Indian Army was a unit in the security system of the British empire and that its administration could not be dissociated from the total armed forces of the empire.[43] Speaking in the Legislative Assembly (lower house) in October 1927, Field Marshal William Birdwood (C-in-C, 1925–30) said:

> The Army in India is one link in the Imperial chain of defence of the empire and naturally, therefore, no alteration in its organization, which might in any way affect its efficiency, can be taken without the fullest consideration of His Majesty's Government, which is ultimately responsible for Imperial security.[44]

The Simon Commission (1930) observed:

> India and Britain are so related that Indian defence cannot, now or in any future which is within sight, be regarded as a matter of purely Indian concern. The control and direction of such army must rest in the hands of agents of the Imperial Government.[45]

The Indian Army maintained a professional profile and concentrated on their assigned duties. The attempt by the political activists to infiltrate the Amy did not succeed. The militancy and agitation in the wake of the partition of Bengal (1905–11), different non-cooperation movements, the Khilafat movement, the activities of the extremist groups and communal troubles did not adversely affect the morale and discipline of the troops. During World War I, the *Gaddar* party activists made several unsuccessful bids to foment rebellion among the Sikh troops. Similarly, the Quit India Movement (1942) of the Congress could not undermine the British war efforts in India in any significant way. The Army personnel held on to their professional ethos and stood by the British administration.

The only exceptions were the formation of the Indian National Army (INA) during World War II and the strike in the Navy (1946). The INA was organized as a 'national liberation force' consisting of Indians living in East Asia and the Indian soldiers captured by the Axis Powers, especially by Japan. Two ICOs, Mohan Singh and Shah Nawaz Khan, played an important role in organizing units of the INA. However, it acquired greater significance when Subhas Chandra Bose, a charismatic Indian leader who developed differences with Gandhi and later joined the Axis Powers, took command of the INA. Some of its units joined with the Japanese when they attacked Burma and the eastern region of India (the Arakan and the Imphal-Kohima battles in 1944 and the Irrawaddy battle in 1945) but it collapsed and many of its members were captured. Some of its officers were put on trial by the Indian government in 1945. Most Indian political parties capitalized on their trials by according them hero's status as freedom fighters. However, after India and Pakistan attained independence, the INA personnel were not taken back in the Army, although they were granted a pension.[46] The naval strike of February 1946 was triggered by the hunger strike of some ratings of the Signal School in Bombay in protest against pay and living conditions. About 3,000 naval personnel went on strike in Bombay and replaced the White Ensign with the flags of the Congress and the Muslim League on the ships, and some of the ship hooters sounded 'Jai Hind'.[47] The strike soon spread to Karachi, Calcutta, Madras and Delhi. The Air Force and the Army personnel in some stations observed a token strike in sympathy with the Navy personnel. In Jabbalpur, about 2,500 Indian troops came out on the streets carrying the Congress and the Muslim League flags.[48] The British troops were sent in to restore order. The situation returned to normal after about a week when the government appointed a committee to look into their grievances.

These incidents, limited to a small section of service personnel, made it clear to the British government that the nationalist sentiments had started penetrating the most powerful institution of the empire. A good number of officers who got into the Army during the war period on emergency commissions were relatively more influenced by the nationalist leaders than those who joined the service before the outbreak of the war. By 1946, the two nationalist parties, the Congress and the Muslim League, were engaged in extensive political mobilization and they had penetrated the main Army recruiting regions. The British realized that time was fast approaching when they might have problems with the loyalties of the troops. Some British officers entertained an additional fear: communal sentiments which had spread widely in the polity might undermine the discipline in the Army, causing conflict along Hindu–Muslim lines.[49] However, such fears proved unfounded and the Indian Army upheld its discipline and professional disposition.

The Army endeavoured to stem the tide of communal killings during the last few weeks of British rule. The British Indian government decided to set up a special Army command as the Punjab Boundary Force (PBF) from 1 August 1947, for maintaining peace and security in the districts of Sialkot, Gujranwala, Sheikhupura, Lyallpur (Faisalabad), Montgomery (Sahiwal), Lahore, Gurdaspur, Hoshiarpur, Amritsar, Jullundur, Freozepur and Ludhiana. It had a mixed communal composition with a Muslim: non-Muslim ratio of 35:65. Though its approved strength was 50,000 personnel, the actual strength ranged from 15,000 to 23,000. The PBF provided some protection to the people in these districts, but it soon became clear that it was not in a position to check communal frenzy. This special command was disbanded on the night of 1/2 September and the task of maintaining law and order in these districts was handed over to the new governments of India and Pakistan.[50]

The government of Pakistan handed over this task to the Army. Its personnel provided protection to refugee convoys moving across the frontier, and undertook relief work in refugee camps by providing food, clothing and medical care in collaboration with the civil administration. Heavy rains and floods in the autumn created additional problems. Army engineers and other personnel were brought in for rescue and relief operations and for restoring communications. The Navy moved some refugees from Bombay by sea; the Air Force performed some support duties for refugee movements and relief operations during the floods. This was the first civic mission the military undertook in Pakistan at a time when the three services were themselves undergoing the process of partition and reorganization and many personnel had lost family members in the communal frenzy that accompanied the establishment of the state.

Division of the Military

The Muslim League demand for the establishment of a separate state of Pakistan for the Muslims of South Asia raised the question of the future of the British Indian military: should this be retained as a single unified force or divided, along with the division of South Asia? The Muslim League put forward the demand for its division in early 1947. Liaquat Ali Khan raised this issue formally with the Viceroy in April 1947, suggesting that a plan be prepared for the division of the military so that it could be readily divided at the appropriate time.[51] Nawab Muhammad Ismail Khan, the only Muslim member of the Armed Forces Nationalization Committee appointed by the Interim Government in November 1946, took exception to the report, issued in May 1947, on the ground that it had completely ignored the issue of partition.[52] Another prominent Muslim Leaguer, Malik Feroz Khan Noon (Prime Minister of Pakistan, 1957–8), demanded the division of the armed forces, ordnance factories and military equipment between India and Pakistan before independence was granted to them, 'because', he maintained, 'whosoever gets the army will get India'.[53]

The opposition to this demand was quite strong in the British circles because the preparation of a plan for the partition of the military at that stage, in their view, would have meant that the British government had accepted the Muslim League demand for the partition of South Asia; the official policy did not change until the announcement of the partition plan on 3 June 1947. The military high command in India was also not in favour of dividing the military. They were of the opinion that a divided military would not be able to attain the degree of professionalism and efficiency that characterized the British Indian military. Field Marshal Claude Auchinleck (C-in-C, 1943–7, Supreme Commander, 1947) was opposed to such a move. He, and most of his senior colleagues, wanted the military to be maintained as a single entity for the defence of both India and Pakistan; its division would lead to chaos and civil strife in the two states, exposing them to serious external threats.

The Congress leaders described the Muslim League demand as unrealistic because they expected the British to grant independence to a single and undivided India. However, some of them maintained that if India was partitioned, the armed forces would have to be divided.[54] The 3 June Plan proposing the establishment of two independent states of India and Pakistan changed the situation altogether. The Congress demanded the division of the military on the lines of the proposed partition. However, some senior Hindu Army officers shared the view of the British officers that the Indian Army should not be divided. K.M. Cariappa, the most senior Indian officer, approached senior Muslim officers with a view to winning them over to the idea of keeping the military intact. The Muslim officers rejected his proposal.[55] Maulana Abul Kalam Azad, a former president of the Congress, supported the move for keeping a joint control of the armed forces.[56] These efforts were bound to fail as the Congress and the Muslim League were equally in favour of the division of the armed forces. Jinnah and Liaquat Ali Khan went to the extent of declining power on independence if Pakistan did not have armed forces under its operational control.[57] Auchinleck, who initially opposed the division of the military, accepted the political decision with the grace of a soldier and presided over the process of division of the military. However, many senior military commanders and civil officials, including Lord Mountbatten, hoped that India and Pakistan would soon agree to joint defence.[58] Later developments, especially the dispute on the division of military equipment and stores, the war in Kashmir and other problems, dashed all such hopes.

The Partition Council, headed by Mountbatten, established the Armed Forces Reconstitution Committee to undertake the division of the military. It was presided over by Auchinleck and had a sub-committee each for the Army, the Navy and the Air Force. The guidelines for the division of the military, approved by the Partition Council on 30 June laid down that the two governments would have armed forces in their own territories under their operational control on the day of independence which would be predominantly Muslim in the case of Pakistan and pre-dominantly non-Muslims in the case of India.

Though Jinnah was willing to accept citizenship rather than religion as the basis of division of the military,[59] the guidelines offered a religion-cum-territorial criterion for division of manpower. Every service personnel was given an option to serve either India or Pakistan. However, there was one restriction. A Muslim from the area that formed part of Pakistan could not opt for India, and a non-Muslim from the area that constituted India could not join the Pakistan military. There was no restriction on a Muslim from Indian territory and a non-Muslim from Pakistani territory to opt for India and Pakistan respectively. A small number of non-Muslim personnel opted for Pakistan and some Muslims decided to stay with the Indian military. However, as communal violence intensified, some of them requested a change in their option, which was granted.

By 15 August, the future of the units had been decided. The only exceptions were the troops that served under the Punjab Boundary Force or those that were still abroad; they were divided later. The ratio for division of the troops was 64:34 for India and Pakistan, excluding the Gurkha troops. As there was no purely Muslim regiment in India, Pakistan did not get any regiment in full strength. The future of the Gurkha troops was decided by a tripartite arrangement signed in November 1947 by Britain, India and Nepal, which allocated four Gurkha units to Britain and six to India. The division of the naval ships and air force squadrons more or less reflected the communal proportion of the manpower, which meant that Pakistan had to be content with a smaller share.

A Joint Defence Council (JDC) was established on 15 August for dealing with the matters relating to division, movement, and the transfer of troops and military assets to India and Pakistan. It performed these and related functions through the newly created office of the Supreme Commander, redesignation of the C-in-C, British India – Auchinleck – to distinguish him from the C-in-Cs of India and Pakistan. The Supreme Commander had no operational control over the troops and he was not given any responsibility for the maintenance of law and order. His primary job included control of the British troops; management of military establishments serving the two countries, and division of troops and stores and their transfer to the governments of India and Pakistan. The moment the troops and equipment reached the respective state, the control of the Supreme Commander ceased to exist. The Supreme Commander was responsible to the JDC, which comprised the Governor General of India (Mountbatten) as an independent chairman, the Defence Ministers of India and Pakistan, and the Supreme Commander.

India and Pakistan developed serious differences on the division of military equipment and stores. Their representatives diverged sharply in the meetings of the sub-committees, the JDC and the Partition Council. At one stage they decided to refer the issue for arbitration. However, they changed their mind and mutually agreed that Pakistan would get roughly a third of equipment and stores. This did not improve the situation because the tendency on the part of India was to surrender as little as possible and Pakistan wanted to obtain as much as possible. In this tussle, India had a clear advantage because most equipment and stores were located there.

The Supreme Commander, Auchinleck, ran into trouble with the Indian government, which accused him of bias towards Pakistan. The senior Indian officials demanded his removal, claiming that he leaned heavily towards Pakistan and that the presence of such a senior officer as the Supreme Commander impeded the autonomous development of their military.[60] India's non-cooperation with the Supreme Commander's headquarters could be gauged from the fact that no guarantee of personal security was given for its Muslim staff, who had to be relieved from duty in the first week of September and moved to a refugee camp in Delhi. The under-training personnel and the staff of the India-based Army training institutions who had opted for Pakistan were released for transfer towards the end of September, although the original decision envisaged the joint use of the training institutions up to April 1948.

When Auchinleck realized that Mountbatten, who had become Governor General of India on 15 August, would not protect him from the vilification campaign of the Indian leaders, he proposed the closure of the Supreme Commander's headquarters on 30 November 1947 rather than the originally scheduled date of 1 April 1948.[61] In the JDC meeting Pakistan opposed the proposal, fearing that the removal of the Supreme Commander would make it extremely difficult for Pakistan to obtain its share of military equipment and stores. India naturally supported the proposal; Mountbatten went along with the Indian demand. The British government decided to wind up the Supreme Commander's headquarters on 30 November.[62] An Inter-Dominion Committee, known as the Executive Committee of the JDC, was set up to complete the unfinished work of the Supreme Commander.

The division of equipment and stores became more problematic after the closure of the Supreme Commander's headquarters. Additional problems were caused by the outbreak of the conflict in Jammu and Kashmir, especially after the Pakistan Army formally moved in. All the 16 ordnance factories were located in India which were transferred to India. Pakistan's bid to obtain machinery for two factories that had not been installed did not succeed. However, India agreed to pay Rs. 60 million to Pakistan as a contribution for setting up an ordnance factory and a security printing press. This amount was transferred to Pakistan towards the end of January 1948. The control of the training institutions was handed over to the country where these were situated. Pakistan obtained seven army training institutions, including the Staff College at Quetta, and Royal Indian Army Service Corps School at Kakul.

Military equipment and stores were transferred to Pakistan in an intermittent manner with frequent delays. Pakistan maintained that its due share was not handed over by India and that a good part of what was sent was useless and damaged; some packing cases contained bricks. The much needed items like tanks, specialist and armoured vehicles and their spares were not received, while the full share of many other important items including transport, guns and ammunition, was not transferred.[63] Even these supplies were suspended in October 1948.[64] Indian sources admitted that the transfer of stores to Pakistan was stopped, but they maintained that Pakistan owed a huge sum of money to India as the price of the surplus stores (the British government stores taken over by undivided India in April 1947 and located in Pakistani territory). India wanted this payment to be made separately, irrespective of differences on the transfer of equipment to Pakistan.[65] Pakistan's contention was that these claims had to be adjusted first against Pakistan's total share of military equipment and stores.

The conflicts that cropped up in the course of division of the military and its equipment reinforced the traditional distrust and bitterness that existed between the leaders of the Congress and the Muslim League. These legacies, coupled with other negative developments in the early years of independence, undermined the prospects of developing an amicable interaction between the newly independent states of India and Pakistan. The military inherited by Pakistan was weak, less organized and ill equipped, but it had to perform internal security duties from the first day and it soon found itself embroiled in an armed confrontation with India in Kashmir.

4
Civilian Institutions and the Military

The first 11 years of independence were crucial to shaping Pakistan's political and administrative profile. A new state structure was created out of the chaos and dislocation caused by the partition of British India, and Pakistan's sovereign status was stabilized, defying the predictions that the new state would collapse under the weight of its problems. However, state building in the difficult circumstances of the early years entrenched the centre and the bureaucratic-military elite at the expense of the political institutions and processes. Pakistan shaped up as a centralized and administrative polity which stifled the growth of autonomous and viable political institutions and processes. The state, though having sufficiently developed apparatus, found it difficult to cope with the participatory pressures and demands for socio-economic equity from a heterogeneous populace and diversified regions.

State Formation and the Security Environment

Pakistan faced serious administrative, political and economic problems in the early years of independence. There was hardly any area free of turbulence caused by the partition and two-way movement of the people – influx of Muslim refugees from India and the departure of non-Muslims from Pakistan. The most difficult problems were their protection on the way and resettlement on their arrival. Any government would have faced serious difficulties in dealing with these problems but, in Pakistan, there was hardly an established government at the centre, and the provincial governments in Karachi, Lahore and Peshawar were completely shaken under the impact of partition and the loss of non-Muslim labour. A new provincial government was being put together at Dhaka. There was a serious shortage of civil servants at the senior level because the Muslim representation in the services was quite poor in British India.[1]

The initial problems, especially the urgent need to set up an effective central government that could save the new state from collapsing, had three major implications. First, the newly established centre made its presence felt by asserting its role in almost all aspects of administration, even if something was in the provincial domain. It relied heavily on the concept of a strong centre as inherited from the British period. Second, a handful of senior and middle-level civil servants were assigned abundant powers to deal with the administrative matters. They were the main instrument for state formation. Third, the military was also associated with the initial efforts to make Pakistan a viable state. The Army personnel helped the civil administration to deal with the law and order situation in the districts bordering India. They also assisted refugee migration and managed their camps. Similarly, the Army and the Air Force undertook rescue, relief and rehabilitation operations when the Punjab faced serious floods within weeks of independence.

The state-building efforts were imperilled by the problems Pakistan developed with India in the first couple of years. These included communal riots and an influx of refugees, protection of religious minorities, the distribution of assets of the British Indian government and the military, the canal water dispute, the evacuee property issue, concentration of Indian troops in the Punjab sector of the Indo-Pakistan border in 1950 and 1951, and the suspension of bilateral trade in 1950. Other developments that were perceived by the Pakistani establishment as a threat to the survival of the state included the dispute over the accession of state of Jammu and Kashmir to India (October 1947) and the first Indo-Pakistan war in Kashmir (1947–8), Indian military action in Junagadh (November 1947) and Hyderabad (September 1948). On top of this were the statements of the Congress Party leaders regretting the establishment of Pakistan; some of them talked of reunification of India in the future. The Pakistani leaders were thus convinced that, after the failure of the Indian leaders to forestall the establishment of Pakistan, they were trying to 'strangle' Pakistan so that the chances of its survival could be reduced to a minimum. The Indian government made no effort to rectify this perception. Rather, its policies often placed Pakistan in an extremely difficult situation at a time when it needed support to put its house in order. Consequently, resentment against India became entrenched in Pakistani minds. Three interrelated developments contributed to shaping the Pakistan military's perception of India as an adversary: the dispute over the division of the assets of the British Indian military, the communal riots and the influx of refugees, and the Kashmir dispute.

Pakistan's external security was also adversely affected by Afghanistan's irredentist claims on Pakistani territory, often described as the Pakhtunistan issue. Rejecting the Durand Line (see chapter 3) as an international border, Afghanistan refused to recognize Pakistan's sovereignty on NWFP and Balochistan, which had a predominantly Pakhtun and Baloch populations. Afghanistan made different demands for these provinces. At times, it demanded that these provinces should join Afghanistan. At other times, it talked about an independent state comprising these two provinces. At still other times, it advocated the right of self-determination for the Pakhtuns and Baloch populations in Pakistan.[2]

Afghanistan manifested active interest in the Pathans living on the east of the Durand Line when it realized that the British were planning to withdraw from India. As early as November 1944 the Afghan government approached London proposing that in the event of India's independence the areas that were annexed by the British government during the nineteenth century should be given the option to become independent states or join Afghanistan.[3] The 3 June, 1947 plan for the division of India provided that NWFP would decide in a referendum either to join India or Pakistan. The Afghan government asked that the Pathans of NWFP should also be given the option of independence. Several Congress leaders sympathized with the demand and the pro-Congress party of NWFP – *Khudai Khidmatgar*, led by Abdul Ghaffar Khan – which was in power in the province at that time, also supported the demand. However, the British went ahead with a referendum as planned; an overwhelming majority of the votes cast opted for Pakistan. The *Khudai Khidmatgar*, who had boycotted the referendum, declared the establishment of 'a free Pathan state' as their goal.[4] When Pakistan applied for membership of the UN, Afghanistan was the only country that voted against it on the ground that it had a territorial dispute with Pakistan. What contributed to Afghanistan's persistence in its territorial claims was the diplomatic support it obtained from India and the Soviet Union.

There were periodic border clashes between the border militia and regular troops of Pakistan and Afghanistan, and the Pakistani Army and the Air Force occasionally took action against the Afghanistan-inspired tribes on the Pakistan–Afghan border. Their diplomatic relations were suspended during October 1955–August 1956 and September 1961–May 1963.[5] The policy-makers in Pakistan never expected a full-fledged military operation by Afghanistan but they were perturbed by the spectre of a two-front scenario – war with India and serious border clashes with Afghanistan or armed revolts in the tribal areas. Furthermore, Pakistan suffered from several security handicaps. The split of the state into two wings of West and East Pakistan (1947–71) separated by 1,000 miles of Indian territory created peculiar security problems. The geographical conditions and terrain in the two wings were so dissimilar that different security strategies were needed for effective defence. The main communications network in West and East Pakistan ran parallel to the frontiers. The important railway link in certain parts of the eastern wing was situated close to the Indian border. The situation in West Pakistan (post-1971 Pakistan) was not much better as the territory lacked strategic depth. The main surface arteries that linked Karachi with Peshawar were at various points within 50 miles of the Indian border or the Line of Control in Kashmir. Some of the major cities were situated very close to the border and there were hardly any natural barriers like rivers and mountains on the Indo-Pakistan border. No Pakistani airfield of military relevance with the exception of Quetta was more than 150 miles from the Indian border.

The following major courses of action were adopted to cope with such a difficult external security environment.

(i) Reorganization of the Military

Reorganization of the military was necessitated by the division of the British Indian military at the time of independence. As the non-Muslim personnel had been transferred to India, almost all battalions and regiments had to be re-grouped. The regiments and battalions with common traditions, class and recruiting areas were amalgamated and the gaps were filled by new recruitment. Greater attention was given to development of *esprit de corps* among them because a good number of them were either brought together from different units or recruited afresh.

There was a serious shortage of officers, especially those with staff experience. Pakistan had only one Major General, two Brigadiers and six Colonels in the immediate aftermath of independence as against the requirement of 13 Generals, 40 Brigadiers and 53 Colonels.[6] The government decided to retain 355 British officers from amongst those already present in Pakistan and the services of 129 officers were obtained from England to meet the immediate shortage of officers. They were given command and staff appointments. The pre-independence practice of appointing one C-in-C for three services of the military was done away with. From 15 August, 1947, the Army, Navy and Air Force were commanded by separate C-in-Cs; they were British officers. For technical services, some British Other Ranks were also employed.[7]

The C-in-C, Army, appointed a Nationalization Committee in October 1947 for advising on the immediate measures for nationalization. Another committee was appointed by the government in February 1948 to review reorganization and other allied matters and to make recommendations for complete nationalization by the end of December 1950. A host of measures were adopted on the advice of these committees for overcoming the problems of officers and technical staff for the Army, the Navy, the Air Force. First, competent officers (KCOs and ICOs) were given accelerated promotions. A good number of officers recruited on emergency or short commission were asked to stay on. Second, a number of junior-commissioned officers were promoted to commissioned ranks. Third, the released officers and men, not in government or essential services, were asked to offer themselves for enlistment. A good number of them were taken back. Fourth, the release of personnel from the armed forces was temporarily stopped, except for medical or special reasons. Fifth, temporary and emergency commissions were initiated, mostly for specialist jobs or to fill some specific types of appointments. Sixth, a small number of qualified army officers of the princely states that had opted for Pakistan were also absorbed.

The headquarters of the British Northern Command in Rawalpindi was changed to the General Headquarters (GHQ) of the Army. In the case of East Pakistan, only two infantry battalions were available there at the time of independence. With the transfer of non-Muslim companies of these two battalions to India, only five Muslim companies were left. A Sub-area Head-quarters for East Pakistan was set up and temporarily housed in the High Court building, Dhaka, with a British officer, Major General Mould, as the commander. Major General Mohammad Ayub Khan was appointed General Officer Commanding (G.O.C.) East Pakistan in January 1948 and served there until November 1949. The first infantry East Bengal Regiment was set up in February 1948. The nucleus was provided by the optees of the Bihar Regiment and the Bengal Pioneer Corps of the British Indian Army. Additional requirement of the Junior Commissioned Officers was fulfilled from the Punjab Regiment. When the required number of Bengali personnel were available they replaced the Punjabis. East Pakistan Rifles, a paramilitary force, and the *Ansar*, a civil armed force, were set up during this period.[8] Later, another civil armed force, *Mujahid* was raised.

Pakistan established new training institutions for the three services to replace those situated in India. The Pakistan Military Academy was set up at Kakul in January 1948 to replace the Indian Military Academy, Dehra Dun. The Air Force College for training pilots resumed at Risalpur in September 1947. The Navy also established its training institutions. As Pakistan did not get any ordnance factories, work on setting up such a factory was initiated in 1948 at Wah, with technological cooperation from Great Britain; it was inaugurated in December 1951. Construction of the first dry dock for the Navy started in Karachi in February 1952 and it was inaugurated in September 1954. A floating dock was also acquired during this period.

The reorganization and nationalization of the Navy and the Air Force proved a longer and more difficult process. There was a serious shortage of officers and personnel with technical know-how. In the case of the Navy, Pakistan got about 50 officers, most of whom had joined the service during the Second World War. The situation in the Air Force was no better. The Air Force had to rely heavily on British officers and technical personnel in the early years. It was in January 1948 that the first Pakistani attained the rank of Air Commodore. General Ayub Khan was the first Pakistani officer to assume the command of the Army on 17 January 1951. The Navy had the first Pakistani C-in-C in February 1953 when Rear Admiral (later Vice Admiral) Muhammad Siddiq Choudri assumed this office. Air Marshal Mohammad Asghar Khan was the first Pakistani to become C-in-C of the Air Force in July 1957.

Much attention was given to their training in order to maintain the professional character of the three services; pre-service and in-service training was emphasized by the services chiefs and their senior staff. This emphasis was not allowed to slacken when Pakistani officers took command of the three services. Discipline, internal cohesion, efficiency, professionalism and *esprit de corps* which were the features of military organization during the British rule and distinguished the military from other sectors of society, were maintained in the post-independence period. A number of officers of the three services were sent to Britain and other Commonwealth countries, later to the US, for training and specialized courses.

(ii) Priority to Defence Requirements

Defence requirements enjoyed the highest priority in Pakistan. No matter whether the government was being run by civilians or generals, defence obtained the largest share of the national budget. Pakistan had seven prime ministers and eight cabinets during 15 August 1947–7 October 1958. They belonged to different political parties and bitterly criticized each other's policies, but they all shared the perspective that Pakistan must have a strong and powerful military for coping with the antagonistic regional environment. The military commanders did not have to engage in much lobbying to obtaining resources.

As early as October 1948, the first Prime Minister, Liaquat Ali Khan (August 1947–October 1951), said, 'the defence of the state is our foremost consideration. It dominates all other governmental activities.'[9] Muhammad Ali Bogra (Prime Minister: April 1953–August 1955) declared in his defence policy statement in August 1953 that he would much rather starve the country than allow any weakening of its defence.[10] Iskander Mirza (Governor General: August 1955–March 1956 and President: March 1956–October 1958) asserted in July 1957 that it was the 'foremost duty of every Pakistani' to strengthen our armed forces so that the country could live in peace.[11] The National Assembly supported the policy of strong defence. The members generally accepted the security perceptions of the government and their speeches reflected a deep anxiety over Indian and Afghan policies. The troubled relations with India, especially the Kashmir dispute and the communal riots in India, and Afghanistan's irredentist claims were often cited as strong evidence of the hostile external environment. The government never faced problems in obtaining the assembly's approval for the defence allocations in the national budget.

Pakistan spent on average 60.69 per cent of its national budget on defence during these 11 years, which was quite high given that the country was facing acute social and economic problems. Some defence-related expenditure was covered under other heads like civil works, roads and highways, and law and order. Additionally, Pakistan began to obtain military equipment and weapons from the US from November 1954 onwards under the bilateral security arrangements which made additional resources available to the military. By 1958, Pakistan had become a typical example of a country where 'a poverty of resources for human needs contrasts with the affluence under which military programmes operate. The threats that touch people in their daily lives – joblessness, crime, illness, hunger – rank lower in the scale of government priorities than preparations for war.'[12]

Table 4.1   Defence Expenditure 1947–58 (in Million Rupees)

	Defence Expenditure	Total Expenditure met from Revenue	Defence Expenditure as Percentage of Total Expenditure
1947–48	153.8	236.0	65.16
1948–49	461.5	647.0	71.32
1949–50	625.4	856.0	73.06
1950–51	649.9	1266.2	51.32
1951–52	779.1	1442.3	54.01
1952–53	783.4	1320.1	59.34
1953–54	653.2	1108.7	58.91
1954–55	635.1	1172.6	54.16
1955–56	917.7	1433.4	64.02
1956–57	800.9	1330.7	60.18
1957–58	854.2	1521.8	56.13

Source: Compiled from *Pakistan Economic Survey*, an annual publication of Government of Pakistan. See also Hasan-Askari Rizvi, 'Pakistan's Defence Policy', *Pakistan Horizon* Vol. 36, No. 1 (First Quarter 1983), pp. 32–56.

The major portion of the defence expenditure was spent on four types of activities. First, the day-to-day requirements of the armed forces which included the reorganization and expansion programme, the absorption of the armies of the princely states that had opted for Pakistan, the building up of the reserves, training and exercises, and pay and allowances of the officers and men. Second, renovation and expansion of various military installations and setting up of various training institutions. Third, the procurement of military stores, equipment and weapons from abroad. Fourth, movement of troops from one place to another in order to meet external threats (i.e. the Kashmir war and other security-related movements) or for assistance to the civil administration, i.e. the maintenance of law and order, relief and humanitarian assistance in case of natural calamities, and other 'aid to civil power' operations.

This left comparatively less for setting up defence-related industry or for establishing major maintenance facilities for the armed forces which slowed down the modernization process. It also made Pakistan more dependent on external sources than India for procurement of weapons and military equipment as well as for specialized training of personnel and for building maintenance facilities.

(iii) Diplomacy and Weapons Procurement

Pakistan's policy makers viewed astute diplomacy and extra-regional ties as essential for dealing with the turbulent regional environment and especially for weapons procurement. Power asymmetry between Pakistan and India to the advantage of the latter, and the former's inability to cope with the security pressures due to the inadequacy of domestic resources, deficient technological-industrial base, and the urgent need of building strong defence, all made Pakistan's policy-makers diligent cultivating external linkages and connections.[13]

Pakistan lobbied a large number of states, especially Commonwealth members, and used the UN forum extensively for mobilizing support for its disputes with India, especially over Kashmir. Pakistan gave much attention to cultivating relations with the Muslim states which was facilitated by projection of its Islamic identity at the international level. Though some Muslim countries were disappointed by Pakistan's participation in the US-sponsored alliance system, most understood the reasons for Pakistan's tilt towards the West. With Iran, Turkey, Saudi Arabia, Jordan and Indonesia, Pakistan developed most cordial relations. Their diplomatic support was a source of strength for Pakistan. On Indo-Pakistan disputes, most Muslim states either maintained a sympathetic disposition towards Pakistan or adopted a non-partisan posture.

Pakistan was most keen to develop cordial relations with countries that could contribute to strengthening its defence, especially in the supply of weapons and equipment. Pakistan's desperate need of arms and ammunition in the early years was underlined in a statement by Ayub Khan that they were so short of ammunition that they 'could hardly allow [the] soldiers even five rounds for their general practice to keep their weapons in order.'[14] Great Britain and other Commonwealth countries were the first choice for weapons procurement and training of its officers. In the initial years, Pakistan had to send its naval vessels to Malta or Great Britain for repairs. The US was approached by Pakistan in October–November 1947 for procurement of weapons and equipment.[15] A similar request was made in early 1948 by both India and Pakistan, but the US administration declined the export of military material to either country because of the ongoing Kashmir conflict.[16] Pakistan purchased stores, ammunition and equipment in the early years from Great Britain, Italy, Spain, Sweden, Japan, France, Malaya, Australia, Canada, Belgium, Holland, Egypt, Ceylon (Sri Lanka) and West Germany.

Pakistan's need to strengthen its defence arrangements led it to join the US-sponsored alliance system in the mid-1950s which facilitated the transfer of sophisticated weapons and equipment from the US and other Western countries for its three services. Pakistan and the US signed Mutual Defence Assistance Treaty in May 1954 which served as the main framework for US arms transfers and military training to Pakistan.[17] In September, Pakistan joined the Southeast Asia Treaty Organization (SEATO) and, one year later, in September 1955, it became a member of another security alliance, the Baghdad Pact (later renamed the Central Treaty Organization, CENTO). In March 1959, Pakistan and the US signed a bilateral agreement of cooperation, an executive arrangement not formally confirmed by the US Senate. It declared that the 'government of the United States of America regards as vital to its national interests and to world peace the preservation of the independence and integrity of Pakistan.'[18] A separate agreement was signed in July 1959, allowing the US to set up a communication facility, i.e. an air base, near Peshawar.[19] Pakistan began to receive American weapons from November 1954, as an outright grant or against soft loans. These included, *inter alia*, tanks, artillery pieces, other arms and ammunition, armoured personnel carriers, and transport for the Army; aircraft, including the F-104, B-57, F-86 and C-130, and some equipment for the Air Force; naval defence equipment, including war ships, for the Navy; and radar and communication equipment. The US Military Assistance Advisory Group (USMAAG) was set up in Rawalpindi to advise and guide modernization of the armed forces. An enormous construction programme was carried out to improve air, sea and land defences. The naval base at Karachi was modernized and some equipment was provided for building another naval base at Chittagong. Training facilities in Pakistan were improved and a good number of Pakistani military officers were sent to the US on training courses. Pakistan's Air Force and the Navy took part in joint SEATO and CENTO exercises.

The security ties with the US helped Pakistan to accelerate the process of modernization of its armed forces and it got military equipment, weapons, aircraft and warships, which added to the military strength. Though the US refused to make any security commitment vis-à-vis India, and the overall regional balance of power continued to remain in favour of India, these security pacts gave Pakistan the much needed confidence that it could withstand India's military and diplomatic pressures. Military assistance was accompanied by generous economic assistance, which gave a boost to Pakistan's faltering economy in the 1950s. However, there was a cost of the alignment option. Pakistan was embroiled in the superpower conflict and the Cold War. The Soviet Union was completely alienated, openly supporting India on Kashmir and bolstering Afghanistan in its dispute with Pakistan.

Pakistan and the US did not fully share each other's goals. The US was pursuing its global agenda against the Soviet Union. Pakistan was concerned about the regional security environment and its major preoccupation was security against India. The containment of communism was not a priority for Pakistan, although its leaders often highlighted their aversion to communism in order to reassure the Americans. The divergence in their perspectives and goals produced strains in their relations soon after the beginning of the pact era. Pakistan developed doubts about the reliability of American commitments as early as 1956. Similarly, questions were raised in the US in 1957 about the advisability of relying on Pakistan as a defender of American interests.[20] However, the two sides neither endeavoured to harmonize their divergent perspectives nor attempted to clarify ambiguities in their relations. They played down their differences and continued to cooperate with each other for different reasons.

(iv) The Strategic Doctrine

Pakistan's strategic doctrine was shaped against the backdrop of an adverse regional security environment: India's military preponderance, Pakistan's security handicaps and the resources constraints, making it difficult to carry on a long-drawn war. Pakistan did not aim at military parity with India which was neither possible nor desirable. It wanted to develop enough military capability and especially the strike-power to make it known to India that Pakistan could withstand India's military pressure and increase the cost of an armed conflict for that country.

A war with India in Kashmir or on the international border was considered a strong possibility. The strategy was to confront the opposing troops right on the borders or to take the war into the adversary's territory because some Pakistani cities were situated close to the border. It had to be a quick operation, not dragging on for months as Pakistan on its own could not carry on a long war due to paucity of resources and especially the limited capacity of its weapons industry.

A short war was possible only if Pakistan had the capability to raise the cost of the war quickly to unacceptable limits for the adversary. The underlying idea was that if the adversary knew that the cost of a war was going to be extremely high, it would be deterred from engaging in a military adventure, and, if war broke out for one reason or another, it could be kept brief.

A prerequisite for this doctrine was the maintenance of a highly professional, trained and well-equipped military with strong fire-power and mobility. An effective air cover and transport facilities that could quickly transfer troops from one sector to another were required. Pakistan's preferred option was to build pressure on India in Kashmir by engaging in a limited military operation there or by extending military support to Kashmiri activists. This strategy was less costly for Pakistan and tied large numbers of Indian troops in Kashmir. India preferred to extend the conflict to the international border as Pakistan was at a disadvantage if military operations were carried out simultaneously in Kashmir and on the India–West Pakistan border.

Pakistan could not pursue its strategic doctrine without external cooperation as it lacked sufficient domestic resources to develop the required capability. It was not therefore surprising that the military attached much importance to Pakistan's security relations with the US. International connections were also important for building diplomatic clout for its disputes with India and Afghanistan.

East Pakistan did not figure prominently in Pakistan's strategic doctrine and no attempt was made to develop an autonomous defence system for that province. The keystone to the defence of East Pakistan was Ayub Khan's statement: 'The defence of East Pakistan does not lie in that part of the country.' He maintained that East Pakistan was not defensible even if the entire military strength was concentrated there as long as West Pakistan was not made strong.[21] The military commanders were of the view that India could not engage in a large-scale war simultaneously on both fronts.[22] If India launched an attack on East Pakistan, the Pakistani military could go on the offensive across the West Pakistan–India border or the ceasefire line in Kashmir, thereby relieving pressure in the east because India could not afford to lose territory in the west. However, skirmishes were not ruled out on the East Pakistan borders. A limited number of troops were stationed in East Pakistan and paramilitary and civil armed forces were created for border security, anti-smuggling drives and assistance to the civilian authorities. The Air Force and the Navy were also stationed there and a naval base was built at Chittagong.

The assumption underlying the defence of East Pakistan was influenced partly by the British military training and partly by the experience in the post-independence period. The military commanders of India and Pakistan were oriented towards the use of heavy armour. The East Pakistan terrain was not suitable for such operations. Given the fact that there were hardly any natural barriers on most of the West Pakistan–India border, it was generally presumed that the Indian armed forces could easily advance in the western sector; the plains of the Punjab were ideal for tank and heavy armour move-ment and Pakistan was most vulnerable there. This perspective was rein-forced by the periodic concentration of troops of the two countries on the West Pakistan–India border, the war in Kashmir and frequent violations of the ceasefire line, and the strained relation with Afghanistan. These factors contributed to the formulation of a West Pakistan focused defence doctrine.

Pakistan had troubled relations with Afghanistan but the latter lacked the military capacity to launch a major offensive to realize its irredentist claims on Pakistani territory. This enabled Pakistan to revise the traditional British policy of a high-profile military presence in the northwest to deter Afghan-istan as well as to maintain a sustained pressure on the Pathan tribes. Pakistan started with the initial advantage of being a Muslim state which eased much tension with the Pathan tribes. The first sign of change in the attitude of the Pathan tribes was visible when Jahawarlal Nehru visited the tribal areas in October 1946 along with the *Khudai Khidmatgar* leaders. He did not receive a cordial welcome and, in some places, his car was stoned.[23] A large number of tribal chiefs declared their loyalty to the new state of Pakistan in the specially convened tribal *jirgas*. Jinnah visited the area several times to build their confidence in Pakistan, assuring them that the government would respect their autonomy and traditions. The government withdrew the regular troops from the outposts in north and south Waziristan by 31 December 1947 and handed over the security responsibilities to the locally recruited paramilitary force. However, the British policy of paying financial subsidies to the tribal chiefs was continued. Pakistan also allocated resources for economic devel-opment and social welfare in consultation with the tribal chiefs and encour-aged the tribal youths to join the Army. This policy paid off as most of the tribal chiefs worked more or less smoothly with Pakistan. Some, like the Fakir of Ipi tribe, defied Pakistan from time to time, mostly with support from Afghanistan. At times, tribal uprisings coincided with increased Afghan propaganda for Pakhtunistan or active movement of Afghan troops on the border. Pakistan acted swiftly by mobilizing its paramilitary force and regular troops for countering such a security situation.

Civilian Institution Building

A centralized polity with an entrenched bureaucratic apparatus and a strong military saved Pakistan from collapsing in the early years of independence. However, this diverted attention from the task of creating viable political institutions and processes that were urgently needed to inculcate a sense of participation in the diversified population and to give endurance and vitality to the nationalist sentiments that manifested in the last stage of the independence struggle. Two constituent assemblies (1947–54, 1955–6) spent about eight years grappling with some of the basic political questions like the role of Islam, especially the nature of the Islamic state, distribution of powers between the centre and the provinces, representation in the federal legislature, the electoral system, the national language and the relation between the legislature and the executive.[24] The delay polarized the situation to such an extent that when the constitutions was finally approved in early 1956 it hardly represented a broad-based consensus in the polity.

The first year of independence was marked by heavy dependence on the charismatic personality of Jinnah; he was Governor General and President of the Constituent Assembly, and, above all, the founder of the state, revered as the Great Leader – *Quaid-i-Azam*. He overshadowed the administrative process at the federal and provincial levels. His death in September 1948, 13 months after independence, did not give him a chance to employ his charisma for establishing and legitimizing constitutional and political arrangements. Liaquat Ali Khan, first Prime Minister, who inherited the mantle of leadership and partially filled the gap, developed problems with the provincial leadership. His assassination in October 1951 left the field to political leaders who lacked national stature and were short on ideas to address difficult political and constitutional problems that bedevilled the country. Their regional power base with little or no political standing outside of the native province made it difficult for them to evolve a consensus on the constitutional issues.

The Muslim League was unable to transform itself from a nationalist movement into a national party that could put the nation on the road to constitutionalism, democracy and stability. This was different from India where the Congress Party succeeded in such a transformation. The roots of these differences can be traced back to the pre-independence period. The Congress Party, established in Bombay on 28 December 1885,[25] had become a mass party by 1920 under the guidance of Gandhi. It served as an umbrella organization for diverse interests and political perspectives ranging from those who believed in non-violence to Hindu hardliners, Marxists and Socialists. It also produced a group of leaders who had sufficiently long experience of working together for the shared goals and evolved ways and means to keep their internal disputes within manageable limits. The Muslim League had a different track record. Founded in Dhaka on 30 December 1906 by a group of enlightened Muslims,[26] the Muslim League maintained an elitist character until 1937 when its leadership began to engage in popular mobilization. It functioned as a mass and popular party for 7–8 years after the Congress provincial ministries resigned in 1939, more so, after the passage of the Lahore Resolution in March 1940 which called for the establishment of a homeland for the Muslims of South Asia. The Muslim League's representative character was often challenged by a couple of Muslim organizations and it penetrated the Muslim majority provinces rather late. A large number of Muslim leaders from the Muslim majority provinces joined the Muslim League in the last seven years or they stopped opposing the Muslim League when it became clear that Pakistan would come into existence. As a result, the Muslim League could neither evolve a viable organizational network nor bring forward a group of committed frontline leaders with sufficient experience of working together as a team nor evolved a general consensus on the political contours of the polity it wanted to create. The Muslim League was heavily dependent on Jinnah who commanded the party and steered it to independence. When the main objective of the Muslim League, i.e. the establishment of Pakistan, was achieved and Jinnah and Liaquat were gone, there was none to keep the Muslim League together.

The Muslim League suffered from another drawback. Most of the senior members of the Muslim League who held cabinet positions at the federal level or dominated the party at the national level came from the Muslim minority provinces and lacked a popular base/constituency in the Pakistani territory, i.e. Muslim majority provinces. They were more comfortable with the bureaucratic elite, most of whom also hailed from the Muslim minority provinces rather than with the leaders hailing from the Pakistani provinces whom they viewed as parochial and lacking sufficient commitment to the party.[27] Consequently, the Muslim League leadership was not in favour of holding early elections. The situation was precarious for them in East Pakistan where their hold was very weak. The Muslim League leadership was fearful of a revolt by the province-based leaders and kept a firm hold over the party by assigning the key offices to the refugees or to those provincial leaders who had been coopted in to the system. Criticism within the party was discouraged. Any opposition to the Muslim League from within the party or from outside was equated with criticism of the state. This strategy did not help the faltering fortunes of the Muslim League. The province-based leadership created personal cliques at the provincial level and their interaction with the national leadership was shaped mainly by their factional considerations, i.e. how far they could use these connections to outmanoeuvre their local rivals. The national leadership did not hesitate to play one faction against another to make its writ effective in the provinces rather than working towards making the party a coherent and effective political machine.

Other political parties, set up mostly by defectors from the Muslim League, did not offer a credible alternative. These parties suffered from all those weaknesses and deficiencies which undermined the Muslim League: the absence of a clear political and economic programme, weak or non-existent organization, and personal and factional feuds. The political parties were ephemeral conglomerates of the political leaders who, along with their loyalists, engaged in struggle for self-aggrandizement and material gains. The democratic norms, political morality and political consistency were not their concerns. They shifted their support from one party to another, from one leader to another within the same party without giving any attention to the consequences of such action on the political process. One of the earliest analysts of Pakistan politics correctly observed that the political scene in the 1950s was dominated by 'a large number of leading persons, who with their political dependents' formed 'loose agreements to achieve power and to maintain it.' Those who disregarded democratic norms but controlled 'legislators, money or influence' prospered.[28] The orthodox and conservative Islamic parties, most of which lost their credibility in the last phase of independence movement due to their refusal to endorse the Muslim League demand for Pakistan, found the confusion in Pakistani politics suitable for staging a comeback by demanding the establishment of an Islamic state on conservatives lines. The Muslim League, unable to cope with the political situation, tried to win them over by yielding to some of their demands. This emboldened them and they began to raise narrow sectarian issues and launched a political onslaught on the Ahmadiya community, demanding they be declared non-Muslims. These controversies further confounded Pakistani politics and accelerated fragmentation and decay of the political process.

Various governments adopted three major methods to obtain and sustain the support of the political leaders and parties. First, the state apparatus was employed to discourage and crush opposition. The political opponents were arrested or restrictions were imposed on their activities for one reason or another or the state machinery was used to harass them or their supporters; the power to ban public meetings and processions was often used to restrict political activities. No traditions of healthy opposition could therefore take firm roots, something that is integral to the democratic process. In 1949, the Public and Representative Offices (Disqualification) Act (PRODA) was enacted, which authorized the Governor General or the provincial Governors to institute proceedings against the elected representatives and those

holding public offices on charges of corruption, misuse of office and maladministration. Any citizen could also ask for initiation of such proceedings on
a deposit of Rs. 5,000. If convicted by a special tribunal, the said leader could
be disqualified from holding any public office for ten years. This law was
used as a political weapon against party rebels and others by the Governor
General and the Prime Minister.[29]

Second, financial and material rewards were offered for political loyalty by
the ruling elite. Import permits and licences for various kinds of commercial
and industrial activity were often issued on political considerations. The
political leaders could obtain these licences and permits and sell these to
businessmen and industrialists, or they made money for facilitating such
licences and permissions to others. At the district level, the licences to keep
arms were given on the recommendation of the members of the ruling party,
especially the ministers and members of the legislatures Third, expansion of
cabinets was a convenient device to sustain support or to cause defection in
the opposition ranks. The government could also win them over by promising to make discretionary appointments or to release funds for development
schemes on their recommendation. This compromised the role of the central and provincial legislatures. Their sessions were brief and discussions
perfunctory, often marked by belligerent idiom and devoid of parliamentary
courtesies.

The real political power concentrated in the head of state (Governor
General 1947–56, and President 1956–8) who directed the political process
with the support of the top echelons of the bureaucracy. The head of state
functioned in the tradition of the British Viceroy rather than the head of
state in a parliamentary system of government. Though Jinnah was the first
to function as a powerful Governor General, his was a special case. Being the
father of the nation, he had enough moral clout and political legitimacy to
play such a role. His successor, Khawaja Nazimuddin (Governor General,
September 1948–October 1951) reverted to the role of a titular head of state.
The situation began to change with the appointment of Ghulam Muhammad, a former bureaucrat belonging to British India's Audit and Accounts
Service, as Governor General in October 1951. He was succeeded by Major
General Iskander Mirza, a bureaucrat with an Army background, in August
1955. They used their knowledge and experience of administration and their
connections with their erstwhile colleagues in the senior echelons of the
bureaucracy to strengthen their position and manipulate the divided and
fragmented political forces. They had close connections with the Army Chief
General Mohammad Ayub Khan who was reluctant to come into the lime-
light, but extended support to them in their resolve to establish a centralized, bureaucratized and administrative polity.

Ghulam Muhammad adopted a domineering political style and removed
and appointed governments at will. In April 1953, he dismissed Prime
Minister Nazimuddin who had got the budget approved by the legislature

a few days earlier. He handpicked Muhammad Ali Bogra, Pakistan's ambassador to the US, as new Prime Minister; six members of Nazimuddin's
cabinet were reappointed and the Muslim League accepted the new Prime
Minister as its leader.[30] The Constituent Assembly attempted to retrieve the
initiative by repealing the PRODA in September 1954 and rushed amendments in the Interim Constitution, 1947, without the prior knowledge of the
Governor General, to deny him the powers to dismiss the government. In
the meanwhile the Constitution Drafting Committee finalized the draft of
the constitution which stripped the head of state of effective powers in the
British parliamentary tradition.[31] Ghulam Muhammad retaliated by dissolving the Constituent Assembly on 24 October, maintaining that having
failed to frame a constitution in seven years, it had 'lost the confidence of
the people'.[32] The President of the Constituent Assembly, Maulvi Tamizuddin Khan, challenged the dissolution order before the superior judiciary,
which started a legal and constitutional wrangling involving the Sindh
Chief Court and the Federal Court. In a series of judgments and advisory
opinions, the Federal Court upheld the action of the Governor General, but
restrained him from imposing a constitution on the country.[33]

Having removed the Constituent Assembly, Ghulam Muhammad asked
Prime Minister Muhammad Ali Bogra to reconstitute his cabinet, but the
cabinet members were selected by him. The new cabinet, described as the
cabinet of talent, was dominated by bureaucratic-military and industrial
elements. The key positions were held by Ghulam Muhammad's friends
like Chaudhri Muhammad Ali (a former bureaucrat who became Prime
Minister in 1955), Iskander Mirza (a former bureaucrat), and M.A.H. Ispahani (an industrialist and Pakistan's first ambassador to the US). The most
significant appointment was that of General Ayub Khan, C-in-C of the Army,
as Defence Minister who continued to head the Army, reviving the memory
of the Viceroy's Executive Council which included the C-in-C as its member.
None of them was interested in promoting parliamentary democracy, adult
suffrage and provincial autonomy.

A new Constituent Assembly was indirectly elected in June 1955, and a
coalition government of the Muslim League and the United Front, headed
by Chaudhri Muhammad Ali (see above), was installed in August. However,
the political institutions and processes could not overcome the shock of the
1954 dissolution. Iskander Mirza, who succeeded Ghulam Muhammad in
August, was no less interventionist. He used his linkages with the Army
Chief and the senior bureaucracy to assert his centrality to the political
process. The introduction of a Parliamentary Constitution on 23 March
1956 did not make any difference to the ground realities. Pakistan had four
Prime Ministers during the lifetime of the Constitution (23 March 1956–7
October 1958) who headed coalition governments comprising the political
parties having no shared ideology or common programme. These coalitions
were put together by Iskander Mirza directly or indirectly, who also forced

the Prime Ministers out of office by causing the erosion of their support base. The most interesting situation was faced by Hussain Shaheed Suhrawardy, who replaced Chaudhri Muhammad Ali as Prime Minister in September 1956. When a coalition partner, the Republican Party, known as the instrument of President Mirza, withdrew its support in September 1957, Suhrawardy wanted to test his strength on the floor of the National Assembly. Mirza refused to summon the National Assembly saying that he knew about the party situation and that if he wanted to avoid a dismissal he should resign.[34] Suhrawardy obliged, and Mirza installed a new coalition government.

The provincial political scene was equally disappointing principally due to rampant factionalism and the domineering role of central government. The Constitution and the political heritage weighed heavily in favour of the central government, enabling it to interfere in the provincial affairs by virtue of constitutional provisions and bureaucratic practices or by manipulation of the divided and faction-ridden provincial leaders. A frequently used power was that of dismissal of the provincial government or suspension or dissolution of the provincial assembly. The first provincial government dismissed by the central government was that of NWFP. On 22 August 1947, the pro-Congress *Khudai Khidmatgar* ministry, led by Dr Abdul Sattar Khan, was dismissed as it had opposed the establishment of Pakistan. It was replaced by a Muslim League ministry led by Abdul Qayuum Khan. Sindh witnessed the second dismissal in Pakistan's history when, on 26 April 1948, Ayub Khuhro was removed on charges of corruption and maladministration. He managed to become Chief Minister of Sindh for the second time in 1951 but he soon developed differences with the centre which forced another dismissal on him on 29 December 1951; the provincial assembly was also dissolved. In the case of the Punjab, the government led by Iftikhar Hussain Mamdot was dismissed and the provincial assembly dissolved on 25 January 1949 because of factional feud within the Muslim League. It was an interesting dismissal as the central and the dismissed provincial governments belonged to the same party. Another ministry in the Punjab, headed by Feroz Khan Noon, was dismissed on 21 May 1955 under direct orders from the Governor General without any consultation with the Prime Minister. Still another dismissal of provincial government was that of NWFP, when on 18 July 1955 Sardar Abdur Rashid was removed from office.[35] The central government continued to use this power in the subsequent period. This was resorted to more often in East Pakistan after the 1954 provincial elections because of rampant factionalism in East Pakistani politics and the centre's distrust of some provincial leaders.

The establishment of an integrated province of West Pakistan by abolition of different administrative units and provinces in October 1955, called the One Unit, showed how the centre could impose its will through blatant manipulation and threats. The central leadership created this to establish its firm grip over the politics in the western wing and to bring it at par with East Pakistan for representation in the national legislature, thereby neutralizing East Pakistan's numerical superiority and making it difficult for the leaders of smaller provinces of West Pakistan to create alliances with East Pakistani parties demanding greater autonomy.[36] The One-Unit scheme was first announced after the Governor General dissolved the Constituent Assembly. The opposition to the One-Unit scheme in Sindh was neutralized by installing Khuhro as the Chief Minister in place of Pirzada Abdus Sattar in November 1954, as the former had promised to deliver the support of the provincial assembly. On 11 December 1954, the Sindh Assembly endorsed the integration of West Pakistan by 100 votes to four. In NWFP, Chief Minister Sardar Abdur Rashid was directed to secure the approval, which he complied with when, on 25 November, the NWFP Assembly unanimously endorsed the scheme, although many political circles were openly opposed to it. There was no problem in securing a unanimous endorsement from the Punjab Assembly because the leading political personalities from this province were piloting the scheme. Similarly, the centre used its political clout to obtain the approval of the states of Khairpur and Bahawalpur, the municipal committee of Quetta and the *Shahi jirga* of Balochistan, Chitral, and *jirgas* from the tribal areas. Dr Khan (NWFP) was offered Chief Ministership of West Pakistan to obtain his support.[37] The new Constituent Assembly enacted a law for the unification of West Pakistan by 43 votes to 13 on 30 September 1955, followed by the inauguration of the new integrated province of West Pakistan on 14 October. Subsequently, the One-Unit was one of the most contentious issues in West Pakistan provincial politics and the political parties changed their positions several times on this issue. In September 1957, the West Pakistan Provincial Assembly passed a resolution demanding the dissolution of the One-Unit.

In East Pakistan, the United Front (UF), comprising the Krishak Sramik Party (KSP), Awami League, the Gantantari Dal, Nizam-i-Islam Party and some small groups, scored a resounding victory in the elections to the provincial assembly held in March 1954, against the ruling Muslim League. However, the UF government could not function smoothly partly because of the intra-UF feuds and partly because the central government was opposed to it. The new UF Chief Minister, Fazlul Haq, leader of the KSP, was removed on 30 May on charge of engaging in 'treasonable activities'[38] and Iskander Mirza who was sent to Dhaka as Governor used authoritarian methods to contain dissent. The centre's rule continued until 6 June 1955, when a new ministry, headed by Abu Hussain Sarkar, a KSP leader, was installed. Lacking sufficient support in the Provincial Assembly it did not convene its session until 22 May 1956, and, in that brief session, the government's lack of support was exposed. The President's rule was imposed on 26 May to authenticate the expenditure for the provincial government for three months. The Sarkar ministry was revived by revoking the President's rule on 1 June, but it could not manage governance and resigned on 30 August, followed by the reimposition of the President's rule. On 6 September, Ataur Rahman Khan, leader of the Awami League, was installed as Chief Minister and the Provincial Assembly had a full-day session on 17 September for the first time since May 1954.

East Pakistan faced a major ministerial crisis during March–September 1958 which set the stage for the collapse of the parliamentary system in Pakistan. On 31 March 1958, after having failed to have the provincial budget approved by the Provincial Assembly, Chief Minister Ataur Rahman Khan asked Governor Fazlul Haq, who belonged to the rival KSP, to prorogue the Assembly. The Governor turned down the request, dismissing the ministry and installing his party man, Sarkar, as Chief Minister. Ataur Rahman Khan approached Prime Minister Feroze Khan Noon for the removal of the Governor. The latter obliged the former so that the Awami League continued to support his government in the centre. The Chief Secretary, a senior bureaucrat, was appointed Acting Governor on 1 April, who dismissed Sarkar and re-installed Ataur Rahman. His government had to resign when the National Awami Party (NAP) defected; Sarkar returned as Chief Minister on 20 June. However, three days later, the new Chief Minister lost on the floor of the Assembly because the NAP refused to support him, and some other members switched sides. The federal government imposed the President's rule on 24 June for stabilizing the situation. Two months later, on 24 August, the President's rule was withdrawn and Ataur Rahman formed a new ministry. He was faced with the uphill task of mustering stable support for his government because, as in the past, the Assembly members and the political parties were ready to change sides if sufficient material rewards or ministerial positions could be assured. When the Provincial Assembly met on 20 September, the ruling Awami League moved a resolution for the removal of the Speaker, who was viewed as being sympathetic to the KSP. Scuffles broke out between the members the ruling party and the opposition during the debate on that resolution; the speaker was assaulted by the members of the ruling party. Three days later, the members again resorted to violence against one another on the floor of the Assembly. The police had to be called in to restore order. Several members were injured; Deputy Speaker Shahid Ali, who was presiding over the session, received serious injuries and died later in hospital.[39]

The ruling elite shied away from the electoral process; no direct elections were held for the Constituent Assembly or the central legislature. They were not keen to hold early elections even after the introduction of the 1956 Constitution. For about two years, the political leaders found one reason or another to delay it. Finally, they scheduled the elections for February 1959 but not many expected the government to honour the schedule. In the case of provincial assemblies, direct elections were held rather reluctantly. The Punjab Assembly was dissolved in January 1949 and new elections were not held until March 1951. The Sindh Assembly was dissolved in December 1951 and new elections were not held until May 1953. New elections for the NWFP Assembly were held in December 1953. The term of the East Pakistan Assembly expired in March 1953. The Constituent Assembly extended it for a year and the new elections were held in March 1954.

The politics in Pakistan was not conducive to the development of democratic and participatory institutions and processes. These conditions also undermined the capacity of the government to cope with the socio-economic pressures; economic planning and development were neglected. By 1958, Pakistan was in the grip of a severe economic crisis. Price hikes, shortages of essential commodities, black marketing, hoarding, smuggling, financial indiscipline and corruption in the government all caused problems for the general population. The situation of foreign exchange reserves was precarious and the overall economy was under serious strains. This was bound to create disillusionment and alienation amongst the ordinary people, who found themselves completely irrelevant to what was happening in the national and provincial capitals.

The Military and the Political Process

The military was integral to state survival and state building from the earliest days of Pakistan. Such a role was not only a carryover from the British period when the military was perceived as the ultimate sanction of the Raj, but it was also shaped by the developments in the post-independence period. The insecurity caused by the troubled interaction with India translated into support for building strong defence and a powerful military. These sentiments were widely shared by the refugee population settled mostly in cities and towns. Others who supported a strong military included the Kashmiris and those involved in the first Kashmir war. The strong religious fervour also created support for building a strong military in order to cope with external, especially Indian, threats.

There was hardly any serious criticism of high defence allocations and the media generally supported the government policy of strong defence. The parliament also endorsed such an approach and neither seriously questioned high defence allocations nor disputed the parameters of the defence policy. Some members did talk of the need for a more effective utilization of defence budget or called for greater involvement of the people in the defence of the country by giving them military training or suggested the establishment of a national militia. Even though the members generally supported the government policy on defence, the government did not encourage debate on defence related matters; the plea of sensitive security matters was used to hold back information on military and security affairs. Some members from East Pakistan regularly raised the issue of the under-representation of Bengalis in the armed forces. They urged the government to adopt effective measures to improve their representation in the armed forces so that they would have a sense of participation in the security of the country.

Defence and security policy making was the exclusive prerogative of the top bureaucrats of the defence ministry and the military top brass. Once the policy outlines were determined, the top brass enjoyed much autonomy in its implementation. The same applied to defence expenditure. Hardly any information was provided on its details and especially on allocations to the different services.

Jinnah and Liaquat did emphasize the primacy of the constitution and the political authority established thereunder. However, the military's opinion was given weight in the making of security policy. In October 1947, the Supreme Commander, Field Marshal Auchinleck, persuaded Jinnah to reverse his order to the C-in-C, Pakistan Army, for sending the Army into Kashmir after India secured its accession and landed its troops there.[40] Later, Pakistan's decision to induct its troops in Kashmir was also made on the advice of the Army Chief. On 20 April 1948, General Douglas Gracey suggested in his report that if the troops were not sent to Kashmir Pakistan's security would be jeopardized. The Government of Pakistan accepted the report and formally committed the regular troops to Kashmir in early May.[41]

The decision to enter into security arrangements with the US and participation in SEATO and CENTO was taken by the political leadership on the initiative of the Army commanders. The latter viewed this as a quick means to obtain modern weaponry and military equipment to strengthen security arrangements. General Ayub Khan began to think about developing close ties with the US as early as August 1951, within seven months of assuming the command, because he felt that Pakistan's precarious security situation underlined the need of having 'a strong and reliable friend'[42] whose interests should be the strengthening of Pakistan.[43] Ayub Khan was closely associated with the negotiations for the security arrangements with the US and accompanied Governor General Ghulam Muhammad and Prime Minister Muhammad Ali Bogra in their separate visits to the US when security arrangements, including the supply of weapons, were discussed. Ayub Khan supervised the procurement of weapons from the US which he perceived to be the core of the Pakistan–US relations. This brought the US Administration and the Pakistan military close to each other and the former were happy that such a professional Army was on their side.

The military extended assistance to the civilian authorities in the non-professional field. Its role could be divided into three broad categories: assistance for coping with natural calamities; help to deal with specific socio-economic problems; and cooperation for the maintenance of law and order and for the restoration of the authority of the civilian government. Cyclones and floods often hit parts of Pakistan and these caused much havoc. The Army and the Air Force undertook rescue and relief operations, providing shelter, food, clothing and medical assistance to the afflicted people. Army engineers helped to restore means of transportation and communication including roads, bridges, railway tracks and telephone lines. They also restored power supplies and repaired the collapsed embankments of canals and rivers. Useful assistance was provided for coping with other natural calamities including earthquakes, major landslides in the mountainous regions or heavy rains.

The Army's assistance for coping with specific problems included an anti-locust drive in NWFP (1951), Sindh (1952) and Quetta (1954), which saved standing crops from the locust onslaught. In 1958, the Army conducted anti-salinity and water logging operations in Sindh. Occasionally, the local administration sought the Army's cooperations in killing wild boars which caused serious damage to standing crops. The Army conducted three major operations in East Pakistan during 1947–58 which effectively demonstrated its capability to carry out its assigned task. In 1952–3, the Army was asked to assist the civil administration in the 5-mile broad belt along East Pakistan's border with India for controlling the smuggling of jute. The Army launched what was described as the 'Operation Close Door' to seal the border and the government authorized the Army officers to arrest and detain any person or seize jute and any other item being smuggled into India. The second assignment was the 'Operation Service First,' launched in 1956 to overcome the shortage of food and grain in parts of the province. The G.O.C., East Pakistan, was appointed the Chief Food Administrator and was given sufficient powers to deal with all aspects of food supply. The officers and men took upon themselves the responsibility of managing and supervising the distribution of wheat, rice and other food stuffs and they also cracked down on hoarders and black marketeers. The third major assignment was the 'Operation Close Door', launched in 1957–8 to check the smuggling of food stuffs, medicine and jute, and the flight of capital to India. The Army swiftly sealed the East Pakistan–India border and controlled smuggling.

The Army responded positively to the calls of the civilian administration for assistance in the restoration of law and order. As political and economic conditions deteriorated and politics became fractionalized, the governments were often faced with street agitation, strikes, riots and similar civic upheavals. The major instances when the regular troops were called out included the riots in Karachi (1949), Dhaka (1950), the language riots in various cities of East Pakistan (1952), the anti-Ahmadiya riots in the Punjab (1953) and labour troubles in East Pakistan (1954).

The Army got the first opportunity to run the civil administration directly in March–May 1953, when martial law was imposed in Lahore, following anti-Ahmadiya riots spearheaded by several orthodox and conservative Islamic groups for declaring the Ahmadis as non-Muslims and removing the then Foreign Minister Zafarullah Khan, who happened to be an Ahmadi. Martial law was declared on 6 March 1953 and Major General Muhammad Azam Khan was appointed Martial law Administrator.[44] The Army authorities brought the situation back to normal within a few days and then launched the 'Cleaner Lahore Campaign' to improve civic conditions. By the time the city was handed back to the civilian administration in mid-May, it was presenting a new and cleaner look.

The military's contribution in the non-professional field had three major implications for civil–military relations. First, the weaknesses and deficiencies of the political institutions and leaders were exposed – that they could not satisfactorily perform their primary duty of political and administrative management. Second, it gave the military firsthand experience of civilian affairs and the machinations of the political leaders – that some political leaders were involved with smugglers, hoarders and other criminal elements. Third, it created a strong impression in the public mind that the military could cope with a difficult situation even when the political leaders failed, thereby giving a boost to the Army's reputation as a task-oriented and efficient entity with a helpful disposition towards the people.

Institutional Imbalance

The institutional imbalance between a powerful bureaucracy and the military on the one hand and weak political institutions and processes on the other, inherited from the British, was accentuated in the post-independence period. The process of political decay and degeneration rendered the political institutions and processes incapable of articulation and aggregation of diverse interests within a national framework; no viable processes and political ethos were developed that enjoyed widespread acceptability. The political institutions and processes suffered from a crisis of legitimacy and could not ensure political participation or pursue meaningful socio-economic policies, thereby further weakening their role in the polity.

The 'over-developed' state structure established its centrality to the political process long before the military assumed power in October 1958.[45] The military maintained its organizational characteristics such as centralization, hierarchy, discipline and professionalism. Ayub Khan and his senior commanders devoted much attention to strengthening the Army and adopted various measures to improve its organization, intercommunication, mobility and strike-power. Pakistan's participation in defence pacts with the US, and procurement of weapons and military equipment from abroad, helped to strengthen the military. Foreign training of its officers and participation in military exercises with the alliance partners accelerated modernization and strengthened professionalism, greatly increasing senior commanders' self-confidence.

Thus, the degeneration and fragmentation of the political institutions and processes were in sharp contrast to the military's professional, task-oriented and confident disposition of a modernized structure with enough technological skills. This accentuated the institutional imbalance to the disadvantage of the political institutions. The political leadership was too weak and divided to assert its primacy over the military whose top commanders had ample freedom to deal with their internal affairs and consolidate their position.

Pakistan had seven Prime Ministers and eight cabinets during 1947–58. However, there was one Pakistani C-in-C of the Army, Muhammad Ayub Khan, who was appointed for a four year term on 17 January 1951. He got another full term in 1955, i.e. up to January 1959. In June 1958, his tenure was extended for two more years, up to January 1961. Such an extended stay in office not only helped him to consolidate his position but also provided him with an opportunity to observe the polarization of politics from close quarters. Invariably, the defence portfolio was held by the Prime Minister which made it possible for the three C-in-Cs, especially that of the Army, to stay in close interaction with the Prime Minister; Ayub himself was Defence Minister from October 1954 to August 1955. Ghulam Muhammad and especially Iskander Mirza relied on the military for support. Ghulam Muhammad could not have dissolved the Constituent Assembly in October 1954 without the support of the military. In fact, Ghulam Muhammad offered to hand over power to Ayub Khan on that occasion, which he declined.[46] He did, however, join the cabinet to demonstrate his support to the Governor General. The influence of the military increased in decision-making during the presidency of Iskander Mirza (1955–8), who himself had a military background; also served as Defence Secretary and was a close friend of Ayub Khan.

Though the military had become an important actor in the decision-making process by 1954, its top brass avoided direct and open involvement in politics. The only instance that showed political activism on the part of some officers was what was later described as the 'Rawalpindi Conspiracy'. Eleven officers and four civilians[47] were arrested in March 1951 on charges of planning to overthrow the government.[48] The evidence suggested that it was an amateurish plan by a group of officers led by Major General Mohammad Akbar Khan (not to be confused with Major General Akbar Khan Rangroot) who diverged from the government policy of seeking a diplomatic solution to the Kashmir problem. Their plan envisaged coercing the Governor General to dismiss the government and dissolve parliament and appoint a military council, which was to hold elections to the parliament for framing a 'democratic' constitution in a year or so. They also planned to resume military action in Kashmir.[49]

The conspiracy was limited to a small number of hotheads. The Army as a whole remained loyal to the established political order and the top commanders. The accused were tried by a special tribunal set up under a law passed by the parliament. The trial lasted for 18 months and they were sentenced to 1–12 years' rigorous imprisonment. A half-hearted attempt was made by some political leaders to launch a signature campaign for the release of the convicted.[50] The movement did not catch on. In October 1955, the Governor General remitted the unexpired portions of their sentences and they were set free.

The military commanders maintained a highly professional profile, emphasizing discipline, efficiency, training and a strong service pride. They were in command of their house, which was orderly and well maintained. This strengthened their position vis-á-vis the political leaders, who were faced with social turbulence and political fragmentation. The civilian leaders were not in a position to assert their leadership over the military. Rather, they attempted to cultivate the military so as to strengthen their position, and, thus, the military was able to play a key role in decision-making not only for the matters that related to its professional interests, but it also influenced priorities in the civilian and political domains.

5
The First Military Regime

The abrogation of the 1956 constitution and the imposition of martial law on 7 October 1958 was a joint decision of President Iskander Mirza and the C-in-C of the Army, General Ayub Khan, taken by the former at the prodding of the latter. Both had come to this conclusion on their own, although they must have discussed the matter with each other as they were close friends. Iskander Mirza had been quite successful in manipulating the divided political leaders since 1954. However, with growing political polarization and deterioration of economic conditions, he was finding it increasingly difficult to sustain his manipulative role. The scheduling of the general elections for February 1959 had caused additional problems for him; he could not be sure of the leadership that was likely to emerge from the general elections, especially in East Pakistan. This threatened his own political future because the constitution had stipulated presidential elections soon after the elections to the National Assembly.[1] Ayub Khan was fully aware of the degeneration of the political process and the growing alienation of the ordinary people. The press and independent political circles had started talking about the need of the military stepping in to salvage the political situation. The echo of such sentiments was also heard amongst Army officers, who felt that the time was fast approaching when the Army would have to do something to contain political turmoil.

There is no evidence to suggest that Ayub Khan and other senior commanders began considering the option of assumption of power before late May 1958. What perturbed them most was the fear that the on-going deterioration of the political and economic conditions might threaten the military's professional and corporate interests and adversely affect its internal cohesion and discipline. The divided political elements might try to cultivate support in the military or drag it into their struggle for power. In order to forestall such a development, an ordinance was issued in June disallowing statements and actions that could impair the discipline of the military personnel. Ayub Khan travelled to different parts of the country during these months and met the local commanders in order to gain a firsthand idea of their assessment of the political situation; in some such visits he also met the civilians. These visits helped him to make up his mind about the expansion of the role of the military. It was after the death of the Deputy Speaker of East Pakistan Assembly in the last week of September that Ayub Khan asked the Chief of the General Staff to prepare a plan for the takeover of the civil administration. Other factors that contributed to this decision included the threat by a Kashmiri leader, Ghulam Abbas, to cross the Ceasefire Line in Kashmir (June), the ultimatum by the Muslim League President Abdul Qayuum Khan to launch a civil disobedience movement and the mobilization of Muslim League National Guards for that purpose (early October), and a confrontation between the Khan of Kalat (former ruler of the state of Kalat which acceded to Pakistan in 1948) and the government of Pakistan (early October). By 3 October, the Army's plan for the takeover was ready.

The coup was executed with traditional secrecy and promptness required for the success of such an action. In addition to Iskander Mirza, who issued the proclamation, and Ayub Khan, only the senior most staff at the Army Headquarters knew about it; the C-in-Cs of the Air Force and the Navy were informed after all arrangements had been finalized. Prime Minister Malik Feroz Khan Noon came to know of the coup when he received a letter from the President the same evening; most political leaders learnt about the change from the morning newspapers. The only person who had an advance knowledge of the coup was the US ambassador to Pakistan, James Langley, a personal friend of Iskander Mirza. The ambassador was informed by Iskander Mirza in advance that he planned to assume all powers and that the Army would support him. He also informed him that in case he did not do so, Ayub Khan might take such an action. However, the date given to the ambassador for the takeover was 8 October.[2] On 11 October, President Eisenhower endorsed the coup in a letter to Iskander Mirza, followed by the visit of the US Defence Secretary to Pakistan on 23–27 October,[3] to reassure the military government of American support. American official and unofficial circles were optimistic that as a pro-West and modernized institution, the military would accelerate socio-economic development, ensure political stability and create conditions for constitutional and democratic rule.

Within a week of martial law, strains emerged in the relations between Iskander Mirza and Ayub Khan. Iskander Mirza resented the loss of power after having appointed Ayub Khan as the Supreme Commander of the armed forces and the Chief Martial Law Administrator (CMLA). While Ayub Khan was on a visit to East Pakistan on 20 October, Mirza contacted his friends in the military to seek their support for retrieving the initiative. This annoyed the ruling generals, who confronted him on this issue,[4] a charge he vehemently denied.[5] In the evening of 27 October, three Lt.-Generals – Azam Khan, Wajid Ali Burki and Khalid M. Sheikh, assisted by Brigadier Bahadur

Sher – went to the President House with the approval of Ayub Khan and asked Iskander Mirza to resign. He obliged without hesitation. The Army authorities shifted him to Quetta the same night and, on 2 November, he was dispatched to London where he lived until his death in November 1969.

A day before Iskander Mirza was forced out of office, he appointed Ayub Khan as Prime Minister and the new cabinet took the oath of office on the morning of 27 October. After Ayub Khan assumed the presidency, the office of Prime Minister was abolished; the cabinet was sworn -in again on 28 October as the presidential cabinet. Ayub Khan surrendered his position as the C-in-C of the Army to General Muhammad Musa.

Martial Law Administration

The CMLA presided over the administrative pyramid and was the source of all authority. A large number of martial law regulations were issued but these did not totally supplant the existing legal and administrative system. The Laws (Continuance in Force) Order provided that the country would be governed as nearly as possible to the abrogated constitution, subject to the overriding powers of the CMLA. The existing laws were non-operative to the extent these conflicted with the martial law regulations and orders. The Supreme Court and the High Courts were allowed to function but these courts could not question any order or action of the martial law authorities or question the judgement of the military courts. The Supreme Court provided legal legitimacy to the military government by declaring in a judgement on 27 October that 'a victorious revolution or a successful coup d'état' was 'an internationally recognized legal method of changing a constitution,'[6] by relying on Hans Kelson's formulation of revolutionary legality, described as one of the basic doctrines of legal positivism.

During 8–27 October, the CMLA was assisted by a senior bureaucrat, designated as the Secretary General Government of Pakistan and Deputy CMLA, and an advisory council consisting of senior bureaucrats. When Ayub Khan assumed the presidency, three C-in-Cs of the Army, the Navy and the Air Force were appointed Deputy CMLAs and a presidential cabinet replaced the advisory council. The country was divided into three martial law zones, each headed by a martial law administrator with the rank of Lt.-General or Major General: Zone A: Karachi and Malir; Zone B: rest of West Pakistan; Zone C: East Pakistan. Two provincial governors for East and West Pakistan headed the civil administration and were responsible to the President/ CMLA. Special and summary military courts were established. The former could impose punishments including the death sentence, life imprisonment, rigorous imprisonment (that is, hard labour) for not more than 14 years, fines, forfeiture of property and lashing. The latter type courts could impose any sentence with the exception of the death sentence or imprisonment exceeding one year. Twenty-six inquiry commissions and committees were appointed to examine the long-term administrative, social, economic and political problems. Their reports were used for initiating new policies. The reports of five expert committees set up before the imposition of martial law were also used for policy-making.[7]

The military regime relied heavily on the civilian bureaucracy for running the administration. In his first address to the nation, Ayub Khan declared that he would use the civilian agencies to the maximum. Major General Umrao Khan, Martial Law Administrator, East Pakistan, said that 'the Martial Law administration did not contemplate any upsetting of the prevailing civil administrative structure. The only change that [the] people would find in the course of time would be the toning up of the administrative machinery that had been demoralized and rendered so ineffective.'[8] The senior commanders knew that they alone could not run the administration and needed the cooperation of the bureaucracy. The bureaucrats realized that it was not advisable to work against the military regime as the latter was capable of retaliating against them by dismissing them or by taking other punitive actions. In fact, punitive action was taken against a number of civil servants as a part of strategy to tone up the administration and to make it known to the civil servants that similar action could be taken against others. A compromise suited both. The bureaucracy cooperated with the military and the latter strengthened their role. Such a marriage of convenience between the bureaucracy and the miliary was the hallmark of military rule and served the professional and corporate interests of both. However, the military commanders did not compromise on their centrality to the martial law administration.

Restrictions were placed on all kinds of political activities, political parties were banned and no public meeting or political marches were allowed. However, the military regime avoided extreme repression and ruthlessness. The reason being that it did not face any resistance at the time of assumption of power, and, during the martial law period, its survival was never threatened by any major agitation or a conspiracy. It did encounter some difficulties, but none could be described as a credible challenge to its authority. There were sporadic student agitations in 1960, 1961 and 1962. An isolated insurgency was launched by a small group of Baloch nationalists in the Jhalawan area in 1959 which was put down by the regular troops. In 1959, a plan to distribute anti-martial law posters in Karachi on the Independence Day (14 August) was uncovered in advance; the accused were sentenced to rigorous imprisonment ranging from 7 to 10 years by a military court. In February 1961, the military government remitted their sentences and set them free.

The press was kept under firm control. Nothing could be published against the regime and its policies. In April 1959, the government took over the Progressive Papers which published two daily newspapers – *The Pakistan Times* (English) and *Imroze* (Urdu), and a weekly *Lail-o-Nihar* (Urdu). The well-known Bengali newspaper of Dhaka, *Ittefaq*, and its editor ran into difficulties with the martial law authorities in September 1959. The Press and Publication Ordinance, 1960, replaced a number of punitive regulations enacted during the British period, but it still gave the government enough powers to muzzle the press. In June 1961, Associated Press of Pakistan (APP), a privately owned news agency, was taken over by the government. A number of political leaders and activists were detained and convicted by the military courts. However, their detention was brief and most political activists did not serve the full term of the sentence. Martial law regulations provided the death sentence for a number of crimes, but no one was executed with the exception of some of those involved in the Jhalawan insurgency.

Administrative Measures

The military regime adopted stringent measures to check hoarding, black marketeering of food items and consumer goods and smuggling of these items across the international border to India and Afghanistan. Army personnel and the police raided the suspected hoarders and smugglers and recovered a large quantity of grain, food items and contraband goods. The estimated value of contraband goods recovered from various parts of West Pakistan in the first two weeks of martial law was Rs. 1,564,000.[9] Later, businessmen and traders voluntarily declared their stocks, a facility extended to them by the military government. The prices of foods items and other goods of daily use were fixed by the martial law authorities and the shopkeepers were asked to display these prominently in their shops.

The martial law authorities moved swiftly to curtail three corrupt practices: illegal possession of foreign exchange, evasion of income tax and other taxes and duties, and the sale and purchase of import permits. Foreign exchange voluntarily surrendered locally amounted to Rs. 40.6 million, and the unauthorized foreign exchange held abroad by Pakistani nationals was Rs. 42 million.[10] The government collected Rs. 240 million as tax on excess income, and undeclared wealth totalling Rs. 1,340 million was brought on record.[11] A ban was imposed on the sale and purchase of import permits, punishable by 10 years rigorous imprisonment.

The military government took punitive action against 1,662 federal civil servants. The largest number (1,303) belonged to the lowest cadre (Class III) of the civil service, 221 were from the middle level (Class II) but only 138 were from the senior cadre (Class I), including 13 officers of the elite Civil Service of Pakistan (CSP), three from the Foreign Service, and 15 from the police service. Only 128 out of these 1,662 civil servants were dismissed; 686 were compulsorily retired who were entitled to all retirement benefits, and punitive action of lesser severity (i.e. stoppage of annual increment, placement on special report or issuance of warning) was taken against the rest.

Two provincial governments also took action on similar lines against provincial civil servants. East Pakistan government penalized 1,343 civil servants, including the dismissal or removal from service of 300 and compulsory retirement for 877. West Pakistan government took punitive action against 544 officials; with the exception of 88, they were dismissed or removed from service.[12]

Three special bodies, Administrative Re-organization Committee (December 1958), Provincial Administration Commission (February 1959) and Provincial Re-organization Committee (August 1961), were appointed to review the existing administrative organization and procedures and to suggest measures for improving efficiency and performance of the civil servants. Most of their recommendations were implemented by the federal and provincial governments gradually. A Pay and Services Commission, headed by Justice A.R. Cornelius, was appointed in August 1959 to review the structure, organization, recruitment, emoluments and other terms and condition of the civil services under the federal government. The report was submitted a few days before the withdrawal of martial law in June 1962. Its recommendations for upward revision of emoluments were implemented by Ayub Khan's post-martial law administration, but the proposals for creating a seven-tier service structure with a single Pakistan Administrative Service at the apex[13] were not implemented because the top echelons of the bureaucracy felt that this threatened their privileged position. The report was not made available to the public until after Ayub Khan's ouster from power in 1969.

A Law Reform Commission was appointed in September 1959 to suggest improvements in the existing legal and judicial system and the structure of the legal profession.[14] Its recommendations were implemented over a number of years. Ten ordinances were issued for improving the administration of justice. Some changes were made in the Civil Procedure Code. The powers of the Union Councils were enhanced to enable these to deal with petty cases and the *jirga* system was introduced in some parts of the country. The jurisdiction of West Pakistan High Court was extended to Balochistan. Another commission of inquiry – Company Law Commission – established in October 1959 recommended changes in the existing Companies Act for providing additional safeguards to the investors. These measures contributed to improving the working of the legal/judicial system but the much trumpeted objective of 'speedy and less expensive justice' remained a far cry. The legal circles were particularly critical of the introduction of the outdated *jirga* system, which did not give a fair opportunity for defence to the defendants. The members of the legal profession were also critical of the military courts and the constraints imposed by martial law on the regular courts.

The military shifted the national capital from Karachi to the *Potwar (Potohar)* plateau, near Rawalpindi, on the recommendation of a commission appointed in January 1959 for reviewing the suitability of Karachi as the headquarters of the federal government. Some government departments were moved to Rawalpindi in October 1959 which was designated as the interim capital. In February 1960, the presidential cabinet named the capital Islamabad. Its master plan was approved by the government in October, and one year later, in October 1961, construction work was resumed. The new capital began to function officially in October 1963 when some federal offices shifted from Rawalpindi to the newly constructed secretariat in Islamabad.[15] The shifting of the capital facilitated closer interaction between Ayub Khan and the Army Headquarters, which was situated in Rawalpindi. It also brought some prosperity to the *Potohar* area as the land was acquired by the government on payment of compensation and new job opportunities were created when the construction work started. The decision to shift the capital was criticized by the commercial and industrial circles in Karachi, who felt that they would encounter much inconvenience in maintaining their business-related interaction with the government. The Bengali civil servants based in Karachi were also unhappy as they had to relocate to the colder climate of interior West Pakistan. The political leaders in East Pakistan felt that the construction of a new capital would divert more resources to West Pakistan, accentuating the existing inter-wing economic disparities.

The military government inherited the problem of resettlement of refugees who had migrated to Pakistan at the time of independence. They were temporarily settled in different parts of the country and the previous government asked them to make compensation claims of the immovable property left by them in India. The value of their claims approved by the government was adjusted by allotting to them the property left by the Hindus and Sikhs who had migrated to India. The people were allowed to sell their unadjusted claims in the market, mostly at a price lower than their face value. However, as there was no reliable method of verifying such claims, the approval and disposal of these claims became a scandalous affair. Most applicants were at the mercy of the officials who had wide discretion for approving or rejecting or reducing the amount claimed. A large amount of illegal money changed hands for seeking approval of these claims and their subsequent adjustment. By the time martial law was imposed, a large number of people were still waiting for the settlement of their claims. Lt.-General Azam Khan was given the Rehabilitation portfolio in the cabinet. He undertook the refugee settlement work on a war footing and threatened to use martial law powers to deal with corruption and mismanagement of the compensation claim affairs. By the time martial law was withdrawn in June 1962, out of total compensation of Rs. 1,950 million payable to the claimants, Rs. 1,230 million had been adjusted against the value of the property transferred to them and Rs. 70 million was paid as cash compensation.[16] A large number of low cost houses were constructed to settle the refugees and others lacking permanent dwellings. The Korangi Township in Karachi was the first such scheme with

15,000 houses completed in one year. About 1,800 small houses were constructed in New Karachi and 7,000 were built in the Malir Extension Scheme. Fifteen low-cost housing schemes were launched in East Pakistan for the homeless and displaced.

The military regime issued two ordinances for excluding the political leaders from the political process. The first ordinance – Public Offices (Disqualification) Order (PODO), issued in March 1959, applied to those who held public office any time since independence. If a person was found guilty of 'misconduct' by an independent tribunal, he could be disqualified from holding a public office for 15 years. He could also be directed to compensate for any loss to public revenue caused by him. The second ordinance – Elective Bodies (Disqualification) Order (EBDO), issued in August 1959 – simplified the procedure laid down in the PODO and covered even those political leaders who were members of the legislature but never held a public office. The EBDO provided that if a person was found guilty of 'misconduct' which meant, *inter alia*, corrupt practices like bribery, nepotism, misuse of powers and wilful maladministration, by a tribunal, he was disqualified from holding any elective office until 31 December 1966. A political leader charged under the EBDO had the option of voluntarily retiring from public life up to the above date. Three tribunals were set up for proceeding against the political leaders: one for the centre and two for the provinces of East and West Pakistan. Each tribunal included a former civil servant and a Lt.-Colonel. The central tribunal was presided over by a judge of the Supreme Court and the provincial tribunals were chaired by a former judge of the High Court of the province concerned. With the exception of a few like H.S. Suhrawardy, C.E. Gibbon and Makhdoom Hassan Mahmud, none contested the charges framed under the EBDO.

The exact number of those excluded from public life under the EBDO is not known. The military government never released these figures. The unofficial claims ranged from 6,000 to less than 1,000. The figure of 6,000 appeared inflated because Pakistan did not have so many members of central and provincial assemblies during 1947–58; a good number of them were elected more than once and all were not indicted. A careful estimate by the present author is that approximately 400 political leaders were disqualified from public life.

The Social Sector

The most important measure adopted in the social sector was the introduction of the Family Laws in 1961, replacing the traditional/Islamic family laws that had allowed much discretion to men regarding marriage, divorce and other related affairs. As early as August 1954, the then civilian government established a Marriage and Family Law Commission, whose report, submitted in June 1956, was not implemented by the then government because the conservative Islamic groups were opposed to changes in the traditional family laws. Ayub Khan took up the report and issued the Family Laws Ordinance, 1961, which introduced far-reaching changes in the laws and procedures that governed different aspects of marriage, family, divorce and inheritance. The Family Laws made it obligatory to register every marriage with the Union Council/Committee (the lowest unit of local bodies) of the concerned locality. The practice of polygamy by men was regulated by the imposition of a condition that approval was needed from the local Union Council/Committee for a second or subsequent marriage. Such permission could be granted if the first wife was dead, or a divorce had taken place, or the family had no children, or the permission of the first wife had been secured. No divorce could take effect unless a written notice was given to the local council with a copy to the wife. The chairman of the local council was to set up an arbitration council with himself as its chairman and the nominees of the husband and the wife as its members. If no reconciliation could be brought about by the arbitration council, divorce was to be effective after 90 days from the date of notice to the local council. A woman could approach the local council to secure maintenance from her husband or to apply for a divorce. The minimum marriageable age for women was raised from 14 to 16 years. The Sunni law of inheritance was amended to enable a grandson to inherit the property of his grandfather if the former's father died while the latter was alive. Special attention was given to controlling the rapid growth of population. An extensive programme of population control was launched with the cooperation and financial support of international agencies.

The conservative Islamic circles were opposed to the Family Laws, but they did not become active for their annulment until after the lifting of martial law. They introduced a bill in the National Assembly in July 1962 for repealing the Family Laws. Several women's organizations protested against the bill and the government opposed it which foiled the bid. Another unsuccessful attempt was made in 1972 when a resolution was moved in the National Assembly against the Family Laws. This led to a lengthy debate in the house but the resolution was rejected. The conservative Islamic groups became more vocal during the period of General Zia-ul-Haq's martial law (1977–85). The General himself criticized the Family Laws and the judgments of the Federal *Shariat* Court, set up by Zia-ul-Haq, neutralized some aspects of these laws.

The military government introduced several changes in the education system on the recommendation of a National Education Commission, set up in December 1958. The course contents at all levels were revised and updated, with a greater emphasis on Pakistani identity, Islam and character-building. The Bachelor's Degree course and the Law Degree were extended from two to three years. A system of monthly tests and class work was introduced at the Bachelor's level which carried weight for determination of the final results. In addition to setting up one engineering and one agriculture university in each province, a number of polytechnic institutes were established to impart functional skills to the young people after their high school education. The government announced a phased plan for introducing compulsory school education and an ambitious programme of financial assistance to outstanding students was launched. Greater encouragement was given to the adoption of Bengali and Urdu as the medium of instruction. These measures were coupled with greater governmental control on the universities and the role of the elected student unions was restricted.

The student community opposed the increase in the duration of the Bachelor's and Law degrees. In September–October 1962, soon after the lifting of martial law, the students took to the streets in many cities against these changes and other demands like expensive text books, high tuition fees and a lack of adequate facilities in the educational institutions. The government withdrew the three-year degree and law programmes in order to pacify them. A year later, when the Dhaka students launched an agitation and demanded that, *inter alia*, the report of the National Education Commission should be scrapped altogether, the government further diluted the education reforms.

Major Economic Measures

Feudalism was the dominant feature of rural life in most of West Pakistan. In Sindh more than 80 per cent agricultural land, in the Punjab, more than 50 per cent, and in NWFP, little less than 50 per cent of land, was owned by a few thousand absentee landlords.[17] As they dominated the executive and the legislature, no land reforms were possible, although different governments promised to abolish feudalism. The military government appointed a land reforms commission for West Pakistan soon after assuming power with a mandate to 'consider problems relating to the ownership and tenancy of agricultural land and to recommend measures for ensuring better production and social justice as well as security of tenure for those engaged in cultivation.'[18] The report of the commission was submitted to the government on 20 January 1959, and, four days later, land reforms were announced by Ayub Khan. The major features of the land reforms were:[19]

(a) No individual could own more than 500 acres of irrigated or 1,000 acres of unirrigated land, or individual total land holding should not exceed 36,000 Produce Index Units (PIUs). Additional land up to 150 acres could be retained as an orchard. The government could also allow the owners to retain the area being used as a stud and livestock farm over and above the ceiling. Furthermore, the excess land could be gifted to the heirs up to 18,000 PIUs. The upper ceiling did not apply to the land owned by a recognized academic institution, any charitable or religious institution.

(b) The land in excess of the above ceiling was to be taken over by the government on payment of compensation ranging from Rs.1 to Rs. 5 per PIU in the form of 'non-negotiable and non-transferable but heritable' bonds redeemable in 25 years with simple interest rate of 3 per cent per annum. Additional compensation was to be paid for any permanent installations and structures on the resumed land which could be used for agricultural purposes.

(c) The acquired land would be sold to the existing tenants who could make the payment in installments. If some land was still available it could be offered to others.

(d) The occupancy tenants were to be made full owners.

(e) A number of measures were announced for the security of tenures for tenants who could not be ejected except by making a recourse to a revenue court on certain specified grounds.

(f) All *jagirs* (land grants) were abolished without compensation.

These reforms were combined with a number of measures to help farmers: consolidation of fragmented pieces of land, encouragement for use of modern methods of farming, improvement in irrigation facilities, i.e. tubewells or supply of canal water, control of water-logging and salinity, better seeds, more credit facilities and improved access to markets.

Over 2 million acres were resumed by the government under these reforms but it was too little to alter fundamentally the existing sharp disparities in land holdings. These reforms were moderate in nature because the military, with links with the landed aristocracy in the Punjab, wanted to trim down the feudals rather than destroy their power. As the basis of the holdings was individual and there were many exceptions granted on one basis or another, the feudals were able to retain enough land to continue commanding the rural society. Moreover, there were loopholes in the implementation process which enabled the feudals to dilute these reforms. A good part of the surrendered land was unsuitable for cultivation. This could not be distributed, and, if some tenants or peasants obtained such land, they did not have resources to make it productive. Nevertheless, the military government should be given credit for initiating the first land reforms in West Pakistan.

A 'Bonus Voucher Scheme' was introduced in January 1959 in order to boost exports and foreign exchange earnings. Any person remitting foreign exchange from abroad or earning it through exports was given an additional financial incentive in the form of foreign exchange entitlement, called the Voucher, at a rate determined by the government, which could be used for payment of imports from abroad or sold in the open market for use by others for import of goods or for foreign exchange payments. These Vouchers were quoted on the Stock Exchange and commanded a high premium. The scheme was first introduced as a temporary measure for one year. It was extended up to the end of the second Five-Year Plan in July 1965. Later, it was further extended for the duration of the third Five Year Plan (1965–70). However, it continued up to May 1972, when the government devalued the currency and withdrew the Bonus Voucher Scheme. This Scheme encouraged exports and discouraged illegal transactions of foreign exchange, but it produced three rates of foreign exchange, the official rate, the Bonus Voucher rate, and the open market rate, which amounted to an unofficial devaluation of the currency. Industrialists and businessmen were able to make additional money without paying much attention to improving quality control and cost-effective management.

The military rulers believed that the considerations of socio-economic development should override the imperatives of political participation. That there was nothing wrong in insulating economic development from day-to-day political pressures or interference. The existing Planning Board was replaced with a powerful Planning Commission, designated as a division in the President's secretariat. The President was made its Chairman and a senior bureaucrat was appointed Vice-Chairman to serve as its operational head. A number of Harvard based American economists were closely associated with economic planning whose growth oriented perspective with full encouragement to the private sector was fully reflected in the second Five-Year Plan (1960–5). In term of absolute numbers, this Plan was a success. All the major targets were either achieved or surpassed. Per capita income increased by 14.8 per cent instead of the target of 12 per cent; the rise in gross national income was 30.4 per cent as compared to the projected target of 24 per cent; and grain production rose by 27 per cent whereas the target was 21 per cent. However, the Plan neglected the distributive aspect of growth. The government had consciously pursued a policy of 'functional inequality' that ignored the equity imperatives on the assumption that such a policy would raise savings, encourage greater accumulation of wealth and promote rapid growth whose rewards, it was claimed, would later 'trickle down' to the lower strata of the society. This resulted in the neglect of the social sector, accentuated the existing economic disparities among different sections of people and increased regional inequities.

Such a skewed economic development coupled with a monolithic nation-building model and a centralized polity caused much alienation in East Pakistan. The military regime did make more funds available for the development of East Pakistan and increased the allocation of foreign exchange to that province. In 1962, the Agricultural Development Corporation was established for each province in order to facilitate the supply of much needed agricultural inputs to farmers and to provide them with necessary technical information and support. In 1962, Pakistan Industrial Development Corporation (PIDC) was divided into two corporations – one each for East and West Pakistan. Similarly, the Water and Power Development

Authority (WAPDA) was divided between the two provinces and two separate Railway Boards were created. However, the overall balance of utilization of resources was tilted heavily in favour of West Pakistan. The emphasis on the private sector and liberal economics accentuated inter-wing disparities. The private sector with a strong profit motive was not keen on investment in East Pakistan due to its poor infrastructure, the climatic conditions, and the confrontational political discourse.

Furthermore, martial law's centralized administration worked to the disadvantage of East Pakistan. West Pakistanis had sufficient representation in the military and the bureaucracy, giving them continued access to the state. The military-bureaucratic channel was not available to East Pakistanis because they were under-represented in the these institutions, especially in the higher echelons of the Army. They had very little access to the policy makers for seeking redress of their economic and political grievances.

The central government emphasized the common bond of Islam and the political struggle of the pre-independence period as the main bases of unity between the two wings. Ayub Khan floated a proposal for a common script for Bengali and Urdu. His preference was for the Roman script, a proposal that faced opposition in both wings. Bengali folklore, culture and history were projected in a selective manner on the state-owned media which annoyed Bengali intellectuals. Several words and terms of Bengali were introduced in Urdu and vice versa, and a scheme of inter-wing scholarships was introduced in order to encourage the students of one wing to study in the educational institutions of the other. Some efforts were made to encourage inter-wing marriages and a programme of settling Bengali peasants in the Ghulam Muhammad Barrage area in Sindh was initiated; the first group of 81 Bengali families were moved to the designated area in January 1960.

These measures could not evoke voluntary support at the popular level due to the absence of credible political mechanisms for strengthening partnership and cooperation between East and West Pakistan. With the exception of those willing to be coopted by the military regime, the politically active circles, especially the new political aspirants, in East Pakistan found themselves practically excluded from the national mainstream.

Political and Constitutional Changes

Ayub Khan had developed definite views on Pakistan politics and society before coming to power because, as C-in-C of the Army, he was in close interaction with the policy-makers and directly observed the degeneration of politics. Three major factors further shaped his political outlook. First, his military background and professional ethos which emphasized discipline, order and authoritarian values rather than political participation and consensus-building through dialogue and accommodation. Second, the experience of military rule reinforced his perception that if political activities were restricted and the role of the political leaders, whom he detested, was minimized, a determined and task-oriented government could ensure socioeconomic and industrial development. Third, his personal ambition to hold on to power and to ensure the continuity of his polices after the withdrawal of military rule led him to introduce a political system that reflected his political views and ensured his continuation in power.

Ayub Khan had prepared a document entitled 'A Short Appreciation of the Present and Future Problems of Pakistan' in October 1954 and presented it to Governor General Ghulam Muhammad. This document, made public in 1960, reflected Ayub's strong dissatisfaction with the parliamentary system and proposed a centralized polity with a powerful head of state who had sufficient powers to deal with the affairs of the state at the federal and provincial levels. An indirectly elected legislature was assigned a limited role. The document further suggested that different provinces and administrative units in West Pakistan should be integrated into a single province, thereby reducing the number of provinces to two – East and West Pakistan – which were given limited autonomy.[20]

After assuming power, Ayub Khan spoke freely against Western-style liberal democracy, especially the parliamentary system of government. He maintained that such a complex system of governance could function only in societies that had attained a high degree of social and political awareness, mass literacy, an advanced system of mass communication, responsible political leadership, and organized political parties. None of these prerequisites existed in Pakistan, he claimed. He described the 1956 constitution as 'a bundle of unworkable compromises',[21] which created a fragmented power structure, making the government dependent on the whims of the political leaders who changed their loyalties on personal and material considerations. He advocated a political system with a strong executive capable of effectively regulating political activity. 'Pakistan needed an executive,' declared Ayub Khan, that was 'popularly elected – and re-elected at fixed periods – but which [could] not be overturned constantly by changing party combination in the legislature.'[22] Another reason for Ayub Khan's opposition to liberal democracy was his strong belief that socio-economic development could not be pursued under this system because it dispersed power in such a way that the much needed effective political and economic management could not be ensured.[23]

In March 1959, Ayub Khan circulated a document to the cabinet members and two provincial governors which outlined his views on the shape of the new constitution. The document, approved by the Governor's Conference in May 1959,[24] could be described as the revised version of the 1954 document and proposed an even more authoritarian and centralized system of governance. After the cabinet endorsed the new political and constitutional agenda, the military government embarked on a phased strategy to implement it in such a manner that it looked like a genuine attempt to create a political order with broad based consultations and support. The first phase involved the introduction of a new system of local self-government, called the Basic Democracies. This led the country to the second phase, when Ayub Khan got himself elected as President through an electoral college comprising the elected members of Basic Democracies. The third phase was initiated with the appointment of a constitution commission which reviewed the political and constitutional history of Pakistan and prepared recommendation for the new constitution. In the fourth phase, the report of the constitution commission was reviewed by the military government and a new constitution was introduced.

(i) Basic Democracies

The Basic Democracies (BD) system was launched on the first anniversary of assumption of power by the military on 27 October 1959,[25] with the objective of building support at the lowest level of the society without ceding any power at the highest level. It was a four-tier[26] semi-representative system that began at the village level and went up to the divisional level; the representative and elective character was carefully neutralized with the presence of official and non-official nominated members and the assignment of some overriding powers to the bureaucracy. 80,000 single member BD constituencies (wards) were established in the country, divided equally between East and West Pakistan. The population of a ward ranged from 1,000 to 14,000 people, and about ten such wards were grouped together to establish the lowest tier of the BD system, known as the Union Council in the rural areas, Town Committee in towns of under 14,000 population, and Union Committee in cities and cantonments. The government could nominate some members to represent special interests, such as women, religious minorities and labour. Their strength could be not more than one-half of the elected members. Each Council or Committee could elect its Chairman from amongst the elected members and was assigned 37 community welfare and development functions.

The second tier of the BD system in the case of the Union Council and Town Committee was the *Tahsil* Council in West Pakistan and the *Thana* Council in East Pakistan. The chairmen of all Union Councils and Town Committees in the *Tahsil/Thana* were its ex-officio members. Its nominated members included the officials of the government departments engaged in social and educational uplift and others nominated by the Deputy Commissioner to provide representation to special interests like women and religious minorities. The senior bureaucrat in the *Tahsil* (*Tahsildar, Mukhtarkar*, Sub Divisional Officer or Assistant Commissioner) presided over its meetings. Its functions included coordination of the work of the lower level councils and performance of any task assigned to it by the District Council. In the urban areas, the second tier was called the Municipal Committee. In the cantonment areas, it was designated as the Cantonment Board. These bodies provided civic facilities or undertook welfare-related work within their municipal limits.

The third level in rural and urban areas was the District Council which covered the geographical area of an administrative district. It comprised official and non-official nominated members. The former included the representatives of the nation-building departments in the district. In the case of the latter, at least half had to be the chairmen of the Union Councils/Committee. It was presided over by the Deputy Commissioner, the most powerful bureaucrat in the district. The District Council performed a wide range of duties relating to education, libraries, health care, agricultural and industrial development, roads, sanitation and other welfare-related work. It could draw up development schemes as well as coordinate the work of the lower level councils in the district.

The Divisional Council was the fourth tier which consisted of official and non-official nominated members. Like the District Council, at least half of the nominated members had to be chairmen of the Union Council/Committees. It coordinated and supervised the work of the lower bodies, scrutinized the development schemes, and reviewed the performance of the administration. The Divisional Commissioner, a bureaucrat, presided over its meetings. The first elections for the lowest level of the BD system were held on the basis of universal adult franchise in December 1959 and January 1960 under strict control of the military authorities. The voter turn out was 69 per cent and out of 144,284 candidates, 17,394 or 12 per cent were elected unopposed.[27] The second BD elections were held in the post-martial law period, in October–November 1964.

The military government wanted BD to perform so that they could claim to have successfully established a new system of local self-governance, bringing forward a new popular leadership. The government was very generous in allocating funds and powers to the BD; the Village AID (Agriculture and Industrial Development) programme was merged with them and they were also associated with the Rural Works Programme. There is no doubt that these institutions undertook useful developmental work in education, health care, water supply, sanitation, road construction, agriculture and cottage industry. However, these could not shape up into a new and autonomous political infrastructure and failed to provide sustainable support to the military government. The BD system's credentials were compromised by its heavy dependence on government funding, awesome presence of the official and nominated members and, above all, the commanding powers of the bureaucracy. Though the principle of nomination was done away with in 1965, the overall control of the bureaucracy was not reduced, making it difficult for these institutions to come out of the 'tutelage' of the bureaucracy.[28]

(ii) The Presidential Referendum

The smooth launch of the BD system gave the military regime enough confidence to seek endorsement of its policies from the BD members. As a prelude, a massive propaganda campaign was launched on the virtues of the new system. The cabinet members travelled extensively, making speeches and contacting the BD members and other influential people. Ayub Khan undertook a tour of West Pakistan in a train, the *'Pak Jamhuriat* Special', from 14 to 21 December 1959, addressing public meetings at every train stop on the achievements of his government and the importance he attached to the 'new democratic experiment', i.e. the BD system. A similar 'meet the people' tour of East Pakistan was undertaken from 21 to 29 January 1960.

A presidential referendum was staged on 14 February 1960. The elected BD members were asked to express their confidence in Ayub Khan by marking either 'Yes' or 'No' on the ballot paper. Out of 79,850 elected BD members, 78,720 casted their votes. 75,283 voted in favour (95.6 per cent of the votes cast), 2,829 voted against (3.6 per cent), and 608 votes were declared invalid.[29] Three days later, on 17 February, Ayub Khan was sworn in as the first elected President.

(iii) The Constitution Commission

Within a few hours of taking the oath of office, Ayub Khan appointed a Constitution Commission comprising ten members and a chairman, Justice Muhammad Shahabuddin, a senior judge of Supreme Court,[30] to formulate proposals for the new constitution after undertaking a comprehensive analysis of Pakistan's political history, especially the circumstances leading to the abrogation of the 1956 constitution, and how such developments could be averted in the future.[31]

The Constitution Commission issued a questionnaire in April seeking views on the problems of democracy in the pre-1958 period and how these could be tackled. The Commission also sought views on a number of specific issues including a federal or unitary system, presidential or parliamentary form of government, bicameral or unicameral legislature, the powers of the President, the electoral process, female representation in the legislatures, appointment and terms of service of the judges of the superior courts, and fundamental human rights and civil liberties.[32]

The questionnaire evoked much interest in politically active circles. Several bar councils debated the issues in their general body meetings and then submitted responses to the questionnaire. Some religious leaders also consulted one another before submitting their responses. A number of well-known political leaders not only responded to the questionnaire but also released their responses to the press, generating a debate between the military regime's supporters and the dissident political elements. The statement of Chaudhri Muhammad Ali, a former Prime Minister, generated much controversy and the cabinet members issued rejoinders.[33] The military authorities were perturbed by this debate because they felt that it adversely affected the work of the Constitution Commission and provided the political leaders with a convenient excuse for engaging in popular mobilization.

In early August, after a stern warning from the military government, the press stopped reporting these issues.[34]

The Constitution Commission received 6,269 replies to the questionnaire and it interviewed 565 people in Dhaka, Chittagong, Khulna, Rajshahi, Quetta, Peshawar, Lahore, Karachi and Rawalpindi. Its report, submitted to Ayub Khan on 6 May 1961, was very critical of the working of the parliamentary system and attributed its failure to several interrelated causes including the deficiencies in the 1956 constitution, absence of proper elections, poor quality of leadership, lack of well-organized political parties, a complete disregard of a democratic ethos by political leaders, excessive involvement of the head of state in politics and the affairs of the government, and undue interference of the centre in provincial affairs. The Commission recommended a presidential form of government with a powerful President and a Vice-President. It proposed a federal system, but assigned overriding powers to the centre, which represented a compromise between the demands for greater autonomy and Ayub Khan's inclinations towards a unitary system. A bicameral legislature was proposed with direct elections for the lower house, President and Vice-President. However, universal adult franchise was to be replaced with a restricted franchise based on literacy and/or ownership of property, and a franchise commission was proposed to determine voters' qualifications. However, the report was of the view that the first elections to the central and provincial assemblies could be held through the BD members so as to expedite the lifting of martial law. The report proposed a religion-based separate electorate and that the existing restrictions on the political parties should be withdrawn. Other important recommendations included an independent judiciary, the enforcement of the fundamental rights through the courts, retention of the Islamic character of the polity, and the continuation of the fiscal arrangements set out in the 1956 constitution.

(iv) Enforcement of the Constitution

The report of the Constitution Commission was scrutinized by a subcommittee of the cabinet[35] for revising the recommendations that diverged from the perspective of the military regime, i.e. direct elections, separate electorate, political parties, enforcement of fundamental rights, and the office of Vice President, etc. Another committee of five senior bureaucrats[36] was asked to look into the administrative aspects of the introduction of the proposed constitutional arrangements. These two review reports were approved by the Governors' Conference, held in the last week of October 1961. The Law Ministry was assigned the task of drafting the Constitution under the supervision of Manzoor Qadir.

The new constitution was announced by Ayub Khan on 1 March 1962. It deviated from the recommendations of the Constitution Commission on a number of issues and created a more authoritarian system than the one envisaged in the report; it was more in line with Ayub Khan's memorandum of October 1954 and the document of March 1959. This came as no surprise because it had been known for some time that Ayub Khan wanted to create a centralized polity with a President as the pivot of the political system. Defending the new constitution, Ayub Khan maintained:

> My own analysis had led me to the conclusion that Pakistan needed a strong government capable of taking decisions which might not be popular but which were necessary for the safety, integrity and, in particular, development of the country. We could not afford the luxury of a system which would make the existence of the government subservient to the whims and operations of pressures groups. On this I was not prepared to make any compromise.[37]

The 1962 constitution stipulated indirect elections for the members of the national and provincial assemblies through an electoral college comprising the elected BD members. The candidates were not allowed to hold public meetings or processions. Instead, the Election Commission arranged 598 meetings in East Pakistan and 302 meetings in West Pakistan during 12–26 April so that the candidates to the national and provincial assemblies could address their voters, i.e. the BD members. With the exception of the workers of the candidates, the ordinary people showed no interest in the indirect electoral exercise. A noteworthy feature was that despite the ban on political parties, a number of people with pre-martial law political affiliations contested the elections and a number of politicians, disqualified under the EBDO, supported their favourites from the sidelines.

The National Assembly polls were held on 28 April and, for that purpose, 445 and 190 polling stations were set up in East and West Pakistan respectively. The elections to the two Provincial Assemblies were held on 6 May, and a total of 668 polling stations were established; 445 in East Pakistan and 223 in West Pakistan. The voter turn-out was 97.3 and 99.7 per cent for the National Assembly and the Provincial Assemblies respectively. The elections to the reserved women's seats in these assemblies were held on 27 and 29 May.[38] On 8 June, the 1962 Constitution was enforced and the elected assemblies began to function, bringing an end to military rule.

6
Authoritarian Clientelism: Post-Martial Law Rule

The introduction of the 1962 constitution was a planned disengagement of the military from power and a careful transition to civilian rule by political and constitutional engineering, a careful tailoring of the political institutions and processes, and a co-option of a section of the political elite. The new political and constitutional arrangements reflected the military's organizational ethos of hierarchy, order and discipline and attempted to regulate political activity; the democratic and participatory considerations were assigned a low priority. The continuity of key personnel and policies from military rule was more conspicuous than the change. The highly centralized political system with concentration of powers in the President established a patron–client relationship between the President on the one hand, and other institutions of the state and the political forces on the other. The authoritarian patron created clients rather than partners in political management.

The Ayubian Political Order

The executive authority of the state was vested in the President, who could exercise it directly or through the officers subordinate to him.[1] Once elected indirectly by an electoral college comprising the elected BD members for a five-year term, the President could exercise substantial powers in respect of administration, law-making, policy execution and key appointments, enabling him to determine the nature and direction of governance at the federal and provincial levels. He appointed members of his cabinet who held office during his pleasure and were not answerable to the federal legislature, i.e. the National Assembly.[2] He was also empowered to make several other key civil and judicial appointments. As the Supreme Commander, the President could raise and maintain the armed forces and their reserve, grant commissions in these services and appoint their C-in-Cs and determine their terms and conditions.[3] He could declare war or make peace without reference to the National Assembly. He had the power to legislate through ordinances which needed the approval of the National Assembly if these were to stay effective after a prescribed period, although there was nothing to stop the President from reissuing the ordinance.

The unicameral National Assembly, whose 156 members[4] were divided equally between East and West Pakistan, were elected indirectly by the same electoral college that elected the President. As long as the National Assembly worked in harmony with the President it could exercise sufficient powers for law-making and amendments in the constitution. If the two diverged, the President had enough powers to restrain the National Assembly. It enjoyed much less financial powers than its predecessor body under the 1956 constitution.[5] The National Assembly could vote only on the 'New Expenditure'; the 'Recurring Expenditure' could be discussed but not voted upon.[6] The latter included expenditure which was required from year to year for some multi-year project. In the first year, such an expenditure would fall in the category of 'New Expenditure'. If the National Assembly passed the expenditure for the first year of a multi-year project, it was deemed to have passed the expenditure for the subsequent years. In this way, the President did not need annual approval for a large part of the budget. The practice of dividing the budget into votable and non-votable portions resembled the British Indian practice during 1921–4[7] and showed Ayub's distrust of the elected legislature. The President acquired dictatorial powers by declaring a state of emergency in the country which he alone was competent to impose and withdraw.[8] Ayub Khan invoked this power in September 1965 on the outbreak of the Indo-Pakistan war and did not lift the emergency until February 1969.

The centre's overriding legislative, administrative and financial powers left little autonomy to the provinces. The provincial Governor was a nominee of the President who appointed his cabinet members with the consent of the President. He enjoyed vast executive and legislative powers, modelled on the President in the centre, and could carry on administration effectively even when he developed differences with the Provincial Assembly. Originally, the Fundamental Rights were incorporated in the constitution as the Principles of Law-Making to serve as guidelines to the law-makers, but, the legislative measures or executive actions could not be challenged in the court of law on the basis of these principles. This caused much furore in political circles and the government had to initiate the first amendment to the constitution in 1963 to change the title of the Principles of Law-Making to Fundamental Rights and to make these enforceable through the courts.

The strong presidency was bolstered by assigning an important place to the bureaucracy in the Ayubian political system. The marriage of convenience that developed between the bureaucracy and the military regime during the martial law period continued in the post-withdrawal period. The bureaucracy was the main beneficiary of the government's decision to expand its role in socio-economic development. The key positions in 22 public corporations and agencies dealing with these matters were held by civil servants and military officers and, in 1964, they constituted 48.3 per cent of the members of the board of directors.[9] While extending the reach of the bureaucracy, the Ayub regime retained enough powers to keep these bureaucrats committed. The retirement age was raised to 60 years in December 1962 but the regime amended the constitution (fourth amendment) in August 1965 to enable the federal and provincial governments to retire a civil servant at the age of 55 or on the completion of 25 years of service. Another amendment (the sixth, approved in March 1966 and further clarified through the eighth amendment enforced in December 1967) granted the federal and provincial governments power to extend the service of a person beyond retirement. These powers were used to ensure the loyalties of the top bureaucrats on whom the Ayub regime relied for governance.

The growing influence of the bureaucracy can be gauged from the fact that the senior bureaucrats convinced Ayub Khan not to implement the recommendations of the Pay and Services Commission which had suggested measures to strip the CSP of its privileged position. The report was shelved and not released to the public until after the displacement of the Ayub regime. One CSP officer went to the West Pakistan Assembly chamber in Lahore and reprimanded a member (some reports accused him of assaulting the member) because the latter had criticized him. The National Assembly and the West Pakistan Assembly pressed for strong action but the officer was not disciplined; rather, he was transferred to pacify the members. Still another indication of the clout of the bureaucracy was the practice of appointing a provincial Chief Secretary (a senior civil servant) as acting Governor whenever the Governor was abroad.

The BD system was another pillar of the Ayub regime. The 1962 constitution designated its members as the electoral college for electing the members of the national and provincial assemblies and the President. The bureaucracy played a key role in ensuring the loyalties of the BD members who were viewed as an extension of the Ayub regime. As the opposition vowed to abolish the BD system, its members sought strength from the regime rather than extending its support base. As long as the Ayub regime was entrenched, the BD members displayed confidence and supported its policies. It was not surprising that Ayub Khan was re-elected as President in January 1965. But, when the Ayub regime was faced with street agitation between November 1968 and March 1969, they could not help the government to tide over the agitation. The BD system suffered from another drawback. It was essentially a rural-based system which was unable to build support for the Ayub regime in the urban areas where the politically active circles, especially the new political aspirants, felt that they had limited opportunities for political advancement except through the regime's cooption process.

Interaction with the Military

Ayub Khan maintained close links with the Army which he viewed as his ultimate strength. General Muhammad Musa who served as the C-in-C of the Army from October 1958 to September 1966 looked to Ayub Khan for guidance and kept a low profile. On his retirement, he was appointed Governor, West Pakistan.[10] His successor, General Agha Muhammad Yahya Khan, had close association with Ayub Khan from pre-martial law days. He got rapid promotions and held important command and staff positions. Though conscious about personal projection and public relations, he did not question Ayub's 'guardianship' until the latter was threatened by massive street agitation in early 1969. Ayub Khan was in regular contact with the Army headquarters and maintained links with the Navy and the Air Force. The C-in-C of the Navy, Vice-Admiral H.M. Siddiq Choudri, developed some policy differences with Ayub Khan and voluntarily sought early retirement in February 1959. He was succeeded by Vice-Admiral Afzal Rahman (A.R.) Khan who served in this post until October 1966 when he assumed the Defence portfolio in Ayub Khan's cabinet. Vice-Admiral S.M. Ahsan who succeeded him as the C-in-C of the Navy, kept his interests exclusively to his professional domain. The Air Force was headed by Air Marshal Asghar Khan when Ayub Khan took over power in 1958, and the Air Marshal, though not involved in the planning and execution of the coup, supported the Army's decision. On his retirement in July 1965, Asghar Khan was appointed President of Pakistan International Airlines (PIA) and Chief Administrator of Civil Aviation and Tourism. He held this position until May 1968. His successor, Air Marshal Muhammad Nur Khan,[11] was another highly professional officer.

The government looked after the welfare and material interests of the military personnel which helped to maintain discipline and professionalism as the personnel were assured of good service conditions and a stable and secure life after retirement. The defence portfolio in the Presidential cabinet was reserved for a person who had held a rank not lower than Lt.-General in the Army or an equivalent rank in the Navy and the Air Force for the first 20 years after the commencement of the constitution.[12] A system of regular induction of military officers to the CSP cadre of the federal services was initiated in 1960. The first batch included five Army officers and by 1963, when this practice was discontinued, 14 Army and Navy officers had been inducted to the CSP; eight of them had close connections with the top echelon of the military.[13] However, the system of contractual appointments and rehiring of military personnel for government and semi-government jobs continued. A number of senior Army officers – Lt.-General, Major General and Brigadier – and their equivalent in the Air Force and the Navy, were appointed to key positions in public corporations, boards and other autonomous bodies after their retirement where they could draw handsome salaries and other perks. The private sector also hired them in order to avail themselves of their contacts and influence with the government. A few went into business after retirement.[14] Some of the senior officers were given ambassadorial assignments abroad. The Army officers and men were also absorbed in the ordnance factories and the industrial enterprises of the *Fauji* Foundation which expanded its operations after the military's assumption of power. In 1960, the federal and provincial governments agreed to fix a quota for ex-servicemen and gave them some relaxation in educational qualifications and age.

The grant of agricultural land for military service, a practice dating back to the British period, remained in operation in the post-independence period. The Veteran Land Settlement Programme was pursued with greater seriousness after the assumption of power by the military. Over 300,000 acres of land were made available in Sindh. Some land was reserved for allotment to military personnel along the Indo-Pakistan border in the Punjab. The land was distributed on a graded formula on the basis of the ranks in the three services. Major General and above or their equivalent were entitled to 240 acres, Brigadiers and Colonels received 150 acres, Lieutenant Colonels 124 acres, Lieutenants to Major 100 acres, Junior Commissioned Officers (JCOs) 64 acres and Non Commissioned Officers (NCOs) 32 acres. When some Army personnel lost their lands due to water logging, they were compensated by new allotments in Nawabshah district. The Navy and the Air Force personnel were also given land in the Guddu barrage and Ghulam Muhammad barrage schemes.[15] Some officers who got land along the Indo-Pakistan border, exchanged it for better land in the interior. All such exchanges were annulled under the 1972 land reforms. The *Fauji* Foundation launched many pre-retirement and post-retirement training programmes for Army personnel to prepare them for new professions after their retirement. The skills taught them included the growing of cash crops, poultry farming, control of plant and animal diseases, dairy farming, manufacturing skills, making of handicrafts and leather goods, electrical and machine working, welding, carpentry, truck driving and vehicle maintenance typing, shorthand and office management. Some of these programmes were also open to their family members.

Ayub Khan was generous towards the military in making necessary funds available to them. The defence expenditure continued to rise during the years of his rule, 1958–69, and the defence allocations were, as in the past, the single biggest item in the national budget. After touching a peak in 1965–6 due to the war with India in September 1965, defence expenditure declined, but it did not revert to the pre-war level; it was more than double the amount spent in the first year after the civilianzation of military rule, 1962–3. The salaries and other facilities of the military personnel were raised, making them better off than their civilian counterparts. This gave rise to a complaint by some politicians in the National Assembly that the officers were leading a luxurious life – a charge vehemently denied by the government. Table 6.1 shows defence expenditure from 1958 to 1969.

Table 6.1   Defence Expenditure, 1958–69 (millions Rupees)

	Defence Expenditure	Total Expenditure Met from Revenue	Defence Expenditure Percentage of Total Expenditure
1958–59	996.5	1,956.5	50.93
1959–60	1,043.5	1,846.5	56.51
1960–61	1,112.4	1,894.2	58.72
1961–62	1,108.6	1,986.8	55.79
1962–63	954.3	1,795.3	53.15
1963–64	1,156.5	2,337.2	49.48
1964–65	1,262.3	2,736.2	46.13
1965–66	2,855.0	4,498.1	63.47
1966–67	2,293.5	3,765.5	60.09
1967–68	2,186.5	4,077.1	53.62
1968–69	2,426.8	4,371.0	55.52

Source: Same as Table 4. 1.

The Ayub regime viewed the military as an instrument of the socio-economic development and modernization of society. The second Five Year Plan (1960–65) envisaged the utilization of the military's skilled and disciplined manpower, technology and organizational resources for developmental work. The Army Engineering Corps was mobilized for overcoming the water shortage in the Quetta region of Balochistan. They constructed a series of dams – Wali Tangi, Kach, Urak Tangi and Sra Khula – for water storage, conservation and distribution, which assured a sufficient water supply for Quetta city and the surrounding areas. This also helped farmers grow more vegetables and fruit.[16] Another important project was the Indus Valley Road from Gilgit to Peshawar and Rawalpindi which connected the northern regions with the rest of Pakistan. In October 1966, Frontier Works Organization (FWO) was set up by the Army for the construction of the Karakoram Highway (KKH), an all-weather road up to the Chinese border. Later, the FWO undertook several other civilian engineering projects.

These tasks were in addition to the Army's role in aid of civil government for the maintenance of law and order and rescue and relief operations in the event of natural calamities like cyclones (East Pakistan), floods and locust attacks on standing crops (East and West Pakistan). It also contributed to the government's efforts to check water logging and salinity in West Pakistan.

The government highlighted the role of the military in the civilian sectors in order to generate and sustain goodwill at the popular level. The armed forces featured prominently on national days. From 1960, the second Sunday in January was designated as the Armed Forces Day. After the 1965 Indo-Pakistan War, 6 and 7 September were declared as the Armed Forces Day and the Air Force Day respectively. The parades of the armed forces, air displays, exhibitions of military equipment and weapons featured on these occasions. Lectures and seminars were held on the role of the military in defence of the country and its contribution to the civilian sectors. The Postal Department issued several stamps featuring the armed forces.

Defence and Security Issues

Pakistan's search for security which shaped its foreign policy options in the pre-1958 period continued to haunt the Ayub regime. The major political developments in and around South Asia in the 1960s led Pakistan to review its avowedly pro-West foreign policy and adopt an independent approach by improving relations with China, the Soviet Union and several other states which had been ignored in the past. It was an attempt to expand policy options by adopting a relatively balanced approach towards regional and global issues. However, the change was that of strategy and tactics rather than the goal of security and territorial integrity of the state. This meant that the military continued to be central to the new foreign policy strategy.

Pakistan continued to have difficult relations with Afghanistan due to the latter's persistence in its irredentist claims on the former's territory. In August 1961, Pakistan suspended transit trade facilities to Afghanistan and severed its diplomatic relations. This stalemate lasted till Sardar Daoud was ousted from power in Afghanistan in March 1963. Pakistan and Afghanistan agreed to revive their diplomatic and economic relations on the initiative of Iran and the US, although Afghanistan did not abandon its territorial claim.

A development of far-reaching consequence for Pakistan's security was the Sino-Indian border conflict, in October 1962, and the decision of the US and other Western countries to supply weapons and military equipment to India to enable the latter to stand up to China. The roots of the Sino-Indian border conflict could be traced to 1953, when a few maps were found in the possession of a Chinese merchant visiting Calcutta which showed parts of Assam and the whole of the north-eastern frontier as part of China. Later, some of the Chinese maps laid claims to about 36,000 square miles of territory in the northeastern frontier region and about 15,000 square miles in the Ladakh region of Kashmir, across the MacMohan Line established in 1914 by the British as a boundary between India and China.[17] The Chinese government disputed the legitimacy of this boundary line, and, by June 1954, Chinese troops periodically intruded into the territory south of the MacMohan Line, claimed by India as its territory. The intermittent bilateral negotiations between China and India could not reconcile their conflicting claims and border skirmishes began to take place as the two sides tried to assert their territorial claims. These escalated into a border war when, in October 1962, the Indian Prime Minister ordered the military to dislodge the Chinese troops from the area. The Indian military could not match the qualitative and quantitative superiority of the Chinese troops and was overwhelmed both on the northeastern border and in the Ladakh area. After the Chinese troops captured the areas they laid claim on, the Chinese government announced a unilateral ceasefire.

The military reverses caused a security panic in India. Its frantic efforts to strengthen security against a stronger China had similarities with Pakistan's search for security in the early 1950s when the latter perceived serious security threats from a stronger India. Now, it was India's turn to approach the US, Great Britain, Australia, Canada, France and the Soviet Union for immediate military assistance. India sought security guarantees, including air cover and surveillance, weapons and military equipment, training facilities and joint military exercises.[18] The first consignment of British weapons arrived in India by air on 29 October. The US President John F. Kennedy also responded promptly by resuming an airlift of weapons on 3 November.[19] The US viewed this as an opportunity 'to snap Nehru out of his obsession with peaceful coexistence',[20] and dilute his non-alignment by bringing him close to the West. Canada and Australia also chipped in for enhancing India's defensive capability. India's long-term security needs were reviewed by American and British expert missions between November 1962 and February 1963, followed by a phased supply of weapons, military equipment, including support to India's first five-year defence plan launched in 1964.[21] The Soviet Union, which began military sales to India in 1961, supplied more weapons, including MiG aircraft, helicopters and transport planes, from early 1963.[22] A programme for the expansion and modernization of indigenous defence industry was also initiated with external cooperation.

As a partner in security arrangements, Pakistan felt betrayed by the American and British decision to supply weapons to India. Pakistan's policymakers maintained that India was exploiting the West's trepidation about China to build its military, which it would use against Pakistan with whom it had a more deep-seated antagonistic relationship and enjoyed military superiority. They further argued that there was no possibility of a full-fledged war between India and China because the latter had no intention of occupying large tracts of Indian territory beyond what it claimed to be its own. This perspective was not acceptable to the US administration, which wanted to upgrade and modernize India's security arrangements to enable it to thwart any future Chinese bid to advance southward, so that a strong India could counteract Chinese influence in the region.[23] Kennedy's repeated assurance that India's enhanced military power would not be used against Pakistan did not allay the latter's security apprehensions.[24]

Pakistan had initiated a review of its policy of alignment with the West after Pakistan faced Soviet ire when they shot down an American U-2 spy aircraft over their airspace in May 1960, which had taken off from Peshawar. Western weapons transfers to India left no doubts in the minds of Pakistan's policy-makers that they must expand their foreign policy options by opening up diplomatic channels with China, the Soviet Union and a number of other countries which had been kept at bay in the past in deference to security partnership with the U.S.

Pakistan's foreign policy began to change in 1961 when agreements were signed with the Soviet Union for Soviet technical cooperation and credit facilities for oil exploration in Pakistan. Two years later, two agreements were signed for another loan and barter trade. An air services agreement was also signed in the same year which enabled Pakistan's national airline, PIA, to start a regular service to Moscow and beyond on 1 April 1964. More significant developments took place in Pakistan's interaction with China when the two countries opened negotiations on demarcation of their boundaries in October 1962.[25] The agreement was finalized by the end of the year, and signed in March 1963. They also signed an agreement on trade, commerce and shipping in January 1963, an air services agreement in August and a barter trade agreement in September. PIA started its regular air service to Beijing and beyond on 29 April 1964, thereby becoming the first non-communist air line to have a regular service to both China and the Soviet Union. These developments caused much concern in the US and other Western countries, which accused Pakistan of causing a breach in the 'free world' solidarity. The US was especially perturbed by Chinese Prime Minister Zhou Enlai's visit to Pakistan in February 1964, and made no secret of its strong displeasure over Pakistan's growing relations with China. Pakistan was equally terse in objecting to American military assistance to India.[26]

In order to placate Pakistan, the US and Great Britain persuaded India to initiate a dialogue with Pakistan on Kashmir. Six rounds of talks at Foreign Minister level were held during December 1962 and May 1963 but these did not produce any result as the two sides showed no flexibility in their traditional positions on Kashmir. Pakistan's policy-makers were convinced that India was not interested in a peaceful settlement of the Kashmir problem and that Western arms supplies had contributed to this 'adamancy'. When Sheikh Abdullah's visit to Pakistan in May 1964 did not facilitate any settlement, all hopes for a peaceful settlement were lost. Several other Kashmir-related developments escalated tension which included the disappearance of the hair of Prophet Muhammad from the Hazratbal shrine in December 1963, the debate on Kashmir in the UN Security Council on Pakistan's initiative in 1964, release (April 1964) and re-arrest (May 1965) of Sheikh Abdullah by India, Kashmir Assembly's decision to take steps for integration of Kashmir with India (March–April 1965), periodic agitation in Indian-administered Kashmir, and bitter diplomatic exchanges between Pakistan and India.

It was in such a charged atmosphere that the armies of India and Pakistan clashed in the Rann of Kutch area in the first week of April, starting the first of the two wars the two countries fought in 1965. The Rann of Kutch, situated on the border of the Indian state of Gujarat and Sindh, is a desolate and infertile territory part of which is under water for most of the year. The dispute pertained to the precise location of the boundary. Pakistan maintained that the boundary was located in the middle of the Rann. India claimed that it ran along the northern edge of the Rann, creating a dispute of about 3,500 square miles of territory.[27] War broke out as the Indian Army established control over a post in Ding, and Pakistan responded by moving its troops to stall the Indian advance. Indian troops were dislodged and a ceasefire was agreed on 30 April, followed by the signing of a formal ceasefire agreement on 30 June through the mediation of British Prime Minister, Harold Wilson. Later, the dispute was submitted to an international arbitration tribunal whose ruling, given in February 1968, was accepted and implemented by the two sides.[28]

The performance of the Pakistan Army in the limited war in the Rann of Kutch was a morale booster for the military. The civil and military authorities launched a massive propaganda campaign to project the military as an invincible force.[29] The top echelons of the Army and the key decision-makers in the Foreign Office were convinced that Pakistan should now challenge India in Kashmir. This sentiment was strengthened by a misperception that Kashmir was seething with so much disaffection that a limited external support would ignite a popular revolt, overwhelming the Indian civil and military establishment there. The Army headquarters and the Foreign Office prepared a plan, later approved by Ayub Khan, for induction of Pakistani/Kashmiri personnel with sufficient paramilitary training into Indian-administered Kashmir to bolster the local Kashmiri activists in their bid to dislodge the Indian administration.

This plan of action, named Operation Gibraltar, was launched on 5 August 1965 when the first batch of Pakistani trained personnel were sent across the ceasefire line in Kashmir. A clandestine radio, most likely installed by Pakistani intelligence, came on air and announced the setting up of a revolutionary council to wage a war of liberation in Indian-administered Kashmir. To the disappointment of Pakistan, the dream of a popular uprising did not materialize, and the infiltrators could not be effective in their operations. On 16 August, Indian troops crossed the ceasefire line and occupied three passes in the Kargil area, alleged to be the infiltration routes. Later, they made more advances in certain parts of Pakistan-administered Kashmir and by the end of August they occupied several strategic posts on the Pakistani side of the ceasefire line, including Tithwal and Haji Pir. The Pakistan Army retaliated by crossing the ceasefire line on 1 September and advanced in the Chamb-Akhnur sector in Indian-administered Kashmir. As the Pakistan Army pressed ahead in this sector, India launched a three-pronged attack in the Punjab sector of the India-West Pakistan border on 6 September in order to relieve pressure in Kashmir. Thus, for the first time, a war broke out on the ceasefire line in Kashmir and the India–West Pakistan border, involving the Army and the Air Force. The naval forces also had a brief encounter near India's Dawarka naval base. There were no hostilities on the India–East Pakistan border.

During the 17-day war (6–23 September), the morale of the two sides was high as both were convinced of the righteousness of their cause. Though the two sides fought to the best of their abilities, they showed restraints by limiting their air attacks to military and semi-military targets; they avoided industry, waterways and dams, and other important economic interests. There was no evidence to suggest that the two sides deliberately targeted the civilian population. Having a common British background and similar combat training, they were using similar tactics rather than taking bold initiatives. Given Pakistan's numerical inferiority and resource constraints, its military put up an impressive show of its capabilities. Both sides achieved some of their objectives. India was able to save Kashmir by expanding the scope of hostilities, but it could not make much territorial gain across the international border, especially in the Punjab, which could have strengthened its bargaining position on Kashmir. Pakistan was unable to stir a rebellion in Kashmir and failed to impose a military solution of the Kashmir problem. However, it foiled India's bid to capture major parts of Pakistani territory.

In January 1966, Ayub Khan and Lal Bahadur Shastri met at Tashkent on the invitation of Soviet Prime Minister Alexei Kosygin and signed a peace agreement called the Tashkent Declaration which suggested ways and means to normalize their relations by dealing with immediate problems including the return of the prisoners of war (POWs), withdrawal of troops and return of the areas occupied during the war, revival of economic relations and resumption of diplomatic relations. It also called upon the two sides to settle their disputes through peaceful means. Kashmir, the main cause of the war, was mentioned in the Declaration in a perfunctory manner, i.e. the two sides presented their perspectives on Kashmir in the context of an understanding that the continuation of tension between the two countries did not serve their interest.

The September war demonstrated that both sides were capable of standing up to each other. This led India and Pakistan to devote more attention to building their military prowess and the acquisition of weapons became an obsession with them. India stepped up its indigenous defence production and procured weapons and military equipment from the Soviet Union, Eastern Europe and several Western countries. It acquired advanced aircraft from the Soviet Union and expanded its Navy to make it a two-fleet force for the Bay of Bengal and the Arabian Sea; Goa was developed as major naval base and the existing naval installations were gradually modernized.

Pakistan also made frantic efforts to obtain weapons and military equipment from abroad. The American decision to put an arms embargo on South Asia on the outbreak of the Indo-Pakistan war had hit Pakistan very hard because it was heavily dependent on American weapons and equipment; the Air Force was almost entirely dependent on the US. Pakistan's own defence industry was underdeveloped. The non-availability of military supplies contributed to Pakistan's decision to accept the UN-sponsored ceasefire. Pakistan therefore decided to expand and modernize its defence industry, and diversified weapons procurement from abroad.

China was the most important new source of weapon procurement. It was towards the end of 1965 or in early 1966 that Pakistan began to receive Chinese weapons and military equipment, including MiG-19 aircraft and T-59 tanks. Pakistan purchased weapons and military equipment mainly from Great Britain, France, West Germany, Italy and Czechoslovakia. It also obtained some weapons through Iran and Turkey. As Pakistan's relations had improved with the Soviet Union, it argued with the Soviet leaders that they should either supply weapons to Pakistan or cease such supplies to India. Pakistan's first military delegation, headed by the C-in-C of the Air Force, Air Marshal Nur Khan, visited Moscow in June 1966 to discuss this issue. Another Pakistani military delegation, headed by the C-in-C of the Army, General Yahya Khan, paid a visit to Moscow in July 1968 and repeated Pakistan's request for the supply of weapons. The Governor of West Pakistan, a former Army Chief, General Musa, was in Moscow on an official visit in September 1968, and, in March 1969, a Soviet military delegation, led by Marshal Grechkov, undertook a visit to Pakistan. These exchanges resulted in the Soviet decision to supply T-54/55 tanks, MI helicopters and their spares, 130 mm guns, jeeps and trucks during 1968–70.

The US eased its embargo in March 1966 by agreeing to sell 'non-lethal' military equipment such as trucks, medical and engineering supplies, etc. This policy was further revised in April 1967, when the US agreed to cash sales of spare parts for the military equipment previously supplied to Pakistan and India on 'a case by case basis', and that no weapons would be supplied as grants. As Pakistan was not in a position to make cash payments, it could not obtain any major weapon system or combat aircraft even after the lifting of the embargo. In 1970, the US made a 'one-time exception' to enable Pakistan to place an order for 300 armoured personnel carriers (APCs), a small number of combat aircraft and some weapons. However, no aircraft was supplied and the APCs were made available in 1973.

This policy of strengthening defence was generally endorsed by the National Assembly and the politically active circles. The Assembly debates reflected a widely shared desire across the political divide to strengthen the armed forces and security arrangements in view of the perceived Indian threat and the fear of another military encounter. The defence expenditure was never subjected to serious scrutiny. However, the poor representation of Bengalis in the armed forces, especially in the Army, was criticized by the members from East Pakistan, who persistently demanded an increase in the recruitment of the Bengalis to the Army. They also felt that the government had not given adequate attention to the defence of East Pakistan, a feeling that intensified after the 1965 Indo-Pakistan war because the eastern wing was virtually isolated from West Pakistan during the war period.

Political Dynamics

The political parties were not revived on the introduction of the Constitution in June 1962. The members of the National Assembly and the two Provincial Assemblies organized themselves as 'the like-minded' groups; one of these supported the government. As the political circles (including the government supporters) mounted pressure for the revival of political parties, the government enacted the Political Parties Act in July which legalized the formation and functioning of the political parties with a proviso that these could neither advocate anything prejudicial to the Islamic ideology, integrity and security of Pakistan nor accept financial assistance from, or affiliate with, any foreign government or foreign agency. The politicians disqualified under the EBDO could not hold any party office until the expiry of their disqualification period. If a political party violated the Act, the government could ban it, followed by a reference to the Supreme Court which had the final word on such a ban. The Act also provided that a member of the National or Provincial Assemblies would have to seek re-election on changing party affiliation. Ayub Khan also agreed to make the fundamental rights enforceable through the courts and the word 'Islamic' was added to the official title of the state, thereby reverting to the practice of the earlier constitution.

Most pre-martial law political parties were revived. The Muslim League was split in two groups. The pro-government members of the Muslim League held a convention in Karachi in September to revive the party, later known as the Convention Muslim League; Chuadhri Khaliquzzaman was appointed its Chief Organizer and President. The Muslim Leaguers who stayed away, held a separate meeting in Dhaka in October to revive the party, later called the Council Muslim League, with Khawaja Nazimuddin as its President. This party served as the main building block of the opposition to Ayub Khan and the EBDOed politicians played an active role in organizing this, although they did not formally join.[30] The Convention Muslim League functioned as the official party. In May 1963, Ayub Khan joined it and assumed its presidency in December.

Ayub Khan had thus created the necessary structure to sustain his post-martial law regime: constitutional arrangements that strengthened his position, the BD system whose members depended on the regime for funds and favours, and a political party comprising the co-opted elite. The state apparatus was available to back up these political arrangements. It was a top-heavy system with a concentration of power in the President. The lower levels of the Ayubian political system derived strength from above rather than serving as the support base for the top leadership. The bureaucracy was the linchpin that kept the BD system and the Convention Muslim League intact and operational; the latter was unable to develop into a viable and autonomous political machine capable of support mobilization, and the articulation and aggregation of interests.

A carrot and stick policy was used to dissuade political adversaries from undermining the political arrangements. In January 1963, an ordinance was promulgated to restrain the EBDOed political leaders from behind-the-scene involvement with the opposition. The new law made them liable to two years' imprisonment if they issued statements of a political nature, addressed a press conference or joined a group engaged in political activity. Another law entitled the President to remove their disqualification[31] – a carrot for encouraging them to support the government.

The regime imposed new curbs on the press in September 1963 by amending the Press and Publication Ordinance/laws issued during the martial law period. The press vehemently opposed these amendments. Ayub Khan offered a carrot by withdrawing some of the new restrictions in October, but the modified laws still gave enough powers to the government to build strong pressures on the dissenting newspapers and magazines. The newspapers and magazines that persisted in open defiance of the government often found themselves in the clutches of various laws, suffered the loss of advertisement revenue or faced harassment from the state apparatus. In 1964, the National Press Trust was formed, which spearheaded the propaganda campaign for the government. A new University Ordinance was enforced in 1963 which further neutralized the autonomy of the universities and allowed the government to withdraw the degree of a student on certain specified grounds. From time to time, the opposition leaders were arrested to restrain them from political mobilization and agitation. In January 1964, Jamaat-i-Islami was banned and its leaders were arrested for engaging in anti-state activities. However, the Supreme Court revoked the ban in September, causing embarrassment to the Ayub regime.

Ayub Khan also benefited from the organizational weaknesses and internal feuds of the opposition which could not project itself as a viable alternative to him. The opposition political parties repeatedly vowed to work to restore 'full and complete democracy' and created many alliances, but these could not last long due to mutual distrust and personality clashes.[32] One of the opposition alliances, the Combined Opposition Parties (COP), established in 1964, posed a temporary but strong challenge by fielding Ms Fatima Jinnah, sister of the founder of Pakistan, as their joint candidate against Ayub Khan in the presidential elections in January 1965. This boosted the image of the opposition as it nominated a venerated and non-controversial person. The election campaign showed that the voters were attracted by the personalities of the two candidates rather than the political parties supporting them. Ayub Khan had a clear edge in campaigning due to his knowledge of administration and politics and the support of the governmental machinery. Above all, the COP stance that they would restore a parliamentary system of government and abolish the BD system deterred the BD members who constituted the electoral college for the presidential elections. Though Ayub Khan won with a comfortable margin, over 36 per cent of the Basic Democrats voted against him. What caused much concern was Ayub Khan's narrow margins in East Pakistan, losing in the districts of Dhaka, Noakhali, Sylhet and Comilla. In West Pakistan, he won in all districts with the exception of Karachi.[33]

The demoralized COP could not maintain its coherence as the elections to the national and provincial assemblies approached. It managed to nominate some candidates jointly for the National Assembly, but it could not even do that for the elections to the provincial assemblies. The elections held in March and May were a virtual walkover for the ruling Convention Muslim League. However, like the presidential elections, the ruling party performed badly in East Pakistan;[34] it won 71 seats as against 84 which were secured by independent candidates. A large number of independent members later joined the government.[35]

1965 was the year of glory for Ayub Khan as he won the presidential elections and his party swept the assembly elections at the national and provincial levels. In September, when India and Pakistan were at war, the opposition extended unqualified support to him. However, the year of glory was also the beginning of the end of the Ayub regime. The September war set in motion the forces that later led to the collapse of the Ayub regime. The government and the Army authorities projected the 1965 war as a major triumph: Pakistani soliders had outstripped their Indian counterparts due to their professionalism, commitment and courage. The performance of the Air Force and the Navy received similar adulation. The Ayub regime became a victim of this propaganda when it signed a peace treaty with India at Tashkent in January 1966 which stipulated the withdrawal of troops, return of the captured territory and normalization of relations, without proposing any concrete step for the solution of the Kashmir problem. The Tashkent Declaration was hardly acceptable to the public who had been made to believe that Pakistan's 'triumph' in the battlefield had strengthened its position in Kashmir. By mid-January, students, labour and other politically active circles were out in the streets demonstrating against the Ayub regime. The opposition could not miss such an opportunity and cashed in on the anti-Tashkent Declaration sentiments. The government reacted in its characteristic manner by using the state apparatus against them.

The 1965 war accentuated East–West Pakistan differences and caused much alienation in East Pakistan. Though there was no war on the India–East Pakistan border, East Pakistan was virtually cut off from West Pakistan during the 17 days of the war. Most East Pakistani leaders complained that had India launched a military offensive, East Pakistan could hardly be defended. This perceived sense of insecurity was articulated by the political leaders to reinforce their demand for greater provincial autonomy. It was in this context that the Awami League advanced its Six-point Formula in March as a solution for economic disparities and for ensuring maximum autonomy to East Pakistan (see the next chapter). In April, a number of East Pakistani leaders, including Sheikh Mujibur Rahman, were arrested. A similar action had already been taken against several West Pakistani political leaders in the wake of the anti-Tashkent agitation.

The Indo-Pakistan war caused economic dislocation and had adverse implications for economic development. The Third Five Year Plan, initiated in July 1965, had to be readjusted to cope with postwar security pressures. This accentuated the already existing economic disparities and imbalances. Pakistan experienced undoubted spectacular economic growth in aggregate terms during the Ayub era. Maximum encouragement was given to the private sector through state subsidies and other incentives which accelerated the pace of economic growth, but these policies ignored the distributive side which resulted in disparities in interpersonal and inter-regional incomes, a trend that sharpened after the 1965 war due to higher allocations to defence and security. The government propaganda was telling the people in 1967–8 about the major economic strides during the last ten years, but the urban professional classes were facing economic hardship due to inflation and price hikes. The educated youths and urban proletariat were completely alienated as they found that the much trumpeted economic development had not improved the quality of life for them. In the case of East Pakistan, the problem of personal income disparity was coupled with an increased inter-wing disparity to its disadvantage. The rate of economic growth being higher in West Pakistan, East Pakistan lagged behind which caused bitterness amongst the Bengalis who felt that the Ayub regime was insensitive to their economic and political predicament and that unless they secured economic and political autonomy from the powerful and entrenched central government, their conditions would not improve.

The heightened interpersonal and inter-wing economic disparities were not the only economy-related problems. As the regime settled down in the post-martial law period, there were complaints about increased corruption in the bureaucratic structure.[36] What especially hurt the regime was the rise of Gohar Ayub, son of Ayub Khan, as an industrial magnate after having secured his release from the Army. He was later inducted into the ruling Convention Muslim League.

The conservative Islamic circles were critical of the Family Laws and the government efforts to popularize family planning and population control. They also resented the decision of the government to take over the management of some important shrines and mosques and their property, and placing these under the control of the newly established *Auqaf* department. The religious elements viewed this as an unjustified government interference in the religious domain and an attempt to control the religious institutions. This sentiment strengthened as the government attempted to regulate the contents of the Friday sermons in the *Auqaf*-controlled mosques.[37] However, the Islamic element did not have political clout to challenge the regime all by themselves. They began to cultivate other political forces as dissatisfaction increased against the Ayub regime.

The end of the period of disqualification for the EBDOed politicians on 31 December 1966 caused an additional headache for the government as most of those who returned to politics joined the opposition ranks. Zulfikar Ali Bhutto, who had left Ayub Khan's cabinet in June 1966 after developing policy differences, organized a new political party – the Pakistan People's Party (PPP) – in November 1967. His sharp critique of the government policies, rabid anti-India rhetoric and articulation of socio-economic grievances built him as the most formidable adversary of Ayub Khan.

The political atmosphere was more combative in East Pakistan where anti-regime sentiments were more pronounced and the opposition was better placed to show its strength. The situation worsened when, in January 1968, the government announced that 28 people including two officers belonging to the CSP, had been arrested in December 1967 in East Pakistan on charges of 'anti-national' activities. Described as the Agartala conspiracy, the accused were charged with planning the secession of East Pakistan in collaboration with India. Sheikh Mujibur Rahman, who was already in detention, was also named as an accused for having participated in the conspiracy through his contact.[38] The shock of the conspiracy news was hardly over when, towards the end of January, Ayub Khan fell seriously ill and could not function as President for over a month.[39] Even after his recovery in early March, he was not in a position to devote himself fully to his work. This not only increased his dependence on the bureaucracy, but also raised the question of his successor. It was not merely the political circles that began to ponder this question, the bureaucracy and the military – the mainstay of the Ayub regime – were forced to think: After Ayub who? After Ayub what?

The Collapse of the Ayub Regime

What sparked the agitation was a clash between a group of students of the Polytechnic Institute, Rawalpindi, who were agitating on a non-political demand, and the police on 7 November 1968. The encounter led to the death of a student, igniting more agitation. Bhutto, who was in Rawalpindi, cashed in on the incident by identifying with the students, which emboldened them. Three days later, when Ayub Khan was about to address a public meeting in Peshawar, a young man fired pistol shots in the direction of the stage; Ayub was not hit and he later addressed the meeting. However, the incident which came in the wake of the student agitation, panicked the regime which responded with heavy hand on the political adversaries and activists. On 13 November, Bhutto, Wali Khan and 11 other leaders were arrested on the charge of 'acting in a manner prejudicial to security, public safety and interest of Pakistan'.[40] The agitation did not subside. The anti-government forces got a big boost when Air Marshal Asghar Khan, a former C-in-C of the Air Force, entered politics in opposition to Ayub Khan and played a leadership role while other leaders were in detention.[41] Later, a number of other well-known people, hitherto not active in politics, joined the opposition ranks. The most prominent among them were Justice S.M. Murshad, a former Chief Justice of East Pakistan High Court, Lt.-General Azam Khan, and Major Generals Akbar Khan, Jilani and Sarfaraz.

By the end of December, the opposition ranks had swollen and the agitation became widespread. In East Pakistan, Maulana Bhashani and his faction of the National Awami Party (NAP) and the Awami League were engaged in an extremely defiant movement. Eight political parties formed a Democratic Action Committee (DAC) in early January 1969 and put forward demands which virtually called for discarding the 1962 Constitution. These included, *inter alia*, the introduction of a federal parliamentary system of government, direct elections to the assemblies, immediate withdrawal of the state of emergency in force since September 1965, full restoration of the civil and political rights, release of all arrested political leaders, and removal of restrictions on the press.[42] The PPP and the NAP (Bhashani) stayed aloof and carried on anti-Ayub agitation as separate entities.

As the agitation virtually paralysed the government, Ayub Khan decided to offer concessions. The detained political leaders were released, and, on 17 February 1969, the state of emergency was withdrawn and an offer of dialogue on the contentious issues was made. Another gesture was his decision on 21 February not to seek re-election. A major obstacle to a government–opposition dialogue was the opposition demand to withdraw the Agartala conspiracy case so that Mujibur Rahman could participate in the dialogue. While the government was considering the demand, one of the accused in the Agartala conspiracy case was shot dead by security guards. The government version that the accused was making an escape bid was hardly acceptable to anyone in East Pakistan where his funeral turned into a massive rally against the regime. The government was hardly left with a choice other than withdrawing the case.

Two rounds of talks between the government and the opposition[43] on 26 February and 10–13 March produced an agreement on the restoration of federal parliamentary system with regional autonomy, and direct elections on the basis of adult franchise. However, there was no respite in the agitation because the opposition, having suffered from the government's high-handed policies in the past, raised a host of other issues and pressed for the immediate removal of Ayub Khan. In West Pakistan, most political parties demanded the break-up of the integrated province of West Pakistan, and, in East Pakistan, demands for autonomy and political and economic justice dominated the opposition discourse. Bhutto who had stayed away from the dialogue was the main crowd-puller in West Pakistan, and Mujibur Rahman and Bhashani were the key players in the agitation in East Pakistan; they did not want to wait for the implementation of the agreed political changes. The situation deteriorated in East Pakistan where anything that symbolized the

Ayub regime was the target of agitators. In addition to looting government property, BD members and activists of the ruling Convention Muslim League were the targets of popular anger; a number of BD members were killed or were forced to resign. In West Pakistan, the agitation continued unabated, although it was less violent. All the major strata of the society in West Pakistan, especially the labour, students and the urban poor, were actively involved in the agitation, pressing for democratization of the polity and restructuring of the economy.

As the regime's legitimacy crisis deepened, the bureaucracy reviewed its relationship with it and adopted a neutral posture, limiting itself to minimum professional duties.[44] The senior bureaucrats started looking towards the post-Ayub era and began to prepare themselves for another accommodation with a new set of leaders. Some of the senior bureaucrats approached the senior Army commanders asking them to take action to pull the country out of chaos.[45]

Ayub Khan used the troops to reinforce the tottering civil administration from time to time during January–March 1969, especially in East Pakistan. In mid-March, he wanted to impose martial law in some cities to cope with the agitation. However, the top brass of the Army refused to support him. In their estimation, he was totally discredited at the popular level. They not only distanced themselves from the regime but also communicated to Ayub Khan that they were not disposed towards imposing martial law while he headed the government. The loss of the Army support convinced Ayub Khan that he would not be able to hold on to power for long.

The 1962 constitution stipulated that in the event of the resignation of the President, the Speaker of the National Assembly would serve as Acting President and the new President was to be elected within 90 days.[46] The political realities obtaining in Pakistan made such a transfer of power impossible. The Speaker of the National Assembly, Abdul Jabbar Khan, a nominee of the ruling party from East Pakistan, was so closely associated with the Ayub regime that he could not be acceptable to the opposition, which wanted to uproot the Ayubian system completely. Moreover, the presidential elections under the existing arrangements, i.e. indirect elections through the BD members, could not be held as these had been rejected by the political parties. The constitution had to be amended to institute direct elections, but the political conditions were hardly conducive for the existing National Assembly to do that. Above all, a constitutional transfer of power could take place without the support of the military, which was not available.[47] By supporting Ayub Khan or a constitutional transfer of power, the top brass of the Army did not want to miss the opportunity to exercise the supreme political power. With the Ayub regime totally discredited and the political leaders having failed to agree on the mechanisms for transfer of power, Yahya Khan considered himself as the natural ruler. By the third week of March, the senior Army commanders had made up their mind to impose martial law.[48] Senior bureaucrats and several members of Ayub Khan's cabinet also wanted the top brass of the Army to step in.

Ayub Khan could read the writing on the wall. He decided to step down in favour of General Yahya Khan on 25 March, before the top brass of the Army forced him to do so. The text of Ayub Khan's letter to General Yahya Khan asking him to take over was shown to the latter before it was officially sent to him and released to the press. Ayub Khan's last address to the nation, announcing his abdication, was recorded for broadcast on radio in the presence of Yahya Khan. After he finished his speech, Ayub Khan walked up to Yahya Khan and shook hands with him.[49] Thus one general passed on the baton to another.

7
The Second Military Regime

The imposition of martial law by General Agha Muhammad Yahya Khan on 25 March 1969 brought the military back to power unimpeded by any constitutional or popular check. The response of the politically active circles was generally positive as most were happy to get rid of Ayub Khan and they viewed the second military regime as a transitional arrangement that would lead to the establishment of a participatory political process. The students, labour, the urban unemployed and other alienated groups that were the mainstay of the anti-Ayub agitation went back to their routine which restored peace and order in the society and revived economic activity. However, this was not the acceptance of military rule; it was a wait-and-see situation that temporarily calmed these elements and gave some political space to the new military rulers.

The Nature and Style of the Military Regime

Yahya Khan designated himself as the CMLA. Initially, the office of President was kept vacant, but, on 31 March, he assumed this office as well. Unlike Ayub Khan, he did not quit the command of the Army, combining three offices – CMLA, C-in-C of the Army and President. The new military regime drew heavily on the previous martial law. Martial law regulations were reintroduced with necessary modifications and the administrative arrangements as set out in the abrogated 1962 constitution were kept, subject to the overriding power of the President/CMLA to make changes as he deemed fit. Special and summary military courts were established to deal with violators of martial law regulations, rules and orders. The ordinary courts were allowed to function but these could not question any order or action of the martial law authorities or the judgements of any military court.

A three-member Council of Administration was set up with Yahya Khan as its chairman. It included Lt.-General Abdul Hamid Khan[1] (Chief of Staff, Army), Vice-Admiral S.M. Ahsan (C-in-C, Navy) and Air Marshal Nur Khan (C-in-C, Air Force), who were designated as Deputy CMLAs. Lt.-General

S.G.M. Peerzada, who was Principal Staff Officer to Yahya Khan, headed the CMLA secretariat. Initially, no provincial governors were appointed and the Martial Law Administrators of West and East Pakistan were authorized to exercise their powers. Soon temperamental differences surfaced between Nur Khan and S.M. Ahsan on the one hand and Yahya Khan, Abdul Hamid and Peerzada on the other on handling the administrative and political affairs. Nur Khan in particular was viewed as being 'radical'. He favoured making drastic policy changes as was evident from his education and labour policies (discussed later). Ahsan favoured the holding of the elections at the earliest. In early September 1969, Nur Khan and S.M. Ahsan were appointed Governors of West and East Pakistan respectively and retired from service. New C-in-Cs of the Navy and the Air Force, Vice Admiral Mozaffar Hassan and Air Marshal Rahim Khan respectively, replaced them as Deputy CMLAs. However, the real power was wielded by the Army generals: Abdul Hamid and Peerzada. Another senior officer, Major General Ghulam Omar, Chairman of the National Security Council, was associated with them. He and Major General Akbar, Chief of Inter-Services Intelligence (ISI), gained greater importance when political activity picked up in the wake of the decision of the ruling junta to hold general elections. Yahya Khan relied heavily on these generals and allowed them reasonable discretion in running the administration because of his impatience with details. They coopted senior bureaucrats for policy making and implementation as well as for administrative management.

A cabinet was appointed on 4 August 1969 which functioned until 22 February 1971. It comprised people with a dubious political base and included a retired Major General, a former Chief Justice, retired bureaucrats, educationists and lesser known political leaders of the 1950s. This did not shift power from the top brass of the Army. The cabinet was more of a 'ceremonial body' which hardly ever discussed important defence, foreign policy or political affairs.[2] The important decisions were 'the preserve of the military brass and a few trusted civil servants'.[3] The CMLA office played a key role in policy-making, first seeking the input of senior civil servants, chiefs of intelligence agencies and military officials, and then, implementing it through the established bureaucratic channels. The CMLA also set the parameters for, and maintained overall supervision of, the provincial administration through the Martial Law Administrators and the provincial Governors, although the day-to-day affairs were left to their discretion.

Major Administrative Measures

The Yahya regime moved swiftly to address the social and economic issues in order to assuage the politically active and vocal groups. As the students and the labour were in the forefront of the anti-Ayub movement, the military government made gestures towards them. The framework of the new education policy was announced by Nur Khan on 27 April 1969 which emphasized students' participation in academic affairs, institutional autonomy and academic freedom for universities, allocation of more resources for scientific, technical and agricultural education. The work on these guidelines slowed down after Nur Khan was appointed Governor, West Pakistan, and the detailed policy was announced in March 1970. Similarly, the new labour policy, announced in July 1969, accommodated some of the major labour demands on collective bargaining, right to strike and lock-out after the failure of negotiations. The number of essential and public utility services where strikes were prohibited was reduced and the right to set up trade unions in the public sector organizations like railway, telephone and telegraph was recognized. The procedure for setting up a trade union was made easy and the condition of recognition of a trade union by the employers as a prerequisite for legal status was done away with. A new three-scale minimum wage structure was fixed and the government floated a new welfare trust with a contribution of Rs. 100 million. The student and labour groups generally welcomed the new policies but the bureaucracy viewed these as 'radical' and slowed down their implementation.

The military government took several steps to accommodate the criticism of Ayub's economic development strategy that had neglected the distributive aspects. In February 1970, the Monopolies and Restrictive Trade Practices (Control and Prevention) Ordinance was issued to check 'undue concentration of economic power, growth of unreasonable monopoly and unreasonably restrictive trade practices'.[4] A new financial institution, the Equity Participation Fund, with headquarters in Dhaka, was established for, *inter alia*, supplementing the capital and resources of small and medium-sized enterprises in the private sector in East Pakistan and the less developed areas of West Pakistan. The head office of the Industrial Development Bank was shifted to Dhaka. The fourth Five Year Development Plan, initiated in July 1970, allocated more than half of the resources for the first time to East Pakistan: 52.5 per cent as against 36 per cent in the third Five Year Plan. However, the political crisis and the civil strife in 1971 rendered this plan totally irrelevant.

Like the predecessor military government, the Yahya regime targeted the bureaucracy for disciplinary action to assert its control and to show that it was sensitive to popular resentment against the bureaucracy. In May, a three-member special committee was appointed to investigate the properties and assets of the senior civil servants and their dependents. A Services Reorganization Committee, headed by Justice A.R. Cornelius, who had presided over the Pay and Services Commission (1959–62), was established in November to review the existing administrative structure. The most drastic step was the dismissal or retirement of 303 senior civil servants in December (later action was taken against a few others) on a number of charges including inefficiency, misconduct, corruption and possession of property disproportionate to known lawful income. Of these 303 officers, 39 belonged to the elite CSP cadre and 17 were from the police service.

The princely states of Chitral, Dir and Swat were merged with West Pakistan in July 1969. The most significant administrative measure was the abolition of the integrated province of West Pakistan (set up in October 1955) and the establishment of four provinces of the Punjab, Sindh, NWFP, and Balochistan on 1 July 1970.

Political Strategies and Elections

The military regime imposed restrictions on political activities and public meetings but it did not ban the political parties and quickly initiated a dialogue with the political leaders. Yahya Khan was particularly careful in handling the potentially volatile political situation in East Pakistan and avoided confrontation until after the failure of the dialogue in March 1971. In September 1969, a confrontation was averted when Yahya Khan 'pardoned' the student leaders in Dhaka whose arrest had been ordered by local martial law authorities for holding a public rally. The government also adopted a lenient attitude when Maulana Bhashani organized a peasant rally in October 1969. Similarly, when the Urdu-speaking activists protested in the streets of Dhaka in November against the publication of the election-related proformas in Bengali only, the government agreed to publish these in Urdu as well. Yahya Khan maintained direct and indirect contacts with Mujibur Rahman and was confident that a political arrangement leading to a peaceful transfer of power was possible. That was the main reason that he did not interfere with the Awami League's highly politically charged electioneering and disregarded the complaints of other political parties that the Awami League hard-core often disrupted their public meetings and electioneering.

The Yahya regime accepted some of the major political demands. These included, *inter alia*, allocation of seats to the provinces in the National Assembly on the basis of population instead of the existing parity formula which had given equal representation to East and West Pakistan, creation of four provinces in West Pakistan, and greater freedom to the political parties after the completion of the initial dialogue and fixation of the election date. The military regime was also sympathetic towards the Bengali complaint of the neglect of East Pakistan by the federal government and their inadequate representation in the bureaucracy and the military. Six Bengali CSP officers were promoted as secretaries in the federal government in May 1969 and orders were issued for doubling the quota for recruitment of Bengalis to the Army.[5] One Bengali officer attained the rank of Lt.-General (Khawaja Wasiuddin) and another became Major General (Iskandural Islam) in the Army during the Yahya years. An ordnance factory, the first in East Pakistan, built with China's cooperation, was inaugurated at Ghazipur, near Dhaka, in April 1970.

Yahya Khan emphasized the transient character of his regime and repeatedly underlined his commitment to hold new elections and transfer power to the elected representatives. A new Chief Election Commissioner (Justice Abdus Sattar) was appointed at the end of July 1969, to make necessary arrangements, especially the preparation of new electoral lists, for the general elections. Full political activity was restored from 1 January 1970, subject to the conditions that no leader would act in a manner 'prejudicial to the ideology, the integrity or security' of Pakistan, or would not preach hatred between different regions, communities, races, sects, castes or tribes and religions.[6] This law was not invoked against any political leader, although some of them did violate these stipulations during the election campaign.

The Legal Framework Order (LFO), issued on 30 March 1970, provided the parameters for the general elections and constitution-making. The strength of the National Assembly was fixed at 313 seats (300 general seats and 13 reserved for women); East Pakistan was given 162 general and seven women seats and West Pakistan had 138 general and six women's seats, which were further divided among its four provinces and the tribal areas. The LFO fixed a time-limit of 120 days for the National Assembly to frame a new constitution and laid down five principles for that purpose. First, the constitution must be federal, guaranteeing independence, territorial integrity and national solidarity of Pakistan. Second, it must incorporate the ideology of Pakistan and that only a Muslim could become the head of the state. Third, the constitution should establish a democratic polity with free elections, direct adult franchise, fundamental rights and independence of judiciary. Fourth, a maximum legislative, administrative and financial autonomy should be granted to the provinces, but the federal government must also have enough legislative, administrative and financial powers to discharge its responsibilities. Fifth, the constitution must ensure participation of the people of all areas in national affairs and it must contain a specific provision for the removal of economic and other disparities among the provinces within a specified period of time. The LFO was silent on the voting procedure for the approval of the constitution. It was generally assumed that a simple majority would suffice. As a check on the powers of the National Assembly, the President retained the final power of authenticating the constitution. The political leaders criticized the time-limit of 120 days, arguing that, given Pakistan's troubled political history, this was a short period. However, the military expected the political leaders to develop a consensus on the constitution before the National Assembly was formally convened. The President's power to authenticate the constitution was described as a negation of the supremacy of the elected representatives. Despite these objections, the political leaders agreed to work with the LFO so that the elections were not delayed and the ruling generals did not have reasons to hang on to power for an indefinite period.

The election campaign started soon after the lifting of the ban on political activities in January 1970 and continued till December when the elections were held,[7] which gave ample opportunity to the political leaders for mobilization of the people on their respective political agendas. The issues raised during the anti-Ayub agitation figured prominently in the election manifestos of the political parties and the speeches and statements of the political leaders. These political parties could be divided into two categories so far as their treatment of the political issues was concerned. One, the ideology oriented parties like the Muslim League and the *Jamaat-i-Islami* talked of Islam and ideology of Pakistan and advocated a strong centre. Two, a number of issue-oriented parties like the Awami League and the PPP did not dispute the connection between Islam and Pakistan but these raised specific socio-economic issues and talked of restructuring the polity.[8] However, there was a wide difference in the tenor of electioneering in East and West Pakistan. In East Pakistan, the emphasis was on the rights, interests and identity of the Bengalis and provincial autonomy vis-à-vis the West Pakistani dominated federal government that was viewed as being callous towards their interests and aspirations. The Awami League, led by Mujibur Rahman, offered the Six-point programme (see the next section) as the charter for the protection and advancement of the Bengali identity and rights. Other political parties which did not subscribe to Bengali ethnicity and interests were marginalized and, on occasions, the Awami League activists disrupted their sparsely attended public meetings. In West Pakistan, the left–right polarization was quite sharp. The rightist political parties raised the slogan of Islam and Pakistan in danger and the left-oriented parties addressed the social and economic issues and talked of restructuring the economy on socialistic lines and promised to create a more participatory and egalitarian system. The political parties also talked of provincial autonomy but this issue did not attract the kind of attention it got in East Pakistan for understandable reasons. The PPP, led by Zulfikar Ali Bhutto, was in the forefront of the election campaign in the Punjab and Sindh. The fourfold slogan of the PPP – Islam is our faith, democracy is our polity, socialism is our economy, and all power to the people – made much impact on those sections of population who had been alienated by the Ayubian political system. In NWFP and Balochistan, the parties with strong local and provincial roots dominated the campaigning, although the PPP maintained a visible presence.

The Awami League and the People's Party swept the polls in East and West Pakistan respectively. What surprised most, especially the ruling generals, was the magnitude of success of these parties.[9] The Awami League captured 160 out of 162 general seats in East Pakistan; it also won seven women seats, raising its strength to 167 in a house of 313 seats. Two non-Awami Leaguers who were elected were Nurul Amin of the PDP and Raja Tridev Roy, a *Chakma* tribe leader who stood as an independent. In West Pakistan, the

PPP won 81 out of 138 general seats; it performed excellently in the Punjab and Sindh.[10] The ruling generals were upset because these results made it difficult for them to force a political settlement through manipulation and cooption of the political leaders. The results were also a setback to the older political parties including the different factions of the Muslim League, and the NAP. Many well-known personalities, including those who had held cabinet positions in the past, lost to the candidates of the Awami League and the PPP; a good number of them were elected for the first time and did not come from the politically established families. The Islam- and ideology-oriented parties performed poorly. The results showed a polarization on East–West Pakistan lines. The Awami League did not get a single seat in West Pakistan; it got 1.60 per cent votes in West Pakistan as compared to 75.11 per cent in East Pakistan. The PPP neither established party organization nor put up a candidate in East Pakistan.

The East Pakistan Crisis

The elections results confirmed that a strong feeling of socio-economic injustice pervaded East Pakistan which was successfully articulated by the Awami League. The Six-point formula was offered by the Awami League as a panacea for the political and economic deprivations of the Bengalis due to over-centralization and domination of the power structure by the West-Pakistan-based elite. For the first time, the politically active Bengalis expected to restructure the polity to make it responsive to their needs and aspirations. They felt that if they could not fulfil their political aspirations after such an electoral triumph, they might never get another chance. The Awami League leaders were therefore determined to implement their political agenda with or without the cooperation of the elected representatives from West Pakistan.

The roots of such an acute alienation could be traced to the dynamics of politics and economy. The pre-independence legacy of a strong and domineering centre continued to be the hallmark of the post-independence political arrangements. The provincial governments were given such limited legislative, administrative and financial autonomy that these could not effectively deal with purely provincial and local matters. The federal government interfered in provincial affairs and imposed its direct rule by dismissing provincial governments from time to time in all provinces, but East Pakistan was its main victim after the ruling Muslim League lost the provincial elections in 1954. Furthermore, the degeneration of the parliamentary system shifted the political balance in favour of the head of state who established his political hegemony with the support of the bureaucracy and the military. The Bengali representation in the federal cabinets during 1947–71 ranged from 25 to 47 per cent (the head of government included) except during the tenure of Suhrawardy (a Bengali, 1956–57), when it was 57 per cent. Out of

138 cabinet members at the federal level during 1947–58, only 58, or 42 per cent, hailed from East Pakistan.[11]

The rise of the bureaucratic–military elite in Pakistan adversely affected the prospects of the Bengalis at the federal level because their representation in these two institutions was very low. Out of 95 Muslim ICS and IPS officers who opted for Pakistan in 1947, only one was Bengali.[12] Their representation was also low in other cadres of the federal civil services. A quota system was introduced to rectify this imbalance but the overall balance of the federal services continued to be tilted heavily in favour of West Pakistan. Moreover, the new entrants from East Pakistan were in the junior positions; the top echelons were monopolized by West Pakistani civil servants, both at the federal level and in East Pakistan. In 1969, for the first time, Bengali civil servants were appointed Secretaries in federal ministries, the highest position in the federal bureaucratic structure.

The Bengali representation in the military, especially in the Army, was no better. The British authorities had classified the Bengalis as a 'non-martial' race and deliberately discouraged their recruitment to the Army; there was no exclusively Bengali regiment and some branches of the Army (i.e. Artillery) did not have a single Bengali. Eastern Bengal had no military cantonment or pre-cadet training institutions or recruiting centres with the exception of those set up during World War II. At the time of independence, the Bengalis constituted only 1 per cent of the total strength of Pakistan's armed forces; their numerical strength in the Army was 155 which rose to 13,000 in 1965.[13] A modest beginning of the Pakistan Army presence in East Pakistan was made by stationing a garrison in Dhaka. An exclusively Bengali Infantry regiment, East Bengal Regiment (EBR), was raised and, by 1968, four such regiments were in place. A pre-cadet training institution was set up in Dhaka in 1952 which was closed down a year later due to a paucity of candidates.

The pace of induction of the Bengalis to the Army was slow; the situation was somewhat better in the case of the Air Force and the Navy. The top brass of the Army were not willing to take bold initiatives for recruitment of Bengali personnel because they could not overcome the hangover of the martial race theory. Serious security pressures in the early years of independence, the paucity of resources, and availability of ample manpower from the Punjab and NWFP militated against new experimentation in recruitment. By 1963, only 5 per cent of the Army officers were from East Pakistan; in the medical corps, their percentage was 23 per cent. In the case of JCOs and Other Ranks their ratio was 7.4 per cent each. Their representation at the officer level in the Air Force and the Navy was 16 and 10 per cent respectively.[14]

The imposition of martial law in October 1958 concentrated power in the hands of the top echelons of the military and the senior bureaucrats, virtually excluding the Bengalis from decision-making, although the military regime did coopt some of them. The centralized polity under the 1962 Constitution provided a limited opportunity to the Bengalis for effective and meaningful participation. The Bengalis could not benefit from the patronage that became available to senior military officers because of their poor representation in the higher echelons.

The policies of the federal government towards the Bengali language and culture also caused alienation. The power elite designated Urdu as the national language and opposed the demand from East Pakistan for granting a similar status to the Bengali language. They had an erroneous impression that the Bengali language was too much under the influence of Hindu culture and that any encouragement to this language would resurrect cultural linkages with Calcutta, which would in turn weaken Pakistani nationalism. The political circles in East Pakistan persisted in their demand, which gave rise to the first exclusively Bengali political movement. This came of age on 21 February 1952, when some protesting Dhaka students were killed in an encounter with the police. It was not until 1954 that Bengali was also recognized as a national language. However, the controversy persisted because the ruling elite continued to entertain doubts about the 'Islamic character' of Bengali and worked for purging what they perceived as Hindu influences on the Bengali language and culture. Some Islamic groups proposed that Arabic should replace Urdu and Bengali as the national language, while others suggested that Bengali should be written in Arabic script. Ayub Khan floated the idea of a common script, with the Roman alphabet for Urdu and Bengali. The government also encouraged the development of East Pakistani literature based on the Bengali literary tradition developed during the Muslim rule, and the work of Hindu intellectuals, especially those belonging to the Renaissance literary movement, was either excluded or downgraded on the ground that they had projected Hindu imagery and culture. These efforts caused strong resentment in literary and academic circles in East Pakistan, who thought that the federal government was using Islam to undermine their linguistic and cultural heritage. Consequently, the Bengali language and cultural identity became the focal points for political and intellectual mobilization, reactivating the hitherto dormant intellectual ties with Calcutta which had traditionally played a key role in development of Bengali literary and cultural traditions.

The major economic grievances included the ever-growing economic disparity between East and West Pakistan, foreign exchange earnings, transfer of resources from East to West Pakistan, and the allocation of development funds to East Pakistan. Economic disparities that existed between East and West Pakistan at the time of independence to the advantage of the latter accentuated over time. Though East Pakistan registered economic development and industrialization during the Ayub rule, the pace of development was so fast in West Pakistan that the economic gap between the two wings increased. The Ayubian development philosophy, which emphasized aggregate economic growth and neglected social justice, increased concentration of wealth in a few hands which further increased regional disparities.[15] Despite a disagreement among economists on the rate and extent of disparity, all agreed that the gap between the two wings increased in the 1960s. In 1959–60, West Pakistan's per capita income was 32 per cent higher than that of East Pakistan; this disparity rose to 61 per cent by 1969–70.[16] Similarly, the question of use of foreign exchange and transfer of resources from East to West Pakistan caused much bitterness. With the exception of five years during 1949–70, East Pakistan earned more foreign exchange than West Pakistan. Except during three years (1967–70) East Pakistan's imports were far less than its exports. The resource allocations for the two wings in various development plans showed a clear bias against East Pakistan: these ranged from 20 per cent during 1950–5 to 36 per cent during 1965–70. There were shortfalls in utilization of the allocated funds in East Pakistan.[17]

Pakistan's economists and political scientists debated the major causes and nature of economic disparities between the two wings and how these should be tackled. The federal government and most West Pakistani economists did not deny inter-wing disparities but they focused mainly on the progress East Pakistan had made since independence, arguing that East Pakistan was much better off in the 1960s than was the case in 1947–8. They attributed East Pakistan's slow development to the historical legacy, especially West Pakistan's initial advantage as being a more developed region, geographic-climatic factors, migration of Muslim entrepreneurs from India to Karachi at the time of independence, an underdeveloped or non-existent infrastructure, the tendency of the private sector to invest more in West Pakistan which offered better prospects of return, and an extremist political rhetoric in East Pakistan which discouraged West Pakistan-based industrialists from investment there. East Pakistani economists did not give much credence to the historical or climatic-environmental factors. They alleged that East Pakistan was a victim of deliberate neglect by the federal government and that it was being kept as a captive market for the goods produced in West Pakistan. A number of them argued that East Pakistan could overcome under-development and check the transfer of resources to West Pakistan only if the two wings were treated as two distinct economies which needed two separate economic and fiscal policies. Described as the two-economies approach, they argued that East Pakistan should be treated as a separate producing and consuming unit for planning and development purposes, enjoying full control over its foreign exchange earnings and expenditure and domestic resources.[18]

The political, economic and cultural grievances fostered alienation in East Pakistan and nurtured East–West Pakistan polarization. Initially, the Bengalis expressed resentment against the monopolization of power by a narrowly based political elite and demanded their share in the decision-making process at the national level and opposed undue interference of the federal government in provincial affairs. These sentiments were repeatedly expressed during the debates of the central legislature. The 1954 provincial elections produced the first broad-based coalition of political forces in East Pakistan which presented a 21–point political agenda for economic, political and administrative autonomy. They were unable to realize their goals due to their internal squabbles and the undue interference of the federal government.

The 1965 Indo-Pakistan war deepened the political cleavage between the two wings. Though there was no war on the East Pakistan–India border, the two wings were practically cut off from each other during the 17 days of the war. East Pakistan's political leaders did not feel reassured when Bhutto, the then Foreign Minister, told the National Assembly that the threat of Chinese intervention dissuaded India from attacking East Pakistan. The Awami League leaders complained that the government did not make adequate arrangements for the defence of East Pakistan which could have been overrun by India. They maintained that the huge defence expenditure was meant only for the defence of West Pakistan and the government was playing up the Kashmir issue to justify high defence expenditure. This blunted the Pakistan government's anti-India propaganda and generated goodwill for India in East Pakistan. The Awami League became vocal in demanding friendly relations with India – a demand that irked the ruling elite at the federal level.[19]

It was against this backdrop that Mujibur Rahman presented the Six-point formula in a meeting of the opposition parties, held at Lahore in February 1966. A pamphlet was released by the Awami League in March, detailing the formula which was later incorporated in its manifesto for the 1970 elections. The Six-point formula was described as a set of 'basic principles' for the solution of 'inter-wing political and economic problems' and for ensuring the legitimate rights and maximum autonomy for East Pakistan.[20] It proposed a very loose federation incorporating the two-economies approach. The federal government was assigned foreign affairs, defence and currency subject to the condition that the two wings would have separate, but mutually freely convertible, currencies. The fiscal policy was to be made by federating units and separate accounts of foreign exchange earnings would be maintained. The federating units would allocate revenue including foreign exchange, to the federal government and they would also maintain their own paramilitary forces.

There was a negative reaction to the Six-point formula in West Pakistan and the federal government smelled secession in it. When Mujibur Rahman launched his movement in April 1966, the federal government came down hard on him. He was arrested and kept in detention until February 1969. During this period he was also accused of being involved in a secessionist plot, labelled as the Agartala conspiracy. In East Pakistan, the Six-point formula caught the imagination of the politically active circles, especially the rising middle classes, intellectuals and educated youth, the emerging commercial elite and the middle-level civil servants who felt that the existing politico-economic processes were working to their disadvantage and that their prospects were blocked by the West Pakistani elite who dominated the top echelons of the government and the private sector.

The Bengali ethno-linguistic identity and their political and economic rights became the focal issues in the 1970 election campaign in East Pakistan. The Awami League and its leader Mujibur Rahman appealed to both positive and negative sentiments. On the positive side, the emphasis was on the Bengali ethnicity and language and the myth of *Sonar* (golden) Bengal. It was argued that the Bengalis must unite and use their electoral strength to assert their political and economic rights and to restructure the polity. On the negative side, the federal government and especially West Pakistan were subjected to bitter and persistent criticism. As the elections approached, the statements of the Awami League leaders were laced with scorn and hatred for West Pakistan. The devastation caused by the cyclone in August and the tidal wave in November enabled the Awami League to build an anti-West Pakistan emotional hysteria.

The landslide electoral triumph of the Awami League further polarized the situation because it had won sufficient seats in the National Assembly to frame the constitution on its own. The hardliners in the Awami League, especially the student leaders, argued for independence. Others thought that a good measure of autonomy would pave the way for independence at a later stage.[21] Still others felt that with such a massive mandate the Awami League should not agree to any change in its Six-point formula. If the Awami League did not frame a constitution of its own choice, it would lose its credentials as the champion of the rights and interests of the Bengalis, they argued. Mujibur Rahman engaged in a delicate balancing of the divergent shades of opinion: he avoided outright independence but pressed hard for maximum autonomy strictly in accordance with the Six-point formula. This explained the hardening of the attitude of the Awami League by the last week of December and the collapse of Mujibur Rahman's personal understanding with Yahya Khan for some adjustment in the Six-points formula after the elections. Yahya Khan got a taste of the Awami League's new mood during his visit to Dhaka (11–15 January 1971) for discussing the modalities of transfer of power and constitution-making. Despite facing a personal disappointment, Yahya maintained cordiality in his relations with Mujibur Rahman. However, he suggested that Mujibur Rahman should seek agreement with Bhutto so that an early transfer of power could be arranged.[22] On his return from Dhaka, Yahya Khan visited Bhutto in Larkana and briefed him on his talks with Mujibur Rahman. Bhutto who had avoided critical comments on the Six-point formula during the election campaign, agreed to visit Dhaka for exploring the prospects of a compromise. His visit in the last week of January proved equally fruitless because Mujibur Rahman, in view of the Awami League's internal dynamics, was not willing to accommodate Bhutto's concerns.[23]

The first round of the negotiations had drawn lines between East and West Pakistan. Whereas Bhutto and Yahya Khan sought flexibility on the part of Mujibur Rahman, the latter described the Six-point formula as non-negotiable.[24] Both sides adopted a two-dimensional strategy. The ruling generals pressed for some adjustments in the Six-point formula as a precondition for transfer of power, but kept the military option as an alternative; if nothing worked, they could use coercion. The Awami League also adopted a similar approach: if the military would not transfer power on their terms, they would defy them and exercise the independence option. While working for a political settlement both sides prepared for the alternative option: the military by reinforcing its position in the eastern wing and the Awami League by strengthening its organizational network, especially its militant units. As both sides had the other option available, there was a little possibility of a compromise. Two developments increased distrust between the generals and the Awami League leadership. As the generals mounted pressure on the Awami League and they developed a shared interest with Bhutto for seeking some changes in the Awami League demands, the latter's fears of a military–Bhutto conspiracy to deny them power deepened. The other development was the hijacking of an Indian Air Lines aircraft to Lahore by two Kashmiris on 30 January 1971. The passengers were released, but the aircraft was destroyed by the hijackers. Unlike the political leaders from West Pakistan, Mujibur Rahman condemned the incident and held the Pakistan government responsible for the destruction of the Indian aircraft. His stance was very close to the Indian position which also blamed the Pakistan government for the incident. This was interpreted by the ruling circles as an attempt by Mujibur Rahman to cultivate India and made them apprehensive of his intentions, thereby widening the existing distrust.[25] India used the hijacking pretext to ban Pakistani aircraft from flying over Indian territory, thereby disrupting communication between the two wings when crucial negotiations were taking place. On 15 March, India also banned foreign aircraft from making direct flights from West to East Pakistan through Indian air space. This was done, India maintained, to discourage foreign aircraft from transporting Pakistani troops to East Pakistan.

Yahya Khan summoned the National Assembly to meet in Dhaka on 3 March, hoping that some understanding would be reached between the leaders of two wings by that date, although some of his Army colleagues had doubts about it. Bhutto, who had been arguing with the ruling generals for not summoning the assembly until a political settlement was arrived at, demanded the postponement of the session or the removal of the deadline of 120 days. Later, he announced a boycott of the session unless he received a firm assurance from Mujibur Rahman for accommodation of his party's perspective on constitution-making.[26] In order to raise the tempo of confrontation Bhutto threatened retribution if any member from West Pakistan attended the session.[27] The ruling generals were divided on the postponement of the National Assembly session. The Islamabad-based generals, including Yahya Khan, were inclined towards accepting Bhutto's demand. Vice Admiral Ahsan and Lt.-General Yaqub Ali Khan, based in Dhaka, who understood the ground realities, opposed the postponement and made their views known to Yahya Khan, maintaining that any postponement would create an explosive, and perhaps an unmanageable, political situation. As a fallback, they suggested that a new date had to be given if the postponement was unavoidable. The Islamabad-based generals advised them to talk to Bhutto on this matter. When Ahsan and Yaqub Khan met Bhutto to mobilize his support, he refused to cooperate. On 1 March, an indefinite postponement of the National Assembly session was announced by Yahya Khan. Ahsan was relieved from his post as Governor (28 February) and the charge was temporarily handed over to Yaqub Khan, who, within a few days, resigned due to differences with Islamabad on handling the East Pakistan situation.[28] Lt.-General Tikka Khan was sent to Dhaka to carry out the policies of the Islamabad generals. In a bid to salvage the situation, the military regime decided on 6 March to convene the National Assembly on 25 March.

The postponement of the National Assembly session – so soon after Bhutto's defiant speech at a public meeting reiterating his boycott decision – convinced the Awami League activists that the ruling generals and Bhutto would not let the assembly frame a constitution. The reaction in East Pakistan was sharp and violent. The Pakistan flag and the portraits of Jinnah were burnt in public and Mujibur Rahman's strike call completely paralysed the administration. There were pressures on Mujibur Rahman by the militant elements in the Awami League to declare independence but he resisted the demand as he did not want to give a convenient excuse to the ruling generals to launch a crack down. He adopted a middle course by transforming the already announced strike into non-cooperation with the administration and the military authorities. On 7 March, he demanded the immediate lifting of martial law, transfer of power to the elected representatives, return of the troops to the barracks, and an inquiry into the killing of the people by the Army firing in the last couple of days. His other demands included cession of transfer of the troops from West Pakistan, non-interference of the military authorities in different branches of the government, and the maintenance of law and order to be left exclusively to the police and the East Pakistan Rifles who could be assisted by the Awami League volunteers.[29] He directed the government and semi-government departments and officials, courts, banks, educational institutions and the private sector to abide by the orders of the Awami League headquarters. On 15 March, the Awami League consolidated its hold on the administration by issuing new directives[30] which amounted to a *de facto* assumption of control of the administration by the Awami League. The writ of the Pakistan government was limited only to the cantonments. When the Chief Justice of Dhaka High Court was asked to administer the oath to Tikka Khan as the new Governor, he refused.[31]

East Pakistan was in the grip of a popular uprising which engulfed almost all sections of the society. Though the mass movement was extremely powerful in Dhaka, other major cities, district headquarters and towns were involved in it. Protest marches, strikes and public reaffirmation of the commitment to fight the Pakistani administration and to offer all kinds of sacrifices for the establishment of Bangladesh were common features of the political landscape. The Bangladesh flag replaced the Pakistan flag on all government buildings in Dhaka and other major cities, with the exception of the Governor House and the cantonment area. The Awami League activists openly gave training in weapon-handling to their workers and looted weapons from the shops of arms dealers and the police armouries. There were some clashes between the Army and the Awami League workers in the first week, but later the Army retreated to the cantonments. The Awami League activists were in full control of Dhaka and other cities. They harassed and killed non-Bengalis and non-conformist Bengalis. The Bengali press resorted to bitter criticism of the military and published slanderous articles. The military personnel were subjected to verbal insults in the streets and the supply of food items and other goods of daily use was suspended to the cantonments. By mid-March, the situation had deteriorated to such an extent that Army personnel in uniform could not walk alone safely in the streets of Dhaka and other cities. 'They were mobbed, abused and jeered at. Even brigadiers and generals in their distinctive uniforms were not spared. They were frequently stopped by the Awami Leaguers, interrogated, even manhandled when unaccompanied by armed escort.'[32]

Yahya Khan came to Dhaka on 15 March for another round of negotiation. The ruling generals and the Awami League agreed in principle to the withdrawal of martial law and the establishment of federal and provincial governments comprising the elected representatives. The National Assembly was to hold a meeting and then split in two committees – one for each wing comprising members from that part – to prepare special constitutional provisions concerning East and West Pakistan, and then, the assembly would again meet as one body to frame a constitution for Pakistan, incorporating special provisions, if any, prepared by the two committees.[33] While the experts from the two sides were dealing with the legal niceties of the proposed arrangement, the hardliners on both sides were dissatisfied. The ones on the government side were perturbed by the idea of a weak centre and those in the Awami League found it be a climbdown from their virtual control of the eastern wing. The Awami League, therefore, proposed a change in the original formula on 21 March, suggesting that they were not interested in setting up a federal government and wanted the military to transfer power at the East and West Pakistan levels. The same day Bhutto reached Dhaka and raised a host of legal objections on the proposed arrangement which further complicated the matter. On 23 March, the Awami League presented a revised proposal suggesting that the members from East and West Pakistan should meet as two separate bodies, each framing a constitution for its part which would later be tied together under the rubric of the Confederation of Pakistan in a joint session of two bodies.[34]

The developments in the streets of Dhaka on 23 March gave some inkling of what was likely to happen. While the government observed it as Pakistan Day, the Awami League declared it to be Resistance Day. A new Bangladesh flag was unfurled which was hoisted on all government and semi-official buildings. Some of the foreign diplomatic missions which hoisted the Pakistan flag were stoned by the Awami League workers. A new paramilitary force – *Joy Bangla Bahini* – was launched by Mujibur Rahman in a special ceremony. Most Bengali political leaders who addressed public meetings in Dhaka demanded the establishment of a sovereign and independent Bangladesh.[35] Mujibur Rahman gave a stern warning to the military commanders: 'If the demands of the people of Bangladesh were not resolved peacefully he would launch such a country-wide movement that not a single exploiter (i.e. West Pakistani) would stay here.'[36] The advisers of Mujibur Rahman and Yahya Khan met briefly on 24 March, but it was quite clear to the two sides that nothing was likely to come out of the exercise. The military commanders had already made up their minds on 23 March to go for the military option because they felt the eastern wing had virtually slipped out of their hands. Yahya Khan left for Karachi in the evening of 25 March, and, a few hours later, the Army moved out of the Dhaka cantonment area to suppress a popular revolt and to re-establish the authority of the federal government.

Civil War and Disintegration

The troops moved first to take control of the telephone exchange, the State Bank, radio and TV stations and other key government installations. They also targeted the headquarters of the police and the East Pakistan Rifles (EPR) in order to disarm their personnel and to take control of their weaponry. A modest resistance put up by Bengali personnel was overwhelmed by the Army; some people were killed while others escaped with weapons and joined the revolt. The Bengali officers and men of the EBR defected and killed their West Pakistani officers and soldiers in Chittagong, Comilla and a couple of other places. Dhaka University was another target of the troops which was considered to be an important base of Awami League militants. The troops used force to take control of the university and the nearby area and found a large quantity of weapons stored in the halls of residence of the students. The offices of the pro-Awami League newspapers that had spearheaded the anti-military campaign were also attacked. Mujibur Rahman was arrested at his residence while other leaders went underground only to reappear in India after a week or so.

The Army took action on similar lines in other cities and, by the second week of April, it was able to reassert its control in Dhaka, Chittagong and other major cities. However, the situation in the rural areas was different. As the Bengali officials, police and others had either defected or left for India, the governmental authority was virtually non-existent in most of the rural areas. The intensity of the resistance put up by the Awami League activists in the first two weeks was beyond the expectation of the military authorities but the latter were successful due to superior weapons, communications and organization.

The initial success of the Army was not sustained for a number of reasons. First, the Army authorities lacked public support. With the exception of the non-Bengali minority, generally labelled as the *Biharis*, and the *Jamaat-i-Islami*, the Bengali populace was either apathetic or hostile towards the Army; most of them viewed it as an occupation force. They were unable to co-opt a Bengali leadership to replace the Awami League. The government made several gestures which included a call to the Bengalis who had crossed over to India to return (May), a promise of compassionate consideration of the cases of the deserters from the police and the armed forces (June), a general amnesty (June and September) and a promise to transfer power to the elected representatives (June). None of these offers had any impact except that a few thousand refugees returned from India. The absence of popular support undermined the efforts to create a credible authority structure and adversely affected the Army's supply and communication network.

Second, the military action transformed the resistance movement into a war of liberation. The Awami League hard-core had favoured a unilateral declaration of independence in early March, but Mujibur Rahman held them back. The March movement reinforced the mobilization that had taken place during the election period and created a broad-based consensus for maximum autonomy or independence and resistance to Pakistani authorities if they did not accept their demands. After such a widespread and effective mobilization, the fragile link with Pakistan, if it still existed, was completely severed when the troops moved out to restore order. The military action was extremely brutal and caused much loss of life and property; the ordinary people who were not involved in the movement suffered heavily. Its severity did not come to an end after the first few weeks, although it was not so visible in the urban areas. The exact number of people killed by the military action and guerrilla activity during March–December may never be known. Bangladesh claimed that three million people were killed and charged the Pakistani troops with genocide, rape of thousands of Bengali women, displacement of several million people, and a heavy damage to property.[37] The Pakistani authorities denied these charges

for understandable reasons and a top Army commander gave an unrealistic-
ally low figure of 30,000 people killed during this period.[38]

Third, India's role was critical to sustaining the insurgency and contributed to tilting the balance against Pakistan. India helped to set up the Bangladesh government-in-exile which functioned from Calcutta and extended
diplomatic and financial support for its projection at the international
level. A radio Free Bangladesh was also set up in the vicinity of Calcutta.
Financial and material assistance was extended through a large number of
voluntary and non-governmental organizations as well as through the state
agencies. India granted facilities to the Bangladesh government-in-exile to
recruit, organize, train and equip its guerrilla force, the *Mukti Bahini*.

The *Mukti Bahini* was formally launched on 11 April with M.A.G. Osmany,
a retired Colonel of the Pakistan Army, as its C-in-C.[39] There was no manpower problem. In addition to the Bengali personnel of the EBR, the EPR, the
police and the members of the *Ansar* and *Mujahid* forces who defected in
March, the young Bengalis in the refugee camps in India came forward in
large numbers for recruitment. After a careful scrutiny of their political
affiliations, these recruits were trained by the *Mukti Bahini* high command
in collaboration with India's Border Security Force (BSF) and the Indian
Army. From July, the Indian Army directly assumed the responsibility of
training and equipping them and extended logistic support.[40] As the trained
and reasonably equipped manpower became available, the guerrilla activity
intensified mainly in the rural areas. By June–July, the *Mukti Bahini* had
stepped up sabotage, targeting the communication and transportation net-
works and government installations. It avoided direct encounters with the
Army except in the border areas where its personnel could easily withdraw to
Indian territory. The urban areas were relatively secure, although incidents
of sabotage, bomb blasts or disruption of supplies to the cities did take place
from time to time.

Pakistan began a desperate search for political settlement in August–
September, primarily on the advice of friendly countries including China,
the US and Iran. In early August, the Pakistan government announced that
88 out of 167 Awami League elected members of the National Assembly
could retain their seats because there were no criminal charges against
them. Similarly, a large number of the Awami League members of the Provincial Assembly were also allowed to retain their seats. The seats of the
disqualified members were to be filled through new elections, which the
government wanted to hold before the end of the year. Tikka Khan was
summoned back to Islamabad and a new civilian Bengali governor, Dr
Abdul Motaleb Malik, was installed on 3 September and appointed a civilian
cabinet. Lt.-General Amir Abdulah Khan Niazi took over as Martial Law
Administrator. An expert committee was appointed to prepare the draft of
the constitution, which the military government planned to present to the
National Assembly for approval.

Yahya Khan established an indirect contact with Mujibur Rahman and the Bangladesh government-in-exile with the objective of exploring the prospects of a political settlement.[41] Some of the Awami League leaders based in Calcutta were inclined towards resuming negotiations.[42] This information was communicated by the US administration to India in November. Yahya Khan conveyed his peace plan to the Indian government through its ambassador in Islamabad, envisaging the release of Mujibur Rahman, a referendum to determine if the Bengalis wanted to be independent, the formation of an all-party government as an interim arrangement, and the return of the refugees under UN supervision.[43] However, India and the hardline Awami League leaders abhorred the idea of any negotiations with Pakistan. It was too late to think of a political settlement. Furthermore, India was too deeply committed to the Bangladesh movement to pull back.

By November, India had come to the conclusion that it would have to undertake direct military action to dislodge the Pakistan military from East Pakistan and establish Bangladesh. Its eastern command was fully geared to launch a military assault across the border. Moreover, if war was inevitable, November and December were the most suitable months. The rainy season had long ended and the soil had hardened to make it possible to move the heavy equipment swiftly. As the winter had arrived, the northern passes were snow-bound, reducing the probability of Chinese intervention to the minimum.

Furthermore, the confidence in the ability of the *Mukti Bahini* to liberate Bangladesh without the direct Indian intervention had waned. The *Mukti Bahini* was quite effective in harassing the Pakistani authorities but it was unable to dislodge them. A major fear was that if the civil strife was allowed to linger, India's policy of sustaining the commanding position of the Awami League in the Bangladesh movement might run into difficulties. The radical left political and guerrilla groups did not see eye to eye with the Awami League leadership, but, as the latter enjoyed the backing of India, the former could not challenge its dominant role. A prolonged guerrilla war could enable these radical groups to lay claims on the leadership of the movement. A Bangladesh established under the leadership of the left radical parties was not in the best interests of India. A more formidable problem was the influx of several million Bengali refugees from East Pakistan to India's bordering states, especially West Bengal. Any delay in the resolution of the civil strife was expected to prolong their stay and escalate socio-economic pressure in the Indian states which were already facing serious problems of governance. Indira Gandhi was convinced that these refugees would not go back until the Pakistani authorities were completely dislodged and the Awami League was installed in Dhaka.[44] During her visit to the US in the first week of November, Indira Gandhi questioned American optimism about the prospects of a political settlement and maintained that the refugees would not return as long as the Pakistan military was present in East Pakistan.

The regional situation also impelled India towards making some decisive moves. Pakistan facilitated the establishment of direct relations between the US and China in July, when Henry Kissinger secretly travelled from Islamabad to Beijing. It was interpreted in India as the emergence of a China–Pakistan–US axis. This impression was further strengthened when a high-powered Pakistan delegation visited China in the first week of November and the Pakistan government tried to create a baseless impression that China would physically help Pakistan if attacked by India.[45] India was perturbed by the July development and sought to counterbalance it by signing a treaty of friendship and cooperation with the Soviet Union in August whose articles 8, 9 and 10 had security implications. There was a perceptible pro-India shift in Soviet policy towards civil strife after this treaty. However, the Soviets began extending full endorsement to India's position in October and responded positively to India's invocation of article 9 of the treaty by supplying new weapons and military equipment in November and December, reinforcing India's confidence to resort to military offensive. China and the US maintained a sympathetic disposition towards Pakistan but none was prepared to step into the conflict because both were convinced that Pakistan's position could not be salvaged in East Pakistan. Furthermore, the hypothetical possibility of China's intervention on behalf of Pakistan was neutralized by the Indo-Soviet treaty.

By the middle of November, Indian troops were frequently crossing the East Pakistan border and engaged the Pakistani troops in collaboration with the *Mukti Bahini*. However, they would return to Indian territory and let the *Mukti Bahini* continue with the operation. On 21 November, a joint force of the *Mukti Bahini* and the Indian Army moved across the border in the Jessore area which resulted in the first open armed clash between the two countries involving ground troops and air forces. The Indian Army which succeeded in pushing back Pakistani troops entrenched itself in the East Pakistan territory. Similar border clashes took place in the Ballurghat-Hilli sector, the Sylhet sector and the Chittagong area during 21–24 November. Within the next couple of days, armed clashes erupted all along the border. After making initial territorial gains in the bordering areas, the Indian Army concentrated on consolidation of its position. The *Mukti Bahini* stepped up its operations behind the Pakistani Army lines. The strategy was to build enough pressure on the Pakistan Army so that it would make a retaliatory move on the West Pakistan–India border, thereby giving a justification for an all-out invasion of East Pakistan. This strategy paid off. On 3 December, Pakistan launched an air and ground attack on India in the west to release pressure on its troops in the east. This led to a full-fledged war in both the regions.

The Pakistani troops – outnumbered, outgunned and outmanoeuvred – could not withstand the well-coordinated and massive Indian advance in the east. The Indian troops advanced rapidly and, by 9 December, had captured many cities, including Jessore and Sylhet, and was within 30–40 miles of Dhaka. India also enjoyed air superiority. By 8–9 December, most Pakistani aircraft in East Pakistan had been destroyed by the Indian Air Force, and all airfields, with the exception of Dhaka, were either put out of action or were under Indian control. For all practical purposes, the Pakistani troops had no air cover. Similarly, the performance of the Pakistan Navy was dismal and India established an effective sea blockade of the eastern wing. By 13–14 December, the Indian troops had reached the outskirts of Dhaka and Pakistan's administration collapsed. The Governor and his cabinet resigned on 14 December while intense diplomatic activity began for the surrender of the Pakistani troops. Two days later, on 16 December, the Pakistani commander formally surrendered to his Indian counterpart, Lt.-General Jagjit Singh Aurora, and Bangladesh came into existence as an independent and sovereign state; 91,634 Pakistani military and para-military personnel and civilians were taken as POWs and moved to the camps in India. The performance of the Pakistan military in West Pakistan and Kashmir was far from satisfactory. Pakistan lost about 5,139 square miles of territory on the international border in the Punjab and Sindh and across the Ceasefire Line in Kashmir. It captured only 69 square miles of Indian territory. The prisoners-of-war in the West were 617 Indians and 542 Pakistanis.[46]

The Yahya rule was the most turbulent period in Pakistan's history. He assumed power as a caretaker ruler with a promise to restore civilian and democratic rule. However, he plunged the country into a bloody civil war and presided over the break-up of Pakistan.

8
Civilian Interlude

The unceremonious exit of the ruling generals and transfer of power to Zulfikar Ali Bhutto, elected civilian leader of the PPP, was a consequence of the military débâcle and the break-up of Pakistan. The political activists of all persuasion staged protest marches in major cities demanding the resignation and trial of Yahya Khan and his close associates. The non-government press endorsed this demand. What really sealed the fate of Yahya Khan was the mood of the officers who wanted the junta to quit. Lt.-General Gul Hasan Khan, Chief of the General Staff, gauged the resentment among the officers, who joined Air Marshal Abdur Rahim Khan, Chief of the Air Force, to impress on Yahya Khan to quit. In the meanwhile, a meeting of the officers of the rank of Major and above posted at the Army headquarters was summoned to review the situation. When General Abdul Hamid Khan, next to Yahya Khan in Army hierarchy and a member of the ruling junta, addressed the meeting, the officers refused to listen to him and demanded the removal of the ruling generals. When Gul Hasan and Rahim Khan communicated these sentiments with their personal endorsement to Yahya Khan, he was effectively left with no choice. They and others who actually controlled the Army headquarters decided to transfer power to Bhutto, who was summoned back from New York where he was representing Pakistan in the UN Security Council debate on the Indo-Pakistan war. Bhutto replaced Yahya Khan in a formal ceremony on 20 December 1971 as President and CMLA. Martial law was not lifted until 21 April 1972, when an interim constitution on presidential lines, approved by the National Assembly, was enforced. The National Assembly later unanimously approved a new constitution with parliamentary system of governance which replaced the interim constitution on 14 August 1973; Bhutto became Prime Minister.

Reassertion of Civilian Supremacy

Bhutto had three major advantages which facilitated the assertion of civilian primacy over the military. First, he had developed a strong popular base with charismatic appeal for the people, who were convinced that he would solve their basic socio-economic problems. His party, the PPP, had a comfortable majority in the National Assembly and the Provincial Assemblies of the Punjab and Sindh. Second, the Supreme Court judgment in April 1972, de-legitimizing the assumption of power by Yahya Khan in 1969, by declaring him a usurper,[1] reversed the court's judgment of 1958, which had endorsed Ayub Khan's martial law.[2] Though the latest judgment was given when Yahya Khan was no longer in power, it strengthened the position of the civilian leadership.

Third, the military débâcle and the break-up of Pakistan had undermined the reputation and image of the military. Most political groups and the press subjected the military to harsh criticism for their involvement in politics and especially for their abysmal performance in the 1971 war. The press published several stories about Yahya Khan's heavy drinking and involvement with women. The civilian government and the PPP leaders cashed in on anti-military sentiments and ridiculed the senior commanders. They vowed to remove the politically ambitious officers and to limit the military to its professional domain. Bhutto and his colleagues also talked of setting up a people's army,[3] although the theme was neither fully articulated nor was it pressed after the first six months. This was a difficult and demoralizing period for the military.

The government appointed a commission, headed by Hamudur Rahman, Chief Justice of the Supreme Court, to inquire into the circumstances leading to the surrender of the Pakistan military in East Pakistan and the ceasefire in West Pakistan.[4] The commission examined 213 witnesses, including Yahya Khan, Bhutto, Nurul Amin, the Chiefs of the Navy and the Air Force and other senior military commanders, and some political leaders. Its report was submitted to Bhutto in July 1972. When Pakistani POWs returned from India, the inquiry was reopened in May 1974 to collect additional information. The commission recorded the evidence of 73 more people and a supplementary report was completed in November 1974. The two-volume report was not made public by the government, on the grounds that it that it contained sensitive security related material. The leaked/un-official information suggested that the report was extremely critical of the senior commanders, especially those posted in East Pakistan, charging them of being 'morally corrupt and professionally incompetent' and that there was a 'criminal neglect of duty in the conduct of war'.[5] Bhutto did not release the report on the recommendation of the military, but he retired the officers criticized by the commission. General Zia-ul-Haq, who assumed power by dislodging Bhutto in July 1977, was not expected to make the report public. Some of the officers associated with the conduct of military operations in East Pakistan held important assignments during the Zia years. Table 8.1 gives the names of the officers retired or removed from service during December 1971 April 1972.

Table 8.1 Senior Officers Retired from Service

	Number	Names
The Army		
General	2	Yahya Khan, Abdul Hamid Khan
Lt.-General	8	Peerzada, Irshad Ahmed Khan, Bahadur Sher, Attiqur Rahman, K.M. Azhar Khan, Riaz Hussain, Rakhman Gul, Gul Hassan Khan
Major General	10	Ghulam Omar, Khudadad Khan, Kiyani, A.O. Mitha, Shaukat Raza, Khadim Hussain Raja, B.M. Mustafa, Shirin Khan, Bilgirami, Muzaffar
	5	K.M. Masud, Kingravi, S.D.K. Niazi, Jahanzeb, Ehsanul Haq (retired in routine)
Brigadier	4	Ghulam Hussain Raja, Inayatul Haq, Shamsul Haq Kazi, Ghazi.
The Navy		
Vice Admiral	1	Mozaffar Hassan
Rear Admiral	4	Rashid Ahmed, U.A. Saeed, M.A.K. Lodhi, Syed Zahid Husnain
Commodore	2	R.A. Mumtaz, S.M. Ahmed
The Air Force		
Air Marshal	1	A. Rahim Khan
Air Vice Marshal	2	Steven Yusuf, Khyber Khan
Air Commodore	3	Abdul Qadir, Salabuddin, T.S. Jan
Group Captain	1	Syed Mansur Ahmed Shah
Total	43	

Note: Lt.-General A.A.K. Niazi, commander of Pakistani troops in East Pakistan, was reduced to his substantive rank of Major General and removed from service in July 1975.

The Bhutto government asserted civilian supremacy in a dramatic manner on 3 March 1972, when it forced the resignations of Lt.-General Gul Hassan, Chief of Army Staff since 20 December 1971, and Air Marshal Rahim Khan, Chief of Air Staff, on policy differences. The catalyst to their removal was their refusal to make the Army and Air Force support available to the civil government during a police strike.[6] Both were given diplomatic assignments abroad. Two years later, in April 1974, another Chief of Air Staff, Air Marshal Zafar Chaudhry, resigned when Bhutto reversed his decision to retire prematurely seven Air Force officers who had been acquitted of charges of involvement in the 1973 conspiracy.

Two major changes were made in the military command structure. First, the designation of the commander of the Army, the Navy, and the Air Force was changed from C-in-C to Chief of Staff in March 1972. Initially the tenure of the Chief of Staff was fixed at four years. In 1975, it was reduced to three years. However, the change did not affect the then service chiefs who had been appointed before the new rule was enforced. The government also decided not to grant extension to any Chief of Staff. Second, individual autonomy of each service was diluted by establishing a permanent post of Chairman, Joint Chiefs of Staff Committee (JCSC) in March 1976. The Chairman did not have any operational control over the troops, but he was assigned an effective role in planning, coordination, and review of military security and strategy, weapons procurement and other matters common to the three services.

A White Paper on Higher Defence Organization, issued by the government in May 1976, streamlined the policy-making structure for defence and security. The ultimate authority was assigned to the Prime Minister, who was assisted by the cabinet and the Defence Committee of the Cabinet (DCC). Another body, the Defence Council, headed by the Defence Minister, was responsible for the implementation of the decisions of the DCC and the cabinet. Other important bureaucratic structures involved in the process were the Ministry of Defence, the JCSC and its Chairman, the service chiefs and the service headquarters.[7] The Naval headquarters was shifted to Islamabad in 1974 to promote greater coordination with the Army headquarters situated in Rawalpindi and the Air Force headquarters located in Peshawar. In 1983, the Air Force headquarters was also shifted to Rawalpindi and later, to Islamabad.

Bhutto incorporated special provisions in the 1973 constitution to provide constitutional safeguards to the primacy of the civil and to restrict the role of the military to its professional field. Article 245 (1) of the constitution provided that the armed forces would 'defend Pakistan against external aggression or threat of war, and, subject to law, act in aid of civil power when called upon [by the federal government] to do so'.[8] The constitution also laid down the oath for the personnel of the armed forces which enjoined them to uphold the constitution and specifically disallowed their involvement in 'any political activities whatsoever'.[9] The constitution also declared that any attempt or a conspiracy to abrogate or subvert the constitution 'by use or show of force or by other unconstitutional means" was high treason.[10] In September 1973, parliament prescribed the death sentence or life imprisonment for high treason.[11] No previous constitution provided such constitutional safeguards, although these provisions did not deter General Zia-ul-Haq from overthrowing the government in July 1977.

The Bhutto government also expanded and strengthened police, intelligence agencies and paramilitary forces to cope with political agitation and to improve internal security without calling out the regular troops. A new intelligence outfit – Federal Investigation Agency (FIA) – was established and the existing intelligence agencies were streamlined. An elite Federal Security Force (FSF) was set up in October 1972 to assist the civil administration in maintaining law and order and reinforcing the police for different assignments, including checking illicit trafficking of arms and food grain. The expenditure on the FSF jumped from Rs. 36.46 million in 1973–4 to Rs. 107.78 million in 1976–7.[12] Its numerical strength increased from 13,875 in 1974[13] to 18,563 in 1976.[14] The equipment made available to the FSF included semi-automatic 7.62 rifles, SMGs and LMGs, 60 mm mortars, handgrenades, tear gas equipment, communication gear and transport vehicles.[15] The government used the FSF to suppress dissent and to harass its political adversaries like the NAP and the Jamaat-i-Islami which gave the FSF a notorious reputation. The Army became sceptical of the rapid build-up of the FSF and it declined to provide training to the FSF personnel and blocked the plans for placing heavy armour, including tanks, at its disposal.[16] It was not surprising that General Zia-ul-Haq disbanded the FSF soon after assuming power.

The Security Imperatives and the Military

Bhutto's efforts to roll back the military were meant to secure his power. He was not anti-military and fully understood its relevance to Pakistan's security and foreign policy. He also viewed the military as the ultimate shield of the state and a support for his government in the event of a serious internal security threat. Once he was firmly in the saddle and the military was tamed, he began to woo the military by promising to make it a strong and well-equipped force, and introduced legislation to check criticism of the military's professional role.

The continuing security pressures in the post-1971 period underlined the need to strengthen the military. The Simla Agreement (July 1972) initiated the peace process between Pakistan and India but periodic suspension of the dialogue, especially the delay in the return of the POWs,[17] caused much bitterness in Pakistan. It accentuated Pakistan's distrust of India and, despite the restoration of diplomatic and trade relations, Pakistan and India could not come out of their traditional adversarial mould. India's military build-up and especially the 1974 nuclear explosion perturbed Pakistan. The Pakistani leaders maintained that the nuclear explosion had added a new and dangerous dimension to the regional security environment.

Pakistan faced additional security pressures after the overthrow of King Zahir Shah in Afghanistan in July 1973. The new ruler, Sardar Muhammad Daoud, a cousin of the deposed king and former Prime Minister, revived the hitherto dormant *Pakhtunistan* issue, refusing to recognize the Durand Line as an international boundary between the two countries and questioning Pakistan's sovereignty over NWFP and Balochistan. His government began to support the dissident groups in these Pakistani provinces and criticized the deployment of Pakistani troops in Balochistan.[18] These developments coincided with a string of bomb explosions in different

Pakistani cities and the law-enforcment agencies intercepted huge quantities of arms and weapons being smuggled from Afghanistan. Pakistan held Afghanistan's intelligence agencies responsible for explosions and gun running. It retaliated by building diplomatic and economic pressures and bolstering the Islam-oriented Afghan groups opposed to the Daoud government. In February 1975, Pakistan's federal government banned the NAP a leading Pakhtun nationalist party, and most of its leaders were arrested on the charge of engaging in anti-state activities. Afghanistan condemned the action and demanded their release as a precondition for any dialogue with Pakistan.

These developments revived the spectre of security threats from two sides, i.e. India and Afghanistan. Bhutto adopted three major strategies to strengthen defence and security: allocation of adequate resources to the military and modernization of defence capability, an effective use of diplomacy, and weapons procurement from abroad. The budgetary allocations to the military showed that Bhutto continued to accommodate the military's demand for resources. The defence expenditure showed a rise of about 218 per cent between 1971 and 1977, although the world-wide inflation and devaluation of the Pakistani rupee in 1972 neutralized some of its benefits.

Table 8.2 Defence Expenditure, 1971–7 (millions Rupees)

	Defence Expenditure	Total Expenditure met from Revenue	Defence Expenditure as percentage of total expenditure
1971–2	3,725.5	6,303.8	59.09
1972–3	4,439.6	7,480.7	59.34
1973–4	4,948.6	11,724.6	42.02
1974–5	6,914.2	16,139.6	42.83
1975–6	8,103.4	17,613.5	46.00
1976–7	8,120.6	18,161.5	44.71

Source: Compiled from different issues of *Economic Survey*, an annual publication of the Finance Division, Economic Advisor Wing, Government of Pakistan.

Pay, allowances and other facilities for the non-commissioned ranks of the three services were revised upwards in April 1972. Similar revisions were made for the commissioned ranks in August 1973. The disturbance and kit allowances for the commissioned ranks were increased in June 1975. The benefits of the disturbance allowance were extended to Lieutenants and their equivalents, the JCOs and the NCOs. In January 1977, pension and some other benefits were raised for military personnel.

A phased programme for expansion and modernization of the three services was adopted. An air wing was established in the Navy in 1972, and new naval equipment including submarines, gun boats and war ships, was procured from abroad. A defence production division was set up in the Ministry of Defence in 1973 for pursuing a comprehensive programme for indigenous defence production. The existing ordnance industry at Wah was expanded and modernized, and new ordnance factories were set up in the vicinity of Wah: an anti-tank ammunition factory at Gadwal, a heavy artillery ammunition factory at Sanjwal, and a propellant factory at Havelian. Preliminary work was resumed for setting up overhaul and production facilities for aircraft, tanks and armoured personnel carriers. These facilities became operational in the post-Bhutto period. The Machine Tool Factory at Landi and the Heavy Mechanical Complex at Taxila were associated with the defence production programme. The work on the first steel mill was resumed with the cooperation of the Soviet Union in December 1973 and it was formally inaugurated in January 1985 with an initial annual capacity of 1.1 million tons. China was the main contributor to building Pakistan's defence-related industry by extending technological assistance and financial support.

The immediate needs of the military and especially sophisticated weaponry, aircraft and warships had to be procured from abroad. That was the major reason that Bhutto did not withdraw from CENTO[19] and expressed the desire to strengthen the existing ties with the U.S. He lobbied the US administration incessantly for the removal of the arms embargo imposed in 1971. The US eased the embargo in March 1973 by allowing the sale of non-lethal equipment and spare parts of previously supplied military equipment which enabled Pakistan to receive armoured personnel carriers and some military equipment. However Pakistan pressed for a total lifting of the embargo. Bhutto took up this issue during his visits to the US in September 1973 and February 1975. Shortly after his second visit, the embargo was lifted, but the US administration maintained that the new demands for military equipment and weapons would be considered on a case-by-case basis and that the weapons could be obtained only on cash payment; no credit or deferred payment facility and no military assistance grant was extended. Pakistan welcomed the decision, but the cash payment condition imposed a severe constraint. Pakistan obtained a limited quantity of weapons from the US during 1975–7. However, Bhutto was able to show the military that his diplomacy had succeeded in removing major obstacles to the procurement of weapons from abroad. Pakistan also obtained weapons and military equipment, including aircraft, from China, France and international arms markets in Europe.

The post-1971 regional environs led Bhutto to view Pakistan's nuclear programme as relevant to security. The efforts to strengthen the nuclear programme began in 1972, but it was not until India's nuclear explosion in May 1974 that Pakistan embarked on upgrading its nuclear programme for acquiring the capability to exercise the weapons option. Pakistan pursued a two-track approach: on the one hand, it launched a massive diplomatic effort at the international level, especially through the UN system, for building support for its security concerns caused by India's nuclear explosion. On the other, Pakistan made a determined effort to develop an independent nuclear deterrent. The Bhutto government entered into an agreement with France in 1976 to procure a reprocessing plant (cancelled by France in 1978 under American pressure), launched a secret plan to build a uranium enrichment facility and resisted American pressure on its nuclear programme. These efforts enjoyed the support of the senior commanders who shared the perspective of the civilian government that Pakistan must develop a matching response to India's nuclear explosion.

Civil-Military Interaction

The military extended support to the civil administration for coping with floods in the Punjab and Sindh in August 1973, August–September 1975 and July–August 1976. In December 1974, a powerful earthquake caused much damage to human life and property in Swat and Hazara districts of NWFP; 5,300 people were killed and 17,000 injured. The Army and the Air Force were asked to undertake rescue and relief operations, including air dropping of supplies, provision of medical assistance and restoration of communications. In 1974, the Army assisted the Rangers (paramilitary force) in checking the smuggling of foodgrain to India and Afghanistan. In 1976, the Frontier Works Organization of the Army replaced the Public Works Department (PWD) of the civilian government for undertaking road construction and related developmental work in the northern areas. It also undertook development work in Balochistan during 1973–5. The Army engineers constructed 350 miles of roads and 2,800 feet of tunnels in inaccessible areas, and repaired and widened 200 miles of existing roads, thereby improving communication in the Marri-Bugti areas. The water supply was improved in a number of areas for drinking and agriculture. Tubewells were installed in Kohlu, Mawand, Kahan and Dera Bugti, a spring-fed water supply project was completed in Dera Bugti and the Kahan dam was constructed to irrigate about 500 acres of land. Fifteen check-dams were constructed on small streams to regulate the flow of rain water. A number of traditional wells were dug or repaired for making water available. The Army also established dispensaries and repaired school buildings and provided teachers for these schools.[20]

The Bhutto government sought the Army's assistance for maintenance of law and order and for restoration of the civilian authority on a couple of occasions. The first major challenge to the civilian authority was posed by the language riots in the urban areas of Sindh, especially in Karachi, in July 1972. The troops were summoned to restore order. A similar situation developed when labour trouble erupted in the industrial areas of Landi and Korangi, both in Karachi, in October–November. Other difficult situations when the regular troops came to the rescue of the civilian administration included the tribal attacks on non-Baloch settlers in Pat-Feeder, Balochistan, in October–November; tribal conflict in Lasbela, Balochistan, in December; anti-Ahmediya riots in the Punjab in June 1974; and the tribal uprising in Dir (NWFP) in October 1976. The most formidable challenge was the tribal insurgency in Balochistan which erupted in May 1973 as a follow-up of the tribal conflict in December 1972 and February 1973 and the dismissal of the provincial government in Balochistan by the federal government (see the next section).

The military high command and the civilian government maintained a working relationship: the former devoted itself to its professional domain and worked for rehabilitation of its reputation; the latter recognized the relevance of the former to external and internal security and made sufficient resources available. There was a general sharing of views on foreign and security policy but Bhutto's government maintained its primacy in decision-making. General Tikka Khan, Chief of Army Staff, March 1972–February 1976, worked towards strengthening the professional character of the Army and urged his officers and men to be loyal to the Constitution and the civilian authority established thereunder.

Some of the right-wing/Islamic political elements, perturbed by Bhutto's socialistic policies and his impatience towards dissent, often looked to the Army to dislodge the Bhutto government. In the course of the language riots in urban Sindh in July 1972, a number of right-wing activists sent telegrams to General Tikka Khan urging him to assume power.[21] Mian Tufail Mohammad, leader of the Jamaat-i-Islami, while addressing a public meeting in Lahore in February 1973, demanded that Bhutto should hand over power to the military which should then hold elections.[22] The senior commanders ignored these calls.

There was some resentment in a small group of officers against government policies towards the military and especially what they viewed as the lack of interest in securing quick repatriation of the POWs from India. In March–April 1973, 21 officers of the Army, including one serving and one retired Brigadier, and 14 officers of the Air Force, including two Group Captains, were arrested on charges of planning to seize power. The Army court martial, chaired by Major General Zia-ul-Haq, acquitted one officer, two were given life imprisonment, 13 were awarded rigorous imprisonment ranging from two to ten years, two were dismissed from the service and the promotion of three officers was stopped.[23] The Air Force court martial dropped the case against one officer and nine were not found guilty; four were sentenced to rigorous imprisonment ranging from five to ten years.[24] The Chief of Air Staff, Air Marshal Zafar A. Chaudhry, ordered the premature retirement of all 14 officers. However, the civilian government reinstated seven of the acquitted officers and the retirement of other officers was declared normal with no restriction on their re-employment. The Air Force Chief resented the action of the civilian government and resigned.[25]

The Political Process and Civilian Institution-building

Bhutto projected himself as the leader of the masses, 'their brother, friend and comrade',[26] and created a broad coalition of industrial labour, urban intelligentsia, students, the disadvantaged urban and rural sections of the populace for establishing a participatory and egalitarian politico-economic system. He built a direct relationship with the masses that bypassed the party leaders and was characterized by high-flying rhetoric, nurturing high expectations for improving the quality of their life. His leadership style was described as 'populist' and 'Bonapartist', 'reformist', 'power-broker' and charismatic.[27] He initiated participatory institutions and processes and introduced a series of socio-economic reforms to satisfy the main elements in his support coalition. However, he did not empower these institutions, diluted their original participatory character and resorted to authoritarian and patrimonial governance.

The expansion of the role of the state in the economic field was at the head of Bhutto's agenda. In January 1972, the emerald mines in Swat and ten basic industries were nationalized, which included iron and steel, basic metals, heavy engineering, heavy electrical, motor vehicle, tractor manufacturing, heavy and basic chemicals, petrochemicals, cement, and gas and oil. The managing and sub-agencies system was also abolished to reduce further the role of the private sector. The life insurance industry was nationalized in March; general insurance was left to the private sector. In June 1973, the rice export trade and the purchase of cotton from growers were taken over by the government. In August, the vegetable oil industry was brought under state control. A new Board of Industrial Management (BIM) was established under the chairmanship of the Federal Minister for Production for managing the nationalised industry. Later, public corporations were set up for managing different types of nationalized industries. In January 1974, all private banks were nationalized and, in July 1976, over 2,000 rice-husking and wheat flour mills and cotton ginning factories were seized by the government.

The land reforms introduced by Bhutto were an advance over the earlier attempt by Ayub Khan in 1959, but these did not in anyway uproot fuedalism. Land could be retained beyond the prescribed limit either by making use of the exemption clauses or by evading the laws in connivance with the local revenue administration. Nevertheless, the government was able to demonstrate that it was working towards reducing land ownership disparities and that it had adopted measures to improve the conditions of the tenants and peasants. The first instalment of land reforms, announced in March 1972, fixed the land holding ceiling on an individual basis at 150 acres for irrigated and 300 acres for unirrigated land. In terms of PIU, the ceiling was fixed at 12,000, with permission to retain an additional 2,000 PIU for owning a tractor or tubewell. The land in excess of the ceiling was taken by the state without compensation for free distribution to tenants and peasants. The landlords were made responsible for payment of land revenue and provision of seeds; water charges were shared by tenants. The land illegally occupied in Pat Feeder, Balochistan, was also vacated. The civil servants surrendered land in excess of 100 acres which they had received from the government during their service. In November 1975, land holders owning up to 12 acres of irrigated and 25 acres of unirrigated land were exempted from payment of land revenue. The second instalment was handed down in January 1977, when the individual ceiling was reduced to 100 and 200 acres for irrigated and irrigated land respectively. The excess land was resumed on payment of compensation at the rate of Rs. 30 per PIU but it was given free to tenants and peasants. The second instalment could not be fully implemented because the Bhutto government was immobilized by a street agitation beginning in March, followed by its overthrow by the military in July.

The new labour policy provided more participation of workers in management and offered better salary and share in profits, including an upward revision of minimum salary. Better deals were offered to labour for bonus, gratuity, leave, compensation, and retirement. The employer was made responsible for the education of one child per worker. The procedures for settlement of industrial disputes were revised, sufficient protection was provided to workers against victimization, and the scope of trade union activity was expanded. The salary, other benefits and pension benefits of the employees in government and semi-government establishments and the nationalized industries were raised more than once during 1972–7. Three strategies were adopted to expand employment opportunities. First, the public sector was asked to create new jobs to accommodate the unemployed. Second, arrangements were made with the Middle Eastern, especially the Gulf, states for absorbing Pakistani manpower. Third, A National Development Volunteer Corps (NDVP) was set up to provide stipends to unemployed educated youth for assignments in the educational and research institutions and government departments till they found regular jobs.

All private schools and colleges were nationalized and the faculty and staff were offered salary and other facilities equivalent to those serving in the government owned educational institutions. New universities and secondary and intermediate boards were established and a University Grants Commission was set up. A new University Ordinance (1973) partly democratized the management of academic and administrative affairs of the universities by strengthening the elected elements in various university bodies; the rotation principle was introduced for chairing academic departments. An ambitious health policy was introduced for making health care available to all, envisaging a network of basic health units in rural and urban areas which were linked with health centres and hospitals at the *tahsil* and district levels. The import, manufacture, sale and prescription of medicines was switched to their generic names in April 1973 to bring down prices. This scheme caused much confusion because most foreign medicines and a large number of locally manufactured medicines could not be switched. Initially, the government threatened to take punitive action or ban these medicines. However, the government soon realized the impracticability of the generic names scheme and exempted a large number of medicines. Later, the scheme was quietly shelved.[28]

The Bhutto government introduced a number of changes in the administrative structure to cut back on the position and clout of the bureaucracy. In March 1972, over 1300 federal and provincial civil servants were dismissed, retired or reduced in rank under the cover of martial law on grounds of corruption, incompetence, subversion or misconduct. A provision was made for internal review of the penalties and, in a small number of cases, the penalties were reviewed. However, no recourse was allowed to any court of law. A system of 'lateral entry' into the civil service was introduced to enable the persons holding mid-career positions in the government, business and industry, universities and in other professions to join the senior positions in the government through a written and oral examination conducted by the establishment division of the federal government. During 1973–5, when the system was in operation, 514 people were inducted into the bureaucracy at the middle and higher levels: 61.4 per cent of these lateral entrants were already in government service, 16.3 belonged to the armed forces, 12.4 per cent to education, and 9.9 per cent to other professions and the private sector. These inductions were resented by the elite cadres of the bureaucracy like the Civil Service of Pakistan (CSP) and Foreign Service because they felt that the 'outsiders' were getting the jobs hitherto reserved for them. The constitutional protection to the service of senior bureaucrats was done away with and they were subjected to normal legislative measures, designating the Prime Minister as the appointing and competent authority for senior civil servants. In August 1973, new administrative reforms were introduced which merged all services and cadres into a unified grading structure with 22 pay scales (a special pay scale, the 23rd, was meant for special appointments, i.e. Secretary General of a ministry). The practice of reserving posts in the secretariat for the CSP was discarded, and joint pre-service training was introduced for the new entrants. The existing service labels were changed, for example, the CSP was changed to District Management Group (DMG) so as to dilute the elite identity of some service cadres.[29]

The impact of these policy measures was moderate because the government was not aiming at a radical restructuring of the socio-economic and political order. The objective was to provide some relief to the middle and lower classes, especially the PPP support base, without completing alienating the upper strata. These policies were criticized by the ideological left and the extreme right for different reasons. The latter was perturbed by Bhutto's emphasis on Islamic socialism and the nationalization policy. The left groups felt that these reforms fell far short of the radical changes that were needed to restructure the society. In their enthusiasm the radical elements within the party and in the labour movement resorted to strikes, takeover of industry and hostage-taking of the employers and administration, declaring that the era of direct control of industry by labour had started. There were more labour strikes and industrial violence in 1972–3 than was the case in any single year in the past. In NWFP, which had the JUI-NAP government, the PPP radicals instigated a 'peasants' revolt against the feudals who supported the NAP. Such a radicalism created a serious dilemma for the government. If it took action against labour it was bound to lose support but, if labour militancy was not checked, industrial productivity was bound to suffer. After some hesitancy, the government decided to put its foot down to restore some semblance of order in the industrial sector.

The nationalization policy faced problems because the top slots in the nationalized industry were handed over to the bureaucracy, which lacked the technical know-how and managerial skills to run industry. Nationalization increased the powers of the bureaucrats who amassed more material rewards without a corresponding increase in industrial productivity. Furthermore, the government policy of providing jobs to its activists created an additional financial burden on the nationalized industry. The industrial and business elite, discouraged by the government policies and labour militancy, were not willing to make new investment or expand what was still left with them. Some of them moved their capital out of the country, especially to the Gulf region, resulting in large-scale disinvestment in the manufacturing sector which adversely affected industrial production and employment opportunities, alienating large sections of the urban population, who felt that nationalization was being used as a political tool to reward some and punish others.[30] Other factors that adversely affected the economy included the devaluation of Pakistani currency (1972), world-wide economic recession (1972–4), oil price hike (1973–4), heavy floods in the Punjab and Sindh in 1973 and 1975, and high defence spending.

Like the socio-economic domain, Bhutto made a good beginning in the political realm. He withdrew the ban on the NAP imposed by Yahya Khan and entered into political arrangements with its leadership in April 1972 to let the NAP form provincial governments in Balochistan and NWFP and agreed to appoint the NAP nominees as governors of these provinces. An interim constitution was enforced and martial law was withdrawn on 21 April. Dialogue and mutual accommodation between the government and the opposition enabled the National Assembly to frame a new constitution within one year which was enforced on 14 August 1973. It established a parliamentary system of government with a very weak President, a bicameral parliament with sufficient law-making and financial powers, adult franchise and direct elections for the lower house of the parliament, independent judiciary, and the fundamental rights. The federal system was adopted with provincial autonomy but the federal government was assigned a number of overriding administrative, financial and emergency powers. Bhutto took over as Prime Minister and a veteran political leader, Fazal Illahi Chaudhury was elected President.

However, the democratic institutions and processes were not allowed to grow as autonomous and viable entities because Bhutto resorted to personalization of power and moulded these to his partisan considerations. The authoritarian style of governance overshadowed the democratic spirit of the 1973 constitution, dissipating the consensus that had developed at the time of adoption of the constitution. The National Assembly should have dissolved itself after the passage of the constitution so that new elections could be held. However, the PPP dominated National Assembly decided to stay on.

The confrontation between the government and the opposition adversely affected institutionalization. The NAP used the provincial governments in NWFP and Balochistan to entrench itself in these provinces at the cost of the federal government/PPP and their local adversaries. The PPP used the resources and powers of the federal government to build pressures on the two provincial governments and encouraged anti-NAP tribal elements in Balochistan to resist the provincial government. By October 1972, Balochistan was in the grip of a crisis. The provincial government headed by Sardar Ataullah Mengal replaced a large number of civil servants hailing from other provinces with local officers and pro-government tribes began to evict non-Baloch settlers in the Pat Feeder area. The provincial government raised a new provincial security force, *Balochistan Dehi Muhafiz* (BDM), consisting mostly of loyal tribesmen, and strengthened its (non-official) tribal militia. These forces were used by the provincial government against their rival tribes, i.e. the Jamotes in the Lasbela area in December 1972 and February 1973. The federal government which had its own axe to grind objected to the transfer of non-Baloch civil servants, and sent troops to protect the settlers in the Pat-Feeder area in October-November 1972. The federal government again sent the troops in December to contain the armed conflict between the provincial government security forces and Bizenjo-Mengal tribesmen on the one hand and the Jamote tribe on the other. This inter-tribal conflict erupted again in February 1973. The federal government asked the provincial government to withhold its operation in the Lasbela area. As the provincial government turned down the advice, the federal government despatched the Army to the troubled area. A day later, a big arms cache was discovered in Iraq's embassy in Islamabad, allegedly enroute to the NAP in Balochistan. On 15 February, the federal government dismissed the ruling NAP government in Balochistan. Its Governors in Balochistan (Mir Ghous Bakhsh Bizenjo) and NWFP (Arbab Sikander Khan Khalil) were also removed. The NAP–JUI coalition government in NWFP headed by Mufti Mahmud resigned in protest against the federal action.

A number of tribesmen and NAP activists recruited by the Balochistan government in provincial security forces absconded with their weapons and joined their tribal fellows in Jhalawan area. There were minor clashes between the regular troops and the tribal elements in February–March which developed into a major tribal uprising by May in the Jhalawan subdivision of Kalat district and the Marri area. Though the Marri and Mengal tribes and their allies constituted the mainstay of the insurgency, a good number of Marxist and nationalist youths, especially those belonging to the Balochistan Student Organization (BSO), who aspired to create Greater Balochistan were also involved. A protracted conflict persisted up to 1977, although its intensity varied and there were periods of lull in the fighting. The government of Pakistan enjoyed the blessings and material support of the Shah of Iran who entertained strong reservations about the NAP as being a pro-Moscow party and was totally opposed to the idea of Greater Balochistan because it also included Iranian Balochistan. His support was an important factor in Bhutto's decision for not relenting on Baloch nationalists.

A new dimension was added to the NAP–federal government dispute when Sardar Daoud's government in Afghanistan not only revived the Pakhtunistan issue, but also championed the cause of the NAP and provided sanctuary to Baloch nationalists. The NAP leaders also maintained a sympathetic disposition towards Afghanistan and often questioned the rationale of the Pakistan state, enabling the federal government to raise doubts about their political loyalties. In February 1975, when Hayat Mohammad Sherpao, provincial PPP Chief in NWFP, was killed in a bomb explosion in Peshawar, the NAP was banned on the charge of working against the solidarity and integrity of Pakistan. Its major leaders including Wali Khan were arrested. A number of Baloch leaders, including Ghaus Bakhsh Bizenjo, Ataullah Mengal and Khair Bakhsh Marri, were already in detention. A reference was made to the Supreme Court on the banning of the NAP, as provided in law, which upheld the ban on 30 October 1975.[31] Some moderate members and sympathizers of the NAP established a new party under the name of National Democratic Party (NDP) on 6 November with Sher Baz Khan Mazari as its convenor as a forum for the 'nationalist, democratic and progressive' people.[32] In the meanwhile, a treason case was registered against the detained Pakhtun and Baloch leaders and a special tribunal was set up for their trial. Its proceedings, held in camera in Hyderabad (the Hyderabad conspiracy case), were not concluded by the time Bhutto was overthrown in July 1977.

The opposition parties set up a United Democratic Front (UDF) in March 1973 which comprised eight political parties, including the NAP led by Wali Khan, Muslim League led by the Pir Pagara, Jamaat-i-Islami led by Maulana Maudoodi and Mian Tufail Mohammad, and Tehrik-i-Istiqlal led by Air Marshal Asghar Khan. A state of confrontation persisted between the government and the major constituents of the UDF. Asghar Khan who was the bitterest critic of Bhutto often faced harassment from the police, the FSF and PPP activists. The Pir Pagara ran into difficulties with the government periodically but could field Hur tribesmen in Sindh to apply counter pressure on the government. The Jamaat-i-Islami engaged in street agitation in the Punjab from time to time by mobilizing the students through its student wing, *Islami Jamiat-e-Tulba*, which dominated a large number of educational institutions in that province. Its leaders also called upon the Army to dislodge the Bhutto government. The government dealt with the opposition activists in a high-handed manner. The press, especially the magazines and newspapers with known linkages with the opposition, were subjected to punitive measures. These included newspapers like *Jasarat* (Karachi), *Shahbaz* (Peshawar), *Jamhoor* (Lahore), *Mehran* (Hyderabad), and magazines like *Urdu Digest* (Lahore), *Zindigi* (Lahore), *Frontier Guardian* (Peshawar), *Outlook* (Karachi) and *Punjab Punch* (Lahore). Such a state of confrontation made it difficult to develop a consensus on the operational norms of the polity which could give endurance to civilian supremacy.

What further prevented the development of accommodative and democratic politics was Bhutto's policy of concentrating power in his own hands and the denial of opportunities to political adversaries to seek judicial redress. Four amendments were introduced in the constitution during 1975–6 to strengthen Bhutto's authoritarianism. One amendment (third amendment, 1975) extended the period of preventive detention from one to three months and another amendment (fourth, 1975) restricted the power of the High Courts to grant pre-arrest or post-arrest bail when the government invoked the preventive detention laws. Two amendments (fifth and sixth, 1976) adversely affected the independence of the superior judiciary. One of these enabled the government to change the Chief Justices of the Lahore and Peshawar High Courts and the other retained the Chief Justice of the Supreme Court, Yaqub Ali Khan, in office, after he reached the age of superannuation.

Another important institution that could strengthen the civilian processes was the PPP which had built a widespread support in the Punjab and Sindh during its formative years, 1967–71. However, it could not transform itself into an autonomous and self-sustaining political machine which could serve as a bridge between the government and the people. This could be attributed mainly to the PPP's internal character and political management by its high command. The PPP was an umbrella organization which accommodated diverse elements. It faced serious discord at the leadership level after coming to power on converting the election promises into policy measures. At the lower levels, problems of discipline and direction haunted the party as its ranks swelled because every body wanted to get on the PPP bandwagon to win favours from the government. This caused much incoherence in the party which already suffered from organizational problems.

Bhutto did not work towards creating a viable organizational network. He relied heavily on his charisma and populist style of going to the people over and above the party leaders and organization. The control of the state apparatus and patronage gave him additional leverage, enabling him to run the party like his fiefdom. Within 2–3 years of coming to power, sharp differences arose between Bhutto and the party ideologue and leftist elements who asked for radical socio-economic reforms and wanted to assign a more active role to the party in policy-making. These elements and others who took exception to Bhutto's personalized political management were forced out of the government and the party.[33] The feudals, industrialists and others who opposed the party in the past made their way into it, transforming the socio-economic makeup of its leadership by 1977, although the party did not change its political rhetoric. The PPP lost 'its effectiveness as an instrument of political participation and recruitment' and was unable to serve 'as an effective channel of communication between the elite and the mass populace'.[34] It was indeed ironic that Bhutto, who enjoyed popular support and was viewed as charismatic by a large number of people, neither used his mass appeal to evolve enduring consensus on the operational norms of the polity nor institutionalized the participatory framework nor established viable political institutions and processes.

The General Elections

The government's decision in January 1977 to hold general elections on 7 and 10 March set in motion the process that exposed the frailty of Bhutto's political edifice. Bhutto and his colleagues were confident of an electoral triumph partly due to what they perceived as the impressive track record of the government and partly because they were convinced that the opposition was too divided to put its act together. A major upset to these calculations was the decision of nine opposition parties on 11 January to establish an electoral coalition, the Pakistan National Alliance (PNA), which included Tehrik-i-Istiqlal (TI), Pakistan Muslim League-Pagara Group (PML-P), Jamaat-i-Islami (JI), Jamiat-ul-Ulema-i-Islam (JUI), Jamiat-ul-Ulema-i-Pakistan (JUP), National Democratic Party (NDP), Pakistan Democratic Party (PDP), Khaksar Tehrik (KT), and Azad Kashmir Muslim Conference (AKMC). Despite ideological differences among the PNA members and the dubious electoral standing of the PDP, KT and AKMC, they shared antipathy towards Bhutto and his economic policies. The PNA leaders were very critical of Bhutto's socialistic rhetoric and the nationalization policy, and highlighted how inflation, price-hikes and corruption in government had created serious problems for the ordinary people. The government was also taken to task for undermining the democratic norms and for suppression of dissent. Other issues raised by the PNA included Bhutto's Western life-style and consumption of alcohol as well as his alleged collusion with Yahya Khan in the break-up of Pakistan. The PNA promised to introduce the Islamic system to improve the lot of the common man and vowed to bring down the prices to 1970 levels.[35]

Most political observers expected the PPP to manage a simple majority. However, the PPP leaders did not want to take any chances and used the local administration to manipulate elections in several constituencies. Three factors strengthened doubts about the credibility of the elections. First, the PPP won 155 out of 200 seats as against 36 seats won by the PNA.[36] The wide margin of the PPP victory created serious doubts about the credibility of the electoral exercise in the minds of those who had closely followed the public meetings and processions of the two sides during the election campaigning. Second, 19 candidates of the National Assembly and 66 candidates of four provincial assemblies belonging to the PPP were elected unopposed. These included Bhutto and four provincial Chief Ministers. In most cases the PNA candidates complained that they were not allowed to file their nomination papers by the local administration and the police. Third, as the Election Commission investigated the PNA complaints and identified some irregularities, the government restricted its powers.

The PNA accused the government of engaging in massive rigging of the elections[37] and boycotted the elections to the provincial assemblies. The success of the PNA call for a nationwide strike on 11 March emboldened its leaders, who aggressively pressed their rigging charges and demanded new elections. Bhutto denied the rigging charge[38] and attempted to contain the opposition protest by arresting senior PNA leaders and a large number of their activists. This snowballed the agitation as it spread to all major cities and towns and the initial demand for fresh elections was superseded by a call for Bhutto's removal. They raised the catch-all slogan of introduction of *Nizam-i-Mustafa* (the system of governance of Prophet Muhammad, i.e. the Islamic system) which meant different things to different people: to orthodox and fundamentalists, it meant a polity that accommodated their religio-political views and guaranteed an effective role to them in governance; for lawyers, journalists and advocates of civil and political rights, it meant the restoration of civil and political rights, rule of law, justice and socio-economic egalitarianism; labour expected to get a better deal that would protect them against inflation, price hikes, and personal insecurity; the business and industrialist community supported this to get rid of Bhutto's socialist economy.

The 1977 anti-Bhutto agitation was more widespread than the 1968–9 anti-Ayub movement because the PNA did not start from the scratch. The PNA mobilizational network, set up in the wake of the election campaigning, was intact and the populace was already in a state of activism. No incubation period was needed and the agitation quickly gained momentum. Though the agitation was strong in major cities, it engulfed the district and *tahsil* headquarters and small towns. It was particularly strong in the market towns where petty businessman, small and middle level shopkeepers and traders and others who had been adversely affected by the increased state intervention in the economy, especially by the nationalization of rice husking and wheat flour mills, were in the forefront.[39] They used their links with and patronage of local *mullah* to activate the religious circles in their support. Financial resources were made available by the business community – shopkeepers and traders – and manpower was made available mainly by the Islamic political parties and groups, including the Islamic schools. The detention of the leading PNA personalities gave an opportunity to the religious elements to play a prominent role. The mosques and Islamic schools where the government could not ban the assembly of people served as the meeting places and mobilization centres. Some of these religious schools were affiliated with the JUI and the JUP and enjoyed the financial support of the business and industrial community.[40] Several processions of women and children, lawyers and Islamic scholars were brought out and, at least on one occasion, blind men paraded the streets demanding the introduction of the Islamic system. The Jamaat-i-Islami used its student wing to mobilize the students in a number of cities in the Punjab and Karachi. Labour, especially those with Islamic orientations, were also involved in the movement. Pakistan National Federation of Trade Unions (PNFTU), Karachi Port Trust and Dock Workers Unions, Pakistan Labour Alliance, the Railway Union, and a host of other groups representing workers, clerks, lower level bank employees, and transporters extended support to the PNA movement.[41]

The police and the FSF could not contain the agitation because the activists not only defied them but also resorted to violence which resulted in casualties on both sides. The PPP proved equally incapable of counterbalancing the opposition as it lacked organizational coherence. Whatever support it enjoyed as the ruling party dissipated as the PNA agitation paralysed the government. Bhutto attempted to salvage the situation by offering a dialogue and made a gesture towards the Islamic elements by imposing a total ban on the sale and consumption of alcohol, proscribing gambling and designating Friday as the weekly holiday instead of Sunday. He also promised to move the country closer to Islamic civil and criminal codes and vowed to enforce Islamic moral codes strictly.[42] He offered to hold elections to the provincial assemblies which the PNA had boycotted and that if the opposition won these elections, new elections would also be held at the federal level. However, the opposition was not prepared to accept anything less than the resignation of Bhutto.

The Military and the Political Crisis

The military's role during this crisis varied, depending on the intensity of the agitation and the high command's perception of the problems of the Bhutto government. Initially, the top commanders supported the government but, as the strife persisted, they reviewed their role and adopted a more autonomous position. The Bhutto government called out the troops to reinforce the police and the FSF within a week of the start of the agitation. However,

the Army's role was limited to assisting the civil administration for controlling the agitators in major urban centres. The turning point came on 21 April
when martial law was imposed in Karachi, Hyderabad and Lahore, and the
Army authorities superseded the civilian administration in these cities.
Bhutto's increased reliance on the military was further exposed when he
secured a public pledge of support from the Chairman Joint Chiefs of Staff
Committee and three service chiefs.[43] Bhutto also involved the Army commanders in the negotiations with the opposition to show the latter that he
enjoyed their support. While the PNA leaders were in detention, the Army
commanders were asked to give them briefings on the regional security
situation, including the Balochistan problem; Bhutto himself attended one
such briefing. The Army Chief, General Zia-ul-Haq, was invited to the cabinet meetings and Bhutto and his senior advisers held separate meetings with
the Army Chief and some of his senior commanders to discuss the political
situation.

Whereas Bhutto tried to demonstrate that the military was on his side, the
PNA leaders impressed on the military commanders not to support a discredited regime. The PNA adopted several methods to delink the military
from the government and to encourage it to adopt an independent posture.
These methods included direct appeals to the senior commanders, indirect
contacts with some of them, and public pressure on the troops performing
law and order duties. The PNA demanded the withdrawal of martial law in
three cities and criticized the use of the troops for police duties. Some of the
leading opposition leaders sought interviews with the Army Chief to explain
their position on the political crisis; this request was not granted. A large
number of telegrams and letters were sent by the PNA leaders and activists to
the Army Chief to withdraw support to the government; some such mes-
sages asked the Army Chief to remove Bhutto from power. A PNA leader and
former Chief of the Air Force, Asghar Khan addressed a letter to the three
service chiefs and the officers in May and managed to have it distributed in
the military. The letter incited the servicemen to revolt against the 'illegal'
government and that the military personnel should not kill the people for
retaining Bhutto in power. It argued:

> It is not your duty to support [Bhutto's] illegal regime nor can you be
> called upon to kill your own people so that [Bhutto] can continue a little
> longer in office. Let it not be said that the Pakistan Armed Forces are a
> degenerate police force, fit only for killing unarmed civilians.... As men
> of honour it is your responsibility to do your duty and the call of the
> duty in these trying circumstances is not the blind obedience of un-
> lawful commands. There comes a time in the lives of nations when each
> man has to ask himself whether he is doing the right thing. For you, that
> time has come. Answer this call honestly and save Pakistan. God be
> with you.[44]

PNA women supporters made telephone calls or wrote letters to the wives of the senior commanders requesting them to prevent their husbands from taking action against the protesters. Anti-Army slogans were stamped on currency notes and the protesters often chanted slogans taunting the Army on its dismal performance against the Indian Army in 1971. These pressures were bound to sap the morale of the solders and officers performing law and order duties in the Punjab and NWFP. The bulk of the troops came from these two provinces and, given their strong ethnic and family ties with the people of these provinces, especially the Punjab, they could not be expected to fire indiscriminately for an indefinite period. Many a time the troops were reluctant to fire into the crowd and three Brigadiers posted in Lahore asked to be withdrawn from internal security duties or offered to resign. The top brass of the Army were cognisant of these strains on the troops and began to express reservations on the continued use of the troops for containing street agitation in their meetings with the Prime Minister and his colleagues.

These developments had a number of implications for civil–military relations. First, the military high command realized that the Bhutto government was facing a serious legitimacy crisis and it could not survive without their support. Second, the PNA demonstrated its street power as well as its determination to dislodge the government through extra-constitutional means. Third, while persuading the military high command not to support the Bhutto government, the PNA leaders gave sufficient indication of their willingness to endorse a coup against Bhutto. What caused much embarrassment to the government and the military authorities was the judgement of the Lahore High Court in early June declaring the imposition of martial law in Karachi, Hyderabad and Lahore as illegal on the ground that martial law could not be declared under the provisions of the constitution. The court also struck down the amendment in the Army Act which had enabled the military to set up courts to prosecute civilians.[45]

The deepening political crisis rekindled desire among the senior commanders to assume an active political role. By May–June, they began to show impatience with the government's handling of the situation while discussing these matters with Bhutto's cabinet members and senior administrators.[46] While advising Bhutto to work out a political settlement with the opposition at the earliest, the top brass of the Army prepared a contingency plan, code named Operation Fairplay, to seize power if the political situation deteriorated.[47] They informed Bhutto of the growing impatience in the Army with the inability of the government to defuse the situation which was, in their assessment, bordering on anarchy.[48] However, General Zia-ul-Haq repeatedly assured Bhutto of his loyalty.

Bhutto made several offers of negotiations to the PNA leaders on the contentious issues[49] but, as they distrusted him, the offers were spurned. In May, the Saudi ambassador to Pakistan, Riyadh al-Khatib, offered his mediation on behalf of King Khalid and Crown Prince Fahd to Bhutto and the PNA. He was later joined by the ambassadors of the United Arab Emirates (UAE), Kuwait and Libya, and the Foreign Minister of the UAE, who talked to the two sides and facilitated the resumption of a dialogue on 3 June.

By 15 June the government and the PNA had agreed on the broad principles of the agreement which envisaged the holding of new elections to the national and provincial assemblies in October, a host of measures to normalize the political situation, and the establishment of an implementation council with Bhutto and Mufti Mahmud as Chairman and Vice-Chairman, each side nominating four members. However, they diverged on the details, i.e. the administrative set-up for the interim period and the role of Bhutto as the head of the implementation council. While the two sides were deliberating on these matters, Bhutto decided to visit Saudi Arabia, Kuwait, Libya, the UAE and Iran (17–23 June) ostensibly to thank their leaders for their help in defusing the crisis in Pakistan. On his way back he also visited Afghanistan. His absence slowed down the negotiations and created the impression that he wanted to delay the settlement. The PNA leaders began to raise new issues. Begum Nasim Wali Khan and Sher Baz Khan Mazari insisted on the withdrawal of the treason case against the Pakhtun and Baloch leaders and the withdrawal of the Army from Balochistan. Bhutto was not opposed to accepting these demands, but the Army Chief, General Zia-ul-Haq, opposed this.[50] Another problem was that Asghar Khan, the Pir Pagara and Begum Nasim Wali Khan detested Bhutto so much that they wanted to get rid of him at any cost and thus played the spoiler's role. They, especially Asghar Khan, made no secret of their preference for a military takeover because they thought that the miliary, rather than Bhutto, could be trusted to hold free and fair elections. The PNA was thus divided and its council did not approve the proposed agreement. The PNA negotiators went back to the government with a couple of new proposals and sought clarifications and assurances on some issues. In a meeting in the evening of 3 July which proved to be the last government–PNA meeting, Bhutto agreed, albeit reluctantly, to give his response after consultation with his colleagues. The cabinet held an inconclusive meeting on these demands in the late afternoon of 4 July which was attended by the Army Chief. Bhutto and the Army Chief also had a brief exclusive session. Shortly after his meeting with Zia-ul-Haq, Bhutto decided to accept the PNA demands. It was not known why he took this decision so suddenly and what was discussed in his separate meeting with Zia-ul-Haq. In a press conference at midnight (4–5 July) Bhutto announced his readiness to accept the PNA demands.[51] There is no evidence to suggest that this information was formally communicated to the PNA and the Army Chief.

The Army Chief, working on the assumption of a stalemate and the possibility of more violence in the days to come, made up his mind after the cabinet meeting to launch the contingency plan 'Operation Fairplay'. He issued some initial instructions and summoned the Rawalpindi-based senior commanders to the Army headquarters by 11 pm who had a brief discussion and, shortly afterwards, the final orders were issued for the takeover. This meant that by the time Bhutto addressed the press conference (midnight, 4–5 July), the Army Chief had already initiated the takeover process. However, it was after 2:00 am (5 July) when all press people, cabinet members and other visitors had left the Prime Minister's house, that tanks and troops rolled out to reassert the predominance of the military.

During the course of the agitation, Bhutto accused the United States of financing and supporting the PNA to dislodge him from power in retaliation for his 'defiance' on the nuclear issue.[52] There is hardly any direct evidence available to suggest American involvement in the anti-Bhutto movement and his overthrow by the military. However, some circumstantial evidence suggested that three policy decisions by the US administration created a strong impression in Pakistan that the US had abandoned Bhutto's government. The US blocked the supply of tear gas to Pakistan in April,[53] and, shortly afterwards, new economic assistance was suspended. In early June, the US withdrew the offer of 110 A-7 aircraft.[54] This was to be the first major aircraft procurement from the US since the early 1960s. The cancellation of this deal against the backdrop of Bhutto's domestic troubles led the Pakistan military leadership to conclude that Bhutto could neither be instrumental in procuring weapons from the US, nor was he in a position to ensure domestic stability. They felt that there was no political or diplomatic cost to his removal from power. However, the key factors that tilted the balance were the legitimacy crisis and Bhutto's inability to quickly clinch a political settlement with the opposition. The fact that several PNA leaders strongly favoured Bhutto's displacement by the military was also a contributory factor.

9
The Third Military Regime

The military takeover was swift and peaceful. Bhutto, his cabinet colleagues and the leading opposition leaders were arrested and kept in the 'protective custody' of the Army until 28 July. Martial law was imposed and the Chief of Army Staff, General Mohammad Zia-ul-Haq, designated himself as the Chief Martial Law Administrator (CMLA). Though President Fazal Illahi Chaudhry was allowed to continue as the titular head of state, the executive authority was vested in the CMLA, whose advice and recommendations were binding on the President. The federal and provincial governments were dismissed and national and provincial assembles were dissolved. The 1973 constitution was suspended (described as held in abeyance) and it was provided that the country would be run as closely as possible to the suspended constitution, subject to the overriding powers of the CMLA. The country was divided into five martial law zones,[1] each with a Martial Law Administrator, directly responsible to the CMLA. The Chief Justices of the provincial High Courts were appointed acting Governors of the respective provinces as nominal heads of civilian administration. A host of martial law regulations, inherited from the earlier martial law regimes, were reimposed with necessary modifications. Special and summary military courts were established to deal with the cases under martial law regulations and orders and had the power to impose various punishments including the death sentence, life imprisonment, confiscation of property, fines and imprisonment for various terms, and lashing. Their judgements could not be challenged in regular courts but the High Courts and the Supreme Court managed to exercise a limited review power until March 1981.

The CMLA was assisted by a Military Council which included the Chairman, Joint Chiefs of Staff Committee, the Chiefs of the Navy and the Air Force, Chief of Staff to the CMLA, and Ghulam Ishaq Khan, a bureaucrat who was designated as the Secretary General-in-Chief of the government. Another important body was the Martial Law Administrators Conference, which met periodically under the chairmanship of the CMLA, and included the Martial Law Administrators of various zones, senior Army commanders holding key positions, and some senior bureaucrats. Still another important body was the Council of the Federal Secretaries (senior bureaucrats) who headed different departments of the government and were responsible for the implementation of the decisions of the other two bodies and looked after the day-to-day affairs of the government. An Election Cell was set up in August, headed by Lt.-General Faiz Ali Chishti, to deal with election-related affairs. It also held regular consultations with different political leaders and prepared position papers for the CMLA on politics and elections; it continued to function until March 1980.[2] In January 1978, the Secretaries stopped meeting as a body and a Council of Advisers was set up which included civilians and some Army commanders. In July, this was reconstituted as cabinet and the representatives of one of the PNA parties, the PML-Pagara, were added. In August, when the cabinet was reconstituted to accommodate other PNA parties, the serving Army officers were dropped. The induction of a purely civilian cabinet did not change the dynamics of power management. The cabinet was nothing more than a public relations exercise and it had very little role in decision-making on key domestic and foreign policy issues. Like the previous martial laws, a combination of the top brass of the Army and the senior bureaucrats ruled the country. Several Army officers were appointed to key civilian posts in the administration to reinforce the dominance of the military.

Political Priorities

Zia-ul-Haq projected himself as a reluctant ruler who had assumed power because the political leaders had failed to resolve the political crisis. That his regime's agenda included the restoration of law and order, reduction of political tension among the competing groups, holding of free and fair elections and the transfer of power to the elected representatives. This was to be a 90-day operation.[3] In a statement, he declared: 'I will not accept [any] political office because I do not think I am fit for that.'[4]

However, as Zia-ul-Haq entrenched himself and outmanoeuvred his adversaries, he expanded the goals of the coup from elections to accountability, Islamization of the polity and induction of decency in politics. He developed a 'saviour' or 'messiah' complex and ruled the country with an aura of a God-ordained mission to transform Pakistani society on Islamic lines. Claiming that he was only accountable to God for his actions,[5] Zia-ul-Haq maintained that nobody could challenge a ruler in an Islamic state (e.g. Zia in Pakistan) if he performed his duties in accordance with the *Quran* and the *Sunnah*,[6] although he never gave an operational criterion for evaluating the performance of a ruler in an Islamic state. He minced no words in emphasizing that he would not hand over power as long as the mission of Islamization and moral renewal of the country was not completed. 'We have no intention of leaving power till the accomplishment of our objectives of Islamization of the national polity and induction of decency in politics. Until then neither I will step down nor will let any one rise.'[7]

The widespread political agitation against the Bhutto government convinced the coup leaders that the PPP had lost support and that Bhutto's ability to manipulate politics would be completely neutralized after he was ousted from power. This assessment was reinforced by the PPP's acquiescence to the coup and some defections from the party. The military leaders did not visualize any problem in organizing new elections within 90 days and transferring power to the PNA which was, in their estimation, bound to win the forthcoming polls. The PNA leadership was confident that it would get a virtual walk-over in the elections. These calculation were upset by the massive turn-out of people on Bhutto's first visit to Lahore, Multan and Karachi after being released from the 'protective custody' of the military regime. Encouraged by resurgent support, Bhutto adopted a defiant posture against the martial law authorities and threatened them with retribution if he was elected.

This created a serious dilemma for the ruling generals. If they ignored Bhutto's defiant posture and clear violations of martial law regulations by his supporters, the credibility of the regime would be compromised and Bhutto would be better placed to sway more votes to his side. If they reacted sharply, a direct confrontation was to develop between the military regime and the PPP. The military commanders who were alarmed by the upsurge of popular support for Bhutto, decided to stop him in the tracks. He was prevented from visiting a shrine in Lahore and later Zia-ul-Haq warned him to control his supporters. As the tension mounted between the military regime and Bhutto, the latter threatened to raise 'fundamental issues of jurisprudence' if any legal proceedings were initiated against him.[8] He questioned the neutrality of the military regime and taunted that there was 'no difference between [the] PNA and [the] PMA' (Pakistan Military Academy).[9]

By an interesting coincidence, it was during these days that the military regime unearthed evidence of Bhutto's involvement in the murder of his political opponents. The military rulers also accused Bhutto of engaging in massive corruption and decided to proceed against him. He was arrested in the first week of September on the charge of directing the FSF in November 1974 to 'eliminate' a political opponent. The PNA leaders and activists were equally perturbed by the resurgence of support for Bhutto. They demanded that Bhutto's trial on the murder and other charges should precede the holding of the elections. The need for such a course of action was underlined by the military government's intelligence reports and the PNA's own assessment that the PPP was expected to perform better than its political adversaries in the elections.[10] The elections were thus postponed indefinitely and the military regime decided to pursue the accountability of the ousted Bhutto regime as the main priority.

While the accountability process was underway, a massive propaganda campaign was launched against Bhutto and his ousted regime. The state-owned radio, television, and newspapers took the lead. Several right-wing newspapers and weeklies joined the campaign. The martial law authorities issued seven white papers spread over 2,771 pages, describing how Bhutto rigged the March 1977 elections and how he, his family and friends undermined the government institutions and procedures, and obtained, or extended to others, illegal favours.[11] Zia-ul-Haq described Bhutto as the 'worst cheat and cold-blooded murderer' who 'had been running a Gestapo-style police state in which kidnapping and political murders had become a routine affair'. He maintained that Bhutto and his colleagues would not be able to escape punishment and that the martial law powers would be used against such 'criminals.'[12]

Bhutto's trial on murder charges lasted from October 1977 to March 1979, and turned into a long-drawn and controversial legal battle.[13] In March 1978, Lahore High Court sentenced him to death. An appeal was filed with the Supreme Court which gave a split verdict – 4 to 3 judges – upholding the High Court judgement on 6 February 1979.[14] A review petition was disposed of by the Supreme Court on 24 March. Zia-ul-Haq, who had given enough indications that he would not exercise presidential power to spare Bhutto's life, prepared carefully for Bhutto's execution. In February, several measures were adopted for the Islamization of the polity and a day before the Supreme Court rejected the review petition, a new date was announced for the general elections so as to mollify the Islamists as well as those who had doubts about the regime's political intentions. The Army high command thoroughly discussed the execution of Bhutto. The Martial Law Administrators Conference recommended the rejection of all mercy petitions. Zia-ul-Haq took up the matter with other service chiefs who agreed with him on the implementation of the court's judgement. This was also discussed in the cabinet meeting and the PNA ministers were unanimous in their demand for hanging Bhutto. After obtaining the endorsement of the top brass and assurance of support from the PNA, Zia-ul-Haq went to Karachi to discuss Bhutto's burial arrangements with Lt.-General S.M. Abbasi, then Governor of Sindh, and other senior Army commanders posted there.[15] He also took up the matter with the Pir Pagara.[16] A large number of PPP activists and leaders, including Nusrat and Benazir Bhutto, were already in detention/house arrest; more arrests were made to pre-empt any agitation in the immediate aftermath of the execution. Once the necessary administrative and precautionary security steps were completed,[17] Bhutto was executed in the early hours of 4 April in Rawalpindi jail and an Air Force aircraft flew his corpse to his ancestral town in Sindh for burial under the watchful eyes of the Army authorities.

While the political parties were gearing up for the new elections scheduled for 17 November, the military government began to change the ground rules for the polls which caused confusion and raised new doubts about the military government's intention to hold the promised elections. The major electoral changes included (i) introduction of a separate electorate for Muslims and non-Muslims; (ii) a declaration of intent to introduce proportional representation; and (iii) an amendment in the Political Parties Act, 1962, which called for (a) registration of the political parties with the Election Commission as a precondition for participation in the elections, (b) submission of party accounts annually to the Election Commission for scrutiny, (c) publication of a formal manifesto, (d) annual election of the party office-bearers, and (e) submission of a list of office-bearers and ordinary members to the Election Commission. A failure to fulfil these conditions resulted in refusal of registration by the Election Commission, which meant that the party could not take part in the elections.

These changes were opposed by most political parties. Some of them, including the PPP, the NDP and the PDP, refused to file registration papers. Amidst these controversies, the military government decided to hold local bodies elections on a non-party basis prior to the already announced general elections. Despite the negative response of the major political parties, the military authorities went ahead with local bodies polls in September. Much to their dismay a large number of people having ties with the political parties, especially with the PPP, were elected. The success of the pro-PPP candidates alarmed the military government which viewed this as an indication of how the party might perform in the forthcoming national elections. The government therefore postponed the elections for the second time declaring that the time was not ripe for any kind of national elections.

During the period from November 1979 to August 1983, the promise to hold elections at an 'appropriate' time was often repeated. The ruling generals offered several reasons for delaying an election and subsequent transfer of power. At times, the military rulers called upon the people to work for the welfare and good of everybody rather than asking for national elections.[18] Sometimes the need for establishment of an 'Islamic system of democracy' was cited as a higher priority[19] and the Islamic elements were encouraged to launch an ideological onslaught on the existing system of elections, representation and political parties.[20] At other times, they emphasized that elections could not be held without a guarantee of positive results[21] – an indirect way of suggesting that no elections could take place unless they were sure of the success of the political groups that shared their political perspective on national and international affairs. At still other times, the regional strategic environment against the backdrop of the Afghanistan crisis was given as the major reason for not holding early elections.[22] On top of all this, Zia-ul-Haq declared that Islam did not believe in the rule of majority and therefore if the majority made a wrong decision, it could be turned down. Only a 'correct' decision needed to be honoured in Islam even if it was supported by a minority, he maintained.[23]

Islamization

The Islamization of the polity was the central concern of the martial law regime. This did not figure prominently in the early days of martial law. Zia-ul-Haq made a brief gesture towards the PNA in his first address to the nation by referring to the Islamic orientation of the anti-Bhutto movement and declared that he considered the introduction of Islamic system 'as an essential pre-requisite' for Pakistan. Martial Law Order No. 5, issued on 8 July, introduced, for the first time, the Islamic punishment of amputation of the right hand from the wrist for theft, robbery and dacoity. However, the military regime projected the holding of elections rather than Islamization as its principal goal in the Nusrat Bhutto Case before the Supreme Court.

As the commitment of the military regime to hold early elections wavered and as confrontation developed with Bhutto and the PPP, the need for Islamization of politics and society began to figure prominently in the policy statements. Once the elections were pushed to the background and the accountability of the ousted regime was initiated, Islamization was employed as the raison d'être of the continuation of martial law. It was an attempt on the part of the military regime to cope with the legitimacy crisis which had been accentuated with the postponement of the elections and the expansion of the goals of the coup. This also facilitated the cultivation of fundamentalist, conservative, *fiqah* (Islamic jurisprudence)-oriented, literalist Islamic elements who wanted to create a puritanical Islamic order. The military regime's Islamic rhetoric also fitted well with the overall resurgence of Islam in the Muslim world and helped to win the blessings of the conservative Arab sheikhdoms like Saudi Arabia, the UAE and Kuwait. The Islamic elements in Pakistan supported the military regime hoping that, with the restructuring of the polity on Islamic lines, a built-in bias in the political system would enable them to dominate the state institutions and processes which they were not expected to achieve under the existing political and electoral arrangements. Their shared hatred of the PPP also brought them closer to Zia-ul-Haq, especially because the PPP appeared to retrieve support after being dislodged from power.

The major focus of Islamization was regulative, punitive and extractive. Very little attempt was made to project other aspects of Islam, i.e. social and economic egalitarianism and accountability of those in power, and thus the socio-economic structural bases of the existing power arrangements remained unaltered. The following steps were taken by the military regime to promote Islamization.

First, the Council of Islamic Ideology (CII) was reconstituted to provide more representation to conservative and orthodox *ulema* (Islamic scholars and priests) for advising the government on Islamization of polity, including the review of the existing laws with the objective of bringing these into conformity with the *Quran* and the *Sunnah*.[24]

Second, the constitution was amended to set up a *Shariat* bench in each of the four provincial High Courts and an Appellate Bench in the Supreme Court in early 1979. One year later, a Federal *Shariat* Court (FSC) replaced the *Shariat* benches. During the next five years (1980–5), several presidential orders were issued to modify the working of the FSC, and it was incorporated in the constitution as a separate chapter – 3A. The FSC could hear cases pertaining to the Islamic laws enforced by the military government, dealt with *Shariat*-related petitions, and adjudicated if a law or administrative action was disputed as being in violation of Islamic injunctions. An appeal against its judgement could be filed with the Appellate Bench of the Supreme Court. The FSC was however debarred from questioning the Constitution, Muslim Personal Laws and fiscal matters, including taxation, banking and insurance. The President exercised wide discretion in the appointment, modification of terms of appointment, tenure and transfer of the judges of FSC which adversely affected its independence.[25]

Third, four laws were issued in February 1979 to enforce Islamic punishments for a number of crimes. Collectively called the *Hudood* Ordinances,[26] these prescribed penalties for various sex-related crimes, wrongful imputation of illicit sexual relations, theft of property and possession of alcohol and prohibited drugs. The punishments ranged from imprisonment, financial penalties, lashing, amputation of the right hand for theft, and stoning to death for adultery and rape. The lower courts including the FSC did award the punishment of amputation of the hand, and stoning to death, but the Appellate Bench of the Supreme Court set aside such judgements and these punishments were not carried out. In October 1984, a new Law of Evidence (*Qanoon-i-Shahadat*) replaced the existing law which dated back to the British period. However, the new law was little different from the earlier law except that it rearranged and reworded the clauses and provided that, in the event of financial or future obligations, the witness of two females was equal to one male; for other matters the courts could treat the witness of both sexes at par. The Law of *Qisas* and *Diyat* also discriminated against women by fixing compensation for bodily injuries or murder as half of what was admissible to men; for proof of murder liable to *Qisas*, evidence of at least two males was essential.

Fourth, an interest-free banking system, described as a Profit and Loss Sharing (PLS) system, was initiated in January 1981. In June 1984, 12 modes of interest-free finance were offered,[27] and by mid-1985, all Pakistani banks switched to PLS banking and other modes of interest-free finance, although this did not apply to the National Savings Schemes of the government. Two Islamic modes of investment, i.e. *Musharika* and *Modarba*, were encouraged, but these did not become popular with the investors.

Fifth, a compulsory tax, *Zakat*, was introduced in 1980 which applied to saving accounts and other investments at the rate of 2.5 per cent per annum.

Another tax, *Ushr,* made operative in 1983, applied to agricultural produce at the rate of 10 per cent of the value of the crop/produce.[28] A *Zakat* Fund was established with the initial amount of 2,250 million Rupees for the help of widows, orphans and other needy persons. The major contribution for this Fund came from Saudi Arabia and the UAE. A network of Zakat Councils was set up from the federal level to provinces, districts and below for management and distribution of *Zakat.*

Sixth, a *Sharia* faculty was established in the Quaid-i-Azam University, Islamabad, in September 1979. Later, a separate Islamic University was set up in Islamabad with the financial cooperation of a number of the Gulf states.

Seventh, the courses and syllabuses of schools and colleges were revised to place greater emphasis on Islamic principles and teachings and Ideology of Pakistan. A promise was made to set up separate universities for women. This was not fulfilled due to a paucity of funds and opposition to the idea by the educators and non-conservative elements.

Eighth, the electronic media and press were directed to reflect orthodox Islamic values. Various cultural activities – art, music, dance, women's sports, women's participation in stage performances – were discouraged. Women TV announcers and newscasters were ordered to cover their heads, and women were discouraged/excluded from various kinds of cultural programmes (i.e. folk dances) on the TV; film censorship was made stricter. A dress code was issued for women and government servants were advised to wear national dress.

Ninth, obligatory prayer breaks during working hours were introduced in government offices and the non-government sector was encouraged to do the same. The government decided to appoint the Organizers of Prayers (*Nazmeen-i-Salaat*) in August 1984 to work as volunteers to encourage people to offer prayers regularly. They were required to submit reports to the provincial governor for onward transmission to the President on the religious conduct of the people in their area.[29] This scheme was never taken seriously by the government and the people; when some enthusiastic Organizers of Prayers began going from door to door for that purpose, not many took them seriously which dampened their zeal.

Tenth, in pursuance of the demand of the orthodox elements, the military regime resorted to a more systematic segregation of the Ahmadis who had been designated as non-Muslims by a constitutional amendment in 1974. In April 1984, an ordinance was issued prohibiting the Ahmadis to use Islamic titles, symbols, practices, titles or *Quranic* verses and they could not designate their places or worships as *masjid.* As the violation of the law was a criminal offence, the conservative and orthodox Islamic elements employed the new law to persecute the Ahmadis at the lower and middle strata of the society. The Ahmadiya community filed a constitutional petition against the ordinance with the High Court which was dismissed on the ground that the High Court could not question the legislative competence of the CMLA. They also approached the FSC against the discriminatory nature of the ordinance but their petition was turned down.[30]

The Islamization process[31] encountered difficulties due mainly to the inability of the military regime to recognize the pluralist nature of Islam with different schools of *Fiqah* and sects. Those not sharing the establishment's perspective resented the lack of adequate attention to their religious sensitivities. The most forceful expression of resentment came from the *Shia* community which, under the leadership of their religious leaders, staged a massive protest in Islamabad in July 1980 against the compulsory deduction of *Zakat*. They disputed the right of the state to collect *Zakat* compulsorily and argued that the individuals were to pay this voluntarily. The government, fearing that the protest might trigger agitation in other cities, with the political parties jumping on the bandwagon, agreed to make payment of *Zakat* to the state voluntary for the Shias. Sectarian tension began to surface more frequently not only between the *Shia* and the *Wahabi/Deobandi* sects but also between the main sects of *Sunni* Islam, i.e. *Brelvis* and the *Wahabi/ Deobandis*.

Several religious and political groups emphasizing participatory decision-making and socio-economic egalitarianism doubted the motives of the military regime and expressed reservations about the enforcement of Islam by administrative decrees. They felt that this was a self-serving strategy on the part of the military to protect itself. They also argued that the military-sponsored Islamization reinforced the socio-economic status quo in society and would, thus, cause alienation at the popular level. A large number of those who shared Zia-ul-Haq's perspective on Islamization also felt frustrated because the military regime firmly kept the initiative in its hands and, at times, wriggled out of the commitments made to them. A controversy developed about the Islamic punishment of *Rajam*, or stoning to death. In March 1981, the FSC declared this to be 'repugnant to the injunctions of Islam' on the ground that it was not prescribed in the *Quran*.[32] This caused much furore among conservative *ulema*, who attributed the judgement to a lack of understanding of Islamic jurisprudence on the part of the FSC, and campaigned against the judgement of the Court.[33] Zia-ul-Haq supported these *ulema* and appointed three of them as judges of the FSC. The reconstituted FSC revised its judgement in June 1982, declaring *Rajam* to be an Islamic punishment.[34]

The left-of-centre groups were the strongest critics of the military government's Islamization policy because this was used to contain and undermine their political activities. This also gave a fillip to activism on the part of educated and urban women who contested the anti-women slant of various legislative and administrative measures under the rubric of Islamization.[35] New womens groups were formed mainly in Lahore and Karachi and the older ones became more active for protection of women rights.

The Politics of Co-option

The Zia regime was the first instance in Pakistan's history when the ruling generals openly declared themselves to be conservative-Islamic in their orientations and cultivated close ties with the political groups of the right, especially those Islam-oriented parties that were prepared to support martial law. The catalyst to the right-military rulers' cooperation was the military regime's decision to initiate accountability of the ousted Bhutto regime – a cherished goal of the PNA – and the Islamization of the polity. The military government felt that a cooperative interaction with these elements would help to legitimize their rule, undercut the support base of their adversaries, facilitate the introduction of fundamentalist Islamic reforms, and gradually bring forward a viable leadership that they could trust for sharing/transfer of power. The military rulers alignment with the right could be divided into two phases.

The first phase was 1978–9, a period of close interaction between a number of PNA parties and the military regime. When the military regime offered to set up a civilian cabinet, the Muslim League-Pagara (PML-Pagara) was first to join it in July 1978; a month later, other PNA parties also joined, ostensibly to facilitate Islamization of the polity and prepare the country for elections. This cooperation, which lasted until two weeks after Bhutto's execution in April 1979, proved useful for the military in dealing with political dissidents and partly civilianized and humanized military rule, at least for the rightist elements. The induction of the political elements in the government was important for the military for another reason. On 16 September 1978, the civilian President, Fazal Illahi Chaudhry, voluntarily resigned, declaring that his staying on would serve 'no useful purpose' because the top brass did not plan to hold elections in the near future and that they were planning to amend the constitution in a manner that would go beyond the scope of 'the doctrine of necessity.'[36] Zia-ul-Haq assumed the presidency promising to step down when 'another suitable man could be found.'[37] With the civilian President gone, the continuation of the PNA civilian ministers in the cabinet gained greater importance. However, the PNA–military combination could not produce an alternative leadership the military could trust. It also failed to eliminate the support base of the dissident left, and those political parties of the right that were not willing to join hands with the military rulers. Several reasons account for this.

First, the PNA decision to join the cabinet accentuated differences within the alliance. Not all of its component parties supported active cooperation with the military regime. The NDP, *Tehrik-i-Istiqlal* and the JUP decided to part company which weakened the alliance. Second, there was a lack of full understanding on goals. The military leaders co-opted the civilians in order to expand their political base and to facilitate the desired politico-economic changes in the polity. The PNA expected to share the 'credit' of Islamization of the polity as well as make use of the state machinery and patronage to strengthen their political influence for cashing it in the elections. However, the PNA ministers soon found out that the ruling generals and senior bureaucrats bypassed them on important policy matters. The PNA President, Mufti Mahmud, admitted that the 'real power,' was with the Army.[38] Third, there were personality, policy and factional conflicts within the PNA, as well as periodic grumbling over the military regime's tilt towards the *Jamaat-i-Islami*, and vice versa.

It was after the introduction of the first set of Islamic laws in February 1979, the fixing of the date for elections (17 November) in March, and the execution of Bhutto in April, that the PNA felt that its initial objectives were achieved. It decided to loosen its links with the regime by withdrawing from the cabinet in April, but the PNA leadership assured the ruling generals of continued support from the outside.[39] A new cabinet was sworn in which included six serving and retired senior military officers, one former bureaucrat (Ghulam Ishaq Khan) and eight non-party civilians; out of six advisers, one was a retired Chief Justice of Pakistan (Hamudur Rahman), one a retired Foreign Service personnel (Agha Shahi), and four civilians, including one woman.

The second phase, beginning in 1979, crystallized the 'like-mindedness' between the *Jamaat-i-Islami* (JI) and the martial law regime. Another component of the PNA, the PML-Pagara, also maintained a very friendly disposition towards the regime, but more significant than this was the understanding that developed between the military rulers and the JI. The roots of this special relationship could be traced to the first phase, when the JI, like the PML-Pagara, was very keen to join the cabinet. Had the PNA not entered the government, the JI would have gone ahead alone to join with the martial law authorities.

After the military government's decision to postpone the elections scheduled for November 1979, some of the rightist groups, especially the JUI whose leader Mufti Mahmud had played a key role in the PNA movement, were disillusioned and began to distance themselves from the regime. By 1980, Mufti Mahmud turned quite bitter about the military regime's policies. The JUP was already alienated from the ruling generals. This made it imperative for the ruling generals to cultivate those Islamic groups which were still sympathetic towards them. This included the JI and the highly conservative and orthodox *ulema*.

Though the JI and the ruling generals did not fully share each other's political goals, they realized that a cooperative interaction would be mutually rewarding. The JI enjoyed relative freedom to engage in low-key political activity and penetrated to varying degrees the bureaucracy, the military, the mass media, and the educational institutions. It also entrenched itself in the educational institutions in the Punjab. In the Punjab University, other student groups, especially those with the left-of-centre orientations, were thrown out by the JI's student wing, i.e. *Islami Jamiat-i-Tulba* (IJT). For the military government, the threat of political agitation by a political party with a highly disciplined cadre was temporarily eliminated. The JI also helped the military regime to undercut the efforts by the political adversaries to launch a street agitation. The JI's support of the military regime was quite crucial in the immediate aftermath of Bhutto's execution. A few hours before Bhutto's execution, the JI Chief, Mian Tufail Muhammad, called on Zia-ul-Haq. It was not known what transpired between them, but what the JI chief said to the newspaper correspondents after the meeting was significant. He asserted that Bhutto deserved to be hanged and that his execution would not lead to any deterioration of the political situation. If that happened, he was confident that his party would take care of that.[40] After Bhutto's execution, the JI and IJT workers and supporters were clearly visible in several urban centres, although they did not have to go into 'action' because the pro-Bhutto demonstrations were sporadic.

The other major group cultivated by the martial law regime comprised extremely orthodox Islamic leaders who were opposed to modern democratic institutions and processes, especially the existing electoral process, political parties and a legislature elected on the basis of universal adult franchise. They supported the use of state power to the maximum for establishing a *Sharia*-based Islamic system which bordered on theocracy. As the military regime could use them to side-track the demand for early elections and the restoration of representative political process, they were encouraged to dispute the politico-legal traditions and the political demands of the adversaries of the regime. The core political and economic issues were pushed to the periphery and many non-central issues began to dominate the political discourse, i.e. female announcers and artists should not be allowed to appear on TV; the photograph of Jinnah on currency notes was un-Islamic; all civil servants should be asked to wear a beard; Arabic should be the national language; complete female segregation, removal of non-Muslims, especially the Ahmadis, from key government positions, etc. Suggestions were also made to inscribe *Kalima* on the national flag and that the independence day should be observed according to the Islamic calendar. The TV started a five minute news bulletin in Arabic and the religious programmes, especially sermons by religious leaders, were increased. The military regime used the *Zakat* fund to support these Islamic elements. As the *Zakat* funds became available, Islamic *madaras* (traditional Islamic schools) proliferated which encouraged Islamic orthodoxy and opposed modern political and social institutions and processes, thereby causing much confusion about the direction of the Pakistani polity.

The Politics of Exclusion

The imposition of martial law raised the question of powers of the superior judiciary, especially because the generals suspended rather than abrogated the 1973 Constitution. The first test came when the Supreme Court admitted for hearing the petition filed by Nusrat Bhutto challenging the legality of the martial law regime. This made the generals somewhat uneasy because the Chief Justice (Yaqub Ali Khan) who had admitted the petition was retained in his present post after the age of superannuation by the sixth amendment in the constitution by the Bhutto government in 1976. Assuming that he would be sympathetic towards Bhutto, the CMLA revoked the amendment; consequently, Yaqub Ali Khan ceased to hold office on 22 September 1977. The next senior judge (Anwar-ul-Haq), who had been adversely affected by the 1976 amendment, was appointed Chief Justice. The reconstituted Supreme Court heard the Nusrat Bhutto petition and extended conditional legal legitimacy to the martial law regime in November by employing the doctrine of necessity. Describing Zia-ul-Haq's coup as 'a case of constitutional deviation' for saving the country from 'chaos and bloodshed,' the Court qualified it with restoration of normality and 'the earliest possible holding of free and fair elections for the purpose of the restoration of democratic institutions under the 1973 constitution.' The Supreme Court did not lay down a timetable for holding the elections but expected that the period of 'constitutional deviation' would be short and that the CMLA would devote his energies towards materializing that goal. The CMLA was authorized to make necessary constitutional changes for that purpose but the superior judiciary retained power to review the actions of the martial law authorities under article 199 of the Constitution.[41]

When the military regime postponed the general elections and expanded its goals, it began to make changes in the constitution and placed restrictions on the powers of the superior judiciary. This gave rise to confrontation between the regime and the legal circles. The former maintained that the Supreme Court judgement gave the CMLA unconditional powers to amend the constitution but the latter maintained that he could amend the constitution to the extent it was needed for holding the promised elections. This confrontation became sharp after the second postponement of the elections in October 1979, when Zia-ul-Haq decided to adopt a more strict policy towards dissent, and the military courts began to impose harsh punishments, including public whipping, with greater frequency. A large number of political activists and some leading political personalities were arrested; the press was put under severe restrictions and some journalists were arrested;[42] academics in the Punjab University and the Quaid-i-Azam University were targeted;[43] and the regime came down hard on lawyers and bar councils which demanded the restoration of democracy.[44]

The grant of limited relief by the superior judiciary against the judgements of the military courts and the actions of the martial law authorities irritated the ruling generals. Two developments precipitated the confrontation and led the military regime to strip the superior judiciary of its powers. Asghar Khan, leader of *Tehrik-i-Istiqlal* filed a petition in the Lahore High Court in

early 1980, challenging the legality of the Zia regime on the grounds that
Zia-ul-Haq had not held the elections on the basis of which his assumption
of power was conditionally validated by the Supreme Court. He wanted the
High Court to rule that 'his [Zia-ul-Haq's] validation and mandate to rule
[had] therefore ended' and that the actions taken by Zia-ul-Haq for restrict-
ing basic human rights and freedoms, political parties, and powers of the
courts, were 'void and of no legal effect.'[45] The hearing of the case was
completed in May but the military government, fearing an adverse judgement, transferred the Chief Justice to the Supreme Court, thereby dissolving
the bench that heard the case.

Another episode pertained to the imposition of the death sentence on an
activist of the Balochistan Student Organization, Abdul Hamid Baloch, by a
military court on dubious evidence for his involvement in a murder. The
Balochistan High Court stayed the sentence and when the military authorities wanted to go ahead with his execution, the High Court reconfirmed the
stay and issued a stern warning to the prison authorities.[46] While the military authorities were having problems with the judiciary, several opposition
parties joined together to establish an alliance, the Movement for the
Restoration of Democracy (MRD), in February 1981 (to be discussed later).
In early March, an underground terrorist group, *Al-Zulfikar*, led by Murtaza
Bhutto (one of the sons of the executed Prime Minister Bhutto) from exile,
hijacked a PIA aircraft to Kabul and then to Damascus.[47] The military government had to free a number of political prisoners to secure the release of
the passengers and the aircraft. This created a siege mentality in the military
regime which geared up to deal with the situation by fortifying itself in
power. A Provisional Constitutional Order (PCO), enforced on 24 March
1981, replaced what was left of the 1973 constitution. It banned all political
parties and completely subordinated the judiciary to the martial law authorities. The judges of the superior judiciary were asked to take a new oath. Four
judges of the Supreme Court, including the Chief Justice; seven judges of the
Punjab High Court; two from the Sindh High Court; and two, including the
Chief Justice, of the Balochistan High Court either voluntarily refused or
were disallowed by the martial law authorities to take oath under the PCO;
they lost their jobs.[48]

The military regime faced political difficulties periodically, although none
could be described as a formidable challenge. The most vocal critics were
lawyers, journalists and the political parties opposed to the military regime.
The members of the legal profession intermittently organized conventions,
protest marches, boycott of the courts and voluntary courting of arrest
during 1980–1. An alliance of the political parties, dominated by the PPP,
was set up in the first week of February 1981 as the Movement for the
Restoration of Democracy (MRD). It included (i) the PPP, (ii) the NDP, (iii)
Pakistan Democratic Party (PDP), (iv) *Tehrik-i-Istiqlal* (v) the PML–Khairuddin-Qasim Group, (vi) *Quami Mahaz-i-Azadi* (QMA), (vii) Pakistan *Mazdoor*

Kisan Party (PMKP), (viii) The JUI, subsequently, it was split on the question of participation in the MRD. One faction, led by Fazlur Rahman, stayed with the MRD.[49] Later, the Pakistan National Party (PNP), the *Awami Tehrik* (formerly *Sindh Awami Tehrik*), and the NAP *Pakhtoonkhwaha* joined the alliance. The first MRD declaration, whose photocopies were quietly circulated as it could not be published in the newspapers, demanded the removal of Zia-ul-Haq, withdrawal of martial law, and the holding of 'free, fair, and impartial elections to the national and provincial assemblies within three months.'[50]

The MRD launched two political movements during the martial law period. The first agitation was launched immediately after its establishment. For a while, it seemed that the Zia regime was in trouble. The hijacking of the PIA aircraft by the *Al-Zulfikar* personnel in March undermined the movement. As the *Al-Zulfikar* was being led by Bhutto's son, the hijacking partially tainted the MRD in general and the PPP in particular with the blame of the hijacking. The regime used the incident to label the PPP as anti-national and arrested a large number of MRD activists.

In August 1983, the MRD launched another movement to dislodge Zia-ul-Haq from power. The popular response to the MRD agitation call was lukewarm in the Punjab, NWFP and Balochistan; limited to small protest marches, periodic boycott of courts by lawyers, and the leaders of the movement offered themselves for arrest. However, it sparked a militant movement in interior Sindh and brought to the surface the simmering discontent and alienation with a strong ethnic and regional slant that permeated the Sindhi-speaking populace in that province. Sindhi resentment could be traced to the execution of Bhutto, continued allocation of agricultural land in Sindh to military personnel and the bureaucrats, the poor representation of the Sindhi-speaking populace in the middle and higher echelons of the Army, and little chances of change in the existing power structure marked by the Punjabi-Pakhtun military dominance. The regular troops, paramilitary force, and the *Hur* tribal volunteers of the Pir Pagara were employed to put down the agitation.

The military regime adopted several other strategies to contain dissent. First, the discouragement of, and restrictions on, the press (including censorship) to publish dissenting views. The distribution of anti-regime pamphlets was declared an offence with punishment for the printers and those responsible for distribution of such material. Second, imposition of restrictions on inter-provincial or inter-city travel on political leaders so that they were not able to establish a rapport with one another. Third, the issuance of a warning to the political activists to dissuade them from activism. At times, even indoor meetings were not allowed. Fourth, periodic house arrests of prominent leaders and especially the detention of the middle and lower-level political activists under martial law regulations; some of them were released after a couple of days while others were kept in detention for longer periods, whether or not convicted by military courts. Fifth, the divisive political, ethnic, sectarian and regional forces were encouraged so that the political appeal of the leaders of the major political parties could be compromised. The conservative and orthodox Islamic groups were successfully employed against the PPP, the MRD and others who questioned the military regime. A number of right-wing and Islamic parties which had suffered under PPP rule and feared the PPP's performance in any electoral contest obliged the military regime by continuing to oppose the MRD/PPP. Sixth, the intelligence agencies, especially the Inter-Services Intelligence (ISI) and the Intelligence Bureau (IB) were employed to monitor and harass the dissident political leaders. These agencies infiltrated and manipulated the political forces and encouraged the parochial, ethnic and other segmented elements to adopt a more active profile in order to weaken the appeal of the major, nation-wide political parties and leaders. The press was infiltrated by the intelligence agencies in a more systematic manner than was the case in the past and journalists at the reporter and sub-editor/editor levels were roped in by offering material rewards. What was described as the *Lifafa* (envelope) culture became a common practice – handing out money in envelopes to the press for publishing a tainted report or news. Seventh, ideological discord and mutual jealousies amongst the MRD parties, and the organizational problems of the PPP, also helped the military regime in deflecting the pressures. The preponderant position of the PPP in the MRD periodically evoked resentment amongst the smaller constituent parties whose leadership complained of an abrasive treatment on the part of the PPP.

Two other factors helped the military regime. First, a fairly reasonable pace of economic development was maintained. More important than this was the inflow of funds in the form of remittances by Pakistanis working abroad, mainly in the Gulf and the Middle Eastern states. The Gulf bonanza dampened the agitational zeal of the poor and provided a useful if temporary safety valve for the military regime. To most, an opportunity of a job in the Gulf states held better prospects for the future than a change of government through street agitation.

Second, the Soviet military intervention in Afghanistan in December 1979 came as a blessing to the military regime. By the end of 1979, Zia-ul-Haq was virtually isolated in the international system as a dictator who had executed his main adversary. He had also developed serious problems with the US on the nuclear issue and the burning down of the US embassy in Islamabad. However, his decision to oppose Soviet adventurism in Afghanistan made him the blue-eyed boy of the Western world and his perception was changed 'from being a medieval tyrant to a bastion of the free world holding back the flood-tide of communism.'[51] American economic aid and weapons helped to boost the fortunes of his regime. The material and diplomatic support of the Muslim countries was equally significant for the economy and in improving the regime's international image.

The key to the invulnerability of Zia-ul-Haq was the support he enjoyed from the senior Army commanders. His modest disposition with streaks of humility and his practice of consulting on important matters gave senior commanders little cause for complaints. Though he was careful routinely to sideline or retire any senior officer who showed signs of disaffection or was suspected of having a soft spot for the PPP, the military regime looked after the material and service interests of the officers. Several senior commanders were retired in 1980, 1984 and 1987, after the completion of their normal or extended tenures in order to facilitate the career advancement of others in the hierarchy; those retired were well rewarded and their post-retirement concerns were taken care of.

There were no visible signs of disaffection in the Army, although some, like Lt.-General Chishti, grumbled at the individual level. An isolated bid to subvert the discipline was made by a retired Major General, Tajammal Hussain Malik, in March 1980. He was arrested and a military court sentenced him to 14 years' imprisonment. However, he was released in October 1988;[52] his son and accomplices were freed earlier. In February 1982, an unsuccessful rocket attack was launched by an *Al-Zulfikar* activist on Zia-ul-Haq's aircraft as it took off from Rawalpindi.[53] In January 1984, a couple of junior Army officers and civilians were arrested in Lahore on the charges of smuggling arms and weapons from a neighbouring country (i.e. India) as a part of the plot to overthrow the government. Two military courts tried 19 accused during 1984–5, but only seven were convicted and sentenced to imprisonment of varying terms.[54] Given the fact that relatively junior officers were involved, one could not be sure of the operational relevance of the plot.

Expansion of the Role of the Military

Zia-ul-Haq argued for the expansion of the role of the military in the polity by declaring time and again that the military not merely protected the geographical frontiers of the country, but was also the guardian of the 'ideological frontiers.' It was the military's responsibility to ensure that Pakistan's Islamic identity was protected and Pakistani society developed on Islamic lines.[55] Addressing the officers in Abbottabad, Zia-ul-Haq argued that, as Pakistan was created on the basis of the two-nation theory and Islamic ideology, it was their duty as the 'soldiers of Islam to safeguard its security, integrity and sovereignty at all costs both from internal turmoil and external aggression.'[56] The ruling generals floated the idea of amending the constitution to enable the military to share decision-making power with the political elite and that the military should be given power to assume governance in times of national emergency.[57]

Zia-ul-Haq expanded the influence of the military by appointing military personnel, especially from the Army, to civilian jobs in a more consistent and extensive manner than was the case in the past. The Army officers, serving and retired, were assigned to the civil administration and to semi-government and autonomous corporations. Many officers of the rank of Brigadier and above were posted as federal and provincial secretaries or they were given top or senior positions in government corporations and bodies, drawing handsome salary and perks. They were also nominated to the elite groups of the Central Superior Services (CSS) on a regular basis. The most common groups selected for their induction included the District Management Group (formerly CSP), Foreign Service and Police Service. During 1980–5, 96 Army officers were admitted to the selected cadres of the CSS on a permanent basis, while 115 were re-employed on contract. In March 1985, a serving Major General (Naik Muhammad) was, for the first time, appointed Director General of the civilian Intelligence Bureau. In mid-1982, 18 out of 42 Pakistani ambassadors posted abroad came from the military, fifteen of them being from the Army.

Material rewards of various kinds were offered to the military personnel as a part of the policy to distribute the rewards of power as widely as possible in the military. These included an assignment in the Gulf States, and pieces of land for construction of a house in cantonments or in other urban centres, especially in the newly established defence colonies; commercial plots and facilities for loans were also made available to them. The most interesting case was that of allotment of plots to the senior officers in the Lahore Cantonment, adjacent to the Sherpao bridge – a prime site – after dismantling an Army depot. A number of officers who had been given residential plots (many got more than one) at cheap rates sold these to the civilians at exorbitant prices. The military regime continued with the policy of allotment of agricultural land to service personnel under various schemes, i.e. border areas, gallantry, military welfare and *ghori pal*. The Punjab government allotted about 450,000 acres of land to 5,538 military personnel during 1977–85.[58] Agricultural land was allotted to service personnel in other provinces, especially in Sindh, but the government did not release data on such allotments (See also chapter 11). The budgetary allocations for the military maintained a steady rise. The rate of increase during the Zia years was higher than that of the Bhutto period. Table 9.1 shows defence expenditure for 1977–88.

Civilianization of Military Rule

One major dilemma the military regime faced was how to bring about the desired constitutional and political changes and civilianize military rule in a manner that Zia-ul-Haq was able to change from *khaki* to mufti without losing the political initiative.

Zia-ul-Haq often talked about the future shape of the political system in terms of clichés and doctrines without fully operationalizing them or allowing an open debate on these matters. These were shaped by his fundamentalist

Table 9.1   Defence Expenditure, 1977–88 (millon Rupees)

	Defence Expenditure	Total Expenditure	Defence Expenditure as Percentage of Total Expenditure
1977–8	9,675	25,452	38.0
1978–9	10,168	29,861	34.0
1979–80	12,665	37,948	33.34
1980–1	15,300	46,349	33.0
1981–2	18,630	51,166	36.41
1982–3	24,566	59,183	41.5
1983–4	26,798	68,949	38.86
1984–5	31,866	90,074	35.37
1985–6	35,606	100,043	35.59
1986–7	41,335	111,856	36.95
1987–8	47,015	136,151	34.53

Source: Economic Survey, 1984–85, 1992–93, and 1992–93 (Islamabad: Finance Division, Economic Advisor's Wing, Government of Pakistan).

Islamic disposition, military background which valued discipline and efficient managerial ability rather than political participation, the experience of military rule which kept the politician in check, and his strong aversion to the left-of-centre groups, especially the PPP. He believed that the presidential system of government was closer to the traditional Islamic system of governance[59] and wanted to exclude the political parties from the political process and change the electoral process for ensuring a pre-election screening of candidates on the basis of an 'Islamic' critera. The military regime held elections to the local bodies in 1979 and 1983, and established a nominated advisory Federal Council in December 1981, but these efforts did not produce a broad-based consensus in support of its political agenda.

Zia-ul-Haq sought the opinion of three committees on the future system of government. The Council of Islamic Ideology (CII) submitted its first report in April 1982 which recommended a federal system, universal adult franchise, separate electorate and party-based elections.[60] Since the report had not endorsed the official perspective on the political parties and the electoral process, it was returned for reconsideration. The revised report, presented to the President in June 1983, endorsed the official views, expressed a preference for a unitary and presidential system, and recommended that a council of Islamic scholars elected by parliament should be vested with the final authority for interpreting 'Islamic injunctions in the light of the Quran and the Sunnah.'[61] Another report was prepared by a 30–member Special Committee of the Federal Council. To the dismay of the ruling generals, it recommended that the 1973 constitution should be adopted with 'minimal essential changes' mainly for creating a reasonable balance of power between the President and the Prime Minister. The report supported party-based elections and a federal parliamentary system.[62] It was not surprising that the report was hardly given any consideration by the military regime.

Zia-ul Haq appointed a commission headed by Maulana Zafar Ahmad Ansari, known for his conservative and pro-regime views, in July 1983, to recommend a suitable system of government. Its report submitted in August, offered very outmoded views on the political system. The recommendations included a presidential system, certain restraints on the powers of the legislature, abolition of party-based elections, proportional representation and separate electorate, qualifications for candidates, an increase in the number of provinces, and some restrictions on women's participation in politics.[63] As these recommendations were close to the views of Zia-ul-Haq, he publicly applauded the report, although its recommendations were not fully accommodated by the military regime.

Zia-ul-Haq announced the plans for the civilianization of military rule on 12 August 1983 which envisaged the holding of elections and transfer of power to the elected representatives by 23 March 1985. He, however, declined to commit himself on the schedule and mode of elections and the amendments he wanted to introduce before restoring the 1973 constitution. These ambiguities were maintained because the General had started toying with the idea of hanging on to power after the rehabilitation of the participatory political process. Some of his cabinet colleagues, right-wing supporters and conservative Islamic groups urged him to stay on in order to complete the Islamization process.

Zia-ul-Haq revealed his plans gradually. In August 1984, he indicated that he might consider staying on as President. Taking their cue from his statement and with a wink from the bureaucracy, several local bodies, elected in 1883 on a non-party basis, passed resolutions urging him to continue in office. This encouraged Zia-ul-Haq to declare in October 1984 that power would be transferred to the elected representatives on the condition that they would continue with the 'present process of Islamization.'[64] He removed all doubts about his future plans when he declared that he would 'share' power rather than 'transfer' it to the representatives to be elected in the proposed elections.[65]

Zia-ul-Haq's decision to stay on as President underlined the need to legitimize his decision by seeking a popular mandate. This was done through a hurriedly organized referendum on 19 December 1984, which used a novel way of seeking a vote of confidence for him. The referendum proposition sought popular endorsement for Islamization and the plans for transfer of power to the elected representatives. A yes vote on this was considered a mandate for Zia-ul-Haq to stay on as President for the next five years.[66] The deserted polling stations on referendum day were indicative of the lack of popular enthusiasm, but the official results showed that the voters' turn-out was approximately 62.15 per cent, with 97.71 per cent endorsing the proposition. The independent sources described the referendum exercise as dubious. Eight years later, the Chief Election Commissioner who had organized the referendum, admitted that it was rigged.[67]

Once Zia-ul-Haq secured his political future, he was prepared to go ahead with national elections, which were held on 25 and 28 February 1985, on a non-party basis under the religion-based separate electorate. The MRD which had boycotted the referendum rejected the non-party elections; the JUP and some other small political parties also boycotted the polls but several of their members participated in the elections in their individual capacity. The military government was able to neutralize the boycott by adopting three measures. First, propaganda against and instigation for the boycott of the polls were made an offence punishable by the military courts. Second, all major MRD leaders were placed under house arrest or imprisoned several days before the general elections. A large number of MRD workers were also arrested. Third, the newspapers were ordered in early February not to publish any statement in favour of the boycott campaign. Similar instructions were issued to private printers who could be prosecuted or their press closed down if they printed any pro-boycott pamphlet or handbill.

As the general elections were being held after eight years much interest was shown by the ordinary people. There was a proliferation of candidates. A large number of them were political non-entities who wanted to try their luck in the absence of the political parties and the major leaders. About one-quarter belonged to the *nouveau riche* category who had made their fortune during the previous 5–10 years, i.e. those engaged in manpower export to the Gulf, transporters, government contractors, real estate agents and the middle-ranking traders and businessmen who had benefited from the openings in the Gulf region. The leading feudal families, tribal chiefs and religious leaders (*pirs* and *sajjadanasheen*), who could not afford to stay out of the power game due to their high stakes in local politics, fielded candidates. The JI nominated candidates who contested the polls in their individual capacity. The PML-Pagara supported a number of candidates. The election campaign was closely regulated by the military government. The candidates were not allowed to use loudspeakers, hold public meetings or take out processions.

The candidates shied away from major domestic and foreign policy issues and focused on local problems and issues similar to those raised in the local bodies polls, i.e. construction of roads, streets and hospitals, improvement of sanitation conditions, installation of street lights, supply of electricity and gas for domestic consumption, etc. The absence of nation-wide themes and the political parties enhanced the relevance of parochial identities like language, ethnicity, religious sect. Local alliances and feuds figured prominently in the election campaign and the candidates often highlighted their personal piety and devotion to Islam.[68] Though these considerations were present in the earlier elections, the political parties diluted their impact. No such process was allowed in 1985. The feudals, tribal chiefs and the religious influentials, most of whom were also feudal, captured a large number of seats in the rural areas, while in the urban areas the candidates with a strong financial background performed better. Later, the newly elected members of the National and the Provincial Assemblies elected the upper house, the Senate, which was also dominated by the traditional feudal and tribal elements, and commercial and business elite.

The next stage of civilianization began on 2 March, when Zia-ul-Haq issued the 'Revival of Constitution 1973 Order' (RCO), which amended or substituted 57 articles, added six articles and deleted two articles from the original 1973 constitution; one schedule (2nd) was substituted, one (7th) was added, and two (3rd and 5th) were amended.[69] The parliamentary system was retained, but the President was assigned so many overriding discretionary powers in relations to the federal and provincial governments that the original character of the 1973 constitution was drastically altered. The balance of power was decisively tilted in favour of the President, making it difficult for the Prime Minister to function autonomously from the President, who was also given discretionary powers to appoint service chiefs, provincial governors, judges of the Supreme Court, High Courts and Federal *Shariat* Court, and a number of other top officials. Even when the President was to act on the advice of the cabinet, he could ask for the the the advice to be reconsidered.

The President could dissolve the National Assembly on the recommendation of the Prime Minister which was binding on him. He could also do away with the National Assembly at his discretion in two situations. One, when after a vote of no confidence no other member in the house was likely to command the support of the majority. Two, article 58–2–b gave him the sweeping power to dissolve the National Assembly at any time if he was of the firm view that the federal government could not be carried on in accordance with the constitution and an appeal to the electorate was necessary. After the dissolution, the President could appoint a caretaker cabinet at his discretion.

The RCO introduced article 270–A in the constitution for validation of all martial law regulations, laws and orders framed by the military regime and all other actions, including the judgements of the military courts, taken under these orders. A National Security Council was established which consisted of the President, Prime Minister, Chairman of the Senate, Chairman, Joint Chiefs of Staff Committee, three service chiefs and four provincial Chief Ministers for making recommendations regarding the declaration of state of emergency, security affairs and any other matter of national importance that the President referred to it in consultation with the Prime Minister.

The civilianized rule was inaugurated on 23 March when the National Assembly held its first session. Zia-ul-Haq took the oath of office as an elected President who appointed Mohammad Khan Junejo, a feudal from Sindh, as Prime Minister. Most members of his cabinet were selected personally by the President. The provincial Chief Ministers (civilian) and their cabinets were appointed by respective military governors with the approval of the President in early April. Despite the induction of the civilian governments, martial law was not withdrawn.

Zia-ul-Haq obtained the approval of the Parliament for two major legislations as a precondition for the lifting of martial law. These were the Eighth Constitutional Amendment and the Political Parties (Amendment) Act. The Eighth Amendment comprised the provisions of the RCO, as modified by the Parliament in the course of the debate in September–October. The National Assembly was given the right to elect a Prime Minister from March 1990 (as against nomination by the President in the RCO). Similar powers were given to the provincial assemblies to elect Chief Ministers from March 1988 onwards. It was also provided that the provincial Governors would be appointed by the President in consultation with the Prime Minister. The RCO stipulation about the National Security Council was omitted. However, the President retained the power to dissolve the National Assembly and dismiss the Prime Minister at his discretion. Article 270–A of the RCO was retained. This extended indemnity of an unprecedented nature to all martial law Regulations, Acts, Orders, including the Orders of military courts and tribunals, and these remained effective after the withdrawal of martial law. Such an indemnity was needed to protect Zia-ul-Haq and other generals from the charge of 'high treason' as stipulated in article 6 of the constitution. The amended constitution specifically mentioned Zia-ul-Haq in article 41 (7) as being entitled to hold the office of President for five years and he could also continue as the Chief of Army Staff. The amendment in the Political Parties Act strengthened controls on the political parties by reinforcing the 1979 rules for their registration with the Election Commission and imposed a disqualification penalty for any elected representative joining an unregistered political party.

The government also decided to strengthen the civilian law-enforcement agencies so as to be ready to deal with any difficult situation after the lifting of martial law. The initial proposal was to set up a new, well-equipped Federal Reserve Police. The proposal was opposed by the provincial governments because they did not want the federal government to establish such a powerful force. Many described it as the resurrection of Bhutto's FSF. The federal government, therefore, agreed to provide funds to the provinces for expanding and strengthening the existing police and other security arrangements.

These measures – the Eighth Amendment and a blanket indemnity, legal cover to hold on to the post of Army Chief, sufficient regulatory powers over political parties, and some strengthening of civilian law enforcing apparatus – gave Zia-ul-Haq confidence to lift martial law on 30 December and the amended 1973 constitution became fully operative. Zia-ul-Haq thus succeeded in establishing a carefully tailored participatory system through constitutional and political engineering and cooption. The official media projected the change as the heralding of a democratic era, although the continuity of the key personnel and policies from the martial law days was conspicuous.

10
Post-Withdrawal Civil–Military Relations

Post-martial law Pakistan represents the typical dilemma of states that have experienced prolonged periods of military rule and where the military transfers power to the civilian elite after securing its future through constitutional and political engineering and cooption of a section of political elite. The civilian regimes that succeed military rule face serious identity crises. On the one hand, these governments want to prove that they are not under the tutelage of the military and can act autonomously. On the other, they cannot afford to alienate the top brass of the military whose goodwill and support are crucial to their survival. Their task is complicated by the fact that once the tradition of direct military intervention in politics is established, the top brass are disinclined to surrender all the power and privileges they enjoyed during the years of military rule; they make sure that there are sufficient guarantees for their entrenched position in the post-withdrawal period. Furthermore, extended military rule creates vested interests and beneficiaries who support authoritarian and non-democratic governance. Military rule also accentuates political fragmentation and divisive tendencies in a multi-ethnic and diversified society especially if there are ethnic and regional imbalances in the military. These factors make the task of political management difficult for any post-martial law civilian regime aiming to establish itself as a genuine democratic government while not alienating the top commanders.

The civilianized system that replaced the longest military rule in Pakistan created a power-sharing arrangement between the political elite and the military. Instead of assuming power directly, although that option is still available, the military has shaped itself into the most formidable and autonomous political actor capable of influencing the nature and direction of political change from the sidelines. The change in the political style of the military came about gradually when it staged a voluntary and planned disengagement in December 1985. The period of transition lasted until August 1988 when Zia-ul-Haq died in an air crash. As long as he was alive, the military worked through him because he combined the offices of

189

President and Army Chief. Zia-ul-Haq described himself as a bridge between the new civilian dispensation and the military establishment and a source of strength for the former. As Army Chief, he guarded the professional and corporate interests of the military and lashed out at the civilian government periodically to keep it in line with his perspectives. When the coopted Prime Minister endeavoured to assert his autonomous role, Zia-ul-haq sacked him.

The decision of the top brass of the military not to assume power after the death of Zia-ul-Haq and leave the constitutional and democratic processes to be effective, facilitated the holding of party-based elections and the subsequent transfer of power to the elected civilian government. The post-Zia Army Chiefs emphasized professionalism and non-involvement of the soldiers in active politics; they supported the democratic process and governance by the civilians. Their decision to stay back was a tactical move based on a realistic assessment of the domestic and international political situations; it did not change the reality of their centrality to the political process.

The Military and Policy-making

The military participates in policy-making through the Army Chief who interacts regularly with the President and the Prime Minister either separately, or the three meet together. The meetings of these three key players have shaped into an important extra-constitutional arrangement to deliberate on key domestic and foreign policy and security affairs. The Army Chief also holds one-to-one meetings with the Prime Minister, and, at times, communicates with him through the President. Another forum that has gained importance is the Corps Commanders' meeting which is summoned and presided over by the Army Chief. The Corps Commanders, Principal Staff Officers at the Army Headquarters and other senior officers holding strategic appointments participate in the meeting and discuss professional and service affairs, security and foreign policy, domestic politics or any other issue of interest. They may simply comment on these matters or develop a broadly based consensus. It is left to the discretion of the Army Chief to operationalize the consensus which strengthens his position when he interacts with the civilian leaders.

A smooth interaction among these three key players and the military's support to the Prime Minister contribute to political stability. If serious differences develop among them, political uncertainty and instability abound. The Prime Minister, who represents the political side of the power-equation, can find him or herself in a difficult situation for three major reasons. First, given the polarized nature of Pakistani politics, the Prime Minister has always found it difficult to pull together all political elements as a counterpoise to the Army Chief. There is hardly any consensus on the operational norms of the polity amongst the political leaders who often engage in a desperate struggle to eliminate one another. Any sign of strains in the interaction between the civilian government and the Army is exploited by the opposition parties to intensify pressure on the Prime Minister. Second, the military with its institutional and organizational strengths is better placed to exert pressure on the civilian government. Third, the 1973 constitution, as revived by Zia-ul-Haq in 1985, had given so many overriding powers to the President, weakening the position of the Prime Minister.

The Prime Minister's position was boosted by the constitutional and political changes in 1997. However, the Prime Minister needs the military's support for effective management of civilian affairs. This dependence has increased in such an unprecedented proportion in the late-1990s that the Prime Minister is obliged to work in harmony with the military. The fact that the military did not assume power despite the abysmal performance of the civilian governments and the governmental crises in 1990, 1993, 1996 and 1997 made it possible for the senior commanders to claim that they were not motivated by power ambition; they separated the feuding politicians to avert constitutional and political collapse.

The military's primary consideration is not governance but protection of its professional and corporate interests which have expanded over the years. If these interests can be protected from the outside, it would like to stay on the sidelines, and given the military's political experience, organizational resources and institutional strengths, the senior commanders are reasonably confident that they can do that without actually assuming power. The parameters of interaction between the civil and the military are flexible; the senior commanders are willing to negotiate their interests and even accommodate the civilian leaders, but what is not acceptable to them is a frontal attack on their institutional and corporate interests as they define them or a deliberate campaign to malign the military or unilateral decision making by the civilian leaders on matters which directly concern them.

The military pursues wide-ranging professional and corporate interests. Its main interests pertain to defence and security. The military has traditionally made a significant contribution in this respect. The nuclear issue, Afghanistan and relations with India, including Kashmir, have been the areas of direct interest. Another foreign policy interest pertains to weapons and equipment procurement from abroad. The military also jealously guards its autonomy and wants civilian non-interference in the internal organizational matters and service affairs. This includes promotions, transfers and postings in the three services and service-related administrative matters. The senior commanders view civilian non-interference as a prerequisite for insulating the military from partisan political influences, and a safeguard for service discipline and the capacity to cope with the political environment as a coherent entity. Another professional interest relates to the acquisition of resources for the military. The senior commanders are opposed to any cuts in defence expenditure unilaterally by the civilian government. The military also favours a free hand in the disbursement of the allocated funds.

The improvement of service conditions and protection of material rewards and perks are also important military interests. The military personnel enjoy more facilities than their counterparts in the civil service and want these to be adequately protected. The civilian governments are generally responsive to their demands. During the first 14 years of civilian governments (March 1985 to March 1999), 15 out of 32 provincial governors came from the Army.

The military expects a civilian government to ensure some measure of socio-political and economic stability. This stems from the assumption that a turmoil-afflicted society cannot sustain a professional military. Moreover, the military's four charitable foundations have expanded their industrial and business operations to such an extent that the military has developed a stake in the government's economic and industrial policies and fiscal management.

The Intelligence Agencies

The military has also benefited from the expanding role of intelligence agencies. The well-known intelligence agencies like Military Intelligence (MI), Inter-Services Intelligence (ISI), Intelligence Bureau (IB), Federal Investigation Agency (FIA), Special Branch have acquired salience in the political system. The MI is a purely military agency and every military service has its own intelligence gathering mechanism. The ISI is semi-military whose Director General is a serving Army officer (Lt.-General or Major General) but he is appointed by the Prime Minister and it reports both to the military and the civilian authorities on specified matters. The rest are civilian agencies. Though the MI focused on military and security affairs, it overstepped its domain during the Zia years by involving itself in domestic political affairs and establishing its cells at the provincial level to collect information on domestic politics. It undertook some political assignments normally given to the ISI, counter-checked the intelligence gathered by other agencies, and played an important role in implementing presidential dismissals of the governments. The ISI grew from a standard intelligence agency to a massive outfit for domestic and international operations under the Zia regime and it gained notoriety because of its active involvement in the war in Afghanistan and the connections it developed with the American Central Intelligence Agency (CIA) from May 1979 for supporting Islamic resistance groups in Afghanistan.[1] The ISI managed the weapons supply to Afghan resistance groups and extended them strategic support, enabling it to amass sizeable material resources and political clout. Its political wing, established in 1975, was employed effectively by Zia-ul-Haq for monitoring domestic politics as well as for encouraging ethnic and sectarian elements in order to weaken nation-wide political alignments. The IB was also employed for the same purpose and for keeping tabs on the dissident political leaders.

Subsequently, the ISI and the IB continued to collect intelligence on domestic political affairs. The Army Chief partly relied on the information gathered by the MI and the ISI to take up internal and external security issues with the civilian government. The President also benefited from the work of these agencies when preparing the charge sheets against the dismissed civilian governments.

The ISI has worked for implementing the military's political agenda. In the 1988 general elections, the top brass of the Army employed the ISI to manage the reunification of the two factions of the Pakistan Muslim League (PML) and to encourage a number of right-wing political parties to join with the PML to set up an electoral alliance, *Islami Jamhoori Ittehad* (IJI) to counterbalance the expected electoral victory of the PPP. The ISI helped the IJI in its election campaign in the Punjab. In September–October 1989, two ISI officers were involved in the 'Operation Midnight Jackals' to sway some of PPP members of the National Assembly to the opposition side for the vote of noconfidence against the Benazir Bhutto government. Similarly, this agency played a role in switching the *Mohajir Qaumi Movement* (MQM) support from Benazir Bhutto to the opposition. During the 1990 general elections, this agency obtained Rs. 140 million (US $6.45 million at the 1990 rate of exchange) from a banker and distributed most of this amount to the IJI and other leaders on the instructions of the then President and with the full knowledge and blessing of the Army Chief. Similarly, the decision of the MQM to withdraw from the National Assembly electoral contest in 1993 was attributed to the pressure from the Army and the ISI (for details, see the discussion on various governments in this chapter).

The political governments also use civilian intelligence agencies against their political adversaries and the civil and military officials. There have been numerous instances of telephone tapping of cabinet ministers, judges of the superior courts and the senior military officers. Even the Prime Minister has been subjected to eavesdropping by the intelligence agencies. However, attempts by the civilian governments to gather information on senior commanders have not been successful because the military neutralizes such efforts; the military has a clear edge on their civilian counterparts in the area of intelligence-gathering. The Army authorities persuaded the caretaker government that was in power from November 1996 to February 1997 to give the military a greater say in the affairs of the IB by inducting more Army personnel in the IB, and giving the MI a greater role in it.

Intelligence-gathering has become increasingly important if the senior commanders want to pursue a non-takeover intervention in politics. It is also needed to protect and advance the professional and corporate interests of the military. How that information will be used depends on the goals of the senior commanders and the requirements of a particular situation. Given their role in domestic politics these agencies could be used, as was the case in the past, to support or oppose a particular political group and to build pressure on the civilian government by encouraging its adversaries to take on the government. Once sufficient pressure has been built on the government, the Army Chief can make a Prime Minister resign or secure the desired policy changes.

Problems of Governance

Much of the fragmentation and incoherence in politics in the post-withdrawal period can be traced to the efforts of the military government of Zia-ul-Haq to discourage nation-wide political interaction and alignments and to coopt a leadership whose worldview was shaped by their local or tribal and *biradari* or ethnicity or religious sect considerations and links. The military government accommodated their limited agendas by making some economic concessions and by activating local bodies. They were later introduced at the national level as an alternative to those who opposed military rule by setting up a nominated Federal Council (a consultative body with no powers to enact laws) in December 1981 and by holding a carefully managed, non-party general elections in February 1985.

These strategies, especially the 1985 non-party elections, 'destroyed the organizational basis of politics in the country and effectively localized it within the confines of electoral constituencies'.[2] A large number of local and district level leaders were suddenly elevated to the national level. They did not develop a vision and stability for functioning at the national level which could be acquired only through graduation from the lower to the higher levels. The military's cooption policy also brought forward those who had earned wealth in the post-1977 period due to the Gulf region boom and the Afghanistan war, i.e. business or a job in the Gulf region, manpower export to the Gulf region, real estate business, contract work on government projects, American aid and Afghan refugees related work, smuggling, drugs and weapons trafficking. This wealth enabled them to build political clout in view of the military government's policy of excluding the established political parties. The co-opted elite brought the ethos of local and district politics to the national level, i.e. a limited and narrow outlook, personal rather than professional approach, more intolerance towards adversaries, and a desire to acquire material and political gains through all possible means. They acted more like local and district councillors than parliamentarians committed to putting the parliamentary and democratic system back on the rails. The civilian governments mustered their support by offering state patronage, non-judicious use of state apparatus and coercion against those who refused to fall in line. Since 1985, every government has surpassed its predecessor in offering material rewards, such as a seat in the cabinet or the grant of ministerial perks and facilities to other political appointees, bank loans or a waiver from repayment of loans, allocation of development funds, allotment of plots of land in the urban areas at concessional rates, quotas of the parliamentarians for jobs, telephone connections and licences for owning weapons. This resulted in a massive misuse of state resources and widespread increase in corruption, which adversely affected the capacity of the civilian leaders to deal with the major political and economic issues on their merits and govern effectively.

Additional problems are caused by the growing ethnic, linguistic, regional and religious-sectarian polarization and the resort to violence by these interests to advance their partisan agenda. Some of these groups are so armed with sophisticated weapons that the civilian authorities need the support of the paramilitary forces or regular troops to assert their writ. The track record of the civilian governments for political and economic management has been extremely poor, if not totally disappointing, and they are unable to cope with the growing problems of governance. These governments constantly seek the military's support for improving their governance and the politicians do not hesitate to cultivate the senior commanders to pressure their adversaries.

The following discussion examines the interaction of various civilian governments with the military in the post-withdrawal period.

The Junejo Government

The co-opted civilian government of Prime Minister Muhammad Khan Junejo (March 1985–May 1988) faced problems in defining its identity and relationship with the military. It wanted to distance itself from Zia-ul-Haq in order to establish its credentials as a popular government that could charter an independent course of action. However, the civilian government did not want to alienate the military altogether because it needed Zia-ul-Haq's support to ward off challenges from the dissident political parties that questioned its legitimacy. These conflicting pressures often created an anomalous situation for the government and created strains in its interaction with Zia-ul-Haq and the dissident political forces.

The new civilian leadership made its presence felt by electing Syed Fakhr Imam as Speaker of the National Assembly in opposition to a candidate who enjoyed the blessings of Zia-ul-Haq. The Speaker tried to run the house in a nonpartisan manner which landed him in trouble with both the Junejo government and Zia-ul-Haq. Another manifestation of the desire of the elected representatives to adopt an autonomous profile was the adoption of resolutions by the National Assembly, the Senate, and the provincial assemblies of the Punjab, Sindh and NWFP for an early lifting of martial law. Zia-ul-Haq advised Junejo to move slowly on this demand. Later, they accommodated each other: Junejo secured parliament's approval for the Eighth Amendment to legitimize the Revival of Constitutional Order (RCO) with some modification, and Zia-ul-Haq withdrew martial law on 30 December 1985.

The Junejo government realized that the continuation of the ban on political parties imposed during the martial law days was a major obstacle to their efforts to cultivate popular support; the government also faced problems in managing the members of the parliament and the provincial assemblies. It therefore adopted a strategy similar to the one pursued by the civilian leaders in 1962 when the ban on political parties was circumvented by organizing the elected representatives in 'like-minded' groups which functioned till the ban on political parties was withdrawn. Junejo organized his supporters in parliament and the provincial assemblies as the Official Parliamentary Group (OPG). Those who did not join the OPG established an Independent Parliamentary Group (IPG). In January 1986, the ban on political parties was lifted, but cumbersome procedures were announced for their registration with the Election Commission as a prerequisite for engaging in open and legal political activities. Junejo took control of the PML-Pagara with the consent of its leader, the Pir Pagara, and declared it to be the ruling party; the press described it as the Official Muslim League (OML). Before the registration formalities were completed, Junejo assumed its presidency, appointed the provincial Chief Ministers as it provincial chiefs and persuaded a large number of the OPG members to join it. This rendered the OPG members, including the Prime Minister and the Chief Ministers, liable to disqualification for joining an unregistered political party. When this issue was raised in the National Assembly by the IPG, the Speaker referred the matter to the Chief Election Commissioner for adjudication. This panicked Junejo, who persuaded Zia-ul-Haq to issue a presidential ordinance in May 1986 to amend the law for allowing the elected representatives to join a political parties whose registration formalities had not been completed. This averted the collapse of the Junejo government. Junejo reciprocated by replacing the Speaker (Syed Fakhr Imam) who had, in February 1986, admitted a privilege motion against Zia-ul-Haq for assailing the National Assembly in a statement.[3] Another gesture was not to object to Zia-ul-Haq's decision to carry on as Army Chief. Zia-ul-Haq maintained that he would continue as Army Chief until the political government was strong enough to hold on by itself and the Army felt itself 'safe and sound' under a civilian government.[4]

The OML was the first party to register; *Jamaat-i-Islami, Tehrik-i-Istiqlal* and *Jamiat-e-Ulema-e-Pakistan* (JUP) also registered. Other registered parties were political non-entities. The MRD and the PPP refused to register themselves. The unregistered parties could take part in political activities but were debarred from taking part in any election. The OML relied on the bureaucratic structure to establish its organization at the district level and below.[5] It periodically boasted about the rapid expansion of its membership and the setting up of its primary units in different parts of the country. In reality, the OML's mainstay were the OPG, the beneficiaries of martial law, a section of the feudal and business elite and other bandwagon riders. It could not develop a viable organizational network and failed to become an effective political machine for delivering voluntary support to the civilian government. Its strength was the backing it enjoyed from the local/district administration and police and its ability to distribute material rewards on partisan considerations.

The government/OML adopted a host of strategies to sustain support which became the standard practice with every civilian government that succeeded Junejo. First, the cabinets were unduly expanded. The federal cabinet had 36 members in 1987–8. The Punjab cabinet included 34 ministers and advisers. The most interesting situation developed in Balochistan where 27 of the 44 members of the provincial assembly held ministerial portfolios (13 ministers, two special assistants, four advisers and eight parliamentary secretaries). If the Speaker and Deputy Speakers who joined the OML were counted, 29 members held official positions. The provincial cabinets in Sindh and NWFP were relatively small: 17 and 13 members respectively. However, the Chief Ministers of these provinces periodically talked about the expansion of the cabinets in order to keep the members of the provincial assemblies in line with the official policy. Second, the federal and provincial governments distributed developments funds as a political bribe. These were placed at the disposal of the members of the parliament and the provincial assemblies. Additional development funds were given to those who established at least 100 primary units of the OML. Third, 138 members of the parliament were allotted residential plots by the federal government at less than market prices,[6] most of which were later sold by them in open market at exorbitant prices. Fourth, the grant of loans by banks and other financial institutions in disregard of the established criteria and procedures was used as a tool for political manipulation and support-building. The outstanding loans of a number of people were written off on political grounds. Fifth, a number of steps were taken to provide some economic relief to the common people. A five-point programme for socio-economic acceleration was introduced and funds were mobilized from domestic and international sources for financing the programme. The government launched a scheme of free distribution of small plots of state land to the poor for construction of houses. A reasonable number of 3.5 and 7 *marla* plots were given to homeless people in the urban and rural areas in 1987. A Rs. 500 million fund was set up in May 1987 for the welfare of widows and orphans. The *Thar* relief fund was created in October with an initial amount of Rs. 2.5 million. Similarly, special grants were allocated for the drought-affected areas in Cholistan.[7]

The Zia–Junejo system faced political challenges from the MRD and especially from the PPP. The MRD demonstrated its popular appeal by holding a well-attended political rally in Lahore on 14 August 1985, and by extending a spirited welcome to Benazir Bhutto when she temporarily returned to Pakistan later that month to take part in the funeral of her brother,

Shahnawaz, who had died in mysterious circumstances in France. Soon afterwards, she was put under house arrest until she went abroad on 4 November. Political dissent manifested again when Benazir Bhutto returned to Pakistan from self-imposed exile on 10 April 1986 to lead the opposition. The tumultuous and emotionally charged welcome on her arrival in Lahore demonstrated that martial law could not erode the Bhutto family's popular appeal. In her public meetings, Benazir Bhutto attacked the generals who staged the 1977 coup and had ruled since then. Demanding the resignation of Zia-ul-Haq, she called for new elections on a party basis under the original 1973 constitution.[8] The first major confrontation between the MRD and the Junejo government developed on 14 August, when the police attempted to foil the MRD's bid to hold a public meeting in Lahore; four people were killed in this clash which sparked trouble in Karachi and some other cities. Several leading opposition leaders, including Benazir Bhutto, and a large number of political activists were arrested. The Punjab witnessed more agitation this time than was the case during the MRD movement in 1983, but it could not become a province-wide agitation. Its support in NWFP and Balochistan was lukewarm. However, it produced a militant anti-government agitation in large parts of Sindh which had strong ethnic and regional overtones.[9] The Army and paramilitary troops were used in several places in Sindh to cope with the agitation.

The civilian government faced additional problems because of the inten-sification of religious sectarian antagonism, ethnic-linguistic conflict, social and economic discontent and serious law and order problems in parts of the country. The conservative and orthodox Islamic groups which were pam-pered during the martial law period continued to obtain financial support, especially the *Zakat* fund,[10] as Zia-ul-Haq kept his links with them. These Islamic elements engaged in mutual recrimination and violence on *fiqah*-related matters or resorted to fascist methods to contain what they viewed as un-Islamic practices. *Anjuman Sipah-e-Sahaba*, set up in 1985 as a breakaway group from the JUI, began to resort to violence in pursuance of its narrowly based Islamic sectarian agenda. Some groups, such as *Tehrik-i-Nifaz-i-Fiqah-i-Jafaria* (TNFJ), later renamed as *Tehrik-i-Jafaria, Pakistan* (TJP) and *Jamaat-i-Ahle Sunnat* (JAS) converted themselves into political parties in July 1987. Another religious party, *Jamaat-i-Ahle Hadith* (JAH) attempted to launch a movement for the arrest of the unknown killer of their leader.

Violence also increased in the wake of the meteoric rise of *Mohajir* (refu-gee) nationalism in urban Sindh. Its main champion, the *Mohajir Quami Movement* (MQM), was established in March 1984 by the activists of the All Pakistan *Mohajir* Students Organization (APMSO), an organization set up in Karachi University in June 1978.[11] The MQM demonstrated its strength by holding its first public meeting in Karachi in August 1986 and another meeting in Hyderabad in October, and swept the 1987 local bodies polls in these cities. The MQM articulated the grievances of the Urdu-speaking populace in urban Sindh, caused by what they described as the gradual erosion of their socio-economic status, the decline in their representation in government jobs and the growing prominence of the Punjabis and the Pakhtuns in the economy of urban Sindh. The unemployed and alienated *Mohajir* youth belonging mainly to the lower and middle strata of the society provided the MQM with a devoted cadre; they often resorted to violence to assert their identity and to confront other ethnic groups.

Another major ethnic-linguistic movement, Sindhi nationalism, gained momentum in the rural areas of Sindh which were dominated by the Sindhi-speaking populace. Though the roots of Sindhi nationalism can be traced back to the early years of independence, it gained strength during the last martial law period. The major causes behind the growing Sindhi alienation included the execution of Z.A. Bhutto by the military government, the extremely poor representation of native Sindhis in the higher echelons of the Army, the growing unemployment of Sindhi youth, and cynicism about the prospects of any significant improvement in their socio-economic conditions under the military government. The allotment of agricultural land to the people from other provinces, especially to military personnel and bureaucrats, was another major irritant for local Sindhis.

These religious and ethnic-linguistic groups obtained sophisticated weapons, siphoned off from supplies to Afghan resistance groups, and used these freely to advance their political objectives. Furthermore, a host of adventurists and a web of organized crime and narcotics, taking advantage of the confusion and administrative laxity in Sindh, resorted to kidnapping people for ransom, dacoity, highway robberies and looting of banks or any other place where they could lay their hands on cash or other valuables. They often engaged in shooting sprees in the cities to create terror or to trigger ethnic riots. There were numerous incidents of bomb blasts in four provinces and the tribal areas during 1986–7. The most devastating explosion occurred in Karachi in July 1987 which left 73 people dead and over 200 injured. The civilian government relied heavily on the paramilitary and the Army for the maintenance of law and order in Sindh. In June and October 1988, the Army was sent to six and twelve cities respectively in addition to Karachi and Hyderabad.

These were not the only obstacles to the assertion of civilian primacy. Zia-ul-Haq kept the Prime Minister under pressure so that he did not develop an autonomous profile. He often lashed out publicly at the government and the elected representatives for slowing down the Islamization process and questioned the suitability of the prevelant democratic system to Pakistan. Describing the parliamentary system as being incomprehensible and divisive, Zia-ul-Haq advised the people to work towards evolving a political system that promoted stability and brought about the 'complete enforcement of Islam in a peaceful and orderly manner.'[12] In another statement, he advised the people not to waste time on political meetings and procession.

Instead, they should regularly offer prayer five times a day and earn their living through fair means.[13] He repeated his reservations about the relevance of the Westminster model of governance for Pakistan and lamented the slow implementation of Islam by the government in his address to the golden jubilee meeting of the Punjab Provincial Assembly in February 1988.[14] Similar views were expressed in his address to the joint session of the two houses of the parliament in April.[15] He also encouraged orthodox and conservative Islamic elements to attack the government for its alleged failure to Islamize the polity.[16]

Junejo trod his path carefully and avoided public debate with Zia-ul-Haq on these issues. However, they were bound to drift apart because they represented diverse interests. Junejo and his colleagues were more sensitive to public demands for political participation and socio-economic justice and wanted to accommodate some such demands so as to strengthen their position. Zia-ul-Haq's basic concern was the continuation of a civilian arrangement under his tutelage and protection and advancement of the interests of his constituency, i.e. the military. As the political process gained momentum and the press acquired freedom, a number of issues relating to the military were subjected to criticism inside and outside parliament. These included induction of the military officers to lucrative civilian jobs, allotment of land and other material benefits to senior officers and the defence expenditure. Another criticism focused on Zia-ul-Haq's decision to hold on to the post of Army Chief. When, in May 1987, the National Assembly resumed discussion on Zia-ul-Haq's address to the joint session of the parliament, several members demanded that Zia-ul-Haq should hold only one office: President or Army Chief.[17]

The defence allocations were subjected to sharp criticism in the press. A host of articles published in 1986–7 emphasized the need to reduce and/or rationalize the defence expenditure and maintained that the current practice of one-line entry of the defence expenditure in the national budget should be replaced with a detailed statement. When the Public Accounts Committee of the National Assembly asked the Ministry of Defence to submit a report on military purchases and related accounts, no reply was given.[18] In early 1988, the Junejo government hinted at reducing the defence expenditure. Earlier, in 1987, while addressing the National Assembly, Junejo asked the generals and senior bureaucrats to replace their high-consumption staff cars with small economy vehicles. His comment that the government would 'put the generals in Suzukis' (small economy cars) incurred the wrath of the senior commanders. A retired Lt.-General published an article in two Pakistani newspapers, taking a strong exception to what he viewed as unjustified criticism of the senior commanders.[19] This article stirred a debate in the press on the role of the military and the lifestyle of the top brass. Most of the follow-up articles and letters to the editor were critical of the senior commanders and their role in politics. The military circles viewed this as a deliberate attempt by the civilian government to whip up anti-military sentiments. These perception were strengthened as Yaqub Ali Khan, Foreign Minister since 1982 and known as the Army's man, resigned on 1 November 1987. However, as a gesture, Junejo did not make a new appointment; the Minister of State carried on the job. The question of setting up a military cantonment in interior Sindh caused some unease between the government and Zia-ul-Haq. The Army's decision to set up cantonments at Pano Aqil and three other places was resented by several Sindhi nationalist groups. Zia-ul-Haq expected Junejo publicly to defend the setting up of new cantonments but he shied away. The first cantonment at Pano Aqil was quietly inaugurated in March 1988; the Army would have liked Junejo to inaugurate it.

Two developments in 1988 accentuated differences between Zia-ul-Haq and Junejo. They disagreed on signing the peace accord on Afghanistan that evolved out the Geneva-based UN supervised indirect talks between Pakistan and Afghanistan. The Junejo government, perturbed by the spillover effects of the Afghanistan war on Pakistan – the refugee problem, Afghan–Soviet air raids and ground attacks in the tribal areas, bomb explosions all over the country, and proliferation of weapons – was in favour of signing a peace accord at the earliest opportunity. Zia-ul-Haq wanted to hold on for some-time so as to extract concessions from the Soviet Union, especially on the formation of an interim government of the resistance groups. What irked Zia-ul-Haq was Junejo's decision to call a round-table conference of Pakistan's major political parties, including the PPP, in the first week of March 1988 for developing a consensus on Afghanistan. Most of these parties supported an early settlement. The domestic support and American blessing emboldened Junejo to sign the peace accord on Afghanistan on 14 April 1988.

An army ammunition depot at Ojhri, known as a major storage of weapons for Afghan resistance, was blown up on 10 April, causing a heavy loss of human life and property in Rawalpindi and Islamabad. Such an accident could not take place without serious lapses in safety arrangements, and the Army was subjected to sharp criticism. There was a public outcry for punitive action against those responsible for such serious negligence. Two inquiry committees were appointed to investigate the matter.[20] It was generally believed in the political circles in Islamabad and Lahore that Junejo would take punitive action against the concerned senior Army officers in order to assuage public resentment. The two officers who were expected to face censure were General Akhtar Abdur Rahman, Chairman, Joint Chiefs of Staff Committee, who had headed the ISI till March 1987, and the serving Director General, ISI, Major General Hameed Gul. Zia-ul-Haq wanted to protect them which set the stage for a showdown between him and Junejo.[21]

These developments threatened Zia-ul-Haq's role as the guardian of the professional and corporate interests of the military. If the civilian government made some cuts in the defence expenditure, reduced the privileges and perks of the officers, or took action against some senior officers, Zia-ul-Haq was bound to lose the support of the military, which was the key to his political survival. He felt that this could also make his own position vulnerable: the civilian government could ask him to step down from the post of Army Chief. Zia-ul-Haq's speech at the launching ceremony of the book *Defenders of Pakistan* in early May was quite significant. He cautioned against any cut in defence allocations and stressed that the armed forces should not be criticized. He also advised the people to cool their tempers on the Ojhri camp accident and remarked, 'The sooner we get out of the feelings and hangover of this tragedy – whether it was an accident or an act of sabotage – the better it will be for the nation as a whole.'[22] An unrelated but important development was a clash between a group of young Army officers and a member of the Punjab Assembly and his supporters in Rawalpindi on 24–25 May. This incident was viewed as symptomatic of the growing tension between the military and the civilian leadership.[23]

Zia-ul-Haq came to the conclusion that the civilian government was not heeding his advice and that it was also ignoring the interests of the military. He was reported to have said that the military 'needed patrons not prosecutors'.[24] On 29 May 1988, he took command of the situation by dismissing the civilian governments at the federal and provincial levels and dissolving the National Assembly and all the provincial assemblies in a coup-like manner.[25] The troops took control of important government installations in Islamabad, including the Prime Minister's house, radio and television stations. Such a drastic step was taken at a time when there was no political or economic crisis in the country and Junejo had just returned from a visit to China.

The Changing Role of the Senior Commanders

Zia-ul-Haq assumed executive powers at the federal level and appointed a cabinet which he himself headed. In his characteristic manner, he invoked Islam for legitimizing his rule by emphasizing the revival of the Islamization process as the major priority. A *Sharia* ordinance was promulgated in June which declared the *Sharia* to be 'the supreme source of law' and a 'Grand norm for guidance for policy-making'.[26] The new government also talked of reviving the economy, decided to scrutinize the assets of the members of the assemblies, and announced that there would be no reduction in the defence expenditure. It was not until 20 July that the date for general elections was fixed as 16 November, thereby violating the generally held view that the constitution obliged the holding of the elections within 90 days of the dissolution of the assemblies.

Junejo was hardly in a position to resist the change as several of his colleagues joined Zia-ul-Haq's government. Zia-ul-Haq appointed his loyalists as provincial Chief Ministers and, through them, he attempted to dislodge Junejo from the OML. When this attempt failed, a parallel Muslim League was set up in early August, with Fida Muhammad Khan as President and Nawaz Sharif (Punjab's Chief Minister) as Secretary General.

Zia-ul-Haq wanted his loyalists to win the elections. This was to be managed through the provincial governments, which were firmly in the control of his loyalists and by keeping the dissident political forces excluded from the political process. This plan received a jolt when, in late June, the Supreme Court struck down the laws pertaining to registration of political parties, thereby allowing the hitherto unregistered parties to contest elections. As an alternative strategy, Zia-ul-Haq began to work towards holding non-party elections, as he had done in 1985. He also toyed with the idea of reducing the role and powers of the parliament. These plans were cut short by his death in an air crash on 17 August.[27]

Soon after Zia-ul-Haq's death, the top brass of the three services held a meeting and decided to ask Ghulam Ishaq Khan, Chairman of the Senate, to assume the presidency, as provided in the constitution. General Mirza Aslam Beg, hitherto Vice Chief of Army Staff, who took command of the Army after Zia-ul-Haq's death, was formally appointed Army Chief. The military commanders laid down five policy priorities for the acting President which included (i) the upholding of the glory of Islam; (ii) continuation of the policies of the Zia era; (iii) rule of law and justice; (iv) support to the current Afghanistan policy; and (v) restoration of democracy.[28] Zia's cabinet was retained and the state of emergency was imposed, but the fundamental rights were not suspended. An extra-ordinary emergency council was established to advise the government on policy-making. It included the President, five federal ministers (the senior-most, Foreign Affairs, Defence, Interior, and Justice and Parliamentary Affairs), three services chiefs, acting Governor of Sindh (a retired general), and four Chief Ministers.

General Aslam Beg expressed his support for constitutionalism and the democratic process and emphasized that the military 'had no lust for power' and that its sole objective was the preservation of the 'security and integrity of the nation'.[29] He issued several statements during August–November to reaffirm the support of the top brass for holding free and fair elections and transfer of power to the elected representatives.[30] Similar views were expressed by Ishaq Khan, who ruled out a formal role for the military in the political domain.[31] The Army and the civil administration worked in close harmony to ensure peaceful and orderly elections.

The emphasis on limiting the military's role to its immediate professional concerns was a departure from the policies pursued by Zia-ul-Haq, who had strongly advocated the institutionalization of an expanded role for the military in the political system. Several factors shaped the decision of the military commanders to restrict their role. First, despite the military's repeated intervention in politics, a traditional sense of professionalism and discipline remained. Most officers believed in a restricted political role, although they would not shy away from taking over if they perceived it as necessary. Second, since Zia-ul-Haq had already announced that the new elections would be held in November, a military takeover would have been awkward. This would have confronted the top brass with several controversial issues in the politically charged environment. Should they hold the elections on a party basis? Should they allow the interim federal and provincial governments appointed by Zia-ul-Haq to carry on or remove them as demanded by some political leaders? Should they adopt an independent or neutral role or, in the tradition of Zia-ul-Haq, cultivate a group of political leaders? The decisions on these and similar issues were likely to produce a confrontation between the generals and the politicians, thereby making it difficult to hold the elections on time. Any postponement would have reinforced the impression that the military was the main obstacle to the restoration of a participatory system.

Third, the senior commanders were conscious of the fact that the military's reputation had suffered through repeated involvement in politics, and especially because of Zia-ul-Haq's 11–year rule. Stories circulated about the acquisition of wealth and lucrative civilian assignments by the senior retired and serving officers. The failure to dislodge the Indian troops from the Siachen Glacier in Kashmir and the Ojhri Camp explosion were often cited as clear proof of the decline of professionalism in the Army. As criticism focused on their involvement in domestic politics, senior commanders clearly felt that a decision to honour the constitution would help to restore their reputation. Fourth, General Beg, the new Army Chief, could not be sure of the support of the Army's senior echelons. Although he had been Vice Chief since March 1987, Zia-ul-Haq, as the Army Chief, had kept the Army as his exclusive preserve by appointing 'his men' to key positions (some died with Zia in the air crash). General Beg, an Urdu-speaking *Mohajir* from Uttar Pradesh facing a majority of Punjabi and Pakhtun senior commanders, needed time to take stock of the situation and consolidate his position. Fifth, the political situation in the aftermath of the plane crash was peaceful and stable. All major political parties and other politically active circles supported the constitutional transfer of power and the decision of the acting President to uphold the previously announced election date. Such a situation did not warrant a coup.

Sixth, the superior judiciary also reinforced the democratic process. In June 1988, the Supreme Court struck down the rules and procedures for the registration of political parties, abolishing the distinction between 'registered' and 'unregistered' parties. In September, the Punjab High Court judged the dissolution of the assemblies as illegal but it refused to restore these bodies and the Junejo government on the pretext that the elections had been announced. The Supreme Court upheld this judgement in

October, and, in another judgement, it directed the government to hold the elections on party basis.[32]

After withdrawal to the barracks, the military influenced the political process in a subtle and mature manner. When the Supreme Court was dealing with the dissolution case (see above), General Beg sent a message to the Court not to restore the Junejo government as the new elections were being held.[33] As the general elections approached, the top brass realized through their intelligence sources that, if the anti-PPP political elements continued to suffer from disunity, the political balance would tilt decisively in favour of the PPP. Given the distrust of the PPP on the part of the senior commanders, they decided to pre-empt the prospects of the PPP's dominance. This task was assigned to the ISI which managed the reunification of the two factions of the Muslim League (hereafter PML) and encouraged nine right-of-centre political parties to set up an electoral alliance, named *Islami Jamhoori Itehad* (IJI), or Islamic Democratic Alliance, with the PML as the core party.[34] The ISI remained associated with the IJI's election campaign and helped to coin anti-PPP slogans in the Punjab.[35] Most of the IJI parties were conservative and Islamic in their orientation and were prepared to identify with Zia-ul-Haq's political legacy and shared a strong aversion towards the PPP. The IJI also benefited from the state patronage because the PML ruled the four provinces.

The ISI's political engineering worked as no political party obtained a clear cut majority in the National Assembly. The PPP emerged as the single largest party with 93 seats, followed by the IJI with 54 seats. The third largest group was that of the independent members who numbered 27. The MQM was fourth with 13 seats, all from Karachi and Hyderabad. In the provincial elections, the PPP obtained a clear majority in Sindh, but no political party got a clear majority in other provinces, although in the Punjab, the IJI was the single largest group.

Benazir Bhutto's First Term

The decision to invite Benazir Bhutto to form the government was jointly made by Ishaq Khan and General Beg. Benazir Bhutto had a meeting with General Beg a couple of days before assuming power. Though no details of the meeting were made available, it was generally believed that General Beg outlined the interests and concerns of the military, while she made her case for prime ministership and stressed the PPP's goodwill towards the military. Benazir Bhutto, installed as Prime Minister on 2 December, made three major gestures towards the military: support for a five-year term for acting President Ishaq Khan (a Zia loyalist) who enjoyed the blessings of the military;[36] retention of Lt.-General Yaqub Ali Khan (Zia's Foreign Minister) in her cabinet in order to assure continuity in policy on Afghanistan; and a promise not to make unilateral reductions in defence expenditure and service conditions.

The Benazir government and the military started with a cordial relation-ship. General Beg repeatedly made statements in support of the government and left no doubt about the military's blessing to the democratic experi-ment. Benazir Bhutto publicly acknowledged the military's role in the restoration of democracy and declared that the military deserved a 'Medal of Democracy' in appreciation of its 'whole-hearted' support to democracy. The budgetary allocations to the military showed a steady increase during her tenure and her government went along with the military on Afghanistan and acquiesced in the military's management of the nuclear policy. Benazir Bhutto did not replace the Governor of NWFP – a retired Brigadier appointed by Zia-ul-Haq – with an ANP nominee because the President and the Army Chief were not in favour of such a change.

Benazir Bhutto developed differences with the top commanders mainly due to her government's political and economic mismanagement and the attempts to tamper with the military's internal and service affairs. Tradition-ally, the civilian government did not interfere with military promotions, transfers, facilities for the personnel, disbursement of the allocated funds, training and organizational matters. General Beg jealously guarded this autonomy. In reply to a question on the powers of the Prime Minister to change the Corps Commanders, General Beg replied that the Prime Minister was not supposed to do that; such changes were made on the recommenda-tion of the Army Chief. He also maintained that the meetings of the Corps Commanders were presided over by the Army Chief and the Prime Minister was invited only 'to watch the proceedings'.[37]

The issue of appointment and retirement developed into a row between the government and the top brass of the military in 1989. They diverged on the replacement of the Director General of the ISI, Major General Hameed Gul. The civilian government felt that the ISI was deeply involved in domes-tic politics and therefore wanted to change its Director General to neutralize its role. General Beg consented to the change only reluctantly and was annoyed by the Prime Minister's decision to appoint a retired Major General, Shamsul Rehman Kallu, as the new Director General instead of a serving officer, as was the practice. Consequently, Kallu faced problems in securing the necessary cooperation of his colleagues. General Beg also resented the government's attempts to persuade the Army not to take punitive action against the officers on their return from self-imposed exile who had been removed from service for indiscipline in the aftermath of the elder Bhutto's execution in 1979.[38]

A serious dispute developed when the government attempted to retire Admiral Iftikhar Ahmad Sirohi, Chairman, Joint Chiefs of Staff Committee (JCSC) on the completion of his three-year term as Admiral in 1989 (he was appointed Admiral and Naval Chief in April 1986, and elevated to the post of Chairman, JCSC, in November 1988). The military's view was that the Chair-man, JCSC, carried a three-year term, no matter when the appointee got his rank and, for that reason, Sirohi would retire in November 1991. What made the situation worse was the public statement on this issue by Nusrat Bhutto, then senior minister, which irritated the senior commanders who felt that the government was raising unnecessary controversies. Ishaq Khan went along with the military and the government had to cut a sorry figure. Similarly, the attempts by the government to tamper with retirement/extension of some senior commanders in June–July 1990 further strained civil–military relations.[39] The military was also wary of Benazir Bhutto's keenness to cultivate Rajiv Gandhi during his visits to Pakistan in December 1988 and July 1989. Its intelligence sources collected enough evidence on the dialogue between the two leaders to lead the Army commanders to view Benazir Bhutto as being 'unreliable' on security-related matters. That was the reason why she was kept in dark about the most sensitive aspects of the nuclear programme. Her government was also accused of providing India with some information on Sikh militants who had developed connections with the ISI.

The Army and the civil government developed differences on the handling of the law and order situation in Sindh. The Army leadership felt that the government was too partisan and wanted to use the troops essentially against its political adversaries. When the Federal Interior Minister provided a list of 'terrorists' to the Corps Commander of Karachi for rounding them up, the latter found out that most of them were *Mohajirs*. The general raised this matter with the Interior Minister which caused a row between the two.[40] An incident that strengthened the perception of the government's partisanship was the firing by the police on an unarmed MQM procession in Hyderabad on 27 May 1990; the unofficial sources claimed that about 100 people were killed. When the troops moved in to replace the police, the MQM supporters welcomed them and, when General Beg visited the city a couple of days later, he was greeted with slogans calling for the imposition of martial law.

The Army commanders asked for no political interference in their law and order work in Sindh, permission to set up military courts and the invocation of article 245 of the constitution which restricted the powers of the superior judiciary to enforce fundamental rights in the areas under army control. The civilian government refused and offered to invoke article 147 which allowed the civilian authorities to regulate the role of the troops on law and order duties. The opposition leaders supported the Army's demands. This caused serious strains in the government's relations with the Army and the Army Chief made several statements on the Sindh situation with strong political overtones.[41] After the dismissal of the Benazir government, General Beg gave an intriguing explanation of the demand for extensive powers for the Army, maintaining that these demands were a 'cover' for requiring the government to initiate a dialogue with its adversaries.[42]

While the government and the Army developed differences,[43] the latter engaged in a massive public relations exercise for building its image at the popular level. General Beg was the most outspoken general, making speeches and statements on all major foreign policy, security and domestic issues which were widely circulated by the Inter-Services Public Relations Directorate (ISPR). The Army encouraged a dialogue on security affairs and the ISPR organized a couple of seminars, inviting leading journalists, scholars and political analysts. A major Army exercise, *Zarb-e-Momin* (1989), was widely publicized and the press people were given extensive briefings on it.[44] These measures helped to create a better understanding between the media and the military and generated goodwill for it at the popular level, which contributed to improving its overall standing in the polity.

The credibility of the civilian government declined because of its inability to ensure effective political and economic management. Benazir Bhutto ruled in a highly personalized manner with the help of an array of ministers, advisers and special assistants, most of whom lacked experience and political vision. The PPP had come to power after a long period of suffering and it was more interested in rewarding its workers at the expense of professionalism and competence. The fear of the collapse of the ruling coalition and an intense confrontation with the opposition adversely affected its governance and accentuated its political problems. Benazir Bhutto faced an uphill task of keeping the diversified coalition intact. The methods which Junejo used to sustain his political support, i.e. expansion of cabinets, partisan distribution of development funds and state patronage, allotment of plots of land at less than market rates, and bank loans, were employed on a larger scale to keep the members of the parliament on the government side. When the government faced a vote of no confidence in October–November 1989, both the government and the opposition were said to be offering material rewards to the members. It was during this period that the ISI launched 'Operation Midnight Jackals' to sway some members from the government to the opposition.[45] The MQM withdrew support to the Benazir government on encouragement from General Beg and the ISI. To their dismay, Benazir Bhutto managed to survive the vote of no confidence.

The Benazir government developed a bitter confrontation with the Punjab government headed by the IJI-PML Chief Minister, Nawaz Sharif. The two governments virtually declared war on each other. The federal government used its powers and resources to pressure the Punjab government; some of the issues that caused much bitterness included the transfer of federal civil servants at the disposal of the Punjab, delays in allocation of funds and mutual recriminations. The Punjab government was equally adamant as it refused to comply with the orders of the federal government on most matters; it established a new bank (the Bank of Punjab) for the province and threatened to set up its own TV station. The Punjab government played up Punjabi regional sentiments and projected Nawaz Sharif as the proponent of the Punjabi identity and interests vis-à-vis the federal government run by a Sindhi.

The top brass of the military, the President and the senior bureaucracy extended their blessing to Nawaz Sharif in order to neutralize Benazir Bhutto. This support emboldened Nawaz Sharif, who used the provincial machinery to embarrass the federal government time and again and the Benazir government often found itself isolated and haunted. The IJI reciprocated the military's covert support by endorsing its position on various issues including the retirement of Sirohi, change of the Director General of the ISI, and the military's demand for extensive powers for the maintenance of law and order in Sindh. The IJI and the Punjab government launched a massive propaganda campaign against the federal government as being soft towards India, a perspective shared by the military.

The President and the Army Chief developed strong reservations about the capacity of the government to perform its basic functions and they also felt that Benazir Bhutto was not willing to listen to their advice. They were particularly perturbed by the government's abysmal performance in the economic sector. The mutual consultations between the President and the Army Chief showed a unanimity of views on the political situation. The conduct and performance of the government came under sharp scrutiny in the meeting of the Corps Commanders in the last week of July; they indicated their willingness to support whatever course of action the President adopted to rectify the situation, i.e. Benazir's removal.[46] The major opposition parties, the PML, which controlled the Punjab, and the MQM, which was entrenched in urban Sindh, were already demanding the removal of the Benazir government; their full support for the dismissal for the government was assured.

Benazir Bhutto was removed from power on 6 August 1990 in a coup-like manner. The Army took control of important government buildings in Islamabad, including the Prime Minister's house and Parliament while Ishaq Khan announced the dismissal of the government and dissolution of the National Assembly.[47] Commenting on the dismissals of Benazir Bhutto and Junejo, General Beg said that the two Prime Ministers had become 'prisoners of their respective close cronies who built a wall of ignorance around them and divorced them from [the] on-ground realities'.[48]

Instead of instituting non-partisan interim arrangements at the federal and provincial levels, President Ishaq Khan handed over power to the opposition parties. Ghulam Mustafa Jatoi, leader of the Combined Opposition Parties and a member of the IJI, was appointed caretaker Prime Minister. The provincial governments were also assigned to the IJI or its allies. These governments, especially the Sindh government headed by Jam Sadiq Ali, were highly partisan in the run up to the general elections. The bureaucratic machinery and state patronage were freely used in favour of the IJI. The interim government initiated legal proceedings against Benazir Bhutto and some of the PPP leaders for misuse of power and corruption. The ISI went into action again. Under instructions from the election cell of the President and with the full knowledge and blessings of the Army Chief, the ISI obtained Rs. 140 million (about US$ 6.45 million at the 1990 rate of exchange) through a banker for use during the elections. Rs. 60 million were directly given to the IJI leaders and some journalists opposed to the PPP and Rs. 80 million were used for unspecified purposes during the elections.[49] Ishaq Khan's address to the nation on the eve of the general elections sounded like a campaign speech for the IJI.

The IJI emerged as the single largest party in the National Assembly with 106 seats (37.37 per cent of the votes cast). The PPP-dominated People's Democratic Alliance (PDA) won only 44 seats (36.83 per cent of the votes cast). Third largest group was that of independents with 22 seats (4.54 per cent votes) and the MQM captured 15 seats (5.54 per cent votes). At the provincial level, the PDA's performance was equally poor. In the Punjab, the PDA/PPP won only 10 seats (29.20 per cent votes) as against 214 seats (55.13 per cent votes) won by the IJI. In Sindh, the PDA/PPP was unable to obtain a clear majority; and won 46 seats (35.46 per cent votes). The MQM obtained 28 seats (28.94 per cent of votes), and the IJI got only 6 seats (8.46 per cent votes). In NWFP assembly, the IJI was the largest party with 33 seats (26.67 percent votes), and its allied party, the ANP, secured 23 seats (14.77 per cent votes); the PDA won only 6 seats (15.79 per cent votes). In the case of Balochistan, 40 general seats were shared by 7 parties and independents.[50] The PDA/PPP leadership charged the interim government with rigging and manipulation of the general elections.[51]

The First Nawaz Sharif Government

Nawaz Sharif became Prime Minister in the first week of November 1990 with the abundant goodwill of the President and the top brass of the military. Groomed during Zia-ul-Haq's martial law, he won the appreciation and support of the senior commanders because of his defiant posture towards the Benazir government. As Prime Minister, he was cautious in dealing with the military's professional and corporate interests and generally maintained a cordial interaction with the senior commanders. However, several irritants developed in their interaction.

The first divergence between the Army Chief and the Nawaz Sharif government developed on Pakistan's policy on the Gulf crisis, 1990–1. The government made 5,000 troops available to Saudi Arabia for security-related duties immediately after Iraq's invasion of Kuwait in August 1990. However, as the crisis deepened and the US-led coalition geared up to attack Iraq, the Pakistan government's clear leanings towards the US were questioned by a large number of Islamic groups and others who described the Gulf crisis as an American attempt to humble a relatively powerful and anti-Israel Muslim state. There were street demonstrations in various cities against the United States. It was in this context that, on 2 December, General Beg propounded his 'strategic defiance' thesis, arguing that an act of defiance (i.e. Iraq's refusal to bow to Western pressures) was a prerequisite for making deterrence effective and credible. He elaborated his views in another address to the officers on 28 January 1991, when he described the air raids on Iraq by the US and its allies as a part of American strategy to destroy the power of the states that could in any way threaten Israel. He maintained that after the destruction of Iraq, the next target could be Iran, and that a day might come when Pakistan would face such wrath.[52] These statements were viewed as an attempt by the general to cultivate the political elements in Pakistan that were opposed to the government's pro-America policy, and thus build pressure on the civilian government. Under normal circumstances, the Army Chief would have been reprimanded for publicly diverging from the official policy. However, the civilian government lacked courage to take such a course of action. The government and the Army Chief diverged again when, in July, General Beg issued a statement on the growing threat of war with India. The government publicly disagreed with the statement by suggesting that there was not any imminent threat of war. It was during this period that rumours circulated in major urban centres that General Beg might dislodge the government before his retirement in August. These rumours proved false and General Beg retired as expected. He was succeeded by General Asif Nawaz Janjua who belonged to a military family of the Punjab's military heartland, i.e. the Salt range region.

General Junjua endorsed the perspective of his predecessor that the military was not interested in governance. However, he was better placed to exert the clout of his office because of his strong roots in the Army. It was not too long that differences began to emerge. In early 1992, Nawaz Sharif interceded on the transfer of Lt.-General Hameed Gul who was moved from corps command in Multan to the Heavy Mechanical Complex in Taxila.[53] The Army Chief declined to change his decision. Another cause of breach was Nawaz Sharif's decision to appoint Lt.-General Javed Nasir, known for strong Islamic orientations, as the Director General of the ISI.

The handling of the law and order situation in Sindh caused strains in their relations. Though the Army agreed to undertake security operations in the province without insisting on wide-ranging powers under article 245 of the constitution, the two sides developed complaints against each other as the security operation proceeded. The Army initiated its security operation on 28 May 1992 against dacoits and other anti-social elements in the rural areas.[54] The federal and provincial governments were happy because rural Sindh was the stronghold of the PPP and thus their adversaries faced the brunt of the security operation. The Army authorities soon realized the political implication of their security operation and also felt that the improvement of the overall situation in the province required a similar action in the urban areas. Therefore, the Army commanders decided, on their own in June, to extend their operation to the cities. This resulted in a direct confrontation between the Army and MQM activists who had entrenched themselves there during 1990–2. The Army with better organization and equipment came down hard on them and exploited intra-MQM conflict to its advantage by encouraging the dissidents to set up a parallel organization, MQM-Haqiqi or MQM(H).

The Army operation in urban Sindh caused much embarrassment for the government because the MQM was its ally. The MQM wanted the federal government to stop the operations, but Nawaz Sharif could not order the Army to pull out of the urban areas. Some of his colleagues publicly criticized the security operation. A federal minister, Chaudhry Nisar Ali Khan, made an ill-advised statement that the operation violated the government's initial understanding with the Army. A couple of other members of the government, including the Chief Minister of the Punjab, Ghulam Hyder Wayne, expressed displeasure at the army operation. The Nawaz Sharif government disassociated itself from these comments. This did not end the controversy; some close associates of Nawaz Sharif talked of removing General Janjua just as the elder Bhutto had removed the Chiefs of the Army and the Air Force in March 1972. Nawaz Sharif admitted in 1995 (when he was no longer in power) that on occasions the Army authorities disregarded the instruction of the civilian government while conducting the security operation in Sindh. In another interview, he complained about the 'insulting' attitude of General Janjua towards his government and charged that the general of 'sponsoring' the November–December 1992 Long March by the PPP.[55] If the civilian government was unhappy with the conduct of the Army, the latter complained about the partisan attitude of the former. The Army authorities felt that the government was more interested in using the troops against its political adversaries.

The government tried to 'buy off' the Army Chief and senior commanders by offering them substantial material rewards.[56] General Janjua sternly resisted these efforts and, in one of the meetings of the Corps Commanders towards the end of 1992, talked about the efforts of the government 'to corrupt the Army'.[57] The military was also concerned about the poor performance of the government in foreign affairs. The US had suspended military sales, military training programmes and economic assistance to Pakistan from 1 October 1990 (one month before Sharif assumed power) by invoking the Pressler Amendment to the Foreign Assistance Act as retaliation against Pakistan's nuclear programme. While agreeing that Pakistan should not unilaterally surrender its nuclear weapon option, the military expected the government to devise a diplomatic solution for weapons procurement from the US. Such a prospect was marred as the US and Pakistan diverged on issues of drug trafficking from and through Pakistan and the activities of Pakistan-based transnational Islamic groups linked with the Afghan resistance movement, known as Afghan war veterans. As they threatened American interests or the governments of the Muslim countries perceived to be pro-US, corrupt and un-Islamic in their policies, the US and these governments asked Pakistan to contain such groups. In 1992, the US Department of State placed Pakistan on the 'watch list' of states allegedly sponsoring terrorism. The military, concerned about Pakistan's image abroad and keen to obtain weapons, felt that the Nawaz Sharif government was not doing enough to counter these difficulties.

The Sharif government's political and economic management was far from satisfactory. It had a two-thirds majority in parliament and controlled all four provincial governments, but its policy-making and policy execution lacked consistency and coherence. The policies of economic liberalization, deregulation and privatization were marred by stories of favouritism, kickbacks and corruption. The government's reputation also suffered because of use of public funds and resources on personal and partisan considerations, and grants of huge loans from banks and other financial institutions to the power elite and their cohorts.

The confrontational style of politics between the PPP and the IJI that developed while Benazir Bhutto was in power continued unabated; their roles had changed as the IJI was now the ruling party. A host of corruption and misuse of power cases were instituted against Benazir Bhutto and her husband, Asif Ali Zardari; the latter spent over two years in prison. A number of other important PPP activists also faced legal proceedings on one ground or another. The Sindh provincial government headed by Jam Sadiq Ali (1990–2) and Syed Muzaffar Hussain (1992–3) joined forces with the MQM to suppress the PPP in that province. The PPP responded with no less hostility and kept the government under strain by questioning the legitimacy of the general elections and by charging the ruling circles of corruption and misuse of state power.[58] It also resorted to street agitation from time to time, demanding fresh elections under a national or neutral government. In November–December 1992, the PPP made an unsuccessful bid through street agitation, described as the 'Long March', to force the government to resign. The government was also weakened because of internal feuds in the ruling IJI; some its constituent elements withdrew or were expelled due to policy differences (i.e. *Jamaat-i-Islami, Hizbe Jihad*), while others extended nominal support.

What kept the problems of the Sharif government within manageable limits was the support of President Ishaq Khan, who helped to contain the political fall out of the differences between the government and the military commanders by acting as a bridge and a buffer. This crucial relationship was damaged when, after having neutralized the PPP-led 'Long March' in December 1992, Nawaz Sharif's young and over-ambitious advisers thought of pushing Ishaq Khan aside so that they could assume full command of the political system. This was an imprudent move because, given the internal weaknesses of the ruling IJI, complaints of misuse of state resources and corruption by senior figures in the government, and a virtual breakdown of relationships with the opposition, the government could not afford to alienate the constitutionally powerful President. Above all, Nawaz Sharif's relations with the senior commanders were not such that he could pull their weight to his side.

Nawaz Sharif's troubles began when General Janjua died of a heart attack on 8 January 1993.[59] He and his associates wanted Lt.-General Muhammad Ashraf, Corps Commander of Lahore (Acting Army Chief after the death of Janjua), or another general of their choice to be appointed as the new Army Chief.[60] Ishaq Khan was aware of Nawaz Sharif's connections with General Ashraf and, therefore, used his discretionary powers to appoint the little known General, Abdul Waheed Kaker,[61] to the position instead.

Nawaz Sharif retaliated by declaring towards the end of January that his government would strip Ishaq Khan of his discretionary powers under the 8th Amendment. This was a reversal of his earlier policy of support to the retention of the President's discretionary powers. Now, Nawaz Sharif decided to work towards reducing the powers of the President and talked of fundamental changes in the political system.[62] Later, the ruling IJI and the Muslim League circles indicated that they might not nominate Ishaq Khan as their candidate in the presidential elections due towards the end of the year.

By early March, an open confrontation had started between Ishaq Khan and Nawaz Sharif on the powers of the President. The government appointed a committee to suggest changes to the constitution and the federal ministers issued statement after statement describing the 8th Amendment as a threat to parliamentary democracy and that the Prime Minister should be entrusted with all the executive powers of the federation. Ishaq Khan defended his enhanced powers and, given his connections in the bureaucracy and political circles, began to pull strings to counter the Prime Minister's moves. This revived the intra-party rift in the ruling PML whose roots went back to the short-lived split after the dismissal of the Junejo government in 1988. The erstwhile supporters of Junejo in the PML sided with Ishaq Khan. The pro-Nawaz leaders who dominated the PML in the Punjab, decided to hold party elections in the Punjab in order to oust pro-Junejo elements. The party chief, Junejo, who was seriously ill, opposed the holding of elections in one province. His death on 18 March resulted in an open struggle for the control of the PML between these groups. Three federal ministers, two ministers of state and one adviser resigned from the cabinet and joined with several members of the National Assembly to declare their support for Ishaq Khan. The PDA and especially the PPP derived grudging satisfaction from the conflict between the erstwhile partners.

In early April, Nawaz Sharif backtracked by offering to nominate Ishaq Khan as the candidate of the ruling party for the next presidential elections and the campaign against presidential powers was stopped. This did not calm Ishaq Khan who felt betrayed by Nawaz Sharif whom he had helped to rise to power. In another bid to defuse the situation, Nawaz Sharif met Ishaq Khan and General Abdul Waheed separately. However, Ishaq Khan was in no mood to forget and forgive; the conflict persisted and adversely affected political management on the part of the government.

On 17 April, Nawaz Sharif delivered a hard hitting speech against Ishaq Khan on radio and television, accusing him of conspiring to dislodge him from power. Such a defiant public posture was ill-advised as he did not have the support of the major political parties other than his loyalists in the PML. He also did not enjoy support in the Army whose top brass were further annoyed by his public denunciation of the President.[63] As expected, Ishaq Khan moved quickly for a decisive blow, first by seeking the blessing of the Army Chief which was readily available, and then by approaching the PPP for support. Benazir Bhutto assured him of her support on the condition of Nawaz Sharif's removal. After securing his flanks, Ishaq Khan dismissed Nawaz Sharif on charges of corruption, nepotism, terrorizing opponents, violation of the constitution and subversion of the authority of the armed forces. The National Assembly was dissolved and new elections were scheduled for 14 July. Balakh Sher Mazari, a member of the dissolved National Assembly, was appointed caretaker Prime Minister. The Army helped to implement the dismissal order by taking control of important government buildings, including the radio and television stations in Islamabad. The Army Chief and Chairman, Joint Chiefs of Staff Committee, were present when Ishaq Khan announced the dismissal.

Two important developments took place in the immediate aftermath of the dismissal of Nawaz Sharif. First, the divide in the PML was formalized when, on 19 April, the supporters of Nawaz Sharif elected him as its President. The press labelled this group as the PML-Nawaz or (N). Those who stayed away were described as the PML-Junejo or (J), who later elected Hamid Nasir Chatha as their President. Second, a revolt against the Chief Minister of the Punjab, Ghulam Hyder Wayne, a protégé of Nawaz Sharif, in the Provincial Assembly led to the passage of a vote of no confidence against him after an extremely noisy session. He was succeeded by Mian Manzoor Ahmad Wattoo, hitherto Speaker of the Assembly with the support of the PML-J, the PPP and some independent members, thereby dislodging the pro-Nawaz Sharif elements from power in the Punjab.

A legal battle ensued when the ousted leadership filed a writ against the dismissal order in the Supreme Court. From the first day, Chief Justice Nasim Hassan Shah created the impression by his comments that the Supreme Court would restore the National Assembly and the government. These statements helped Nawaz Sharif to sustain political support and reinforced doubts in the establishment as to the advisability of the dismissal. In a meeting of the Corps Commanders after the dismissal, some commanders expressed partial reservations on the dismissal decision and underlined the need to maintain an absolutely neutral posture in the power struggle between the President and the Prime Minister. However, they agreed that the conflict had negative implications for stability and security and decided to monitor its 'fall-out' closely.[64]

The Supreme Court by a majority of ten to one delivered the judgement on 26 May that the President was 'not within the ambit of the powers' conferred on him by the constitution and that his action was 'without lawful author- ity'. The National Assembly and the government of Nawaz Sharif were restored.[65] The judgement conferred legal legitimacy on the Sharif govern- ment, but it continued to suffer from a crisis of political legitimacy. The confrontation with the President did not attenuate and the restored federal government made no secret of its desire to get rid of Ishaq Khan. In this effort the Sharif government developed problems with the provincial gov- ernments of NWFP, Sindh and the Punjab which distanced themselves from Nawaz Sharif's anti-Ishaq disposition.

A major confrontation developed in the Punjab when the Sharif camp tried to take control of that province by ousting the pro-Ishaq government of Manzoor Wattoo. In order to pre-empt such an attempt, the Governor, a nominee of Ishaq Khan, dissolved the provincial assembly on 29 May on the recommendation of Chief Minister Wattoo while the pro-Nawaz elements filed a motion for a vote of no confidence against Wattoo and abducted the Secretary of the Punjab Assembly who could verify the time of submission of the no confidence motion. They also filed a writ in the High Court main- taining that as they had submitted the notice for a no confidence motion before Wattoo had recommended dissolution to the Governor, the Assembly could not be dissolved.[66] Though the Secretary of the Assembly was not available to verify the timing of the notice, the Punjab High Court restored the Assembly and Wattoo's government on 28 June. Shortly afterwards, the Governor again dissolved the Assembly on Wattoo's recommendation before the PML-N could file a new no confidence motion.

Nawaz Sharif adopted another strategy to capture the Punjab. On 29 June, a joint session of parliament was summoned to discuss some routine matters as a smoke screen while Nawaz Sharif called on Ishaq Khan to ask him to remove the Punjab Governor, Chaudhry Altaf Hussain, and appoint his nominee, Mian Muhammad Azhar, in his place. When Ishaq Khan refused, Nawaz Sharif went to the parliament house and asked his Minister for Parliamentary Affairs to move a resolution which had already been secretly prepared, calling for the takeover of the Punjab government by the federal government. The resolution was adopted in the face of strong protest by the opposition with 145 votes in favour out of total of 287 members.

The resolution laid the groundwork for the takeover of the Punjab by the Nawaz Sharif government. It called on the President to assume all the powers of the Governor and the Chief Minister under article 234(1) of the Constitution who would then authorize Mian Muhammad Azhar (des- ignated as Administrator) to exercise all the executive powers of the province. The provincial assembly would be restored and Wattoo would be asked to seek a vote of confidence. If he failed to do so, a new Chief Minister would be selected as laid down in the constitution.[67]

Nawaz Sharif and his associates knew that Ishaq Khan would not issue such a Presidential Proclamation. They decided to bypass him by issuing a Presidential Proclamation the same night (29–30 June) without his knowledge or authorization. Mian Muhammad Azhar was appointed Administrator of the Punjab, although there was no such office in the constitution. A new Chief Secretary and I.G. Police were appointed and the federal government ordered that the Rangers (paramilitary) be placed at their disposal for implementation of the Proclamation. Later, Mian Azhar approached the Chief of the Rangers (a senior Army officer) and the Corps Commander, Lahore, for that purpose.[68] In the meanwhile, Governor Altaf Hussain and Chief Minister Wattoo approached Ishaq Khan who informed them that he had not authorized any such Proclamation. The same information was communicated to the Army Chief and the Lahore Corps Commander, who refused to make the Rangers available which foiled the bid to take over the Punjab.

The Army commanders sought expert opinion on the legal aspects of the action which disputed the legality of the Presidential Proclamation issued by the federal government without the approval of the President. The Army Chief and other senior commanders decided to step in to contain the crisis. A special meeting of the Corps Commanders was held on 1 July, which underlined the need to use constitutional and legal methods for resolving the political crisis. They favoured the holding of fresh elections as suggested by most political circles. The consensus of the senior commanders was communicated to the President and the Prime Minister by the Army Chief.

The PDA was infuriated by the federal government's attempt to take over the Punjab government. It reiterated the demand for holding new elections at the earliest and decided to undertake a 'Long March' to Islamabad and blockade the capital on 16 July in support of its demand. As the PDA enjoyed the support of the Punjab and NWFP governments, the 'Long March' was expected to succeed.

The Army Chief held several meetings with the President and the Prime Minister for a satisfactory solution of the President–Prime Minister conflict against the backdrop of the PDA threat to blockade Islamabad. A summary of these meetings during 11–18 July is given below:

11 July: General Abdul Waheed held a meeting with Ishaq Khan.
The federal government asked the Army and the paramilitary forces to take up security duties for Islamabad on 16 July in order to cope with the PDA 'Long March'.

12 July: Ishaq Khan and Nawaz Sharif met twice.

13 July: Nawaz Sharif held separate meetings with Ishaq Khan and General Abdul Waheed.

14 July: Troops moved into Islamabad, as the federal government requested.
15 July: Ishaq Khan, Nawaz Sharif and General Abdul Waheed held joint and separate meetings.

Benazir Bhutto flew from Lahore to Islamabad in an army aircraft for a meeting with General Abdul Waheed. He assured her that the Army was working towards settling the modalities for holding fresh elections and that the postponement of the 'Long March' would facilitate its task. Benazir Bhutto called off the 'Long March', which won her the goodwill of the Army.

16 July: Ishaq Khan, Nawaz Sharif, and General Abdul Waheed held a meeting. Benazir Bhutto called on Ishaq Khan. The Chief Ministers of the Punjab and NWFP met with General Abdul Waheed.
17 July: Ishaq Khan, Nawaz Sharif and General Abdul Waheed met, at least twice.
18 July: Ishaq Khan, Nawaz Sharif and General Waheed met to finalize the modalities of transfer of power. This was followed by the dissolution of the National Assembly, resignation of Nawaz Sharif, appointment of a caretaker Prime Minister, and resignation of Ishaq Khan.

Nawaz Sharif maintained a defiant posture in the initial stages of the negotiations and insisted on the removal of Ishaq Khan who was accused of being responsible for the political crisis. The government-controlled media launched a propaganda offensive against Ishaq Khan. Some of Nawaz Sharif's well-known supporters advised the Army to cleanse the presidency of conspiracies and that Ishaq Khan should be removed the way Iskander Mirza was ousted by the senior generals in 1958.[69] Even after agreeing to the Army's proposal for new elections Nawaz Sharif wanted Ishaq Khan to be removed from office and that he should continue as caretaker Prime Minister during the election period. This was not acceptable to the PDA; it wanted a non-partisan caretaker administration.

The Army Chief brokered an arrangement that both Ishaq Khan and Nawaz Sharif would resign and new elections would he held under a non-partisan administration. Nawaz Sharif insisted that Ishaq Khan should resign first and that he would tender his advice for the dissolution of the National Assembly as well as his resignation to the acting President. Ishaq Khan maintained that as the head of state he would resign after announcing the dissolution of the National Assembly and administering the oath of office to the caretaker Prime Minister. The Army commanders were favourably disposed towards the second course of action and the Army Chief assured Nawaz Sharif that Ishaq Khan would quit after his resignation. He also suggested that he could secure Ishaq Khan's resignation but that would be announced after the caretaker Prime Minister had been installed. However, Nawaz Sharif would not budge and insisted that Ishaq Khan should resign first. When the Army's efforts to resolve the crisis appeared to be faltering, two senior aides of General Abdul Waheed told Nawaz Sharif in a threatening tone that he should stop dragging his feet. Nawaz Sharif caved in, albeit reluctantly.[70] Dr Moeen Qureshi, a Pakistani economist who served the World Bank in a senior position, was selected as caretaker Prime Minister with the consent of the the PML-N, the PDA and the top brass of the Army.

It was late at night on 18 July that Nawaz Sharif submitted his advice for the dissolution of the National Assembly along with his resignation to Ishaq Khan in the presence of the Army Chief. Ishaq Khan dissolved the National Assembly and announced the holding of new national and provincial elections on 6 and 9 October respectively. It was after midnight, when the new date, i.e. 19 July, had started, when Ishaq Khan administered the oath of office to the caretaker Prime Minister, Dr Moeen Qureshi, and then submitted his own resignation which was to become effective after he availed of four months leave. The Chairman of the Senate, Wasim Sajjad, assumed the presidency in an acting capacity. New Provincial Governors and caretaker Chief Ministers assumed power the next day.

Benazir Bhutto's Second Term

The October 1993 elections reconfirmed the pre-eminent position of two political parties: the PPP and the PML-N, although none was in a position to form a government on its own. The PPP won 86 seats in the National Assembly and its allied party, the PML-J, got 6 seats. The PML-N secured 73 seats; 15 seats went to independent candidates. The MQM boycotted the National Assembly elections and participated only in the Provincial Assembly elections in Sindh. Its party leaders maintained that they were forced by the Army/ISI to boycott the National Assembly elections. In the case of the Provincial Assemblies, no political party got an absolute majority except in Sindh where the PPP secured a clear majority with 56 seats. In the Punjab, the PPP won 94 seats and its allied party, the PML-J, got 18 seats. The PML-N captured 104 seats. The position of the major political parties in the NWFP Assembly was: PPP 22, ANP 21, PML-N 15. The situation in Balochistan was quite confused because 40 general seats were shared by 11 political parties and independents, with the PML-N and *Jamhoori Watan Party* (JWP) topping the list with six and five seats respectively; the PPP won only three seats.

The PPP and the PML-J formed an alliance – Pakistan Democratic Front (PDF) – and obtained the support of some small parties and independent members to cobble together a majority, making it possible for Benazir Bhutto to assume power for the second time on 19 October. The PDF also formed governments in the Punjab and Sindh. The PML-N and the ANP formed a coalition government in NWFP, but, in almost six months, the PPP managed to dislodge this government and installed its own government. A coalition government headed by a PML-N leader was formed in Balochistan.

The presidential elections were held on 13 November and the PPP candidate, Sardar Farooq Ahmad Khan Leghari, was elected with a comfortable majority.

Benazir Bhutto thus started her second term with a clear advantage of having two (later three) provincial governments under her control and the party nominee was holding the presidency; the military was also willing to extend the necessary support to the newly elected government. However, by 5 November 1996, when her government was dismissed, she was more isolated than was the case when her first government was removed. Much of this can be explained with reference to her personalized style of rule, not being amenable to advice, political management through a group of cronies (most of whom were non-elected), and the interference of her husband (Asif Ali Zardari) in government affairs. Other factors that contributed to her downfall included the failure to cope with the political and economic crises, intense confrontation with the opposition, ethnic and religious sectarian violence, corruption in government, and confrontation with the superior judiciary and the President.

Unlike her first term, Benazir Bhutto avoided interference in the internal affairs of the military and generally respected their autonomy. The Troika functioned smoothly until early 1996. The President, the Prime Minister and the Army Chief used to meet periodically to discuss important foreign policy and security issues and domestic affairs. The relationship with the military was so cordial that the civilian government offered a one-year extension of service to General Abdul Waheed, which he declined. General Jehangir Karamat, the most senior officer, succeeded him on 13 January 1996. Benazir Bhutto was reported to be initially inclined towards another general but consultations with Farooq Leghari resulted in consensus on Jehangir Karamat.

The government continued to assign priority to the requirements of the defence services and the budgetary allocations were not reduced despite strong pressure from the International Monetary Fund (IMF) and the World Bank. There was no change in the policy of inducting serving and retired military personnel to civil services and other lucrative jobs. During 1995–6, three out of four provincial Governors were retired senior officers of the Army.[71] The 1994–5 budget gave a 35 per cent rise in salaries of the civil servants and the military personnel. In the case of the latter this was made effective on the passage of the budget, but the former were given this rise in two instalments spread over a year.

Two foreign policy issues of direct interest to the military were dealt with in a satisfactory manner by the Benazir government. Its active diplomacy resulted in the removal of Pakistan's name from the US Department of State's watch list of states sponsoring terrorism. Benazir Bhutto's visit to the US in April 1995 set the stage for the passage of the Brown Amendment, which released the military equipment and weapons withheld in the US since October 1990 when the Pressler Amendment was invoked to block these transactions. The US also agreed in principle to return the money Pakistan had paid for the purchase of F-16 aircraft by selling these to some other country. The Pakistan–US Consultative Group on security matters was revived. These developments served the military's professional interests.

The Army's security operation in Sindh (initiated in May 1992 when Nawaz Sharif was in power) was brought to an end on 30 November 1994, by the Army's own decision, although the provincial government wanted this to continue for another six months or so. The provincial government relied on the reinforced Police and the Rangers to deal with the law and order situation in Sindh but, on occasions, it had to summon the regular troops. The Army was associated permanently with anti-narcotics operations.

The government benefited from the repeated criticism of the Army by the PML-N in 1993–4. Nawaz Sharif and the PML-N leaders, bitter at the loss of power, were very critical of the role of the Army commanders. Some of them claimed that Benazir Bhutto's July 1993 threat to blockade Islamabad had the blessings of the Army. This relationship was further soured by Nawaz Sharif's two statements in 1994. In a public meeting in Azad Kashmir, on 23 August, he attempted to subvert the dialogue between Pakistan and the US for removal of obstacles to weapons procurement by announcing that Pakistan possessed nuclear weapons.[72] In September, Nawaz Sharif accused the senior commanders of proposing the sale of narcotics, i.e. heroin, in order to generate funds for their covert operations. This was a *Washington Post* story, which quoted him as saying that, in early 1991, the then Army Chief, General Beg, and the then Director General of the ISI, Lt.-General Asad Durani, had made such a proposal.[73] This was categorically denied by the Army and the officers named in the statement.[74] These efforts by Nawaz Sharif to get even with the Army damaged his reputation with the military, enabling the government to project itself as a friend.

What got the Benazir government into trouble in 1996 was its abysmal performance in the civilian sector and its failure for the second time to provide an effective and transparent administration. Initially, the government adopted some measures for socio-economic development, and projects were launched for health care, the advancement of women and environmental improvement. Some financial relief was provided to the small investors who had lost their investments due to the collapse of several private finance development institutions (the Taj Company and the cooperative investment companies).[75] New projects were approved for power-generation and improvement of infrastructural facilities, partly with foreign collaboration. However, it was not long before these programmes lost their momentum due to defective planning, poor management and resource constraints. Inflation, price hikes, devaluation of the Pakistani currency by 7 per cent in October 1995 and periodic downward adjustments of the Rupee's exchange value in 1996, imposition of new taxes in the 1995 and 1996 budgets, and enhanced duties on several import items increased economic pressures on the middle and lower middle levels of the society. The much talked about New Social Contract and a new administrative set up at the district level were not implemented. The local bodies suspended by the caretaker government were not revived. When, in June 1996, the Supreme Court restored the local bodies in the Punjab, the government rushed a law through the assembly to neutralize the judgement.[76]

The government played up economic and political mismanagement and corruption by the Sharif government (1990–3). From time to time, investigative reports were released to show how Nawaz Sharif, his family members and close associates obtained bank loans and other material benefits to build their financial and industrial empires and how they obtained kickbacks or engaged in an indiscrete use of state resources. However, it was not long before similar stories began to circulate about some of the leading figures in the PPP government, including the husband of Benazir Bhutto, Asif Ali Zardari. The news about the purchase of a huge mansion in Surrey, England, by Benazir and Zardari in June 1996, damaged the reputation of the government.

Ethnic violence intensified in Karachi and Hyderabad in 1995–6, as the MQM activists and the law enforcement agencies (the police and the Rangers) confronted each other. Amid this confrontation a nexus among organized crime, drug mafia, Afghan war veterans and the MQM hardcore developed, resulting in indiscriminate killings by unidentified gunmen, arson and looting of government and private property. Unable to find a political solution,[77] the government gave a relatively free hand to the police and Rangers, who used excessive force to control the situation. A number of accused died in police custody or in encounters with the police under mysterious circumstances, described by the press as 'extra-judicial' killings.

The writ of the government was also challenged by orthodox Islamic groups, some of whom secured weapons through their connections with the Afghan resistance groups. During 1994–5, extreme religious groups in Malakand and the Khyber Agency took up arms in pursuance of their demand for the implementation of the *Sharia* (Islamic religious) law in their areas. Other type of religion-oriented violence pertained to the invoking of the blasphemy law of the Zia era against religious minorities and physical assaults on the Ahmadis; the government was often unable to protect them. In order to release pressure on the minorities, the government decided to make changes in the blasphemy law. The PML-N and the Islamic groups joined together to resist the proposed changes, forcing the government to abandon the effort. Some violence resulted from religious sectarian killings, mainly but not exclusively in the Punjab as two extreme groups of the *Shia* and the *Sunni* Muslims engaged in armed gang warfare. In November 1995, the Egyptian embassy in Islamabad was destroyed in a bomb blast the responsibility for which was taken by three Arab militant groups who threatened to take similar action against Pakistan if its government did not relent on the Arab volunteers associated with the Afghan resistance groups.

The ruling PPP and the opposition PML-N continued to engage in combative political discourse. The latter confronted the PPP government on each and every issue. Its members engaged in rowdyism on the floor of the assemblies and openly preached defiance of the government, accusing Benazir Bhutto of being a threat to national security. For about a year, the government maintained a low-key posture towards the opposition. When the confrontation did not subside, it decided to hit back by using the state apparatus. A number of opposition leaders and activists, including the father and brother of Nawaz Sharif, were involved in criminal cases, arrested or harassed by the state agencies. Such a state of affairs mounted serious strains on the political process and accentuated the problem of political management.

Benazir Bhutto created additional problems by antagonizing the superior judiciary when her government appointed 20 judges to the Lahore High Court in August 1994, 13 of whom were PPP activists and three PML-J supporters. Some of them did not regularly practise law at the High Court level and had a dubious professional reputation. Nawaz Sharif had also appointed his loyalists to the High Court during 1990–3; these appointments were criticized in legal circles and some of these judges were not confirmed. Benazir Bhutto was more determined to 'pack' the upper judiciary with her loyalists, which irked the superior judiciary. Instead of allaying their concerns, the government built pressures on Chief Justice Sajjad Ali Shah (appointed to this post by the Benazir government) to dissuade him from taking up an appeal filed against the appointment of new judges.[78] The Supreme Court judgement, announced on 20 March 1996, drastically curtailed the powers of the executive to appoint and transfer the judges of the superior judiciary.[79] Later, in pursuance of this judgement, the Chief Justices of different High Courts did not recommend the confirmation of all the judges appointed in 1994. Meanwhile, a couple of other judgements, reflecting a new mood of activism on the part of the judiciary, exerted serious pressures on the government.[80] Benazir Bhutto viewed this as a conspiracy and refused to implement the Supreme Court judgement on the appointment of judges. The Chief Justice approached President Farooq Leghari who persuaded Benazir Bhutto to endorse the recommendation of the Chief Justice on the appointment/confirmation of the judges.

Farooq Leghari's insistence on the implementation of the judgement caused a breach between him and Benazir Bhutto. Their differences widened when Farooq Leghari raised the issue of illicit money-making by senior members of the government, including her husband, Asif Zardari's involvement in various kickback scandals. He also asked Benazir Bhutto to set up a parliamentary select committee to look into the corruption problem.[81] Benazir Bhutto rejected the advice and inducted Asif Zardari in her cabinet as Investment Minister, thereby giving him a direct role in senior policy-making. Leghari responded by proposing to the Chairman of the Senate, Wasim Sajjad, and the Speaker of the National Assembly, Yousaf Raza Gilani, to set up a permanent commission for investigation into political corruption. Leghari also wrote directly to the Provincial Governors on the deteriorating law and order situation and rampant corruption in the government. He built additional pressures by sending communications to the Prime Minister on her government's policy lapses and failures to fulfil constitutional obligations. It was in this setting that Benazir's estranged brother, Murtaza Bhutto, who had set up his own faction of the PPP, was killed along with his security staff in an encounter with the police in Karachi on 20 September. Benazir viewed the murder of her brother as a part of the conspiracy to dislodge her government and hinted at the involvement of Leghari and the MI.[82] Leghari and Benazir Bhutto had several meetings in October and early November, but they could not resolve their differences. The two sides used the intelligence agencies in their confrontation. The Benazir government used the IB to tap the telephones of the President and his son, the Chief Justice, and some senior civil and military officials. A similar strategy was adopted by Leghari, who relied on the ISI for monitoring the Prime Minister's house.[83]

The opposition parties were happy to see Leghari and Benazir Bhutto on the warpath. They cultivated Leghari to encourage him to dismiss Benazir Bhutto.[84] The *Jamaat-i-Islami* mobilized its cadre to stage a massive sit-in in Islamabad on 27–28 October, which exposed the fragility of support for the government. Some unofficial circles floated the proposal to set up a government of technocrats for coping with the economic crisis. What jolted the besieged Benazir government and raised serious doubts about its future was the Punjab High Court's judgement on 3 November restoring the Wattoo government in the Punjab in place of the Nakai government, which the PPP had installed a year earlier.

General Jehangir Karamat did not take sides in the Leghari–Benazir dispute. However, the top brass were perturbed by the confrontation Benazir Bhutto had instigated with the Chief Justice and the President. They were also concerned about corruption and economic and fiscal mismanagement. The government's reputation with the military was further damaged by the fast deteriorating law and order situation[85] and the ongoing confrontation with the opposition. In August, the Army submitted its assessment of the economic conditions to the President warning him of an economic disaster unless some remedial measures were adopted.[86] By mid-October, the senior commanders were convinced that the government was no longer in a position to cope with the economic crisis and that it could not ensure a minimum socio-political stability. Under these circumstances, Leghari had no difficulty in enlisting the Army Chief's support to dismiss the Benazir government.

The dismissal on 5 November was carried out in coup style. The Army took control of the Prime Minister's house and secretariat, and Benazir Bhutto was not allowed any communication with her colleagues for several hours. The

Army also took over the headquarters of the IB and other important government installations. For the first time, all airports were closed and mobile phones were shutoff. In Lahore, the Army cordoned off the Governor's official residence where Asif Ali Zardari was staying. He was taken into custody and handed over to the civilian authorities; the Governor was put under virtual house arrest and subsequently resigned. Within a few hours, the regular troops were replaced in Lahore with a paramilitary force. The Army Corps headquarters in the four provincial capitals were open throughout the night of dismissal and passed on the initial instructions of the presidency and the Army headquarters to top civil servants.

The President framed several charges against the Benazir government in the dismissal order. Some of these were familiar while others were new and included non-implementation of the judgement of the Supreme Court, attempts to destroy the independence of judiciary through the proposed accountability law, the bugging of telephones of senior officials and judges, and 'extra-judicial' killings.[87] Later, Leghari identified the 'imminent economic collapse' as another cause of the dismissal of the government.[88]

Leghari consulted Jehangir Karamat on the appointment of Malik Meraj Khalid, a veteran PPP leader now alienated from Benazir Bhutto, as caretaker Prime Minister; two provincial Governors and all Chief Ministers were also replaced. The Army extended support to the caretaker administration and entrenched itself by inducting more officers in the senior civilian jobs,[89] including induction of more military personnel in the IB, thereby minimizing the autonomy of this civilian intelligence agency.[90] The Army also proposed the setting up of a security council as a forum for accommodating the top brass in the decision-making process during the interim period.[91] Leghari, who wanted more tangible identification of the military with his caretaker set-up, established a full-fledged Council for Defence and National Security (CDNS) in the first week of January 1997 without consulting the caretaker Prime Minister. Modelled on Zia-ul-Haq's National Security Council, the CDNS was assigned an advisory role on foreign and security policies and internal affairs.[92] It evoked such a sharp criticism from the political circles that the Army Chief distanced himself from the decision and the CDNS did not meet after the elected government of Nawaz Sharif took over in February, although it was not formally abandoned.

Nawaz Sharif's Second Term

The general elections were held on 3 February 1997 after a lacklustre campaign which focused on the performance of the Benazir government and especially its economic mismanagement and corruption. The Army helped the civilian administration in the conduct of the elections, which were generally peaceful and orderly. The turn-out was very low. The official sources claimed it to be 35.92 per cent., but the unofficial sources maintained that not more than 25 per cent of the electorate voted. As expected, the PPP lost badly at both the national and provincial levels. What surprised most was the magnitude of the PPP defeat – the biggest ever in its history. It won only 18 seats in the National Assembly, all from Sindh. Its performance was equally disappointing in the provincial elections, winning two seats in the Punjab, one each in NWFP and Balochistan and 34 in Sindh. The PML-N performed exceptionally well at both the national and provincial levels, and Nawaz Sharif emerged as a truly national leader. In the National Assembly, the PML-N won 134 out of 207 general seats. It swept the provincial polls in the Punjab (211 out of 240 general seats). In NWFP, it obtained 32 seats and its allied party, the ANP, won 29 seats. It made considerable gains in Sindh, although the PPP and the MQM had an edge with 34 and 28 seats respectively.

Nawaz Sharif became Prime Minister for the second time on 17 February, obtaining 177 votes in a house of 217 members; the PML-N was able to obtain the support of the MQM, the ANP and some independent members. The PML-N also assumed power in three provinces: a totally PML-N government in the Punjab led by Shahbaz Sharif, younger brother of Nawaz Sharif, and coalition governments in Sindh (PML, MQM and Independents) and NWFP (PML, ANP, and independents). In Balochistan, two regional parties, the Balochistan National Party (BNP) and *Jamhoori Watan Party* (JWP), formed a coalition with the help of a number of smaller groups. In August 1998, this government was replaced with a PML-N led coalition.

The new government started with popular support and goodwill of the military and the President. A host of measures were adopted for socio-economic development. These included the March 1997 economic package, the loan retirement scheme, the 2010 Programme for good governance and socio-economic transformation, the June 1998 National Agenda for a cut-back in expenditure on administration, recovery of overdue bank loans and job opportunities for unemployed youth. Some tax and tariff reliefs were provided in 1997 to encourage ecnomic activity and steps were announced to broaden the tax base. The government secured a low-interest loan of $1.6 billion from the IMF under the Extended Structural Adjustment Facility (ESAF), subject to several structural changes in the economy. The first two instalments of this loan were received in October 1997 and March 1998.

However, these efforts did not produce the desired results because the government lacked the political will to pursue the policy measures, especially tax collection and recovery of overdue bank loans from the politically influential people. The deteriorating law and order situation also adversely affected the economy. Above all, Nawaz Sharif's obsession with power took precedence over all other considerations, compromising the imperatives of transparent, judicious and effective governance. Haunted by the fear of another dismissal, Nawaz Sharif used his parliamentary majority to concentrate power in his hands at the expense of other state institutions. This disturbed the delicate balance of power at the highest level, producing new strains in the political system.

A constitutional amendment (13th), approved by parliament in a couple of hours on 1 April 1997, withdrew the power of the President to dismiss the government and to dissolve the National Assembly at his discretion. The President's power to appoint the chiefs of the three services and some other key government functionaries was also curtailed; he could no longer set aside the recommendation of the Prime Minister for such appointments. Another amendment (14th), approved in a brief session in July, equipped Nawaz Sharif with enough power to contain dissent within the ruling party. The amendment empowered the party leader to remove his party member from parliament or a provincial assembly on a number of grounds, i.e. violation of party discipline, defection, voting against or abstaining from voting when the party had issued its directive, and involvement in activities against the party interest. The party leader was made the final authority to judge the conduct of the members on these matters with no recourse to the judiciary or any independent authority available to the accused. This virtually created the dictatorship of the party leader and secured Nawaz Sharif against any intra-party dissension.

The new accountability law passed by parliament in May diluted the autonomous role of the accountability process established by the caretaker government. The power to appoint the Chief Accountability Commissioner shifted from the President to the Prime Minister and the latter's secretariat was given a key role in initiating and investigating the charges of corruption against the political leaders and senior civil servants. Furthermore, the period from 1985 to 1990 was excluded from the purview of the accountability law, thereby sheltering Nawaz Sharif's tenure as the Punjab's Chief Minister when he had used the state patronage in a highly partisan manner.[93] As expected, the Prime Minister's Accountability Bureau, headed by a business man and close friend of Nawaz Sharif who was also elected to the Senate on the PML-N ticket, targeted the PPP, and especially Benazir Bhutto and her husband, and senior civil servants who held key positions in the Benazir government.

An Anti-Terrorism Act (ATA) was introduced in August which empowered the law enforcement agencies *inter alia* to conduct house searches and arrest without warrant. Special courts were established to decide the cases under the ATA within 30 days. However the level of violence did not decline nor were these special courts able to dispose of the cases within the prescribed time frame. Human rights groups and the opposition objected to the arbitrary powers of the ATA and the superior judiciary took exception to the setting up of special anti-terrorist courts. It was not until October 1998 that some of the arbitrary features of the ATA were diluted.

While strengthening its position, the government took care to avoid triggering negative reaction from the military. Before introducing the 13th constitutional amendment, the Prime Minister consulted the Army Chief General Jehangir Karamat.[94] He was also consulted before the government asked the Naval Chief to resign over his alleged involvement in kickbacks in defence deals in April 1997, and on the appointment of a new Naval Chief. The government continued with the established practice of inducting military officers into the civil services and other important jobs. The initial approval of re-employment of several senior Army officers granted by the caretaker government was confirmed and it also agreed to the induction of officers between the ranks of Captain and Colonel on a permanent basis into the police, the IB and the Federal Investigation Agency (FIA).[95] This enabled the Army to accommodate officers denied promotion or due for retirement. Another gesture was the appointment of Lt.-General Moeenuddin Haider as Governor of Sindh in March 1997 within a week of his retirement, although the Prime Minister wanted to appoint an MQM nominee to this post. Lt.-General Muhammad Arif Bangash, appointed Governor of NWFP in November 1996 by the caretaker administration, was kept in post. A significant move by the government was the acceptance of the Army headquarters' proposal to allow the Army Chief simultaneously to hold the post of Chairman of Joint Chiefs of Staff Committee when its incumbent Air Chief Martial Farooq Feroz Khan retired on 9 November 1997. The May 1998 decision to make Pakistan an overt nuclear weapons power was taken by the Prime Minister on the recommendation of the top commanders.

The top brass were favourably disposed towards the powers of the President to dismiss the government because this made it easy for them to bring about a change of government without actually assuming power. They agreed to the change out of respect for the electoral mandate of Nawaz Sharif and to give him a fair chance to prove his capabilities. The military made another gesture by not insisting on the revival of the CDNS and agreed to a nominal increase of 2 per cent in the 1997–8 defence expenditure. Yet another gesture was to let the government seek the resignation of the Naval Chief. The top brass agreed to this as a damage control operation in view of the media focus on kickbacks in defence purchases and the arrest of an Air Force officer on a charge of drug trafficking in the US. They wanted to show civilians that they did not protect the alleged corruption of their colleagues. However, the Army Chief took strong exception to the propaganda against the military and the attempt to drag the Air Force Chief into a similar kickback scandal. The Prime Minister assuaged the Army Chief by dissociating the government from the propaganda.[96]

Nawaz Sharif's strategy caused a serious conflict with the senior judiciary when he attempted to curtail the powers of the Chief Justice of the Supreme Court for the appointment of new judges. In August 1997, Chief Justice Sajjad Ali Shah recommended that the vacant positions in the Supreme Court be filled by elevating three Chief Justices of provincial High Courts and two senior judges of the Lahore High Court. The government did not want to promote at least two of them, one of whom had in the past given judgements that adversely affected Nawaz Sharif's industrial empire. It scuttled the recommendation by reducing the strength of the Supreme Court by issuing an executive order. As the legal circles protested, the government withdrew the executive order, but threatened to do the same in parliament. This triggered a serious confrontation between the senior judiciary and the executive. Later, the Prime Minister agreed to appoint the judges recommended by the Chief Justice on the prodding by the President and the Army Chief.

Taking advantage of the confrontation, opposition leaders filed several court challenges against Nawaz Sharif and the constitutional and legal changes he had introduced. The Supreme Court took up these cases and, on 29 October, suspended the 14th constitutional amendment on the defection of the members of the parliament. The government viewed this as an attempt by the court to dislodge it from power. Nawaz Sharif described the court's order as 'illegal and unconstitutional', which would revive 'horse trading' in parliament. He also said that the Chief Justice had created an 'unfortunate' and 'undemocratic' situation.[97] The Supreme Court initiated contempt proceedings against Nawaz Sharif and others, who in turn retaliated by amending the contempt of court law through parliament. When President Leghari delayed signing the new legislation by invoking his constitutional powers to keep the bills pending for 30 days, the ruling party decided to impeach the President and reprimand the Chief Justice through the parliament.

Some of the judges who disagreed with the Chief Justice's strategy of confrontation with the government[98] were encouraged by the government to revolt. This caused the first ever split in the Supreme Court, with pro-government and pro-Chief Justice judges passing orders against each other. When the government supporters raided the court of the Chief Justice on 28 November to disrupt the contempt proceedings against the Prime Minister,[99] the Chief Justice asked the President and the Army Chief to deploy troops for the security of the court.[100] As the President endorsed the demand,[101] the battle-lines were clearly drawn between the government on the one hand and the Chief Justice and the President on the other. The opposition parties supported the Chief Justice.

The Army Chief played an autonomous and moderating role by advising the two sides to show restraint. He held meetings with the President, the Prime Minister and the Chief Justice either separately or together. When the Prime Minister threatened to initiate impeachment proceedings against the President and hinted at reprimanding the Chief Justice through parliament, the Army Chief again stepped in to restrain the Prime Minister. The respite did not last long and, as the Chief Justice continued with the contempt proceedings, the government managed to get the order for the suspension of the Chief Justice from two judges opposed to him. The Prime Minister then asked the President to appoint a new Chief Justice, which he refused. While the government repeated its threat to impeach the President, the Chief Justice restored the power of the President to remove the government. This order was immediately suspended by the pro-government judges. The Chief Justice in return suspended the order of the rival bench.

Without the Army's support, the President could neither avoid impeachment nor remove the Prime Minister. All previous government dismissals had been implemented through the Army. This time, the Army Chief decided not to support the President and adopted a neutral posture, enabling Nawaz Sharif to carry on with his quest for power. The Army's decision was based on a careful consideration of the political situation. Removing the Prime Minister and the dissolution of the National Assembly within one year of the elections would have been embarrassing, especially because the government's support – both in the parliament and outside – was still intact. Therefore, the ongoing confrontation was expected to persist and the caretaker administration would have faced problems in holding new elections. This was bound to affect the already faltering economy. The senior commanders therefore concluded that the exit of the President was the least problematic resolution of the conflict. On realizing this, the President decided to step down on 2 December. Subsequently, the Chief Justice was eased out because the acting President, Wasim Sajjad, accepted the government's recommendation for the appointment of a new Chief Justice. Nawaz Sharif also replaced the Leghari-appointed Acting Chief Election Commissioner because he had rejected the nomination papers of the ruling party's Presidential candidate.[102] Nawaz Sharif, with a comfortable majority in parliament and the four provincial assemblies, installed a family friend and political non-entity, Muhammad Rafiq Tarar, as President on 1 January 1998. The 'rules of business' were changed further to restrict the role of the President, and the Prime Minister's secretariat closely monitored the interaction between the President and the political parties.

Nawaz Sharif's quest for power and his personalized and whimsical political management alienated his political allies from the smaller provinces and ethno-national groups. The ANP was the first to withdraw support in February 1998 when the federal government refused to re-name NWFP as Pakhtoonkhwa. The ANP alleged that Nawaz Sharif had backed out of a commitment made in 1997 for this change. Another ethnic party, the MQM, which had joined the federal and Sindh provincial cabinets in 1997, developed serious differences with the ruling Musilim League on the handling of law and order in Karachi. As violence escalated and unidentified gunmen engaged in killing sprees, both random and targeted, which resulted in the deaths of several government functionaries, including a former provincial governor, the federal government accused the MQM hardcore of involvement in these killings. This caused a breach between the

MQM and the Sharif government. A small regional party, the JWP of Balochistan, also withdrew support and vowed to resist the centralized and authoritarian governance from Islamabad.

The imposition of a state of emergency on 28 May 1998, after Pakistan's nuclear tests, enabled Nawaz Sharif's federal government to amass more power. Though the Supreme Court restored fundamental rights in July, the Sharif government retained enough power to rule by decree and interfere in provincial governmental affairs. A change of government was manoeuvred in Balochistan in August and, on 30 October, the federal government assumed executive power in Sindh by imposing the Governor's rule, ostensibly to improve the law and order situation. In June 1999, the federal government transferred the provincial executive authority to a federal minister and senior member of the PML-N, although it was a minority party in Sindh. The MQM and the PPP, which had a majority in the provincial assembly, protested against this but the federal government neutralized the role of the provincial assembly under the provisions of the Governor's rule.

Pakistan faced a paradox. Nawaz Sharif had accumulated more power than any previous Prime Minister since Pakistan began its transition to democracy in 1985. However, the government's ability to evoke voluntary support at the popular level was on the decline and it presided over a weak and fragmented polity which faced a serious political and economic drift. Pakistan's predicament was accentuated with the imposition of economic sanctions by the international financial institutions and most donor states in the aftermath of its nuclear explosions. An abysmal management of the post-explosion political and economic situation, inflation, price hikes, poor revenue collection and fiscal mismanagement, corruption in government and heavy domestic and foreign debt burden haunted the polity. Additional challenges were posed by the stepped up Islamic sectarian violence mainly but not exclusively in the Punjab, and ethnic killings in Karachi.

The military high command was perturbed by these trends, especially by the growing alienation in the smaller provinces and polarization on regional lines. Furthermore, the deteriorating economic conditions had started adversely affecting the professional and corporate interests of the military. The Army Chief, Jehangir Karamat, publicly talked about the injurious implications of the economic drift and political dissension on internal stability and external security, and raised these matters with the government,[103] but to no effect. In the first week of October 1998, he vented his frustration by publicly underlining the need to create an institutional arrangement at the highest level for devising effective policies for coping with the ongoing problems. He maintained that such a body, a national security council, should be backed by a 'a team of credible advisers and a think tank of experts', and that Pakistan needed a 'neutral, competent and secure bureaucracy and administration at the federal and provincial levels'. He warned that Pakistan 'could not afford the destabilizing effects of polarization, vendettas and insecurity-expedient policies'.[104] This was a strong indictment of the government. When Nawaz Sharif expressed displeasure on the statement, the General decided to step down three months ahead of his retirement rather than withdraw his remarks. He was replaced by General Pervez Musharraf, an Urdu-speaking *mohajir* from Karachi, superseding two senior Pakhtoon and Punjabi generals. As the views expressed by Karamat represented the corporate opinion of the senior commanders, the new Army Chief was expected to pursue these. However, Nawaz Sharif hoped that a *mohajir* Army Chief presiding over a predominantly Punjabi-Pakhtoon high command would not build pressure on him. The official circles erroneously projected the episode as the triumph of the elected government over the military. This euphoria proved short lived. In November, the Sharif government sought the support of the Army to cope with the acute law and order situation in Karachi. It gave the Army a relatively free hand under Article 245 of the Constitution, including the powers to conduct criminal-investigations and set up military courts whose judgements could not be challenged in any civilian/regular court.[105] However, in February 1999, the Supreme Court declared the military courts to be unconstitutional.

The Sharif government's credibility eroded further on launching an ill-advised military expedition across the Line of Control in the Kargil sector of Kashmir in May 1999, and then, withdrawing its troops and volunteers under intense international pressure. Nawaz Sharif's domestic political adversaries, especially the Islamic parties, threatened to foment street agitation for his removal. The Army was also unhappy because the withdrawal decision was made by Nawaz Sharif without consulting the top brass.

In the meanwhile, the government leaned heavily on the Army to improve administrative efficiency and economic management Several civilian institutions were handed over to the Army and a large number of army personnel were inducted into civilian assignments.[106] Such an unprecedented induction of military personnel into civilian jobs and duties had not taken place even under military governments. This may temporarily save the polity from collapsing but it erodes the credibility of the civilian institutions and leaders. These problems and uncertainties of the civilian sector and the military's stake in policy-making enable the military to continue as a formidable political actor. The manifestation of this role will vary, depending on the orientations of the senior commanders (including their assessment of the available options), domestic political and economic conditions, and the international factors impinging on domestic politics.

11
The Changing Parameters

Long years in power have enabled the military to spread out so widely in the civilian institutions of the state and society that its presence is firmly established in all walks of life. It has carved out a role and position in the public and the private sectors, industry, business, agriculture, education and scientific development, health care, communications and transportation. Such an omnipresence ensures an important role for the military in the state and society even if the generals do not directly control the levers of power. Several factors have contributed to this. First, the military inducted its personnel in government and semi-government jobs and civilian professions. The private sector was encouraged to accommodate them. The military also contributed to improving their socio-economic conditions by distributing material rewards and facilities. Second, the military controls a vast industrial and business empire which has enabled it to amass sufficient clout in the economy and to develop a capacity for looking after the welfare of its personnel without relying on the civilian government. Third, the close links of the military personnel with the people of the Punjab and NWFP have also contributed to its political clout. This makes the study of ethnicity and recruitment pattern of the Army interesting and relevant to politics. Fourth, the civilian governments at the federal and provincial levels, overwhelmed by the problems of governance, seek the military's support more often than was the case in the past for the performance of their basic functions which in turn adds to the relevance and importance of the military for the orderly functioning of the polity.

This chapter examines how the military has been able to spread out into the government and the society. It analyses the policy decisions and strategies adopted by the military governments to assign their personnel to lucrative civilian jobs and to distribute the rewards of power as widely as possible in the military. The military's burgeoning industrial and business empire and its growing stakes in the economy are also looked into in order to understand the role of the military in Pakistan. As the military's ethnic homogeneity has helped its political profile, recruitment to the Army has also been discussed. It is argued that the Punjab and NWFP continue to dominate the Army, but there are significant changes in the Army's recruitment pattern and the socio-economic background of its officers. Similarly, the relationship between Islam and professionalism is undergoing a change.

Civilian Jobs and Material Rewards

The military has become a ladder for lucrative civilian jobs in almost all states that have experienced the military's rise to power. Pakistan is no exception. Ayub Khan adopted this strategy during his rule and appointed senior officers, mostly retired, to senior jobs with high salaries and perks in the government and semi-government corporations or autonomous bodies. He also inducted 14 Army and Navy officers to the elite Civil Service of Pakistan (CSP) during 1960–3. Yahya Khan continued with the policy of appointing serving or retired officers to senior civilian jobs and diplomatic positions. Zia-ul-Haq distributed the rewards of power more consistently and extensively in the Army because, unable to develop alternative sources of support, his regime had to rely heavily on the military. He institutionalized the induction of military personnel into civilian jobs in a manner that the succeeding civilian regimes could not reverse. This has led to what Finer describes as the 'military colonization of other institutions' whereby 'the military acts as a reservoir or core of personnel for the sensitive institutions of the state'.[1] The higher echelons of the military have emerged as the most privileged caste in Pakistan.

In 1980, a 10 per cent minimum quota was fixed for military personnel in civilian jobs which provided a basis for their induction into all government and semi-government services. Three major methods are adopted for appointment of military personnel to the civilian jobs. First, a number of serving officers are given prize government jobs or top assignments in semi-government corporations and agencies (i.e. WAPDA, PIA, National Shipping Corporation, Karachi Port Trust) for a specified period after which they return to their parent service. Second, retired military officers are recommended by the service headquarters to the government for re-employment. They are also given diplomatic assignments abroad. At times, the civilian government on its own appoints military officers to senior jobs, a practice discouraged by the service headquarters. For the lower-level jobs, various government departments and semi-government institutions are directed to make arrangements for appointment of ex-service personnel by reserving some posts for them or by giving them some credit for military service when they compete with civilians.[2] Third, young officers up to the age of 32 years are inducted permanently in the elite cadres of the Central Superior Services (CSS) on the recommendation of a military selection board. They join the combined training of the CSS probationers and get the advantage of their military service in seniority; the service cadres generally preferred by them include District Management Group (DMG), Foreign Service and Police Service. Since 1980, 8–12 officers are inducted every year under this arrangement. A large number of them are blood relations of the senior commanders or have served them as their ADCs. In a few cases, connections with the privileged political elite have also helped. For example, Nawaz Sharif's son-in-law, a Captain in the Army, was inducted in the DMG.[3]

These measures have enabled the military to make significant inroads into senior government and semi-government jobs. In mid-1982, 18 out of 42 ambassadors posted abroad came from the military. In 1992–3, half the members of the Federal Public Service Commission were ex-Army officers and, during 1995–6, three out of four provincial governors had Army backgrounds. Two of the elite research institutes – Strategic Studies and Regional Studies – have traditionally remained under the tutelage of retired senior military officers or senior bureaucrats. The third reputed institute – Pakistan Institute of International Affairs – was headed by a retired Major General for some time. Four universities had retired Army officers as their Vice Chancellors.[4] Some Brigadiers were given academic appointments in Quaid-i-Azam University, Islamabad, in the 1980s by changing the rules. The practice of inducting serving and retired officers to civilian intelligence agencies was strengthened during 1996–7. A plan was prepared in 1997 to appoint Army officers between the ranks of Captain and Colonel to the police, the FIA and the IB.[5] It was also decided in 1998 to induct the retired personal of the Special Services Group (SSG) into the newly created 'Special Force' of the Police Department.[6]

The tradition of allotment of agricultural land to service personnel went back to the British period when the government distributed large tracts of land as a reward for military service. This practice continued in the post-independence period. Land in the Thal desert under the colonization scheme of the Punjab government was given to the military for settling ex-servicemen families. Similarly, land was given to service personnel in various schemes in different barrage areas in Sindh and the Punjab, i.e. Ghulam Mohammad, Gudu, and Taunsa. The government gave land in Campbellpur, Jhelum, Kohat, Rawalpindi and Hazara districts to local ex-servicemen who developed this with the help of the Army.[7] Land was also allotted to them along India–Pakistan border in the Punjab. The practice of land grants under various schemes to military personnel, senior bureaucrats and other well-connected people in various land development schemes in Sindh and the Punjab continued under Zia-ul-Haq (see chapter 9).

Agricultural land was also awarded for gallantry. Various military decorations entitled the officers or other ranks to land. For example, the recipient of *Hilal-e-Juraat*, *Sitira-e-Juraat* and *Tamgha-e-Juraat* were entitled to 50 acres, 25 acres and 12.5 acres of land respectively. Later, cash awards partly replaced land allocations.[8] Other material rewards offered during the Zia period included assignments in the Gulf States, plots of land for construction of houses in cantonments and urban centres, commercial plots and facilities of loans, etc. A large number of officers got more than one plot at cheap rates, which they sold to civilians at exorbitant rates. In June 1982, the armed forces housing scheme was launched to provide houses for retiring officers at a cost to be paid in easy instalments. The first project was completed in early 1984.

A number of senior officers benefited from the military government's decision to allow the Presidents, Governors, Chairmen of the Joint Chiefs of Staff Committee, Chiefs and Vice Chiefs of the three services to import one luxury car each free of custom duty, other taxes and surcharges. Twenty-seven Army officers (13 Generals, 10 Lt.-Generals, 2 Major Generals, and 2 Brigadiers), 10 Navy officers (7 Admirals and 3 Vice Admirals) and 6 Air Force officers (4 Air Chief Marshals and 2 Air Marshals) took advantage of this facility during 1977–97.[9]

Industrial and Commercial Interests

The military has expanded its role in the economy by active involvement in industry and business, developing a stake in the government's economic policies and industrial and commercial strategies. The Army's industrial and commercial interests can be divided into three major categories: those directly under the administrative control of the Army Chief; those looked after by the Defence Production Division of the Ministry of Defence but headed by the serving officers appointed by the Army Chief; four charitable trusts set up for the welfare of ex-service personnel which operate in an autonomous manner in the private sector.[10]

The first category includes the Frontier Works Organization (FWO), Special Communication Organization (SCO) and National Logistics Cell (NLC). The FWO, set up in October 1966 and staffed by the Corps of Engineers, undertook the construction of the Korakoram Highway (KKH) as its first project. Later, it completed several civilian engineering projects, notably road construction in the Northern areas and Balochistan, and civilian work for the Kot Addu power station. It made its manpower and technical know-how available for the clearing of anti-personnel mines in Kuwait in the aftermath of the 1991 Gulf war. The SCO is manned by the Signals Corps which looks after telecommunication facilities in the Northern areas and Azad Kashmir. The NLC, set up during the Zia years, is the biggest road transport organization which moves goods for the military and the civilian sector, competing effectively with the railways and other transport companies.

Pakistan Ordinance Factories (POF) and heavy defence industry are major industrial enterprises which not only serve the military by producing weapons, equipment and a lot of other goods and services but also make some goods available to the civilian sector; their products are also exported. These establishments are taken care of by the Defence Production Division of the Defence Ministry but the top positions in the POF and to a large extent in heavy defence industry are manned by serving Army officers appointed by the Army Chief. Another important establishment working under the Defence Production Division is the Aeronautical Complex, Kamara, for manufacture and rebuilding of aircraft and related equipment, and accommodating service personnel particularly from the Air Force.

The Army's most remarkable contribution is the setting up of two charitable foundations for generating funds for the welfare of retired army personnel and their families and for creating employment opportunities for them. These are the *Fauji* Foundation and the Army Welfare Trust. These trusts are based on the concept that the military must look after the interests and welfare of its personnel even after their retirement. Originally, three main agencies were engaged in the work for the welfare of ex-service personnel. These were the Welfare Directorate, the Post-War Reconstruction Fund and the Armed Services Boards. These agencies were reorganized and their role expanded.[11] The Post-War Reconstruction Fund was established by the British in April 1942, for making funds available to the provincial governments for the welfare of the war veterans. In the post-independence period, the Pakistan Army decided to invest most of this fund to generate resources on a permanent basis.[12] The *Fauji* Foundation was set up which acquired or established industrial concerns. Starting with one industrial unit, the *Fauji* Foundation has became the single largest industrial conglomerate in Pakistan with assets of Rs. 8,005.87 million in 1996.[13] It has eight fully owned industrial projects and four shareholding projects.[14] The *Fauji* Foundation is also benefiting from current economic globalization by undertaking three joint ventures with foreign companies.[15]

These industrial projects are an important source of employment for ex-service personnel, although civilians are also hired. The Foundation claims that about eight million ex-service personnel and their family members have benefited from its welfare activities and that it spends approximately 70 per cent of its profits on such activities; the remainder is reinvested. Its advertisements describe the *Fauji* Foundation as the 'biggest welfare-industrial group' and claim that it has given 200,000 educational scholarships to the children of ex-service personnel. It has established two colleges and 58 schools in different parts of the country. Four technical training centres and 60 vocational training centres teach various skills suitable for post-retirement life. Its other projects include a 600-bed hospital at Rawalpindi, a 164-bed hospital at Peshawar and a 146-bed hospital at Karachi. It also manages nine hospitals and 46 mobile dispensaries in rural areas. A number of day-care centres are also functioning under its supervision.[16]

Another charitable organization – the Army Welfare Trust – is engaged in a host of commercial activities. A late entrant to the field, it is gradually shaping up as another commercial empire with the motto 'Serving the

Forces and the Nation in All Spheres'. Its projects include sugar and woollen mills, cement plants, agro-industry, pharmaceutical industry, power generation, petrochemicals, aviation and a shoe factory. It has also established financial institutions like Askari Commercial Bank, a general insurance company, a leasing company and share registration. It is also experimenting with small-scale business ventures like catering (restaurant and bakery), travel agency, petrol pump and security services to provide armed guards and related assistance. Its most flourishing business relates to real estate development, i.e. housing and commercial market schemes.[17]

The Air Force established its charitable trust – *Shaheen* Foundation – in 1977 with an initial grant of Rs. 3.5 million from the Air Force and Rs. 2 million from the government, which increased to Rs. 1,680 million in 1998.[18] The *Shaheen* Foundation owns the second national air line, *Shaheen* Air International (SAI), which also resumed international service from Peshawar and Islamabad to Dubai in February 1995 and June 1998 respectively. The other projects include Airport Services (set up in 1982); Air Cargo Service (1992); a knitwear factory (1981); the Aerotraders for import and export business, maintaining a bonded warehouse of Chinese aircraft parts and representing several foreign industrial and commercial concerns; Hawk Advertising Consultants established in 1977; the *Shaheen* Systems established in 1989 for providing expertise in computer technology; *Shaheen* Pay TV launched in 1996 as the first cable network in Pakistan and FM-100 (joint projects with other companies); and an insurance company launched in 1996. Its first real estate development project is a commercial centre in Karachi. Similar projects are being planned for Lahore, Rawalpindi and Quetta. In 1998, it was planning a joint venture with some foreign partners to set up a maintenance and overhauling facility for C-130 and other aircraft at Chaklala.[19] The profits from these ventures are used for financing welfare activities like scholarships for students, establishment of vocational schools for women, health and medical facilities, financial support to the families of those killed on duty, construction of mosques, and *Haj* visits to Saudi Arabia for serving and retired personnel and their families. It has also created employment opportunities for retired personnel and sent about 450 personnel overseas for assignments with other air forces.

The youngest and the smallest of the charitable organizations is the *Bharia* Foundation, set up by the Navy. Its subsidiaries include *Bharia* Tour and Travel Company, *Bharia* Paints Limited, *Bharia* Lubricants Limited and *Bharia* Complex Limited. In November 1993, it entered into its first joint venture with a German company to set up a plastic card facility at Hub. It launched two township schemes in Rawalpindi and Lahore.[20] As it generates funds from these projects, the *Bharia* Foundation is expected to expand its operations.

A military-managed National University of Science and Technology (NUST) was set up in 1991 as a decentralized multi-campus centre of excellence which includes nine institutions: College of Engineering, Risalpur; College of

Signals, Rawalpindi; College of Electrical and Mechanical Engineering, Rawalpindi; Army Medical College, Rawalpindi; Pakistan Navy Engineering College, Karachi; College of Aeronautical Engineering, Risalpur; National Institute of Transportation, Risalpur; Institute of Environmental Sciences and Engineering, Rawalpindi; and NUST Institute of Management Sciences.[21] The President of Pakistan is its Patron-in-Chief, the Prime Minister is its Chancellor, and the Board of Governors is headed by the Army Chief. The Rector is a retired senior Army officer. The NUST began functioning in 1993 and offered BSc, MS, and PhD degrees. The 1998 tuition fee rate for MS and PhD students was Rs. 7,500 per month with a one-time admission fee of Rs. 5,000, comparable to the tuition rates of the private sector.[22] The three services run their professional training institutions for pre-service and in-service training. The Army Education Corps and the Air Force and the Navy also run a number of schools and colleges for general education which are open to civilians. An Army medical college is functioning in Rawalpindi. These institutions are known for good academic standards and discipline in sharp contrast to the faltering academic quality in the state run civilian universities and colleges. The Army Medical Corps runs a network of hospitals and medical centres which provide quality medical facilities primarily to serving and retired military personnel and their families. It has also established specialized medical care facilities like institutes of cardiology and heart diseases.

The civilian governments rely heavily on the Army for managing civilian affairs and for strengthening public welfare services. The second Sharif government inducted more army personnel into civilian jobs and duties than was the case in the past. The Punjab government contracted the Army's FWO and NLC in 1997–8 for road rehabilitation and construction work in Faisalabad, Multan and Lahore. In early 1998, it asked the Army to undertake a thorough survey of the primary schools in the province so that the government had a detailed report on how many were actually functioning and what their deficiencies were in terms of manpower and physical facilities. The Punjab government made plans to involve Army personnel in teaching and management work in primary and high schools, and for extending health care facilities in the rural areas. The Army helped the civilian government conduct the national census in March 1998.[23] In December 1998, about 35,000 Army Junior Commissioned Officers and Commissioned Officers were inducted into WAPDA to manage power distribution and check 'pilferage and theft' of electricity and related corruption. A serving Lt. General and a serving Major General were appointed Chairman and Vice Chairman of WAPDA and eight serving Brigadiers headed its distribution companies.[24] The development of Karachi's water supply schemes was also handed over to the Army. These assignments were in addition to the usual aid to civil power functions like maintenance of law and order, rescue and relief operations after natural calamities like floods and earthquakes, anti-terrorist operations and containment of narcotics trafficking.

Ethnicity and Social Background

Pakistan officially discarded the British concept of martial races for recruitment to the Army and somewhat expanded the recruitment base. However, ethnic imbalances persist in the Army. The Punjab continues to provide the bulk of officers and other ranks; unofficial estimates put its share as 65 and 70 per cent respectively. The Punjab is expected to sustain its entrenched position because it constitutes 56 per cent of Pakistan's population. The Pathans or Pashtuns are the second largest group in the Army, constituting about 22–25 per cent of its officers and other ranks. NWFP and the tribal areas are 16 per cent of Pakistan's population; if the Pathans living in Balochistan are added, their ratio is expected to rise to about 19 per cent. The Baloch and Sindhi-speaking people (3 and 13 percent of Pakistan's population respectively) are under-represented in the Army, especially in the higher echelons. The Urdu-speaking populace of Sindh, i.e. *Mohajir*, approximately 6–7 per cent of Pakistan's population, is fairly represented at the officer level but there are very small number of *Mohajir* at the solider level. They are known to be over-represented in the Air Force and the Navy.[25]

Traditionally, the Salt Range and the Potwar (Potohar) region of northern Punjab and the adjoining districts of NWFP are known as the Army heartland, providing a large number of soldiers, commissioned and non-commissioned officers. In the present-day administrative set-up, the districts/tehsils of Jhelum, Chakwal and Pinddaden Khan, described as the Salt Range area, coupled with Attock, Campbellpur, Rawalpindi and Gujrat in the Punjab and Kohat, Mardan and Peshawar in NWFP, have established their reputation as the major suppliers of manpower for the Army. The tribal agencies, the Northern Area and Pakistan-administered Kashmir also offer some manpower. Over the last three decades, other areas in the Punjab and north-western region have made manpower available for recruitment. The Punjab's districts of Sargodha, Khushab and Mianwali provide a reasonable number of recruits, especially for other ranks. Furthermore, officers and other ranks also come from urban districts like Lahore, Gujranwala, Faislabad and the Canal Colonies. In the case of NWFP, the districts of Kohat, Mardan and Bannu are still the main recruiting areas,[26] although other regions are gradually coming up.

Thus, the recruitment base within the Punjab and NWFP has expanded. The Punjabis and the Pathans continue to dominate the Army as they have a decisive edge over the Baloch, Sindhis and *Mohajirs* in population.

In pre-1971 Pakistan, the under-representation of the Bengalis caused much criticism of the recruitment policy in East Pakistan. The British treated the Bengalis as a non-martial race and their recruitment was deliberately discouraged. At the time of independence, the Bengalis constituted 1 per cent of the total strength of Pakistan's armed forces; their numerical strength in the Army was 155 which rose to 13,000 in 1965. First infantry East Bengal

Regiment (EBR) – Senior Tigers – was set up in February 1948, but, in the initial stages, a number of West Pakistanis were assigned to it as officers and NCO and JCOs. Later, Bengalis replaced them and, by 1968, four such regiments were in place. However, the Bengali representation remained inadequate in the Army, especially from the middle to the upper level. In 1955, only 14 out of 908 Army officers of the rank of Major or above were Bengalis. In 1963, they constituted only 5 per cent of the Army officers and the percentile at the JCOs and other ranks level was 7.4 which improved slightly in the post-1965 period. Only one Bengali attained the rank of Lt.-General and another became Major General at the beginning of 1971. Their representation was much better in the Air Force and the Navy, although it was never more than one third.[27] The continued ethnic imbalance to the disadvantage of the Bengalis was the main reason that the breach between the Bengalis and the military which developed during the British period could not be overcome during the Pakistan days. The military was always perceived by ordinary Bengalis as an outside and alien force.

Ethnic imbalances generate controversy because the Army has been instrumental in creating a centralized and authoritarian polity which ensured its dominance of the state power. Whenever the ethnic and regional elite asserted their ethnic identity and regional rights, the power elite perceived it as a threat to the state and mobilized the state apparatus, especially the Army, to suppress these efforts ostensibly to 'protect national integrity'.[28] These trends were reinforced with the establishment of military rule which 'precluded political participation' for the ethnic and regional identities.[29] Those who suffered under these political arrangements questioned the role of the military.

Regional and ethnic imbalances also attract attention for other reasons. The military offers good salaries and perks to its personnel and has developed an elaborate system to look after their material interests during service and after retirement. It is a major 'employer' in Pakistan, a ladder for jobs in the civilian sectors and a source of patronage. The prosperity and welfare of many areas and families in the Punjab and NWFP are closely linked with the military. For many peasants, the Army offers a 'safety net' against poverty.[30] This works to the advantage of the ethnic groups and the regions well represented in the military, giving a cause of complaint to the under-represented ones.

Some efforts are now being made to improve the representation of Sindhis and Baloch in the three services, especially in the Army. A Sindh Regiment was established and, for some time, the Army recruited illiterate Sindhis as soldiers.[31] The quota for recruitment of soldiers from Balochistan and Sindh was raised to 15 per cent in 1991.[32] The height and educational criteria for recruitment to Other Ranks was reduced for Balochistan and interior Sindh; minimum height was reduced from 5 feet 6 inches (fixed for the Punjab and NWFP) to 5 feet 4 inches, and the minimum educational qualification was reduced from Secondary School Certificate (Matric) to the Middle level (Class 8). However, in December 1998, the Army was still short of about 10,000 Other Ranks from Balochistan and interior Sindh.[33] The Army increased its presence in Sindh and Balochistan. It faced some opposition from the nationalist elements when its first cantonment was established in interior Sindh at Pano Aqil in 1988. New cantonments were set up at Dadu, Pataro, Chore and Sakrand which did not face opposition because the local population realized that these created job and business opportunities. The Army improved communication in the *katcha* area, primarily to facilitate its mobility, but the local population also benefited. The Army is now getting more recruits from interior Sindh than was the case in the past. However, the Army has a long way to go before an adequate number of Sindhis and Balochs are on its pay roll.

The socio-economic composition of the Army officers has a undergone a transformation. Stephen Cohen talks of three military generations: British, American and Pakistani. The British generation included the pre-independence officers trained at the Royal Military Academy, Sandhurst (i.e. the King's Commissioned Officers, or KCOs) and the Indian Military Academy, Dehra Dun (called the Indian Commissioned Officers or ICOs) and those given emergency commissions during the Second World War. The American generation (1950–65) refers to the period when Pakistan joined the alliance system and the military obtained American weapons and technology and its officers were exposed to American training and influences. The post-1972 officers have been described as the Pakistani generation.[34] The British were careful in inducting Indians into the officer cadre. Those sent to Sandhurst came from loyal, prestigious and upper strata families who joined the Army as a matter of prestige rather than to earn a living. The British also sent the sons of the Viceroy Commissioned Officers (VCOs) who did not necessarily have affluent backgrounds. The social base of recruitment slightly expanded with the start of the Dehra Dun academy in 1932, but it was predominantly upper and upper-middle and the families with military-service tradition. The outbreak of the Second World War (1939–45) further expanded the base of recruitment; a large number of Indians were granted emergency commissions after a short period of training.

The Anglicized KCOs and the ICOs (in addition to the British officers) filled the senior slots in the Pakistan Army at the time of independence and set its tone which was British in training and professional orientation. However, the communal riots that accompanied the establishment of the state, the dispute with India over the division of military equipment and weapons, and the war in Kashmir had a profound impact on their psyche and outlook and 'Pakistanized' them in their attitude towards their counterparts in India. The American connection that developed in the mid-1950s exposed them to American military equipment, training and cultural influences, which eroded British influence, especially in the case of those who joined the

Army in the early years of independence. However, the basic pattern of ideas and orientations of the Pakistan Army inherited from the British survived. They could not break out of the British mould in such a decisive manner that one could talk of a distinct American generation.[35] The Air Force which relied more heavily on American aircraft and equipment was more Americanized in social orientations. This was also partly true of the Navy.

The major shift began to take shape as the Army expanded in the late 1960s, more so since the early 1970s. Most of those who joined the officer corps in the 1970s and later came from modest rural backgrounds and urban lower-middle and lower class backgrounds as job opportunities declined in the civilian sector. They looked on the Army more as a career opportunity than as a family tradition or love for the profession. Their strong career orientation was coupled with their exposure to the politicized environment of educational institutions. Some of them had engaged in active political activity on the campus or outside during their student days. This new element was thus more politicized and ambitious than their predecessors, who came from a relatively better social background and were not directly exposed to political pressures in their pre-military days.

The new officers who would occupy top staff and command positions by the end of the first decade of the twenty-first century have a different orientations towards the society. They are quite materialist in their orientations and are eager to enjoy the good life, i.e. a house, car, bank account, modern luxuries and foreign trips or assignments. Some of them tasted power during the Zia years. A large number of officers and men of the Army and the Air Force were posted in the Middle Eastern states, especially in the Gulf region, in the 1970s and the 1980s. This brought them an economic windfall. As the openings in the Gulf region have declined in the 1990s, the younger officers are not likely to get as many opportunities to earn money through foreign assignments. They consider themselves poorer as compared with their counterparts of a decade ago. The UN peacekeeping assignments cannot be a substitute for the openings in the Gulf region. Not are only these opportunities much too limited, but also the assignments are more hazardous. This is causing frustration at the middle and lower levels, especially because they joined the military profession, *inter alia*, to improve their quality of life. The military will therefore have to maintain a strong reward and benefit system to keep them quiet. To make things worse, the ostentatious life-style of the top commanders and the upper strata of the civil society, especially those in power, does not set a good precedent. As in the civilian sector, the distinction between the personal and public domains is fast eroding in the military. The misuse of official transport, manpower and regimental resources and facilities by the senior officers and their families is quite common which gives a licence to the junior officers to do the same.

The traditionally cautious approach towards politics and the civil society is disappearing. The junior officers freely make partisan political statements and express low, often contemptuous, opinions about civilians. Similarly, the instances of junior officers disregarding civilian laws or picking fights with policemen or junior civilian officials are no longer rare.[36] The erosion of professional conduct and the craving for material gain have caused concern within military circles. A retired officer lamented that the motto 'Service before Self' has been changed to 'Self before Service'.[37] Another retired officer wrote in the *Pakistan Army Journal*: 'Our military leadership in the past ten years has become increasingly materialistic like the rest of the society. Money, property and luxurious life styles are now the endemic part of the senior rank structures. The juniors pick on the crumb and grow more disgruntled with time'.[38] A retired general suggested that senior officers who 'blatantly lived beyond their means' should be taken to task.[39]

These development and the military's high political profile have led to what Heeger describes as the 'demystification' of the military. Its image as being above politics is seriously undermined, and it is seen as one of the contending groups engaged in power politics.[40] The growing civilian criticism focuses on the alleged money-making by the officers on martial law duties during the Zia years, the perks and privileges of the military personnel, a craving for quick material gains, and the decline in professional conduct and moral fibre of the young officers. In 1987, a construction company advertised for a retired general as its executive director. A satirical article in a Karachi newspaper under the title 'An open application from a retired general' enumerated the qualifications and experience of the General as: the break-up of the country in 1971, supervision of construction of personal houses in defence societies, management of several ranches overseas, engineering experience acquired by helping to engineer successful coups against civilian governments, and sufficient executive experience including the execution of an elected Prime Minister. Describing the physical features of the general as 'fat and flabby, overfed on power', the article said that the sky was the limit of the salary acceptable to the applicant and that it was to be deposited in a Swiss bank account.[41] The entrepreneurial activities of the charitable trusts, like real estate development, housing schemes, and small-scale business, are also criticized. Another criticism focuses on kickbacks in defence purchases. In 1996–7, the Chiefs of the Navy and the Air Force were accused by the press of involvement in corruption scandals; the Naval Chief resigned in April 1997. In August 1997, three former Air Force Chiefs called upon the Prime Minister to adopt tough legislative measures to 'eliminate the menace of kickbacks and commissions from defence purchases'.[42]

Of late, the political circles have criticized high defence allocations on two major counts. First, Pakistan's deteriorating economy in the late 1990s and especially the growing debt pressures made many in Pakistan look critically at the resources being made available to the military. The review proposals have ranged from suggestions for organizational changes in the military, reduction in defence expenditure to its rationalization and a stricter control on its disbursement. There are demands that the annual budget statement should contain some details of the defence expenditure rather than the current practice of a one-line statement. Second, there is a growing realization that more resources should be made available to the social sector, health care, education and environment if a strong and vibrant society is to be created. Societal security is no less important than military-oriented external security. This expanded concept of security calls for rationalization of the defence expenditure, adoption of political measures to defuse tension in the region, and allocation of more resources to socio-economic development. However, as long as India and Pakistan do not resolve their major problems amicably and the regional security environment does not improve, a major shift away from external territorial security is not expected, assuring the military's continued relevance to policy-making.

Islam and the Military

Islam is integral to Pakistan military ideology. Islam was repeatedly invoked during the wars in 1965 and 1971 to galvanize the soldiers and the civilians for the defence of the country. When Zia-ul-Haq assumed command of the Army in March 1976, he gave the motto of *'Iman'* (faith), *'Taqwa'* (piety and abstinence), and *'Jihad-fi-sibilillah'* (holy war in the name of God), which reflected his strong religious inclinations. However, this was not a major departure because Islamic principles, teachings, history and Muslim war heroes and their battles have always been a part of military education, training and ideology. The commanders that preceded or followed him highlighted Islamic ideals and teachings and urged the soldiers to imbibe Islamic values and military traditions. They emphasized Islam as an identity and a motivational force coupled with professionalism and service discipline. Religious extremism and linkages with Islamic movements or groups were discouraged. The military presented the moderate and liberal face of Islam.

Four major developments during the Zia years had far-reaching implications for the role of Islam in the Army. First, Zia-ul-Haq used Islam and conservative Islamic groups to legitimize his rule and encouraged Islamic conservatism and orthodoxy in the Army. This fitted with the changes in the orientations of the new breed of officers who came from the middle to lower strata of the society, hailing mainly from small towns and urban areas with conservative religious values. Furthermore, assignments in the Gulf region also strengthened religious orthodoxy, although these personnel relished consumerism and the good things of life. The institution of 'regimental priest' was upgraded and strengthened and the bias in favour of Islamic conservatism influenced the promotion policy. Second, some of the Islamic groups were allowed to make inroads into the Army, something of an anathema in the past. Zia-ul-Haq had a strong inclination towards the *Tableghi Jamaat* (a purely religious organization which does not involve itself in politics), and he was the first head of state to attend its annual congregations at Raiwind. Encouraged by this, a good number of officers and men began openly to associate with the *Tableghi Jamaat*, attended its annual meetings and made it a point to demonstrate their religious disposition in public. Other conservative Islamic sectarian groups were also able to develop connections with the personnel of three services, especially the Army. Some of these officers engaged in preaching of Islam within and outside their service in their spare time in collaboration with the *Tableghi Jamaat* and a host of other religious groups. The other group that gained access to the Army and the bureaucracy was the *Jamaat-i-Islami* which had a favourable disposition towards the Zia regime and was associated with the government's Afghanistan policy. The *Jamaat-i-Islami* with its overt Islamic political agenda penetrated these institutions, and many officers began to express their fascination for the *Jamaat*'s ideology and the writings of its founder, Maulana Maudoodi. Religion thus became an important part of the public profile of the in-service personnel.

Third, the Islamic Revolution in Iran (1979) had a profound impact on civilians as well as military circles in Pakistan. It strengthened the conservative Islamic elements and created an environment which in part facilitated Zia-ul-Haq's efforts to push through his Islamization programme. A number of retired and serving officers (like many civilians) talked of an Islamic Revolution in Pakistan, although none was clear on the methods for effecting a revolution and institutional arrangements for the post-revolution phase.

Fourth, the Afghanistan experience reinforced Islamic zeal among Army personnel, especially those working with the Afghan resistance groups. The ISI was involved in transferring weapons to the Afghan resistance, and advised them on strategy against the Soviet troops in Afghanistan. The support of the Muslim world for the Afghan cause and the participation of Muslim activists from several countries in the Afghan struggle generated pan-Islamic sentiments. The exit of the Soviet troops from Afghanistan in February 1989 created a sense of euphoria among them and the thinking process of many Army personnel, including some senior officers, was frozen in the Afghanistan experience. They often argued for an Afghanistan-style armed resistance to bring an end to non-Muslim domination of the Muslims, especially in Kashmir.

The changes in US policy towards Pakistan and Afghanistan after the Soviet withdrawal also strengthened religious zealots inside and outside the military. The US suspended military sales and economic assistance to Pakistan and distanced itself from the Afghan resistance movement. The slowing down of interaction between the militaries of Pakistan and the US and especially the discontinuation of the US-directed or based military training programmes, also strengthened the religious elements. Islamic sentiments were also strengthened due to the growing resentment against the stalemate in Kashmir, US-directed military action against Iraq, Russia's use of military against the Chechnyan Muslims, the agony of the Bosnian Muslims and Israel's aggressive policy towards the Palestinians. The Islamic elements began to view the US as an adversary of the Muslims and felt that the Pakistan government and the senior commanders did not adopt a forthright position against the US. A small group of religious zealots in the Army were arrested in September 1995 for planning a takeover of the Army headquarters and the civilian government in order to establish a strict Islamic order.[43] One Major General (Zahirul Islam Abbasi) one Brigadier (Mustansar Billah), and two other officers were convicted by court martial; one got 14 years' rigorous imprisonment and the others received imprisonment ranging from two to seven years.[44] Some Islamic groups and parties issued statements in their favour, accusing the Benazir government and the Army top brass of 'witch hunting' the Islamic elements. Their efforts did not evoke any sympathy or support within or outside the Army.

As long as Islam is coupled with professionalism and service discipline, it is a source of strength. However, whenever the imperative of military profession are subordinated to extraneous considerations, no matter what is their source, the military faces internal problems. If the professional and corporate interests of the military are to be protected, no principles and ideas can be allowed to flourish independent of professional and service ethos. Commenting on the policies of Zia-ul-Haq, a retired general wrote that his policies 'gave rise to religious orthodoxy among a cross-section of the armed forces. For this small group, ideology can be stretched to radicalism and takes precedence over professionalism. Their attitude needs to be countervailed otherwise it will erode the very foundation of a cohesive, professionally competent, and technologically adept armed forces'.[45] A prolific analyst of military affairs asserted that Islam could serve as a 'force multiplier' for a Muslim army when it was not being used as a 'substitute for the essential hard and software in the shape of weapons and training.'[46] The Army top brass were conscious that some elements in the Army had taken to substituting professionalism and discipline with Islam-oriented activism. General Asif Nawaz Janjua (Army Chief: August 1991–January 1993) and his successors slowly began to push back the politicized Islamic elements and reasserted the age-old tradition of keeping Islam and professionalism together and treating the former as a component of the latter; they continued to acknowledge the role and importance of Islam in military ideology. Islam influences the military mind in two other ways: its pan-Islamic character is viewed as a basis of solidarity that could strengthen the role of the Muslim states at the global level; and a cooperative interaction with Afghanistan, the Central Asian republics and Iran enables Pakistan to develop strategic-geographic depth, so strengthening its security.

The major challenge the military faces in the twenty-first century is the maintenance of a professional and cohesive disposition as the new breed of officers takes over its command. The delicate balance between Islam and service discipline is going to be another important concern, especially because a number of Islamic groups continue to work on the new breed of officers and other ranks. This calls for a renewed emphasis on professional excellence, organization and service ethos and strong moral fibre of the officers and men. How the military addresses ethnic imbalances within its ranks is also important for developing smooth interactions with the civil society. As materialism and consumerism spreads in the wake of trade liberalization and globalization, the military will have to pay more attention than ever to the material welfare of its personnel both in service and after retirement. The military's capacity to generate resources through its industrial and commercial empire or to accommodate its personnel in civilian jobs therefore gains much importance, and it will maintain strong interests in political decision-making to protect its interests. All this is needed to fulfil the military's obligations towards its personnel in return for their loyalty and professional commitment. However, no military can sustain itself unless it is backed by a strong and stable civil society capable of ensuring socio-economic security for its members. The imperatives of human development and societal security cannot be ignored.

Notes

Chapter 1:   Introduction

1   Ayesha Jalal, *The State of Martial Rule* (Cambridge: Cambridge University Press, 1990), pp. 295–6; see by the same author, *Democracy and Authoritarianism in South Asia* (Cambridge: Cambridge University Press 1995), p. 54.

2   For a perceptive analysis of the 1954–5 constitutional crisis and the judgement of the federal court, see Allen McGrath, *The Destruction of Pakistan's Democracy* (Karachi: Oxford University Press, 1996), pp. 102–17.

3   Stephen P. Cohen, 'State Building in Pakistan', in Ali Banuazizi and Myron Weiner (eds), *The State, Religion and Ethnic Politics* (Lahore: Vanguard Books, 1987), p. 315.

4   They were: K.M. Cariappa (January 1949–January 1953), Maharaj Rajendra Sinhji (January 1953–May 1955), S.M. Srinagesh (May 1955–May 1957), K.S. Thimayya (May 1957–May 1961), R.N. Thapar (May 1961–November 1962), J.N. Choudhuri (November 1962–June 1966), P.P. Kumaramangalam (June 1966–June 1969), S.H.F.J. Manekshaw (June 1969–January 1973).

5   Saeed Shafqat, *Civil–Military Relations in Pakistan: From Zulfikar Ali Bhutto to Benazir Bhutto* (Boulder: Westview Press, 1997), pp. 7–8, 34.

6   Shireen M. Mazari, 'Militarism and Militarization of Pakistan's Civil Society', in Kumar Rupesinghe and Khawar Mumtaz (eds), *Internal Conflicts in South Asia* (London: Sage Publications, 1996), pp. 96–108 (p. 98).

7   Omar Noman, *Pakistan: Political and Economic History since 1947* (London: Kegan Paul, 1990), p. 118.

8   They were: Asif Nawaz Janjua (August 1991–January 1993, died in office). Abdul Waheed Kaker (January 1993–January 1996), Jehangir Karamat (January 1996–October 1998), Pervez Musharraf (October 1998–the present).

9   Iftikhar H. Malik, *State and Civil Society in Pakistan* (New York: St. Martin's Press, 1997), p. 4; see also Rasul B. Rais, 'Security, State and Democracy in Pakistan', in Marvin G. Weinbaum and Chetan Kumar (eds), *South Asia Approaches the Millennium: Re-examining National Security* (Boulder: Westview Press, 1995), pp. 64–78; Richard Ponzio, *A Peace Dividend in South Asia? Prospects and Strategies* (Geneva: Graduate Institute of International Studies, 1997).

Chapter 2:   Civil–Military Interaction

1   See, J.J. Johnson (ed.), *The Role of the Military in Under-developed Countries* (Princeton: Princeton University Press, 1962).

2   Guy J. Pauker, 'Southeast Asia as a Problem Area in the Next Decade', *World Politics* (Vol. 11, No. 3, April 1959), pp. 325–45; see also G. Kennedy, The *Military in the Third World* (New York: Charles Scribner, 1974), p. 59; Daniel Lerner and R.D. Robinson, 'Swords and Ploughshares: The Turkish Army as a Modernizing Force', *World Politics* (Vol. 13, No. 1, October 1960), pp. 19–44.

3   H. Daalder, *The Role of the Military in the Emerging Countries* (The Hague: Mouton, 1962), p. 19; see also J.C. Hurewitz, *Middle East Politics: The Military Dimension*

(New York: Praeger, 1969), pp. 419–35; Edward Shils, *Political Development in the New States* (The Hague: Mouton, 1968), pp. 44–5.

4   A.S. Cohen and A.D. Mckinlay, 'Performance and Instability in Military and Non-Military Regime Systems', *American Political Science Review (APSR)* (Vol. 70, No. 3, September 1976), pp. 850–64.

5   R.W. Jackman, 'Politicians in Uniform: Military Governments and Social Change in the Third World', *APSR* (Vol. 70, No. 4, December 1976), pp. 1078–97; see also D. Shah Khan, 'Role of Armed Forces in National Affairs', *Defence Journal* (Vol. 8, Nos. 10 & 11, October–November 1982), pp. 15–29.

6   Nicole Ball, 'Third World Militaries and Politics: An Introductory Essay', *Cooperation and Conflict* (Vol. XVll, No. 1, March 1982), pp. 41–60.

7   Edward Shills, 'The Military in the Political Development of the New States', in Johnson, *op. cit.*, p. 9; see also David E. Apter, *Rethinking Development* (Newbury Park, California: SAGE Publications, 1987); Howard Handelman, *The Challenge of Third World Development* (Upper Saddle River, N.J.: Prentice Hall, 1996).

8   For a discussion of political development and democratization, see Myron Weiner and Samuel P. Huntington (eds.), *Understanding Political Development* (Boston: Little, Brown & Co., 1987); Leonard Binder, et al., *Crises and Sequences in Political Development* (Princeton: Princeton University Press, 1971).

9   For an incisive discussion of the problem of national integration, identity and institution building in the developing states, see Christopher Clapham, *Third World Politics: An Introduction* (London: Croom Helm, 1985); Fred R. Von der Mehden, *Politics of the Developing Nations*, 2nd edition (Englewood Cliffs: Prentice Hall, 1969); John Hutchinson and Anthony D. Smith (eds.), *Nationalism* (New York: Oxford University Press, 1994).

10 Samuel P. Huntington, *Political Order in Changing Societies* (New Haven: Yale University Press, 1968), p. 196.

11 S.E. Finer, *The Man on Horseback* (London: Pall Mall, paperback edition, 1969), p. 10.

12 J.P. Lovell and C.I.I. Kim, 'The Military and Political Change in Asia', *Pacific Affairs* (Vol. XL, Nos. 1 & 2, Spring and Summer 1967).

13 Samuel P. Huntington, *The Soldier and the State: The Theory and Politics of Civil–Military Relations* (New York: Vintage Books/Random House, 1957), pp. 83–5, 260–1.

14 Amos Perlmutter, *The Military and Politics in Modern Times* (New Haven: Yale University Press, 1977), pp. 9–17.

15 A.R. Luckham, 'A Comparative Typology of Civil–Military Relations', *Government and Opposition* (Vol. 6, No. 1, Winter 1971), pp. 5–35.

16 Eric A. Nordlinger, *Soldiers in Politics: Military Coups and Governments* (Englewood Cliffs: Prentice Hall, 1977), p. 193; Edward Feit, *The Armed Bureaucrats: Military-Administrative Regimes and Political Development* (Boston: Houghton Mifflin, 1973), p. 18; Huntington, *op. cit.* (fn.11), p. 194.

17 Paul Cammack, David Pool and William Tordoff, *Third World Politics: A Comparative Introduction*, 2nd edition (London: Macmillan, 1993), pp. 151, 165.

18 Amos Perlmutter, 'The Praetorian State and the Praetorian Army', in Norman W. Provizer (ed.), *Analyzing the Third World* (Cambridge, Mass: Schenkman Publishing Co., 1978), pp. 303–9; Feit, *op. cit.*, pp. 3–4.

19 Morris Janowitz, *Military Institutions and Coercion in the Developing Nations* (Chicago: University of Chicago Press, 1977), pp. 107–50.

20 Edward Feit, 'Military Coups and Political Development: Some Lessons from Ghana and Nigeria', *World Politics* (Vol. 20, No. 2, January 1968), pp. 179–93.

21 For a discussion of the US military assistance to the developing countries during the Cold War period, see Henry Bienen (ed.), *The Military Intervenes: Case Studies in Political Development* (New York: Russell Sage Foundation, 1969), pp. xlll–xxlll (Introduction by Bienen); Nicole Ball, 'The Military in Politics: Who Benefits and How', *World Development* (Vol. 9, No. 6, June 1981), pp. 569–82.

22 Arturo Valenzuela, 'A Note on the Military and Social Science Theory', *Third World Quarterly* (Vol. 7, No. 1, January 1985), pp. 132–43.

23 Finer, *op. cit.*, pp. 89, 118.

24 Lucian W. Pye, 'Armies in the Process of Political Modernization', in Johnson, *op. cit.*, p. 80.

25 Samuel P. Huntington, 'Reforming Civil–Military Relations', *Journal of Democracy* (Vol. 6, No. 4, October 1995), pp. 9–17.

26 Bengt Abrahamson, *Military Professionalization and Political Power* (Beverly Hills: SAGE Publications, 1972), p. 79.

27 Nordlinger, *op. cit.*, p. 119.

28 Joseph P. Smaldone, 'The Paradox of Military Politics in Sub-Saharan Africa', in Charles L. Cochran (ed.), *Civil–Military Relations* (New York: The Free Press, 1974), p. 219.

29 Alfred Stepan, *The Military in Politics: Changing Patterns in Brazil* (Princeton: Princeton University Press, 1971), pp. 229–30.

30 S.E. Finer, 'The Retreat to the Barracks: Notes on the Practices and the Theory of Military Withdrawal from the Seats of Power', *Third World Quarterly* (Vol. 7, No. 1, January 1985), pp. 16–30, see pp. 23–4.

31 Talukdar Maniruzzaman, *Military Withdrawal from Politics: A Comparative Study* (Cambridge, Mass: Ballinger Publishing Co., 1987), p. 80; Karl P. Magyar, 'Military Intervention and Withdrawal in Africa: Problems and Perspectives', in Constantine P. Danopoulos (ed.), *From Military to Civilian Rule* (New York: Routledge, 1992), pp. 239, 241.

32 William Gutteridge, 'Undoing Military Coups in Africa', *Third World Quarterly* (Vol. 7, No. 1, January 1985), pp. 78–89.

33 Henri J. Barkey, 'Why Military Regimes Fail: The Perils of Transition', *Armed Forces and Society* (Vol. 16, No. 2, Winter 1990), pp. 169–92.

34 For a review of writings on the military's withdrawal from power, see Claude E. Welch Jr, 'Military Disengagement from Politics: Paradigms, Processes or Random Events', *Armed Forces and Society* (Vol. 18, No. 3, Spring 1992), pp. 323–42; see also by the same author, 'Long Term Consequences of Military Rule: Breakdown and Extrication', *The Journal of Strategic Studies* (Vol. 1, No. 2, September 1978), pp. 139–53.

35 Claude E. Welch, Jr, *No Farewell to Arms? Military Disengagement from Politics in Africa and Latin America* (Boulder: Westview Press, 1987), p. 20; Maniruzzaman, *op. cit.*, pp. 31–2, 208.

36 See, for example, Robert Hamburg, 'Military Withdrawal from Politics', in Constantine P. Danopoulos (ed.), *Military Disengagement from Politics* (London: Routledge, 1988), p. 1; Welch, *op. cit.*, pp. 22–4.

37 Christopher Clapham and George Philip (eds.), *The Political Dilemmas of Military Regimes* (London: Croom Helm, 1985), pp. 12–13.

38 Robert H. Dix, 'Military Coups and Military Rule in Latin America', *Armed Forces and Society* (Vol. 20, No. 3, Spring 1994), pp. 439–56.

Chapter 3:   The Heritage

1   Philip Mason, *The Men Who Ruled India*, 1st abridged American edition (New York: Norton & Co., 1985), p. 4; Percival Griffiths, *The British Impact on India* (New York: Archon Books, 1965), p. 50.

2   Raymond A. Callahan, *The East India Company and Army Reforms, 1783–1798* (Cambridge, Mass: Harvard University Press, 1972), p. 1.

3   K.M.L. Saxena, *The Military System of India, 1850–1900* (New Delhi: Sterling Publishers, 1974), p. 3.

4   George F. MacMunn, *The Armies of India* (London: Adam & Charles Black, 1911), pp. 4–5.

5   Stephen P. Rosen, *Societies and Military Power: India and its Armies* (Ithaca: Cornell University Press, 1996), pp. 173–7.

6   See Raymond A. Callahan, *op. cit.*, pp. 12–14; S.T. Das, *Indian Military: its History and Development* (New Delhi: Sagar Publications, 1969), pp. 83, 85. As early as 1762, a contingent of Madras Army captured Manila. More such missions were sent in the last decade of the eighteenth century and the first decade of the nineteenth century. see George MacMunn, *op. cit.*, pp. 14–16.

7   For a discussion of the Sindh Frontier Force and the Punjab Frontier Force, see, T.A. Heathcote, *The Indian Army: The Garrison of British Imperial India, 1822–1922* (New York: Hippocrene Books, 1974), pp. 27–9.

8   For a detailed study of the armies of the East India Company, see Roger Beaumont, *Sword of the Raj: The British Army in India, 1747–1947* (New york: The Dobbs-Merrill Co., 1977); Madan Paul Singh, *Indian Army under the East India Company* (New Delhi: Sterling Publishers, 1976); Seema Alavi, *The Sepoys and the Company: Tradition and Transition in Northern India 1770–1830* (Delhi: Oxford University Press, 1995); S.L. Menezes, *Fidelity and Honour: The Indian Army from the Seventeenth to the Twenty-first Century* (New Delhi: Viking, 1993), pp. 1–187.

9   Stephen P. Cohen, *The Indian Army* (Delhi: Oxford University Press, 1990, 1st edition, 1971), pp. 38–40; see also, Saxena, *op. cit.*, pp. 89–91, 263.

10 The army in India adopted different organizational systems: (i) The general mixed composition system: each company in a regiment consisted of different races and castes which were mixed together irrespective of caste or creed. (ii) The class company system: each company in a regiment had soldiers of one caste and social class. In this way, each company was pure; different castes and classes were kept separately at the company level. (iii) The class regiment system: the whole regiment comprised men of one distinct social class or caste. At times, a regiment could have soldiers enlisted exclusively from one district/region.

11 A.L. Venkateswaran, *Defence Organisation in India* (New Delhi: Publication Division, Ministry of Information & Broadcasting, 1967), p. 21; Das, *op. cit.*, p. 120–2.

12 *Ibid.* (Venkateswaran, pp. 21–2; Das, pp. 124–6.)

13 David Omissi, *The Sepoy and the Raj: The Indian Army, 1860–1940* (London: Macmillan, 1994), pp. 10, 15, 19.

14 David Omissi, *op. cit.*, p. 12.

15 Cited from Stephen P. Cohen, *op. cit.*, p. 46; see also T.A. Heathcote, *op. cit.*, pp. 88–92.

16 General O'Moore Creagh, *Indian Studies* (London: Hutchinson & Co., n.d.), p. 233 (the author was C-in-C, India, 1909–14); T.A. Heathcote, *op. cit.*, pp. 92–3; David Omissi, *op. cit.*, pp. 28–9.

17 For an in-depth analysis of the under-development explanation of recruitment from the Punjab, see Mustapha Kamal Pasha, *Colonial Political Economy: Recruitment and Under-development in the Punjab* (forthcoming); see also David Omissi, *op. cit.*, pp. 49–52.

18 For an excellent study of the establishment of the canal colonies and the distribution of land by the British Indian government, see Imran Ali, *The Punjab under Imperialism, 1885–1947* (Princeton: Princeton University Press, 1988), see especially pp. 109–26.

19 *Report of the Indian Statutory Commission, 1930*, vol. 1, Survey, p. 61.

20 *Punjab Administration Report, 1921–22*, Vol. 1 (Lahore: Government of the Punjab, 1922), p. 28, see also S.D. Pradhan, 'Indian Army and the First World War', in DeWitt C. Ellinwood and S.D. Pradhan (eds.), *India and World War I* (New Delhi: Manohar Publications, 1978), pp. 49–67; Krishan G. Saini, 'The Economic Aspects of India's Participation in the First World War', in *ibid.*, pp. 141–76.

21 The statistical data have been taken from the official publication of the Government of India: *India in 1929–30* (Calcutta, 1930), p. 61.

22 Philip Magnus, *Kitchener: Portrait of an Imperialist* (London: John Murray, 1958), pp. 201–2.

23 For details, see Stephen P. Cohen, 'Issue, Role and Personality: The Kitchener–Curzon Dispute', *Comparative Studies in Society and History* (Vol. X, No. 3, April 1968), pp. 337–55.

24 David Omissi, *op. cit.*, p. 216.

25 *Punjab Administration Report, 1921–22*, Vol. 1 (Official Publication of the Government of the Punjab), p. 20. The unofficial sources put this figure much higher.

26 *Report of the Indian Statutory Commission, 1930*, Vol. II, p. 173.

27 Lorne J. Kavic, *India's Quest for Security: Defence Policies, 1947–1965* (Berkeley: University of California Press, 1967), p. 9.

28 Two detailed security plans were evolved by the British government to counter what was described as the 'Russian military menace' in 1927 and 1931. The first was named as the Blue Plan (1927) which proposed an Army advance into Afghanistan in the direction of Kabul and Kandahar from North West Frontier Province and Balochistan. The second plan, labelled the Pink Plan (1931), envisaged a limited military action in the bordering areas of Afghanistan. For details, see, N.C. Sinha and P.N. Khera, *India's War Economy – Supply, Industry and Finance* (Official History of the Indian Armed Forces in the Second World War, 1939–45, general editor, Bisheshwar Prasad) (New Delhi: Orient Longmans, 1962), pp. 15–16.

29 For a study of the British policy towards the tribal areas, see James W. Spain, 'Political Problems of a Borderland'. in Ainslie T. Embree (ed.), *Pakistan's Western Borderlands* (Durham: Carolina Academic Press, 1977), pp. 1–23; see by the same author, 'The Pathan Borderland', *The Middle East Journal* (Vol. XV, No. 2, Spring 1961), pp. 165–77.

30 *Report of the Indian Statutory Commission, 1930*, Vol. l, p. 94.

31 Quoted from Douglas M. Peers, *Between Mars and Mammon: Colonial Armies and the Garrison State in India, 1819–1835* (London: I.B. Tauris, 1995), p. 1.

32 Seema Alavi, *op. cit.*, p. 3.

33 The military expenditure figures have been quoted from N.C. Sinha and P.N. Khera, *op. cit.*, pp. 293–302, 320–39.

34 Chandar S. Sundaram, 'Preventing "Idealness": The Maharaja of Cooch Behar's Proposal for Officer Commissions in the British Army for the Sons of Indian

Princes and Gentlemen, 1897–1898', *South Asia* (Vol. XVIII, No. 1, June 1995), pp. 115–30; Byron Farewell, *Armies of the Raj: From the Mutiny to Independence, 1858–1947* (New York: W.W. Norton, 1989), p. 217.

35 Major General Iskander Mirza, who became Governor General (1955–6) and President (1956–8) of Pakistan, belonged to the first batch of Sandhurst graduates. In 1926, he was selected to the Indian Political Service and served mostly in NWFP during the British period.

36 General K.M. Cariappa, first Indian Army Chief of the Indian Army (1949–53), got the King's Commission in 1919 after graduating from the Indore College.

37 David Omissi, *op. cit.*, p. 176.

38 For the views of the British commanders on Indianization, see R.J. Moore, *The Crisis of Indian Unity, 1917–1940* (Delhi: Oxford University Press, 1974), p. 9; Rajesh Kadian, *India and its Army* (New Delhi: Vision Books, 1990), p. 33; Stephen P. Cohen, *op. cit.*, pp. 116–18; Byron Farewell, *op. cit.*, pp. 295–8.

39 The eight units selected for induction of Indian officers were: 7th Light Cavalry (late 28th Light Cavalry), 16th Light Cavalry (late 27th Light Cavalry), 21 Madras Pioneers (late 64th Pioneers), 4–19th Hyderabad Regiment (late 98 Infantry), 5th Maratha Light Infantry (late 117th Royal Marathas), 1–7th Rajput Regiment (late 2nd Queen Victoria's Own Light Infantry), 1–14th Punjab Regiment (late 19th Punjabis), and 2–1st Punjab Regiment (late 66th Punjabis).

40 For a study of the Skeen Committee with an emphasis on the role of Jinnah, see Riaz Ahmad, 'Quaid-i-Azam Jinnah and Indianisation of Officer Ranks of Army', *Pakistan Army Journal* (Vol. 35, No. 3, Autumn 1994), pp. 3–21.

41 For details, see Hasan-Askari Rizvi, *The Military and Politics in Pakistan* (Lahore: Progressive Publishers, 1986), pp. 31–2.

42 A.L. Venkateswaran, *op. cit.*, pp. 161–5.

43 *India in 1920*, pp. 16–17; *India in 1921–22*, pp. 13–14. (These are official publications of the Government of India.)

44 *Journal of the Parliaments of the Empire* (Vol. VIII, No. 4, October 1927), pp. 1930–1.

45 *Report of the Indian Statutory Commission, 1930*, Vol. II, p. 174.

46 See Peter Ward Fay, *The Forgotten Army: India's Armed Struggle for Independence, 1942–1945* (Ann Arbor: University of Michigan Press, 1993); Stephen P. Cohen, 'Subhas Chandra Bose and the Indian National Army', *Pacific Affairs* (Vol. 36, No. 4, Winter 1963–4), pp. 411–29; S.L. Menezes, *op. cit.*, pp. 372–402.

47 *Manchester Guardian*, 20 February 1946; *The Observer*, 24 February 1946; see also Penderal Moon (ed.), *Wavell: The Viceroy's Journal* (London: Oxford University Press, 1973), pp. 215–16.

48 *New York Times*, 28 February 1946.

49 A senior British officer, Lt.-General Francis Tuker, entertained such apprehensions and expressed these to the C-in-C. See Mary D. Wainwright, 'Keeping Peace in India, 1946–47: The Role of Lt.-General Sir Francis Tuker in Eastern Command', in C.H. Philips and Mary D. Wainwright (eds.), *The Partition of India: Policies and Perspectives, 1935–47* (London: George Allen & Unwin, 1970), pp. 127–47.

50 Robin Jefrey, 'The Punjab Boundary Force and the Problem of Order, August 1947', *Modern Asian Studies* (Vol. 8, No. 4, October 1974), pp. 491–520; see also H.V. Hodson, *The Great Divide* (London: Oxford University Press, 1969), pp. 408–9, 490.

51 Chaudhri Muhammad Ali, *The Emergence of Pakistan* (New York: Columbia University Press, 1967), pp. 131–2, 187; Allan Campbell-Johnson, *Mission with Mountbatten* (London: Robert Hale, 1951), p. 58.

52 *Statesman*, 22 May 1947.
53 *Ibid.*, 4 April 1947.
54 Sardar Baldev Singh's statement, *Statesman*, 26 May 1947.
55 See, Muhammad Ayub Khan, *Friends Not Masters* (London: Oxford University Press, 1967), p. 19; Chaudhri Muhammad Ali, *op. cit.*, p. 187; S.L. Menezes, *op. cit.*, p. 423.
56 Abul Kalam Azad, *India Wins Freedom* (New York: Longmans, Green, 1960), p. 236.
57 *The Memoirs of General the Lord Ismay* (London: Heinemann, 1960), p. 428; Campbell-Johnson, *op. cit.*, p. 125; Larry Collins and Dominique Lapierre, *Freedom At Midnight* (New York: Simon and Schuster, 1975), p. 210.
58 Ayesha Jalal, *The State of Martial Rule: The Origins of Pakistan's Political Economy of Defence* (Cambridge: Cambridge University Press, 1990), p. 38.
59 Chaudhri Muhammad Ali, *op. cit.*, p. 186; V.P. Menon, *The Transfer of Power in India* (Bombay: Orient Longmans, 1968), p. 406.
60 See Mountbatten's letter to Auchinleck: John Connell, *Auchinleck* (London: Cassell, 1959), pp. 915–19; S.L. Menezes, *op. cit.*, p. 436; V.P. Menon, *op. cit.*, pp. 406–7.
61 For Auchinleck's views on the hostile environment, see his report sent to London on 28 September. Connell, *op. cit.*, p. 921. Andrew Roberts writes in *Eminent Churchillians* (London: Weidenfeld and Nicolson, 1994), that Mountbatten's 'covert bias' in favour of India was known to the British officers during the partition days. Auchinleck said in September 1947 that 'Mountbatten is no longer impartial and that therefore the sooner we go the better'. Sir George Cunningham narrates in his diary on 7 November that General Messervy, C-in-C, Pakistan Army, said to him that 'Mountbatten is daily becoming more and more anathema to the Muslims and it certainly seems as if he could see nothing except through Hindu eyes' (p. 110).
62 Campbell-Johnson, *op. cit.*, p. 249.
63 See for details, Fazal Muqeem Khan, *The Story of the Pakistan Army* (Karachi: Oxford University Press, 1963), pp. 39–40.
64 *Ibid.*; see also the statement of Prime Minister H.S. Suhrawardy: *Parliamentary Debates: National Assembly of Pakistan* (Vol. 1, No. 13, 22 February 1957), p. 916.
65 See A.L. Venkateswaran, *op. cit.*, pp. 63–4.

Chapter 4:   Civilian Institutions and the Military

1 The strength of the Indian Civil Service (ICS) and Indian Political Service (IPS) was 1,157 officers at the beginning of 1947. Out of this only 101 were Muslims; 95 of the Muslim officers opted for Pakistan. They were joined by one local Christian officer, 50 British officers and 11 Muslim army officers who had opted for the political service before independence. Of these 157 officials, only 136 were available for administrative assignments as others were holding judicial or diplomatic postings. These 136 available senior officers were strengthened by the addition of about ten non-ICS/IPS officers, bringing their total of the senior officers to 146.
2 For the Afghan official case on the Durand Line and Pakhtunistan, see Rehman Pazwak, *Pakhtunistan: The Khyber Pass as the Focus of the New State of Pakhtunistan* (London: Afghan Information Bureau, n.d.), 153 pages; and by the same author: *Pakhtunistan: A New State in Central Asia* (London: Royal Afghan Embassy, 1960), 28 pages. The map between pages 6 and 7 in the first publication shows all the territory between the Indus river and the Durand Line as Pakhtunistan.

3   S.M. Burke, *Pakistan's Foreign Policy: An Historical Analysis*, 2nd edition (Karachi: Oxford University Press, 1990), p. 72.

4   Shortly after the establishment of Pakistan, they began to talk of an autonomous unit within Pakistan, although some elements continued to toy with the idea of an independent state. See, for the analysis of the politics of referendum in NWFP, Stephen A. Rittenberg, *Ethnicity, Nationalism and the Pakhtuns* (Durham: Carolina Academic Press, 1988), pp. 234–48.

5   See, for details, Mujtaba Razvi, *The Frontiers of Pakistan* (Karachi: National Publishing House, 1971), pp. 45–63; Shirin Tahir-Kheli, 'Pakhtoonistan and its International Implications', *World Affairs* (Vol. 137, No. 3, Winter 1974–5), pp. 233–45; Khalid B. Sayeed, 'Pathan Regionalism', *The South Atlantic Quarterly* (Vol. LXlll, 1964), pp. 478–504.

6   Fazal Muqeem Khan, *The Story of Pakistan Army* (Karachi: Oxford University Press, 1963), p. 222.

7   *Ibid.*, p. 223; Chaudhri Muhammad Ali, *The Emergence of Pakistan* (New York: Columbia University Press, 1967), p. 247.

8   See, Mohammad Ayub Khan, *Friends Not Masters: A Political Autobiography* (London: Oxford University Press, 1967), pp. 22, 30; Chaudhri Muhammad Ali, *op. cit.*, p. 377; Fazal Muqeem Khan, *op. cit.*, p. 46.

9   *News Chronicle*, 9 October 1948.

10   *Dawn* 17 August 1953.

11   *Ibid.*, 1 August 1957.

12   Ruth Leger Sivard, *World Military and Social Expenditure 1977* (Leesburg, Virginia: WMSE Publications, 1977), p. 5.

13   Hasan-Askari Rizvi, 'Pakistan's Threat Perception and Weapons Procurement', in Thomas Wander, Eric Arnett & Paul Bracken (eds), *The Diffusion of Advanced Weaponry: Technologies, Regional Implications, and Responses* (Washington, D.C.: American Association for the Advancement of Science, 1994), pp. 193–210.

14   Quoted from Aslam Siddiqi, *Pakistan Seeks Security* (Lahore: Longmans, 1960), p. 55.

15   Pervaiz Iqbal Cheema, *Pakistan's Defence Policy, 1947–1958* (London: Macmillan, 1990), pp. 84, 113–14.

16   *Foreign Relations of the United States, 1948*, Vol. V, Part 1 (Washington DC: U.S. Government Printing Office, 1975), pp. 496–7 (Memorandum by the Secretary of State to President Truman, dated 11 March 1948). See also the memorandum of conversation between the U.S. Acting Secretary of State and India's Secretary General, Ministry of External Affairs, dated 2 April 1948, pp. 506–8.

17   See, *Department of State Bulletin* (Vol. 30, No. 779, 31 May 1954), pp. 850–1.

18   Three Agreements of Cooperation with identical texts were signed with Pakistan, Iran and Turkey. For the text of the agreements see *ibid.* (Vol. XL, No. 1030, 23 March 1959), pp. 417–18.

19   *Foreign Relations of the United States 1958–60*, Vol. XV (Washington DC: U.S. Government Printing Office, 1992), p. 615.

20   Shirin Tahir-Kheli, *The United States and Pakistan: The Evolution of an Influence Relationship* (New York: Praeger, 1982), p. 6.

21   *Dawn*, 18 January 1955.

22   Air Marshal Mohammad Asghar Khan (C-in-C, Pakistan Air Force, 1957–65) writes in his book *Pakistan at the Cross Roads* (Lahore: Ferozsons, 1969), pp. 4–5: 'The distance between the two wings of Pakistan is so great that rapid movement of forces from one theatre to the other is not practicable. The two Indian theatres of

operation in the east and west are, therefore, likely to remain for all practical purposes, independent of each other and not mutually supporting. The two wings of Pakistan, therefore, lend strength to each other's defence and together impose a strain on India's offensive capability which could prove decisive against the two halves of Pakistan separately. In military terms, therefore, Pakistan's division into two halves lends strength to her defence and enhances her security.'

23 Abul Kalam Azad, *India Wins Freedom* (New York: Longmans, Green, 1960), p. 200; Penderel Moon (ed.), *Wavell: The Viceroy's Journal* (London: Oxford University Press, 1973), pp. 361–2, 377–8.

24 For a discussion of these constitutional issues, see Inamur Rehman, *Public Opinion and Political Development in Pakistan* (Karachi: Oxford University Press, 1992), part 1; Lawrence Ziring, *Pakistan: The Enigma of Political Development* (Boulder: Westview Press, 1980), pp. 167–93; Richard S. Wheeler, *The Politics in Pakistan: The Constitutional Quest* (Ithaca: Cornell University Press, 1970), pp. 91–121; G.W. Choudhury, *Constitutional Development in Pakistan* (London: Longmans, 1969), pp. 35–101.

25 Most of the delegates to the first meetings were upper caste Hindus and Parsis, including some wealthy landowners and merchants, and professionals. A number of Englishmen were also involved, including A.O. Hume, a retired ICS officer, described as the 'Father of the Congress', a confidant of Viceroy Lord Rippon, see Stanley Wolpert, *A New History of India*, fifth edition (New York: Oxford University Press, 1997), pp. 257–8.

26 The founding delegates belonged to the upper strata of the Muslim community. They were titled nobility, wealthy landed owners, and professionals like lawyers, educators and journalists.

27 Mohammad Waseem, *Politics and the State in Pakistan* (Islamabad: National Institute of Historical & Cultural Research, 1994), pp. 89–90, 108; Omar Noman, *Pakistan: Political and Economic History since 1947* (London: Kegan Paul International, 1990), pp. 9–10.

28 Keith B. Callard, *Pakistan a Political Study* (London: Allen & Unwin, 1957), p. 67; see also by the same author, *Political Forces in Pakistan* (New York: Institute of Pacific Relations, 1959), pp. 5–26.

29 Seven cases were instituted against the political leaders during the five year life of the PRODA (1949–54). Four of them were convicted. They were Muhammad Ayub Khuhro, Kazi Fazlullah and Ghulam Nabi Khan Pathan (all from Sindh), and Hamidul Huq Choudhry (East Pakistan). Cases were also instituted against Iftikhar Hussain Mamdot (Punjab), Ghulam Ali Talpur (Sindh), and Mian Mumtaz Khan Daultana (Punjab); they were not convicted. The Governor General had the power to withdraw restrictions imposed under the PRODA which he did in the case of Khuhro.

30 See, *Pakistan News Digest*, 1 October and 1 November 1953.

31 The draft constitution was ready by the time the Constituent Assembly was dissolved. It was signed by the members of the committee two days after the dissolution. see Tamizuddin Khan, *The Test of Time: My Life and Days* (Dhaka: University Press, 1989), p. 151.

32 *Pakistan News Digest*, 1 November 1954.

33 For an analysis of the legal battle on the dissolution of the Constituent Assembly, see Allen McGrath, *The Destruction of Democracy in Pakistan* (Karachi: Oxford University Press, 1996); Paula R. Newberg, *Judging the State: Courts and Constitutional*

Politics in Pakistan (Cambridge: Cambridge University Press, 1995), pp. 43–68; Tayyab Mahmud, 'Praetorianism and Common Law in Post-Colonial Settings: Judicial Responses to Constitutional Breakdowns in Pakistan,' *Utah Law Review* (Vol. 1993, No. 4, 1993), pp. 1226–1305 (see pp. 1233–42).

34 Iskandar Mirza's autobiography was serialized in *Weekly Meyaar* (Karachi) in 1976 under the title 'Iskander Mirza Speaks: An Autobiography'. Later, it was published as a book by the same magazine. In 1996, *Newsline* (Karachi) published excerpts from Iskander Mirza's detailed interview with Hasan Ispahani recorded in September 1967. See 'Memoirs of a President', *Newsline*, May 1996, pp. 130–41 and June 1996, pp. 133–6. Both the memoirs mention the Suhrawardy affair. Iskander Mirza says, 'I issued an ultimatum [to Suhrawardy]: he must resign within two hours or I would dismiss him.' *Weekly Meyaar* (Vol. 1, No. 24, 29 May–5 June 1976, p. 20; and *Newsline*, May 1996, pp. 131–3. See also M.H.R. Talukdar (ed.), *Memoirs of Huseyn Shaheed Suhrawardy* (Dhaka: University Press, 1987), p. 119.

35 For a review of dismissals of the provincial governments, see K.K. Aziz, *Party Politics in Pakistan, 1947–58* (Islamabad: National Commission on Historical & Cultural Research, 1976), pp. 1–28.

36 Prime Minister Muhammad Ali Bogra, while announcing the decision of the government to integrate the provinces and states of West Pakistan into a single province of West Pakistan, maintained that this would promote national integration, eliminate provincialism, reduce administrative expenditure, and simplify the task of constitution-making. He argued that a unitary system was better for Pakistan but given the fact that the two wings were separated by a distance of one thousand miles of India, it could not be adopted. Therefore, he was giving 'the next best thing to a unitary system', he asserted. 'As it [was] not possible to unify the whole of Pakistan we should at least unify the whole of West Pakistan.' For the text of his address to the nation on radio, see *Pakistan News Digest*, 1 December 1954.

37 For the details of the politics of the formation of the integrated province of West Pakistan, see Ayesha Jalal, *The State of Martial Rule: The Origins of Pakistan's Political Economy of Defence* (Cambridge: Cambridge University Press, 1990), pp. 197–202; Khalid B. Sayeed, *op. cit.*, pp. 76–81.

38 It is interesting to note that Fazlul Haq accused by the central/federal government of making anti-Pakistan statements in May 1954, was appointed Interior Minister in the federal cabinet of Chaudhri Mohammad Ali in August 1955, and in March 1956, he was sent to East Pakistan as its Governor.

39 For an insightful analysis of Pakistan's political conditions, see Lawrence Ziring, *Pakistan in the Twentieth Century: A Political History* (Karachi: Oxford University Press, 1997), pp. 98–216; Khalid B. Sayeed, 'Collapse of Parliamentary Democracy in Pakistan', *Middle East Journal* (Vol. 13, No. 4, Autumn 1959), pp. 389–406; K.J. Newman, 'Pakistan's Preventive Autocracy and its Causes', *Pacific Affairs* (Vol. 32, No. 1, March 1959), pp. 18–33; *Report of the Constitution Commission, 1961* (Karachi: Manager of Publications, Government of Pakistan, 1962); Ayesha Jalal, *op. cit.*, pp. 136–276.

40 Allen Campbell-Johnson, *Mission With Mountbatten* (London: Robert Hale, 1851), p. 226.

41 Chaudhri Muhammad Ali, *op. cit.*, pp. 305–6.

42 Fazal Muqeem Khan, *op. cit.*, p. 154.

43 See *Dawn*, 18 January 1955; Mohammad Ahmad, *My Chief* (Lahore: Longmans, 1960), pp. 73–6.

44 See the press note on the imposition of martial law: *Dawn*, 8 March 1953. Chief Minister Mian Mumtaz Daultana said: 'Lahore had to be handed over to the Army when it was fully realized that any further control of the situation by the police would involve a heavy loss of life and property.'

45 See, Hamza Alavi, 'The State in Crisis', in Hassan Gardezi and Jamil Rashid (eds.), *Pakistan: The Roots of Dictatorship* (London: Zed Press, 1983), pp. 40–93 (see pp. 65–6); see by the same author, 'The Army and the Bureaucracy in Pakistan', *International Socialist Journal* (Vol. 3, No. 14, March–April 1966), pp. 149–88; 'The State in Post-colonial Societies: Pakistan and Bangladesh', *New Left Review* (No. 74, July–August 1972), pp. 59–81.

46 Ayub Khan, M., *Friends Not Masters* (Karachi: Oxford University Press, 1967), p. 52; Fazal Muqeem Khan, *op. cit.*, p. 189; see Ayub Khan's first address on the radio after assuming power on 8 October 1958. Iskander Mirza, in his two autobiographies, published in *Weekly Meyaar* and *Newsline*, noted in n. 34, talks about such a proposal by Ghulam Muhammad but he thought that it was not a serious offer. *Weekly Meyaar* (Vol. 1, No. 22, 15–22 May 1976), p. 30; *Newsline*, June 1966, p. 139.

47 The officers were Major General Mohammad Akbar Khan, Major General Nazir Ahmad Khan, Air Commodore M.K. Janjua, Brigadier M. Latif, Brigadier Siddique Khan, Lt.-Col. Ziauddin, Lt.-Col. Niaz Mohammad Arbab, Major Ishaq, Major Hasan Khan, Captain Khizar Hayat, and Captain Zafrullah Poshni. The civilians were: Faiz Ahmad Faiz (Chief Editor, Progressive Papers Ltd., known for its Marxist orientation), Sajjad Zaheer (Secretary General Pakistan Communist Party), Mohammad Hussain Ata (a communist activist) and Mrs Nasim Akbar Khan (acquitted).

48 For the official views on the Conspiracy see *Keesing's Contemporary Archives*, 1951, pp. 11396, 11494; *Pakistan Times*, 10 March 1951; Ayub Khan, M., *op. cit.*, pp. 36–39.

49 In 1972, Major General Akbar Khan admitted that they had worked on the idea of dislodging the government and establishing a military dominated government which was to initiate military action in Kashmir, hold new elections for the constituent assembly and frame a constitution. He, however, maintained that they did not envisage arresting or killing anyone in pursuance of their plans. See his article in Urdu entitled '*Phali Jang-i-Kashmir ki Fire-bandi aur Pindi Sazish Case*' published in monthly *Hikayat* (Lahore) (Vol. 5, No. 1, September 1972). See also his interview in *Defence Journal* (Vol. Xl, No. 6–7, June–July 1985), pp. 10–28. He maintained that they did not want to establish a military dictatorship but wanted to force the Governor General to take certain actions as desired by them. Even these plans had been abandoned in the meeting held at his residence in February. However, in the same interview he claimed: '...If the Pindi Conspiracy had succeeded the country would have had a democratic constitution by 1952 and Kashmir would have become a part of Pakistan' (p. 26). Akbar Khan joined the Awami League after his release from prison. Later, he opted for the Pakistan People's Party (PPP) and served as a Minister of State for National Security in Z.A. Bhutto's government.

50 *Dawn*, 28 October 1953.

Chapter 5: The First Military Regime

1 *The Constitution of the Islamic Republic of Pakistan, 1956* (Karachi: The Manager of Publications, Government of Pakistan, 1956), Article 222(1).

2 *Foreign Relations of the United States, 1958–60* Vol. XV (Washington, DC: U.S. Government Printing Office, 1992), pp. 664–5, 669 (Telegram from the US embassy in Pakistan to Department of State, dated 5 October 1958; and Memorandum from the Director of the Office of South Asia Affairs to Assistant Secretary of State for Near Eastern Affairs, dated 7 October 1958); see also Altaf Gauhar, *Ayub Khan: Pakistan's First Military Ruler* (Lahore: Sang-e-Meel Publications, 1993, 1994), pp. 147–8.

3 For the text of President Eisenhower's letter see *ibid.*, pp. 673–4, and Defence Secretary Neil McElory's visit: p. 678.

4 Mohammad Ayub Khan, *Friends Not Masters: A Political Autobiography* (Karachi: Oxford University Press, 1967), pp. 73–5; Mohammad Asghar Khan, *Generals in Politics: Pakistan 1958–82* (New Delhi: Vikas Publishing House, 1983), pp. 8–9. (The author, C-in-C of the Air Force in 1958, maintained that his Chief of Staff, Air Commodore Maqbool Rabb was contacted by Iskander Mirza for mobilizing support against Ayub Khan. Rabb informed Asghar Khan and the Army colleagues of this development.) See also the interview of Lt.-General K.M. Sheikh: *Nawa-i-Waqt* (magazine section), 10–16 May 1985.

5 See Iskander Mirza's autobiography entitled 'Iskander Mirza Speaks: An Autobiography' *Weekly Meyaar* (Vol. 1, No. 26, 12–19 June 1976), p. 49; and excerpts from his interview entitled 'Memoirs of a President–part ll' *Newsline*, June 1996, pp. 133–41 (p.141).

6 The State vs. Dosso and another: *P.L.D., 1958, Supreme Court*, pp. 533–70 (p. 539). For a comparative analysis of conferment of legality to coup d'état by courts, see Tayyub Mahmud, 'Jurisprudence of Successful Treason: Coup d'état and Common Law', *Cornell International Law Journal* (Vol. 27, No. 1, Winter 1994), pp. 51–140; Paula R. Newberg, *Judging the State: Courts and Constitutional Politics in Pakistan* (Cambridge: Cambridge University Press, 1995), pp. 73–78.

7 For the names of the commissions and committees, see Ralph Braibanti, *Research on the Bureaucracy of Pakistan* (Durham: Duke University Press, 1966), table between pp. 312–13; Ayub Khan, *op. cit.*, p. 249. Appendix V.

8 *Pakistan News Digest*, 15 October 1958.

9 Herbert Feldman, *Revolution in Pakistan: A Study of Martial Law Administration* (London: Oxford University Press, 1967), p. 7.

10 *Pakistan under the New Regime* (Karachi; Pakistan Publications, n.d.), p. 7.

11 Feldman, *op. cit.*, p. 52.

12 Ralph Braibanti, *op. cit.*, p. 293; see also *Dawn*, 28 June 1959; *Pakistan Times*, 3 July 1959.

13 *Report of the Pay and Services Commission, 1959–62* (Karachi: Printing Corporation of Pakistan, 1969), pp. 1–2, 46, 60–2.

14 *Twenty Years of Pakistan* (Karachi: Pakistan Publications, 1967), p. 733.

15 N.A. Faruqui, 'Pakistan's New Capital', in H.B. Khokhar (ed.), *20 Years of Pakistan* (Karachi: the editor, 1967), pp. 77–8.

16 *Pakistan 1962–63* (Karachi: Pakistan Publications, 1963), p. 91. In April 1960, Azam Khan was appointed Governor, East Pakistan, and the Rehabilitation portfolio was transferred to Lt.-General K.M. Sheikh.

17 Ayub Khan, *op. cit.*, p. 87.

18 *Report of the Land Reform Commission for West Pakistan* (Lahore: Government of West Pakistan, 1959), see the introductory note without page numbers. The commission was headed by Akhtar Hussain, Governor, West Pakistan, and included eight senior bureaucrats as its members.

19 For the recommendations of the Land Reforms Commission and the government's policy decision, see *ibid.*, pp. i–ix, and 1–12 of part 2.

20 For the full text of the document, see Ayub Khan, *op. cit.*, pp.186–91; and Mohammad Ahmad, *My Chief* (Lahore: Longmans, 1960), pp. 86–83.

21 Ayub Khan, *op. cit.*, p. 207.

22 Ayub Khan's interview with Guy Wint: *Observer*, 19 April 1959.

23 For Ayub Khan's views on governance, democracy and economic development, see Rais Ahmad Jafri (ed.), *Ayub Soldier and Statesman* (Lahore: Mohammad Ali Academy, 1966); *Speeches and Statements by Field Marshal Mohammad Ayub Khan*, Vols. l–Vlll (Karachi: Pakistan Publications, n.d.); Ayub Khan, 'Pakistan Perspective', *Foreign Affairs* (Vol. 38, No. 4, July 1960), pp. 547–56; see also Ayub Khan's article, 'A New Experiment in Democracy in Pakistan', *The Annals of the American Academy of Political and Social Science* Vol. 358, March 1965), pp. 109–13; Ayub Khan's autobiography, cited earlier, gives an insight into his political ideas, see pp. 204–5, 207.

24 Altaf Gauhar, *op. cit.*, pp. 162–5.

25 It was on this day, i.e. 27 October 1959, that the presidential cabinet elevated Ayub Khan to the rank of Field Marshal.

26 Two Provincial Development Advisory Councils were set up in May 1960 for East and West Pakistan to coordinate the development work undertaken through Basic Democracies. Their members were nominated by the President on the recommendation of the concerned provincial Governor. These councils were abandoned in June 1962, when the provincial assemblies began to function after the introduction of the 1962 Constitution.

27 Shahid Javed Burki, 'Vital Role by Basic Democracies', in H.B. Khokhar, *op. cit.*, pp. 45–8 (see p. 48).

28 See Hamid Yusuf, *Pakistan: A Study of Political Developments, 1947–97* (Lahore: Academy of Administrative and Social Sciences, 1998), p. 72.

29 *Pakistan News Digest*, 1 March 1960.

30 The members of the Constitution Commission were: Justice Muhammad Shahabuddin (Chairman). Members from East Pakistan: Azizuddin Ahmad (a former central minister), D.N. Barori (a leader of Hindu Scheduled Castes), Abu Sayeed Chaudhry (a barrister who later became a judge of High Court), Obeidur Rahman Nizam (business-commercial background), Aftabuddin Ahmad (an agriculturist). Members from West Pakistan: Muhammad Sharif (a former judge of Supreme Court), Tufail Ali Abdul Rahman (a lawyer from Sindh who later became a judge of High Court), Arbab Ahmad Ali Jan (a retired District and Session Judge from NWFP), Sardar Habibullah (an agriculturist from the Punjab), Naseer A. Sheikh (an industrialist from the Punjab). Several honorary advisers were appointed to assist the Commission. These included Sharifuddin Pirzada, G.W. Choudhury, Khawaja Sarwar Hasan, Begum Jahanara Shahnawaz, and Begum Shamsunnaha Mahmud.

31 *Report of the Constitution Commission, 1961* (Karachi: Government of Pakistan Press, 1962), p. 1.

32 For the full text of the questionnaire, see *ibid.*, pp. 143–6.

33 For the text of Chaudhri Muhammad Ali's response to the questionnaire, see Salahuddin Khan (ed.), *The Task before Us: Selected Speeches and Writings of Chaudhri Muhammad Ali* (Lahore: Research Society of Pakistan, Punjab University, 1974), pp. 143–6.

34 For a review of the debate sparked by the questionnaire, see Edgar A. Schuler & Kathryn R. Schuler, *Public Opinion and Constitution Making in Pakistan 1958–62* (East Lansing: Michigan State University Press, 1967), pp. 61–81.

35 The members of the cabinet sub-committee were: Manzoor Qadir, Minister for Foreign Affairs; Mohammad Shoab, Finance Minister; Zulfikar Ali Bhutto, Minister for Fuel, Power and Natural Resources; Mohammad Ibrahim, Law Minister; Abul Kasem Khan, Industries Minister; Habibur Rahman, Minister for National Reconstruction; Akhtar Hussain, Minister for Education and Scientific Research.

36 The bureaucrats were: N.A. Faruqui, Cabinet Secretary; Qazi Anwarul Haq, Chief Secretary, East Pakistan; Muzaffar Ahmad, Additional Chief Secretary, West Pakistan; Ghulam Ishaq Khan, Chairman WAPDA: and Aftab Qazi, Secretary Finance.

37 Ayub Khan, *Friends Not Masters*, p. 213; see also his address to the inaugural session of the National Assembly on 8 June 1962.

38 *Pakistan General Elections, 1962* (Karachi: Government of Pakistan Press, 1963), pp. 47, 52, 54, 55.

Chapter 6: Authoritarian Clientelism: Post-Martial Law Rule

1 *The Constitution of the Islamic Republic of Pakistan, 1962* (Karachi: The Manager of Publications, Government of Pakistan, 1968), Article 31.

2 The ministers could sit in the National Assembly and address it. Article 104 (1) provided that if a member of the National or Provincial Assemblies was appointed minister at the federal or provincial level, he would lose his seat in the assembly. Within a few days of the promulgation of the Constitution, the President removed this restriction by invoking his powers for removal of difficulties in the enforcement of the Constitution. Several members of the National and Provincial Assemblies joined the federal and provincial cabinets. The action was challenged in the East Pakistan High Court which held in April 1963 that the President's action was unconstitutional on the grounds that the article on removal of difficulties could not be used for amending the Constitution. This judgement was upheld by the Supreme Court in May. Several ministers lost their membership of the National and Provincial Assemblies, but they continued to participate in the proceedings of the National and Provincial Assemblies without the right to vote.

3 *The Constitution*, Article 17.

4 The eighth amendment, approved in December 1967, increased the strength of the National Assembly to 218, equally divided between East and West Pakistan. In the same year, the strength of the elected BD members was raised to 120,000. These changes were to be effective from the next general elections due in 1969–70 which could not be held because the military assumed power in March 1969.

5 Khalid B. Sayeed, *The Political System of Pakistan* (London: Oxford University Press, 1967), p. 109.

6 *The Constitution*, Articles 40–2.

7 M. Rashiduzzaman, 'The National Assembly of Pakistan under the 1962 Constitution', *Pacific Affairs* (Vol. XL, No. 4, Winter 1969–70), pp. 481–93.

8 *Ibid.*, Article 30.

9 Mumtaz Ahmad, *Bureaucracy and Political Development in Pakistan* (Karachi: NIPA, 1974), pp. 102–3; see also Ralph Braibanti, *Research on the Bureaucracy of Pakistan* (Durham: Duke University Press, 1966), table between pp. 236–7.

10 General Musa was designated as Pakistan's ambassador to Iran in July 1966. In September, a few days before his retirement, the government decided to appoint him Governor of West Pakistan.

11 Prior to his appointment as the C-in-C of the Air Force, Nur Khan was President/ Managing Director of PIA, a position he handed over to Asghar Khan. When Asghar Khan left PIA in May 1968, his replacement was another Air Force officer, Air Vice Marshal M. Akhtar. Nur Khan was again appointed to the top job in PIA in 1974.

12 *The Constitution*, Article 238.

13 Shahid Javed Burki, 'Twenty Years of the Civil Service of Pakistan', *Asian Survey* (Vol. 9, No. 4, April 1969), pp. 239–54.

14 Two well-known cases of retired officers making fortunes in business were those of Captain Gohar Ayub, son of Ayub Khan, and his father-in-law Lt.-General Habibullah Khan. Their success led to an allegation against Ayub Khan in 1968–9 that his family members were engaged in money-making. For the details of Gohar Ayub's financial assets in 1968–9, see Herbert Feldman, *From Crisis to Crisis: Pakistan 1962–69* (Karachi: Oxford University Press, 1972), Appendix B on pp. 305–6, see also pp. 286–8.

15 Raymond A. Moore, 'The Army as a Vehicle for Social Change in Pakistan', *The Journal of Developing Areas* (Vol. 2, No. 1, October 1967), pp. 57–74; see also *Twenty Years of Pakistan, 1947–67* (Karachi: Pakistan Publications, 1967), pp. 520–1.

16 For details, see Raymond A. Moore, 'The Use of the Army in Nation-building: The Case of Pakistan', *Asian Survey* (Vol. 9, No. 6, June 1969), pp. 447–56; also by the same author 'Military Nation Building in Pakistan and India', *World Affairs* (Vol. 132, No. 3, December 1969), pp. 219–34.

17 *India–China Border Problem* (Delhi: Ministry of External Affairs, Government of India, n.d.), p. 4.

18 For Nehru's letters to Kennedy, see *Foreign Relations of the United States, 1961–63*, Vol. XIX (Washington, DC: U.S. Government Printing Office, 1996), p. 352 (document, no. 182), p. 361 (document no. 188), p. 397 (document no. 203). On Nehru's letters, see also Altaf Gauhar, *Ayub Khan: Pakistan's First Military Ruler* (Lahore: Sang-e-Meel Publications, 1994), pp. 497–517.

19 Norman D. Palmer, *The United States and India: The Dimensions of Influence* (New York: Praeger, 1984), p. 28; *Foreign Relations of the United States, 1961–63*, Vol. XIX, pp. 363–8 (document no. 190, see especially p. 366).

20 Vernon M. Hewitt, *The International Politics of South Asia* (Manchester: Manchester University Press, 1992), p. 67.

21 An American fact-finding mission visited India in November 1962. The Chief of the British Imperial Staff, General Hull, came to India during the same month. A team of Air Force experts from the US and the Commonwealth undertook a comprehensive survey of India's air defence in January–February 1963. Earlier on 20 December 1962, President Kennedy and British Prime Minister Harold Macmillan met at Nassau and agreed to earmark $100 million for supplying military hardware and weapons to India. In June–July 1963, the two countries agreed to allocate more funds for strengthening India's security. For the summary of the dialogue between Kennedy and Macmillan at Nassau, see *Foreign Relations of the United States, 1961–63*, Vol. XIX, pp. 448–58 (documents nos. 230 and 231); see also *Hindu*, 23 December 1962; *Guardian*, 5 March 1963.

22 Ian C.C. Graham, 'The Indo-Soviet MIG Deal and its Repercussions', *Asian Survey* (Vol. IV, No. 5, May 1964), pp. 823–32.

23 For a review of Pakistan's security concerns in the context of Western arms assistance to India, see Khalid Bin Sayeed, 'Pakistan's Foreign Policy: An Analysis of Pakistani Fears and Interests', *Asian Survey* (Vol. IV, No. 3, March 1964), pp. 746–56; Shaheen Irshad Khan, *Rejection Alliance?* (Lahore: Ferozsons, 1972), pp. 85–116.

24 See Ayub Khan's letter of 5 November 1962 to Kennedy: *Foreign Relations of the United States, 1961–63*, Vol. XIX, pp. 377–80 (document no. 195).

25 Pakistan raised the boundary demarcation issue with China in 1959, and in March 1961, it made a formal proposal for border talks.

26 *Foreign Relations of the United States, 1961–63*, Vol. XIX, see document no. 315 (pp. 628–31) summary of the conversation between Ayub Khan and US Ambassador Walter McConaughy in Quetta on 7 August 1963. The concluding paragraph on p. 630 states: 'Main theme on each side came out again at the end of meeting when Ayub solemnly enjoined me on his behalf to urge [the US] President "not to drive us to the wall" and I adjured him not to take any action which would have the unnatural effect of putting Pakistan's immediate interests out of line with U.S discharge of its regional obligations.' For America's negative reaction to Pakistan's improvement of relations with China, see document no. 332 (pp. 679–80) for the highlights of Foreign Minister Bhutto's conversation with President Kennedy and senior staff of the Department of State on 3–6 October 1963, and document no. 341 (pp. 694–6) for Bhutto's talks with President Johnson on 29 November 1963.

27 S.M. Burke, *Pakistan's Foreign Policy: An Historical Analysis* (Karachi: Oxford University Press, 1973), p. 324.

28 For the full text of the ceasefire agreement and the award of the tribunal, see Mujtaba Razvi, *The Frontiers of Pakistan* (Karachi: National Publishing House, 1970), Appendices VII and VIII, pp. 266–82; see also *Pakistan News Digest*, 15 July 1965 and 1 March 1968.

29 For the Army's image-building efforts in the aftermath of the Rann of Kutch war, see A.R. Siddiqi, *The Military in Pakistan: Image and Reality* (Lahore: Vanguard Books, 1996), pp. 84–92.

30 For revival of the political parties and related political activities, see Lawrence Ziring, *The Ayub Khan Era: Politics in Pakistan 1958–69* (Syracuse: Syracuse University Press, 1971), pp. 31–5; Saleem M.M. Qureshi, 'Party Politics in the Second Republic of Pakistan', *The Middle East Journal* (Vol. 20, No. 4, Autumn 1966), pp. 456–72.

31 *Keesing's Contemporary Archives*, 19–26 October 1963, p. 19693.

32 The major opposition alliances during 1962–9 included: National Democratic Front (NDF) 1962, Combined Opposition Parties (COP) 1964–5, Pakistan Democratic Movement (PDM) 1967, and Democratic Action Committee (DAC) 1969.

33 Ayub Khan polled 21,012 and 28,939 votes in East and West Pakistan respectively (63.31 per cent of the votes polled). Ms Fatima Jinnah got 18,434 and 10,257 votes in East and West Pakistan respectively (36.36 per cent). There were two independent candidates in the race: K.M. Kamal and Mian Bashir Ahmed who secured 183 and 65 votes respectively. See *Report on General Elections in Pakistan, 1964–65*, Vol. 1 (Islamabad: The Election Commission, 1967), p. 68.

34 For an insightful analysis of the elections, see Sharif-al Mujahid, 'Pakistan's First Presidential Elections', *Asian Survey* (Vol. 5, No. 6, June 1965), pp. 280–94; and 'The Assembly Elections in Pakistan', *ibid.*, (Vol. 5, No. 11, November 1965), pp. 538–51.

35 The National Assembly elections results were: Convention Muslim League 124 seats, the COP 15 and Independents 17. East Pakistan Provincial Assembly: Convention Muslim League 71, Independents 84; the COP did not put up any candidate. West Pakistan Assembly: Convention Muslim League 104, the COP 1, and Independents 50; the COP had put up only 6 candidates. See *Report on General Elections, op. cit.*, p. 211.

36 Talukder Maniruzzaman, 'Crisis in Political Development and the Collapse of the Ayub Regime in Pakistan', *The Journal of Developing Areas* (Vol. 5, No. 2, January 1971), pp. 221–37.

37 For the controversies on the role of Islam between the government's perspective on the role of Islam in the polity, see Fazlur Rahman, *Some Islamic Issues in the Ayub Khan Era*, Occasional Paper Series (Chicago: Muslim Studies Sub-Committee of the Committee on Southern Asian Studies, University of Chicago, 1972); Jamal Malik, *Colonialization of Islam* (New Delhi: Monohar Publishers, 1996), pp. 34–7, 59–61, 66–7, 123–8.

38 *Pakistan News Digest*, 15 January 1968; Herbert Feldman, *op. cit.*, pp. 184–9; Lawrence Ziring, *op. cit.*, p. 90. A special tribunal was set up through a presidential ordinance which started the trial of the accused in June 1968. However, the proceedings could not go beyond the preliminary stages as anti-government agitation broke out towards the end of the year. The tribunal included Justice S.A. Rahman, a former Chief Justice of the Supreme Court (Chairman) and two judges of East Pakistan High Court: M.R. Khan and Maksumul Hakim.

39 S.M. Zafar, *Through the Crisis* (Lahore: Book Center, 1970), p. 128. The author was Law Minister in Ayub's cabinet in 1968.

40 *Dawn*, 14 November 1968.

41 While announcing his decision to enter politics on 17 November 1968, Air Marshal Asghar Khan declared in a press conference: 'I have been watching, for some time, the deterioration in the political, social and economic conditions in the country. Corruption, nepotism, graft and administrative incompetence are affecting the lives and happiness of millions of our countrymen. Social inequality and economic disparity is increasing and the gap between the rich and the poor is widening day by day.' For the full text, see Mohammad Asghar Khan, *Pakistan at the Cross Roads* (Lahore: Ferozsons, 1969), pp. 97–9. In another statement, he said, 'At present the whole structure stinks. It is not a healthy system . . . There is no criticism. The press is completely suppressed, there is no check on the government. We are bordering on a police state.' *Times* (London), 26 November 1968.

42 The political parties in the DAC included the Awami League (Mujibur Rahman), National Awami Party (Wali), Jamiat-e-Ulema-i-Islam, Nizam-i-Islam Party, Awami League (Nsrullah), Jamaat-i-Islami, National Democratic Front, and Council Muslim League.

43 Bhashani and Bhutto boycotted the dialogue and continued with their agitation against the Ayub regime in the streets.

44 Robert Laporte, Jr, 'Succession in Pakistan: Continuity and Change in a Garrison State,' *Asian Survey* (Vol. 9, No. 11, November 1969), pp. 842–61.

45 See, Altaf Gauhar, *op. cit.*, p. 447.

46 *The Constitution*, Articles 16(1) and 165(4).

47 See, Altaf Gauhar's statement in the Sindh-Balochistan High Court, *Daily Sun*, 29 September 1972; see also his book, *op. cit.*, pp. 471, 473–4.

48 A.R. Siddiqi, *op. cit.*, pp. 148–56.

49 Altaf Gauhar, *op. cit.*, pp. 476–7.

Chapter 7:   The Second Military Regime

1 Abdul Hamid Khan was made a full General on 1 January 1971, but he continued to serve in the post he held as Lt.-General. In this way, for the first time the Army had two serving Generals.

2 G.W. Choudhury, *The Last Days of United Pakistan* (Bloomington: Indiana University Press, 1974), p. 57.

3 Fazal Muqeem Khan, *Pakistan's Crisis in Leadership* (Islamabad: National Book Foundation, 1973), p. 20.

4 *Pakistan News Digest*, 1 March 1970.

5 *Pakistan News Digest*, 15 November 1969; G.W. Choudhury, *op. cit.*, p. 54; Herbert Feldman, *The End and the Beginning: Pakistan 1969–1971* (Karachi: Oxford University Press, 1975), pp. 18–19.

6 Martial Law Regulation No. 60, issued on 20 December 1969.

7 Originally the elections were scheduled for 7 October. The date was shifted to 7 December in view of a cyclone that hit East Pakistan in August, causing much loss of human life and property. A tidal wave hit parts of East Pakistan in late November. Some political leaders favoured another postponement but the military refused to shift the date.

8 Mohammad Waseem, *Politics and the State in Pakistan* (Islamabad: National Institute of Historical and Cultural Research, 1994), pp. 244–5.

9 For an analysis of the election campaign and the results, see: Sharifal Mujahid, 'Pakistan's First General Elections', *Asian Survey* (Vol. Xl, No. 2, February 1971), pp. 159–71; Craig Baxter, 'Pakistan Votes', *ibid.* (Vol. X1, No. 3, March 1971), pp. 197–218.

10 *Report on General Elections, Pakistan, 1970–71*, Vol. 1 (Karachi: Manager of Publications, Government of Pakistan, 1972), pp. 204–5.

11 Safdar Mahmood, *Pakistan Divided* (Lahore: Ferozsons, 1984), pp. 38–41, 255–65; see by the same author, *The Deliberate Debacle* (Lahore: Sh. Mohammad Ashraf, 1974), pp. 41–2, 244–56.

12 Ralph Braibanti, *Research on the Bureaucracy of Pakistan* (Durham: Duke University Press, 1966), p. 49; Khalid Bin Sayeed, *Pakistan: The Formative Phase, 1958–1948* (London: Oxford University Press, 1968), p. 275; Richard D. Lambert, 'Factors in Bengali Regionalism in Pakistan', *Far Eastern Survey* (Vol. XXVll, No. 4, April 1959), pp. 49–58.

13 These figures have been taken from the official statements of the government of Pakistan in the National Assembly in July 1965 and June 1967. See, for details on the Bengali representation in the military Hasan Askari Rizvi, *The Military and Politics in Pakistan, 1947–86* (Lahore: Progressive Publishers, 1987), pp. 137–8.

14 For details of the representation of the Bengalis in the bureaucracy and the military and how East Pakistan was treated by the federal government in the political, administrative and economic domains, see Hasan Zaheer, *The Separation of East Pakistan: The Rise and Realization of Bengali Muslim Nationalism* (Karachi: Oxford University Press, 1994); Kamal Matinuddin, *Tragedy of Errors, East Pakistan Crisis, 1968–71* (Lahore: Wajidalis, 1994); Siddiq Salik, *Witness to Surrender* (Karachi: Oxford University Press, 1979).

15 For an analysis of the policies of the Ayub regime and its implications for East Pakistan, see Rounaq Jahan, *Pakistan Failure in National Integration* (New York: Columbia University Press, 1972), pp. 51–89.

16 *Reports of the Advisory Panels for the Fourth Five Year Plan*, Vol. 1 (Islamabad: Planning Commission, Government of Pakistan, 1970), p. 22.

17 For details, see *ibid.*, pp. 25, 143; M. Anisur Rahman, *East and West Pakistan: A Problem in the Political Economy of Regional Planning* (Cambridge, Mass., Center of International Studies, Harvard University, 1968); Hanna Papanek, 'Sources of

Economic Exploitation of East Bengal', in S. Kashyap (ed.), *Bangladesh: Background and Perspectives* (New Delhi: National, 1971), pp. 159–68.

18 For a two-economy perspective, see Rehman Sobhan, 'Two Economies in Pakistan', *Morning News* (Dhaka), 22 March 1971 (Special Supplement); see by the same author, 'The Challenge of Inequality', *Pakistan Observer*, 12, 13 and 15 June 1965; and 'East Pakistan's Revolt against Ayub', *The Round Table* (No. 235, July 1969), pp. 302–7; Anisur Rehman, *op. cit.*, pp. 1–2; Ralph Braibanti, *op. cit.*, p. 52.

19 Hasan Askari Rizvi, *Internal Strife and External Intervention: India's Role in the Civil Strife in East Pakistan (Bangladesh)* (Lahore: Progressive Publishers, 1981), p. 90; G.W. Choudhury, *op. cit.*, p. 8.

20 Sheikh Mujibur Rahman, *6–point Formula: Our Right to Live* (Dhaka: General Secretary, East Pakistan Awami League, 1966), p. 1.

21 Wayne Wilcox, *The Emergence of Bangladesh* (Washington, D.C.: American Enterprise Institute for Public Policy Research, 1973), p. 19.

22 Rehman Sobhan, 'Negotiating for Bangladesh: A Participant's View', *South Asian Review* (Vol. 4, No. 4, July 1971), pp. 315–26.

23 For Bhutto's point of view, see Z.A. Bhutto, *The Great Tragedy* (Karachi: Pakistan People's Party, 1971), pp. 21–6; A.H. Kardar, *People's Commitment: Politics in Pakistan, 1970–71* (Lahore, 1971), pp. 76–7.

24 See, David Dunbar, 'Pakistan: The Failure of Political Negotiations', *Asian Survey* (Vol. Xll, No. 5, May 1972), pp. 444–61; Robert Jackson, *South Asian Crisis: India, Pakistan and Bangladesh* (New York: Praeger, 1975), p. 25.

25 A few days before the hijacking incident, India and Pakistan expelled each other's diplomats on espionage charges. For the text of the report of a Pakistani commission of inquiry on the hijacking incident, see William L.F. Rushbrook, *The East Pakistan Tragedy* (London: Tom Stacey, 1972), pp. 121–6 (Appendix 4).

26 Bhutto, *op. cit.*, p. 28.

27 *Dawn*, 1 March 1971.

28 Ahsan had already retired from the Navy. Yaqub Khan was retired from the Army shortly after his return to Islamabad.

29 *Morning News*, 8 March 1971.

30 *Pakistan Observer*, 16 March 1971.

31 The same Chief Justice agreed to administer the oath to Tikka Khan on 9 April after the Army reasserted its control in Dhaka.

32 A.R. Siddiqi, *The Military in Pakistan: Image and Reality* (Lahore: Vanguard Books, 1996), p. 189, see for detailed comments, pp. 184–90.

33 G.W. Choudhury, *op. cit.*, p. 166; see also *White Paper on the Crisis in East Pakistan* for details of this and the subsequent proposals.

34 For details of the final Awami League plan, see *ibid.*, pp. 172–7; Richard Sisson and Leo Rose, *War and Secession: Pakistan, India and the Creation of Bangladesh* (Berkeley: University of California Press, 1990), p. 131.

35 See *Morning News* and *Pakistan Observer*, both dated 24 March 1971.

36 *Ibid.*

37 Mujibur Rahman claimed in an interview with the BBC that three million Bengalis were killed during the military operation. *Outlook* (Karachi) (Vol. 1, No. 3, 22 April 1972).

38 General Tikka Khan's statement: *Dawn*, 10 March 1972.

39 The antecedents of the *Mukti Bahini* could be traced back to the last quarter of 1970, when the Awami League established a military committee which created a semi-armed group. This consisted of the Awami League activists, pro-Awami

League students and some former personnel of the *Ansar* and *Mujahid* forces. Their major function was to organize and lead political processions, maintain discipline in the public meetings and disrupt the meetings of the other political parties. The armed groups proliferated during the March movement and military training was provided to the youth in several places, including the Dhaka University. It was during this period that weapons were collected in anticipation of military action by the Pakistani authorities. A number of ammunition shops in major cities were looted and the armouries of the police, the *Ansar* and the *Mujahid* forces were broken into, while crude bombs were manufactured by the university students in their laboratories. These elements had also been getting weapons through their transnational linkages in West Bengal from the last quarter of 1970. While the political negotiations were going on in Dhaka in mid-March 1971, Colonel Osmany sent a secret message to the Bengali officers of the East Bengal Regiment through Major Khaled Musharaf, advising them to stay low-key, avoid involvement in political controversies, not to let the authorities disarm them, and that they should strike as hard as possible if the Pakistani authorities launched a military action. On 23 March, a new paramilitary force, *Joy Bangla Bahini*, was brought into the open by the Awami League. For the details of the launching of the Mukti Bahini and its background, see *Bangladesh Documents* (New Delhi: Ministry of External Affairs, Government of India, 1971), pp. 282–6; Colonel Osmany's interview: *Illustrated Weekly of India*, 19 December 1971, pp. 21–3, 40–1; D.K. Palit, *The Lightning Campaign: The India Pakistan War* (New Delhi: Thompson Press, 1972), p. 53; Siddiq Salik, *op. cit.*, pp. 57–8, 99–105; Fazal Muqeem Khan, *op. cit.*, pp. 65, 73; and Hasan Askari Rizvi, *op. cit.*, pp. 190–9.

40 See, D.K. Palit, *op. cit.*, p. 64; Pran Chopra, *India's Second Liberation* (Delhi: Vikas Publishing House, 1973), p. 155; Wayne Wilcox, *op. cit.*, p. 32.

41 Wayne Wilcox, *op. cit.*, pp. 43–4; G.W. Choudhury, *op. cit.*, pp. 195–7. The Government of Pakistan also started the trial of Mujibur Rahman on 11 August in a special military court. Though there was no official announcement about the completion of the trial or its judgement, some nonofficial sources claimed after the establishment of Bangladesh that, by December, the military court had sentenced Mujib to death.

42 Zillur R. Khan, *Leadership in the Least Developed Nation: Bangladesh* (Syracuse: Maxwell School of Citizenship and Public Affairs, Syracuse University, 1983), p. 36.

43 G.W. Choudhury, *op. cit.*, pp. 198–9.

44 For a detailed study of different aspects of India's support to the Bangladesh movement and the decision to launch the military operation in November, see Hasan Askari Rizvi, *op. cit.*, pp. 162–213.

45 See Yahya Khan's statement: *Pakistan Times*, 9 November 1971; *The Statesman Weekly*, 13 November 1971.

46 While surrendering in East Pakistan on 16 December, the Yahya regime vowed to carry on the war in the west. However, a day later, it agreed to a ceasefire. For territorial gains and losses and the POWs, see Hasan Askari Rizvi, *Pakistan and the Geostrategic Environment: A Study of Foreign Policy* (London: Macmillan, 1993), pp. 23, 30.

Chapter 8:   Civilian Interlude

1 Asma Jilani vs. the Government of the Punjab and Others *PLD, 1972, Supreme Court*, pp. 139–270.

2 See chapter 5: First Military Regime.

3 See Bhutto's statement: *Pakistan Times*, 29 March 1972.

4 Other members of the commission were: Justice Anwarul Haq, Chief Justice of Lahore High Court, and Justice Tufailali Abdur Rahman, Chief Justice of High Court of Sindh and Balochistan.

5 The copies of the Hamudur Rahman Commission (HRC) report were said to have been destroyed by Bhutto. However, Bhutto kept one copy in his possession. Two days before Bhutto was executed by the military regime in April 1979, the security forces raided his residences in Karachi, Larkana and Naudero and recovered a large number of important state documents, including the copy of the HRC report. See, K.M. Arif, *Working with Zia: Pakistan's Power Politics, 1977–1988* (Karachi: Oxford University Press, 1995), pp. 213–14. One Pakistani newspaper alleged that Bhutto tampered with the report after receiving it from the commission by replacing the pages that contained his criticism. See *ibid.*, p.47. For a report of the raid on Bhutto's residences, see *New York Times*, 4 April 1979.

   An Indian journalist claimed that he read some photocopied sections of the HRC report while consulting official documents in Washington for his research on the American role in the 1971 Indo-Pakistan war. He wrote in an article that the HRC report charged 'the army commanders and military leaders of "betrayal" of Pakistan who had "lost the will, the determination and the competence to fight".' The report described the events of 1971 as 'a military defeat' as well as 'a colossal political failure and a moral disaster'. It proposed the court-martial or public trial of several senior army officers. See J.N. Parimoo, 'Night of the Generals', *Illustrated Weekly of India*, 23 October 1988, pp.20–3.

6 See Air Marshal Rahim Khan's interview: *Daily Jang* (Lahore), 20 March 1984. In an interview in January 1998, Lt.-General Gul Hassan Khan said that he developed differences with Bhutto from the beginning because the latter interfered with the internal service affairs. He claimed to have told Bhutto to 'keep his nose out of the Army'. He and Air Marshal Rahim Khan were summoned to the presidency and asked to sign the resignation papers placed before them. They signed the papers and were taken from there straight to Lahore by a close associate of Bhutto. Explaining his decision to resign, Gul Hassan said, 'If the head of state and the head of the army do not see eye to eye, the best thing is for the junior chap to quit.' He ruled out the possibility of a coup against Bhutto at that stage. He said, 'Making a coup is not a joke, half of the Army was sitting on the border. We had just lost a part of our country and a war. Even the troops would have refused.... I was not interested in taking over from Bhutto, so I just left.' See Gul Hassan's interview with Faiza Hassan: *The Friday Times*, 30 January–5 February 1998, p. 24.

7 For the text of the White Paper, see Hasan-Askari Rizvi, *The Military and Politics in Pakistan* (Lahore: Progressive Publishers, 1987), pp. 294–302.

8 The military is also to be summoned in aid of civil power under article 147.

9 *The Constitution of the Islamic Republic of Pakistan*, 1973, Article 244 and Third Schedule.

10 *Ibid.*, Article 6.

11 *Nawa-i-Waqt* (Lahore), 15 September 1973.

12 Khalid B. Sayeed, *Politics in Pakistan: The Nature and Direction of Change* (New York: Praeger, 1980), pp. 107–8.

13 See the statement by Federal Home Minister in the Senate: *Nawa-i-Waqt*, 5 December 1974.

14 *White Paper on the Performance of the Bhutto Regime*, Vol.III (Islamabad: Government of Pakistan, 1979), p. 26.

15 *Ibid.*, pp. 26–7.

16 Omar Noman, *Pakistan: Political and Economic History since 1947* (London: Kegan Paul International, 1990), pp. 59, 70.

17 Pakistan and India signed an agreement in August 1973 for the repatriation of Pakistani POWs which included personnel of the military, paramilitary force, police, and civilian internees. Bangladesh threatened to put 195 Pakistani POWs on war trial and India supported this. They were repatriated between 19 September 1973 and 30 April 1974. Bangladesh abandoned the war trial demand as a part of an arrangement brokered by the Secretary General of the Organization of Islamic Conference (OIC) whereby Pakistan recognized Bangladesh. Approximately 1,220,000 Bengali civil servants, military personnel and their families were repatriated from Pakistan to Bangladesh. About 119,000 non-Bengalis (Biharis) stranded in Bangladesh or escaped to Nepal were airlifted to Pakistan. Later, Pakistan accepted more Biharis, raising their number to 169,000 by 1982.

18 See *Asian Recorder*, 20–26 August 1974, p. 12153; 15–21 October 1974, p. 12243; and 12–18 November 1974, p. 12287.

19 Pakistan withdrew from the SEATO in early 1972 but retained membership of the CENTO till 1979.

20 For the Army's developmental work in parts of Balochistan, see A Correspondent, 'Maiwand Road Begins a New Era for Balochistan', *Pakistan Times*, 4 May 1975; see also *ibid.*, 11 May 1975; *Dawn*, 21 July 1976 (Supplement on Balochistan in Transition); *White Paper on Balochistan* (Rawalpindi: Government of Pakistan, 1974), pp. 28–32.

21 See General Tikka Khan's interview: *Weekly Meyaar* (Vol. 1 No.10, 21–28 February 1976, p. 7.

22 *Dawn*, 19 February 1973. For the full text of his speech, see *Lail-o-Nehar* (Lahore), 25 February 1973.

23 *Nawa-i-Waqt*, 3 March 1974.

24 *Pakistan Times*. 2 February 1974.

25 See the text of the official press release: *ibid*, 16 April 1974.

26 Anwar H. Syed, 'Z.A. Bhutto's Self Characterization and Pakistani Political Culture,' *Asian Survey* (Vol. 18 No.12, December 1978), pp. 1250–1266.

27 See, Anwar H. Syed, *The Discourse and Politics of Zulfikar Ali Bhutto* (Houndmills, Basingstoke: Macmillan, 1992), pp. 3–4, 249–250; Saeed Shafqat, *Political System of Pakistan and Public Policy* (Lahore: Progressive Publishers, 1989), pp. 203, 215; Khalid B. Sayeed, *Politics in Pakistan*, pp. 84–91.

28 For a detailed analysis of Bhutto's socio-economic policies, see Saeed Shafqat, *Civil-Military Relations in Pakistan: From Zulfikar Ali Bhutto to Benazir Bhutto* (Boulder: Westview, 1997), pp. 130–59; Shahid Javed Burki, *Pakistan Under Bhutto, 1971–77* (New York: St. Martin's Press, 1980), pp. 109–68; by the same author, 'Politics of Economic Decision Making During the Bhutto Period', *Asian Survey* (Vol. 14 No. 12, December 1974), pp. 1126–40; W. Eric Gustafson, 'A Review of the Pakistani Economy', in Manzooruddin Ahmed (ed.), *Contemporary Pakistan, Politics, Economy, and Society* (Durham: Carolina Academic Press, 1980), pp. 145–62.

29 For a comprehensive analysis of the administrative reforms, including the lateral entry system, see Charles H. Kennedy, *Bureaucracy in Pakistan* (Karachi: Oxford

University Press, 1987), pp. 54–150; see also by the same author, 'Politics of Ethnic Preference In Pakistan', *Asian Survey* (Vol. 24 No.6, June 1984), pp. 688–703.

30 See, Omar Noman, *Economic and Social Progress in Asia: Why Pakistan Did Not Become a Tiger*, (Karachi: Oxford University Press, 1997), pp. 35,179.

31 *Asian Recorder*, 23–29 April 1975, p. 12556, and 8–14 January 1976, p. 12966. The Supreme Court heard the government reference against the NAP in the open, and the press reported the proceedings in detail during March-September 1975.

32 For the text of the manifesto see, *National Democratic Party Pakistan, ka Manshoor* (Urdu) (Lahore: Secretary General, National Democratic Party Pakistan, n.d.)

33 The well-known leaders who left the PPP included Mukhtar Rana, Meraj Mohammad Khan, J.A. Rahim, Mahmud Ali Kasuri, Khurshid Hassan Meer, Dr. Mohashir Hassan, Haneef Ramay, and Iftikhar Tari.

34 Maliha Lodhi, 'Pakistan in Crisis', *The Journal of Commonwealth and Comparative Politics* (Vol. XVl No.1, March 1978), pp. 60–78; see also Mohammad Waseem, *Politics and the State in Pakistan* (Islamabad: National Institute of Historical & Cultural Research, 1994), pp. 309–13.

35 For the PNA campaign themes see, *Guardian*, 26 February and 4 March 1977; *Economist*, 5–11 March 1977; *Christian Science Monitor*, 2 and 7 March 1977; *Far Eastern Economic Review*, 25 February 1977, pp. 33–4.

36 For analysis of the election campaign and the results, see Shariful Mujahid, 'The 1977 Elections: An Analysis', in Manzooruddin Ahmed (ed.), *op. cit.*, pp. 63–91; Lawrence Ziring, 'Pakistan: The Campaign before the Storm', *Asian Survey* (Vol. 17 No. 7, July 1977), pp. 581–8; Marvin G. Weinbaum, 'The March 1977 Elections in Pakistan: Where Everyone Lost', *ibid.*, pp. 599–618.

37 *Guardian*, 8 March 1977; *Manchester Guardian Weekly*, 13 March 1977. The PNA leader, Asghar Khan had said in a pre-poll statement that the ruling PPP would engage in manipulation of the elections. See *New York Times*, 27 February and 8 March 1977.

38 Bhutto knew that the elections were manipulated in 30–40 constituencies. See Kausar Niazi, *Aur Line Cut Gai* (Urdu) (Lahore: Jang Publishers, 1987), pp. 41–2.

39 In May 1977, the government decided to return 1,523 rice husking units to their former owners but retained some 549 units under its control. This gesture came rather late and it was viewed as a first sign of success of the campaign against Bhutto's socialism. See, *Pakistan Affairs* (Publication of the Embassy of Pakistan, Washington, DC), 1 June 1977.

40 For an insightful analysis of the agitation in 1977, see Khalid B. Sayeed, *op. cit.*, pp. 157–64.

41 See reports by Ghauri in *Far Eastern Economic Review*, 8 April 1977, pp. 13–14, and 1 July 1977, pp. 10–11.

42 *New York Times*, 18 April 1977.

43 For the full text of the statement, see *Dawn Overseas Weekly*, 1 May 1977. In an interview in 1985, General Zia-ul-Haq said that the statement was issued to reassure the then government but that did not mean that the military was willing to support Bhutto no matter what happened in the country. When the political conditions deteriorated, the military commanders could not stay indifferent and let the situation go from bad to worse. *Quami Digest* (Lahore), May 1985, pp. 26–76.

44 For the full text of the letter, see Mohammad Asghar Khan, *Generals in Politics: Pakistan 1958–1982* (New Delhi: Vikas, 1983), pp. 116–18.

45 *Philadelphia Inquirer*, 3 June 1977; *New York Times*, 8 June 1977; For the summary of the Lahore High Court judgement, see *Defence Journal* (Vol. 11, Nos. 4–5, April–May 1985), pp. 77–8.

46 On numerous occasions, the Army commanders bluntly told the government that the law and order was very bad and that the people hardly trusted the government. They advised Bhutto to hold new elections. In one case, he was told that 'he should go for re-elections, otherwise the Army would have to take over as an institution.' Faiz Ali Chishti, *Betrayals of Another Kind* (Delhi: Tricolour Books, 1989), pp. 15, 57–8. See also Khalid Mahmud Arif, *Working with Zia: Pakistan's Power Politics, 1977–1988* (Karachi: Oxford University Press, 1995), p. 80.

47 The corps commanders unanimously authorized the Army chief to impose martial law if the situation demanded it. However, they emphasized that such a step would be taken only for holding new elections. See Faiz Ali Chishti, *op. cit.*, p. 70.

48 See General Zia-ul-Haq's interview: *New York Times*, 9 July 1977, and his address to the seminar on National Integration held at Lahore: *Nawa-i-Waqt* (Lahore), 15 April 1984; see also Lt.-General Faiz Ali Chishti's interview; *ibid.*, 15 September 1983, and *Jang* (Lahore), 24 September 1984.

49 In mid-May, Bhutto offered to hold a referendum on whether he should stay in power. The constitution was amended to authorize the Prime Minister to hold referendum on any matter. The offer was rejected by the opposition.

50 See Yahya Bakhtiar's interview in Munir Ahmad Munir, *Sayasi Autar Charaao* (Urdu) (Lahore: Atashfeshan Publications, 1985), p. 45.

51 For the details of the last stage of negotiations and the connections between some PNA leaders and the Army, see Kausar Niazi, *op. cit.*, pp. 181–203; Prof Abdul Ghafoor's interview: *Saeyara Digest* (Lahore), January 1986, pp. 18–42, and his statement: *Nawa-i-Waqt* (Lahore), 8 November 1983; *Guardian*, 4 July 1977; *Financial Times*, 6 July 1977; *Far Eastern Economic Review*, 15 July 1977, pp. 10–12; General Zia-ul-Haq's interview: *Urdu Digest*, September 1977, pp. 15–32.

52 *Guardian*, 27 April 1977; *Washington Post*, 29 April and 8 May 1977; *New York Times*, 29 April 1977; Farrukh Sohail Goindi, *Garrison Democracy* (Lahore: Jamhoori Publications, 1991), pp. 21–5.

53 *New York Times*, 21 April 1977.

54 *Washington Post*, 4 June 1977.

Chapter 9: The Third Military Regime

1 The Martial Law Zones were: A: Punjab, B: NWFP, C: Sindh, D: Balochistan, E: Northern Areas.

2 The Election Cell had three members: one serving and two retired Major Generals: Jamal Said Mian (in service), Rao Farman Ali Khan and Ihsanul Haq Malik.

3 For Zia-ul-Haq's statements, see *Dawn Overseas Weekly*, 10 and 24 July, 14 and 21 August, and 25 September 1997.

4 *Philadelphia Inquirer*, 8 August 1977.

5 Zia-ul-Haq's statement in a press conference in Hyderabad in April 1978, see 'Martial Law: A Select Chronology of Events', *Defence Journal* (Vol. IV, Nos 6 & 7, June–July 1978), p. 61.

6 Zia-ul-Haq's interview to the BBC: *Dawn*, 18 October 1982.

7 Press Conference by Zia-ul-Haq: *Jang* (Lahore), 22 March 1982; *Muslim*, 22 March 1982; *Far Eastern Economic Review*, 1 April 1982.

8 *Financial Times*, 27 August 1977.

9 *Far Eastern Economic Review*, 26 August 1977 (Report by Salamat Ali).

10 See, Sir Morrice James (Lord Saint Brides), *Pakistan Chronicle* (London: Hurst and Co., 1993), pp. 202–3; William L. Richter, 'Persistent Praetorianism: Pakistan's Third Military Regime', *Pacific Affairs* (Vol. 51 No. 3, Fall 1978), pp. 406–26; Salman Taseer, *Bhutto: A Political Biography* (New Delhi: Vikas, 1980), pp. 174–5; Mohammad Asghar Khan, *Generals in Politics: Pakistan 1958–82* (New Delhi: Vikas, 1983), p. 143.

11 The following White Papers were issued by the military government: (1) White Paper on the Conduct of General Elections in March 1977, July 1978, 1449pp; (2) Summary of White Paper on the Conduct of the General Elections in March 1977, July 1978, 118pp; (3) White Paper on Misuse of Media, August 1978, 363pp; (4) White Paper on the Performance of the Bhutto Regime, Four Volumes: Vol. I: Mr. Z.A. Bhutto, His Family and Associates, January 1979, 179pp; Vol. II: Treatment of Fundamental State Institutions, January 1979, 353pp; Vol. III: Misuse of the Instrument of State Power, January 1979, 228pp; Vol. IV: *The Economy*, January 1979, 81pp. See also Sameel Ahmed Qureshi, 'An Analysis of Contemporary Pakistani Politics: Bhutto versus the Military', *Asian Survey* (Vol. 19, No. 9, September 1979), pp. 910–21.

12 Zia-ul-Haq's interview: *Urdu Digest*, September 1977, p. 28; see also his interview: *Times*, 8 September 1977; for the murder charges, *Washington Post*, 4 September 1977; *New York Times*, 7 September 1977.

13 See, Ramsey Clark, 'The Trial of Ali Bhutto and the Future of Pakistan', *Nation* (Weekly), 19–26 August 1978, pp. 136–140; Hugh Trevor-Roper, 'Bhutto's Fate', *New York Times*, 24 June 1978.

14 The lengthy judgement was written by Chief Justice Anwarul Haq with three judges concurring: Mohammad Akram, Karam Illahi Chauhan, Dr. Nasim Hasan Shah. The dissenting judges were: Dorab Patel, Ghulam Safdar Shah, and Mohammad Haleem.

The Supreme Court bench initially comprised 9 judges. One of them, Qaiser Khan, retired from the Court in July 1978. Another judge, Waheeduddin Ahmad, had a serious heart attack in November and was unable to return to the Court. For the full text of the main and dissenting judgements, see *PLD, Supreme Court, 1979*, vol. 31, pp. 53–710.

15 Khalid Mahmud Arif, *Working with Zia: Pakistan's Power Politics 1977–1988* (Karachi: Oxford University Press, 1995), pp. 198–203.

16 Azhar Sohail, *Pir Pagara ki Kahani* (Urdu)(Lahore: Ferozsons, 1987), p. 80.

17 Two days before Bhutto's execution, the security forces raided his residences in Karachi Larkana, and Naudero and took possession of a large number of official documents and their photocopies which Bhutto had kept there. The military regime knew that a copy of the Hamudur Rahman Commission Report was not destroyed and it was believed to be in Bhutto's possession. This copy was recovered in this raid.

18 *Dawn Overseas Weekly*, 12 April 1980.

19 *Dawn*, 14 April 1982.

20 For a review of perspectives of different Islamic groups on western notions of democracy and polity, see Mumtaz Ahmad, 'Parliament, Parties, Polls and Islam: Issues in the Current Debate on Religion and Politics in Pakistan', *American Journal of Islamic Social Science* (Vol. 2 No.1, June 1985), pp. 15–28.

21 *Dawn*, 13 May 1982; *Viewpoint*, 21 October 1982.

22 Zia-ul-Haq's interview *Washington Post*, 9 December 1982. See the statements of the Interior Minister, Mahmud Haroon: *Jang* (Lahore), 25 February 1982 and *Muslim*, 11 April 1982.

23 *Viewpoint*, 30 September 1979 and 23 September 1982. Zia-ul-Haq said that western style of democracy did not suit Pakistan and he wanted to create a democratic system that fitted 'the psyche of the Pakistani people', *Dawn*, 20 March 1979.
24 For an insightful analysis of the composition and role of the Council of Islamic Ideology, see Jamal Malik, *Colonialization of Islam: Dissolution of Traditional Institutions in Pakistan* (New Delhi: Manohar, 1996), pp. 33–54.
25 *The Constitution of the Islamic Republic of Pakistan*, Articles 203B and 203C.
26 These were: The Offence of *Zina* Ordinance, the Offence of *Qazif* Ordinance, the Offenses Against Property Ordinance, and the Prohibition Order.
27 According to a circular of the State Bank of Pakistan, issued on 20 June 1984, the admissible modes of interest-free finance were: Mark-up, Mark-down, Buy-back, Leasing, Hire-Purchasing, Development Charges, *Musharika*, Equity, Term Certificate, Rent-Sharing, *Qarz-e-Hasna*, and Service Charges.
28 Zakat and Ushr Ordinance, 1980, No. F.17(1)/80–Pub., *The Gazette of Pakistan, Extra-ordinary*, 20 June 1980.
29 *Dawn*, 13 August 1984; *Muslim*, 14 August 1984. Zia-ul-Haq said, 'By making the *Namaz* movement successful, we can create an atmosphere of religious devoutness that would be the envy of others.'
30 *Dawn*, 13 August 1984; for the full text of the judgement, see *Jang* (Lahore), 4, 5, 6, 8, 9, 11, 12, 13, 14 November 1984; see also Tayyab Mahmud, 'Freedom of Religion and Religious Minorities in Pakistan: A Study of Judicial Practice', *Fordham International Law Journal* (Vol. 19, No. 1, October 1995), pp. 40–100.
31 For a review of various Islamization measures, see Charles H. Kennedy, 'Islamization and Legal Reform in Pakistan, 1979–89', *Pacific Affairs* (Vol. 63 No. 1, Spring 1990), pp. 62–77; Mumtaz Ahmad, 'Islamic Revival in Pakistan', in Cyriac K. Pullapilly (ed.), *Islam in the Contemporary World* (Notre Dame: Indiana Cross Road Books, 1980), pp. 261–73; David Taylor, 'The Politics of Islam and Islamization in Pakistan', in James P. Piscatori (ed.), *Islam in the Political Process* (Cambridge: Cambridge University Press, 1983), pp. 181–98.
32 Hazoor Bakhsh v. Federation of Pakistan *PLD, FSC, 1981*, vol. 33, pp. 145–176.
33 See an advertisement by a number of prominent religious leaders calling upon their colleagues to emphasize the Islamic nature of *Rajam* in their Friday sermons: *Nawa-i-Waqt* (Lahore), 27 March 1981; for statements on this issue, see *ibid.*, 28 and 31 March 1981.
34 *Nawa-i-Waqt*, 21 June 1982. Only one judge of the previous bench was part of the new bench that accepted the review petition, see Federation of Pakistan v. Hazoor Bakhsh: *PLD, FSC, 1983*, vol. 35, p. 255.
35 For the perspectives of urban-based elitist women groups on Islamization, see, Khawar Mumtaz and Farida Shaheed, *Women of Pakistan: Two Steps Forward, One Step Back?* (Lahore: Vanguard Books, 1987), pp. 71–120.
36 For the text of the letter of resignation, see *Far Eastern Economic Review*, 29 September 1978. pp. 28–9 (Report by Salamat Ali); see also *Dawn Overseas Weekly*, 23 September 1978.
37 *Dawn Overseas Weekly*, 23 September 1978.
38 *Guardian*, 27 November 1978; In an interview Prof. Ghafoor Ahmad, said that when they joined the government they fully recognized that no minister could enjoy full powers under martial law. *Saiyara Digest* (Lahore), January 1986, p. 42.
39 *Jang*, 16 April 1979. The PNA President, Mufti Mahmud said that the alliance would cooperate with the military government in the larger interest of the country as well as to complete the implementation of the Islamic order. *Dawn*, 10 June 1979.

40 *Nawa-i-Waqt*, 4 April 1979.

41 For the text of the judgement, Begum Nusrat Bhutto v. Chief of Army Staff, etc. *PLD, 1977, Supreme Court*, pp. 657–763.

42 See Zamir Niazi, *The Press in Chains* (Karachi: Royal Book Company, 1986), pp. 175–220. One well-known case was that of Salamat Ali, a correspondent of *Far Eastern Economic Review* who was sentenced to rigorous imprisonment by a military court in November 1979 for writing an article on the situation in Balochistan. He was later released by the military regime and allowed to leave the country.

43 In the case of the Punjab University, three professors were transferred and one temporary professor had his contract terminated in 1979. Three Quaid-i-Azam University professors were convicted by a military court in 1981 for distributing anti-martial law posters. In May 1996, the Benazir Bhutto government lifted the ban on their re-employment.

44 See, *Pakistan: A People Suppressed* (New York: Pakistan Committee for Democracy and Justice, September 1981); *Zia's Law: Human Rights under Military Rule in Pakistan* (New York: Lawyers Committee for Human Rights, July 1985); Aitzaz Ahsan, 'July Five 1982: The Five Years of Martial law', *Muslim*, 5 July 1982; see by the same writer, 'Martial Law's 10th Anniversary: Uncertainty is the only Reality', *Nation*, 5 July 1987.

45 The statement of Mohammad Asghar Khan to the Lahore High Court, dated 2 February 1980. mimeographed text. See also his book, *op. cit.*, p. 163.

46 For details of the Hamid Baloch case, see *Far Eastern Economic Review*, 13 March 1981, pp. 21–2 (Report by Lawrence Lifschultz). After the introduction of the Provisional Constitutional Order, the military authorities carried out the death sentence.

47 For a firsthand account of the working of the *Al-Zulfikar* and the hijacking incident, see Raja Anwar, *The Terrorist Prince: The Life and Death of Murtaza Bhutto* (London: Verso, 1997), pp. 95–120.

48 The judges who did not take oath were: Supreme Court: Anwar-ul-Haq (Chief Justice), Dorab Patel, Fakhuruddin G. Ibrahim, Maulvi Mushtaq Hussain; Punjab High Court: Zakiuddin Pal, K.M. Samadani, Aftab Farukh, Ameer Raza Khan, Khawaja Habibullah, Khalilur Rahman, Khurshid; Sindh High Court: G.M. Shah, Abdul Hafeez Mamin; Balochistan High Court: Khuda Bakhsh Marri (Chief Justice), and M.A. Rashid. (The Balochistan High Court had three judges; two of them opted out). In the case of the NWFP High Court, all the judges took the oath. The Chief Justice of Federal Shariat Court, Aftab Hussain, was removed from office in October 1984. The Acting Chief Justice of Balochistan High Court, Abdul Qadeer Chaudhry, was transferred to Sindh High Court in March 1985.

49 Originally, the Muslim Conference led by Sardar Mohammad Abdul Qayyum also joined the MRD. He withdrew from the alliance within a month.

50 *MRD Declaration*, 6 February 1981, photocopy and mimeographed sheet.

51 Emma Duncan, *Breaking the Curfew: A Political Journey through Pakistan* (London: Michael Joseph, Penguin Group, 1989), p. 70; see also by the same writer, 'Pakistan: Living on the Edge', *Economist*, 17 January 1987.

52 See *Nation*, 29 October and 9 November 1988; Tajammal Hussain Malik, *The Story of My Struggle* (Lahore: Jang Publishers, 1991).

53 See Raja Anwar, *op. cit.*, pp. 134–5.

54 For the details, see *Nawa-i-Waqt*, 15 July 1985; *Pakistan Times*, 15 July 1985; *Far Eastern Economic Review*, 20 September 1984, p. 17 (Report by Lawrence

Lifschultz). For the details of the plot, see the interview of one of the implicated officers, Major Sadiq, in *Weekly Pakistan Express* (New York), 3 April 1998.

55 See, *Muslim*, 27 May 1982, 16 September 1983, and 14 March 1984; *Nawa-i-Waqt*, 20 May 1984. See also the statements of General K.M. Arif and General Rahimuddin Khan on the same subject: *Muslim*, 11 April 1984; *Dawn*, 30 March 1984.

56 *Muslim*, 21 May 1984.

57 For Zia-ul-Haq's statements on the constitutional role of the military, see *Defence Journal* (Vol. 8, No.12, December 1982), pp. 35–8; *Pakistan Times*, 15 September 1977; *Nawa-i-Waqt*, 22 June 1979; *Jang* (Lahore), 23 April 1982; *Dawn*, 7 May 1982; *Dawn Overseas Weekly*, 9 December 1982.

58 Official statement of the Punjab Government, dated 17 January 1988.

59 As early as 1 September 1977, Zia-ul-Haq stated in a press conference that he considered a presidential form of government most suitable for Pakistan because it was very close to Islamic concept of *Amir*. See 'Martial Law: A Select Chronology of Events', *Defence Journal* (Vol. 4, Nos. 6 & 7, June–July 1978), p. 52.

60 Though not officially released the press was able to get a summary of the first report of the CII, see *Muslim*, 27 July 1982.

61 *Constitutional Recommendations for the Islamic System of Government* (Islamabad: Council of Islamic Ideology, June 1983).

62 *Report of the Special Committee of the Federal Council on the Form and System of Government in Pakistan From Islamic Point-of-View* (Islamabad: Federal Council Secretariat, 1983).

63 *Ansari Commission Report on form of Government* (Islamabad: Printing Corporation of Pakistan Press, 1983).

64 *Dawn*, 26 October 1984.

65 *Muslim*, 1 November 1984; for another statement, *Jang* (Lahore), 2 November 1984.

66 The referendum proposition read: 'Whether the people of Pakistan endorse the process initiated by General Mohammad Zia-ul-Haq, the President of Pakistan, to bring in laws of Pakistan in conformity with the injunctions of Islam as laid down in the Holy *Quran* and *Sunnah* of the Holy Prophet (Peace be upon him) and for the preservation of Ideology of Pakistan, for the continuation and consolidation of that process for the smooth and orderly transfer of power to the elected representatives of the people?'

67 *Nation*, 2 January 1993.

68 For an analysis of the elections campaign and the results, see Hasan Askari Rizvi, 'Third General Elections in Pakistan, 1985', *Pakistan Journal of Social Sciences* (Vols. 11 & 12, 1985–6), pp. 1–21.

69 For details of the changes in the constitution, see Abrar Hasan, *The Constitution of Pakistan: Defiled-Defaced* (Karachi: Asia Law House, 1995), pp. 12–13.

Chapter 10:   Post-Withdrawal Civil–Military Relations

1 For the ISI's connections with the CIA, see Lawrence Lifschultz, 'Dangerous Liaison: The CIA–ISI Connection', *Newsline*, September 1989, pp. 49–54; see also *United States Policy toward Afghanistan* (Hearing before the Sub-Committee on Europe and the Middle East and Asian and Pacific Affairs of the Committee on Foreign Affairs, House of Representatives, second session, 7 March 1990). Washington, DC: US Government Printing Office, 1990), pp. 127–31. The report

said that ISI, CIA and Saudi intelligence services under Prince Turki cooperated for supporting the Afghan resistance groups.

2   Mohammad Waseem, 'Pakistan's Lingering Crisis of Dyarchy', *Asian Survey* (Vol. 32, No. 7, July 1992), pp. 617–34.

3   The move to remove the Speaker enjoyed the blessings of Zia–ul-Haq and four provincial Chief Ministers who lobbied for his removal. The stalwarts of the Zia–Junejo system argued that the Speaker's conduct was prejudicial to the existing power arrangements. See the cover story entitled 'House-Cleaning' in *Herald*, June 1986, pp. 43–57.

4   See, Zia-ul-Haq's statement: *Nation*, 27 July 1987.

5   The OML's claim to be the genuine Muslim League was disputed by its other factions. These included the reactivated Pagara group, the Khairuddin-Qasim group, Council Muslim League (Fatima Jinnah group), the Qayuum Khan group, Sheikh Liaquat group, and the Forward Bloc. Some of these groups were non-entities with hardly any popular following or organization.

6   See the statement of the Federal Minister of Justice and Parliamentary Affairs in the Senate: *Dawn Overseas Weekly*, 18–24 August 1988; see also *Nation*, 12 June 1988.

7   Hasan-Askari Rizvi, 'The Zia–Junejo System Holds on', *Muslim*, 31 December 1987; see by the same author, 'After Martial Law: The Civilianization of Military Rule', *Nation*, 28 November 1986.

8   Hasan-Askari Rizvi, 'Civilianization of Military Rule in Pakistan', *Asian Survey* (Vol. 26, No. 10, October 1986), pp. 1067–81.

9   For a review of the MRD movement, see the cover story by various correspondents in *Herald*, September 1986, pp. 41–67; *Far Eastern Economic Review*, 4 September 1986, p. 18 (Report by Husain Haqqani).

10 *Zakat* allocations to Islamic schools in the Punjab rose from Rs. 9.40 million in 1980–81 to Rs. 68.96 million in 1986–87. The number of such schools increased from 636 to 2,084 during the same period.

11 See the interview of the MQM leader, Altaf Hussain: *Weekly Mayar*, 29 November–5 December 1986, pp. 11–14.

12 *Muslim*, 24 February 1986.

13 *Jang*, 18 March 1986.

14 *Nation*, 2 February 1988.

15 *Jang*, 8 April 1988.

16 *Jang*, 3 July 1985.

17 *Muslim*, 5 May 1987.

18 See the statement of Sardar Asif Ali, a member of the Public Accounts Committee, *Nation*, 5 February 1987.

19 Ejaz Azim, 'This General-bashing Must Stop', *Nation*, 25 June 1987; *Muslim*, 26 June 1987.

20 A technical committee was headed by Lt.-General Imranullah Khan and the other was a cabinet sub-committee; see Tehreem Butt, 'Sitting on a Powder Keg', *Herald*, June 1988, pp. 35–6.

21 Khalid Mahmud Arif, *Working With Zia: Pakistan's Power Politics, 1977–1988* (Karachi: Oxford University Press, 1995), pp. 388–90. See also, Tehreem Butt, *op. cit.*

22 Hasan-Askari Rizvi, 'Pakistan's Domestic Scene in 1988: The Year of Change', *Muslim*, 31 December 1988; see also *Pakistan Times Overseas Weekly*, 29 May 1988.

23 Soon after the dismissal of the Junejo government and the dissolution of the assemblies, the said member of the provincial assembly was arrested.

24   Maleeha Lodhi, 'Zia's Move: Reasserting Authority, Reshaping Politics', *Muslim*, 4 June 1988.

25   Zia-ul-Haq accused the Junejo government of three failures: the slowing down of the momentum of Islamization; inability to maintain law and order resulting in the 'tragic loss of innumerable valuable lives as well as loss of property', which threatened the integrity and ideology of Pakistan; and rampant corruption and deterioration of public morality.

26   For the text of the ordinance, see *Muslim*, 17 June 1988.

27   Zia-ul-Haq's aircraft exploded in mid-air within minutes of taking off from Bahawalpur, a city in southern Punjab, where he had gone to witness the performance of a new American tank. Several senior Army officers were also killed. They included, *inter alia*, General Akhtar Abdul Rahman (Chairman Joint Chiefs of Staff Committee), Lt.General Mian Mohammad Afzal (Chief of General Staff), three Major Generals: Mohammad Sharif Nasir, Abdus Sami, Mohammad Hussain Awan, five Brigadiers: Najib Ahmed, Moinuddin Khawaja, Siddiq Salik, Mohammad Latif, Abdul Majid. The American ambassador Arnold Raphael and the Defence Attaché Brigadier General Wassom Mike were also killed. Shortly after the aircrash, the Army took control of the Bahawalpur radio station as a precautionary measure.

28   General Beg's address to the Army officers: *Nation*, 26 August 1988; for the full text of his address, see *Urdu Digest*, September 1988, pp. 73–82.

29   *Ibid.*

30   See, General Beg's statements: *Muslim*, 2 October 1988; *Nation*, 13,28 and 30 October 1988; *Dawn Overseas Weekly*, 20–26 October 1988.

31   *Business Recorder*, 21 August 1988; *Dawn Overseas Weekly*, 25–31 August 1988.

32   The Punjab (Lahore) High Court observed that the grounds given for the dissolution of the assemblies by the President were 'so vague and non-existent that they were not sustainable in law'. However, the Court declared that it was not possible to restore the assemblies. For the text of the judgement, see *Pakistan Times*, 2 and 3 October 1988. For the Supreme Court's endorsement of this judgement, see *Nation*, 6 October 1988. In another judgement, the Supreme Court observed that 'every political party shall be eligible to participate in the elections to every seat in the National and Provincial Assemblies'. *Ibid.*, 3 October 1988 and *Muslim*, 3 October 1988.

33   This information is based on General Beg's statement in 1993, claiming that he sent the message indirectly so that the scheduled elections could be held. See *Nation*, 9 February 1993; *Dawn*, 10 February 1993; see also Hasan-Askari Rizvi, 'The Military and Power Politics,' *Nation*, 8 February 1993.

34   See, Iftikhar H. Malik, *State and Civil Society in Pakistan* (New York: St. Martin's Press, 1997), p. 98. In an interview in May 1995, General Beg admitted that, in 1988, the Army did not trust the PPP. As the PPP was expected to win the elections, the Army decided to balance the situation by creating the IJI. He said that the IJI failed to get a majority at the federal level but its success in the Punjab created the 'balance'. See *Nation*, 9 May 1995.

35   Maleeha Lodhi and Zahid Hussain, 'Pakistan's Invisible Government', *Newsline*, October 1992, pp. 22–34; *Time* (Weekly), 27 March 1989.

36   Ghulam Ishaq Khan was elected President with the PPP support on 12 December with an impressive majority.

37   *Business Recorder*, 14 December 1988.

38   General Beg claimed that he kept his *danda* (stick) under control on three occasions. First, when he did not assume power after the death of Zia-ul-Haq; second,

when Benazir Bhutto sought reprieve for the officers who had been dismissed from the Army for indulging in indiscipline after the elder Bhutto's death; third, when she appointed a retired officer as the head of the ISI. *Daily Pakistan*, 27 April 1995.

39 One well-known case was that of Lt.-General Alam Jan Mahsud, Corps Commander at Lahore. The government wanted an extension in his service and appointment to a senior position at the Army headquarters. The top brass viewed this as an interference in the Army's internal affairs.

40 Abbas Nasir, 'What is Going On', *Herald*, July 1990, pp. 24–35 (sse p. 31).

41 General Beg said in a statement on 1 July 1990 that given the legal authority, the Army will restore 'absolute peace and harmony' in Sindh 'in the shortest possible time'. He further said, 'We do not believe in chasing shadows. We believe in hitting at the root cause of evil and eliminating it, once for all.' For this and a number of other statements by the Army and the civilian government, see 'Army in Aid of the Civil Power', (Documentation), *Defence Journal* (Vol. 16 Nos. 7 & 8, July–August 1990), pp. 37–49, 57–8; see also Iftikhar H. Malik, *op. cit.*, pp. 242–3.

42 *Dawn*, 16 August 1990.

43 See, Hasan Askari Rizvi, 'Civil–Military Relations Under General Beg', *Defence Journal* (Vol. 17, Nos. 6 & 7, August 1991), pp. 17–21; Abbas Nasir, 'The Invisible War', *Herald Supplement*, August 1990, pp. 9–13.

44 Reflecting on the *Zarb-e-Momin* exercise, General Beg wrote in August 1997: 'The idea which propelled us to undertake this massive exercise was to communicate the message to the nation that the Army was fully alive to its responsibilities and could face the challenges. . . . Its professional spirit was intact and had assumed a new dimension of competence. . . . A very vital objective was to send our neighbour a clear message that should it ever [resort to] aggression against Pakistan, its Army will reply back aggressively, carrying the war into enemy territory. This capability was amply demonstrated during [the exercise] under the concept of Offensive Defence.' He maintained that he had adopted the policy of openness so as to remove the 'feeling of estrangement' that had developed between the Army and the people due to the long years of martial law. See Mirza Aslam Beg, '50 Years of Pakistan Army: A Journey Into Professionalism', *Muslim*, 22 and 23 August 1997.

45 For the details of the Operation Midnight Jackals, see Shaheen Sehbai, 'The day of the Night Jackals', *Dawn*, 11 September 1992 (Magazine section); Rashed Rahman, 'Operation Midnight Jackals', *Nation*, 30 September 1992 (Midweek section); Maleeha Lodhi and Zahid Hussain, 'The Night of the Jackals', *Newsline*, October 1992, pp. 32–3.

46 Maleeha Lodhi, '*Benazir Hakoomat ki bartarfi kaa Asbab*' (Urdu), *Jang*, 16 August 1991. In an interview in 1992, General Beg said that in one of his meetings with the President he obtained the copies of the letters the President had written to Benazir Bhutto and read their excerpts in the meeting of the Corps Commanders in late July. According to him, the general consensus in the meeting was that the President should take the final decision on the future of the government since he was the best judge of the situation. *Newsline*, October 1992, p. 38. In another interview, General Beg said that he was perturbed by the corruption charges against the Benazir government which he discussed with the President and that he obtained the copies of the letters the President had written to Benazir Bhutto on corruption and other issues. See *Jang* (Lahore), 16 September 1992. See also Roedad Khan, *Pakistan – A Dream Gone Sour* (Karachi: Oxford University Press, 1997), p. 109.

47 While dismissing the Benazir government, Ishaq Khan cited several reasons including corruption and nepotism; wilful undermining the constitutional arrangements and usurpation of the authority of the provinces resulting in deadlock and confrontation; failure to maintain law and order in Sindh; violation of various provisions of the constitution; and a failure of the National Assembly to discharge 'substantive legislative functions' mainly because of internal discord, dissension, corrupt practices, and the buying of political loyalties by offering material inducements. See for the text: *Address to Nation and Dissolution Order* (Islamabad: Directorate of Films and Publications, Ministry of Information & Broadcasting, Government of Pakistan, 6 August 1990). An appeal filed against the dissolution order was rejected both by the Punjab High Court and the Supreme Court.

48 *Dawn*, 16 August 1990.

49 The then ISI Chief, Major General Asad Durani, gave a list of the political leaders and journalists who received funds during the 1990 general election in an affidavit submitted to the National Assembly in June 1996. The list included several prominent political leaders including Nawaz Sharif (Rs. 3.5 million); Ghulam Mustafa Jatoi, the then caretaker Prime Minister (Rs. 5 million); Junejo (Rs. 2.5 million); Mir Afzal Khan (Rs. 10 million); *Jamaat-i-Islami* (Rs. 5 million); Jam Sadiq Ali (Rs. 5 million); the Pir Pagara (Rs. 2 million). For other names, see *Herald*, July 1996, p. 15. A statement containing these names was submitted to the Supreme Court in November 1997, see *Dawn*, 7 November 1997. In a statement before the Supreme Court in February 1997, General Beg maintained that it was a practice with the ISI to support certain candidates during the elections under the directions of the President, and, that during the 1990 elections the ISI did make funds available to the IJI leaders. *Muslim*, 25 February 1997. In another statement before the Supreme Court, General Beg maintained that the ISI distributed Rs. 60 million to the political parties while Rs. 80 million were used as special fund. *Pakistan Times*, 17 June 1997; *Pakistan Link* (Los Angeles), 4 July 1997. In a statement in 1993, General Beg hinted at some kind of rigging in the 1990 elections when he remarked that the winners and the losers did not know about 'the angels who had played the trick and disappeared'. *Nation*, 9 February 1993.

50 For details of the election results, see *Report on the General Elections, 1990*, two volumes (Islamabad: Election Commission of Pakistan, 1991), see vol. 2, pp. 101–39, 289, 381, 457, 523; see also *Facts and Figures Relating to the General Elections, 1990* (Islamabad: Election Commission of Pakistan, n.d.).

51 For the PDA critique of the 1990 general elections, see *How An Election was Stolen: PDA White Paper on Elections 1990* (Islamabad: PDA, 1991). The IJI rejected these charges. At the time of the 1990 elections, the PDA included the PPP, *Tehrik-i-Istiqlal*, PML-Qasim Group, and TNFJ.

52 For a summary of General Beg's speeches, see *Pakistan Horizon* (Vol. 44, No. 1, January 1991), pp. 146–53; see also his article entitled 'It is Now Iran's Turn', *Muslim*, 8 January 1996.

53 On transfer from the ISI in May 1989, Hameed Gul was appointed the Corps Commander, Multan. In December 1991, he was transferred as chief of the Heavy Mechanical Complex, Taxila, a position considered off the Army's mainstream. Unhappy at the transfer, Gul decided to go on leave. Nawaz Sharif wanted to keep him in some mainstream position. The Army Chief did not agree and recommended his retirement in January 1992 which the Sharif government accepted rather reluctantly.

54 The Army's security operation in Sindh lasted from 28 May 1992 to 30 November 1994. The federal government contributed Rs. 457.39 million and the Sindh government paid Rs. 272.88 million towards the cost of army deployment during this period.

55 See Nawaz Sharif's conversation with the press: *Nation*, 22 August 1995; *Pakistan*, 22 August 1995.

56 A widely circulated story and believed to be true in political circles was that as strains surfaced in civil–military relations, Nawaz Sharif, in his characteristic style of offering expensive gifts to build goodwill, was said to have offered an expensive luxury car to the Army Chief, which he flatly refused.

57 Ahmed Rashid, 'Death of a Pragmatist', *Herald*, January 1993, pp. 55–56a.

58 The PPP issued a report detailing how the leading personalities of the ruling IJI built their industrial and financial empires. See *The Plunder of Pakistan* (Lahore: Central Information Bureau, PPP, 1991).

59 The widow of General Janjua claimed that her husband was poisoned by the people who viewed him as a threat to their power. Later, she accused two close associates of Nawaz Sharif (Chaudhry Nisar Ali, Special Assistant and Brig. Imtiaz Ahmad, chief of the IB) of the possible involvement in the plot to poison him. A subsequent inquiry by the government showed that the general died of a natural cause.

60 Some reports indicated that Nawaz Sharif's other choice was Lt.-General Rahamdil Bhatti.

61 General Kaker superseded four Lt.-Generals: Rahamdil Bhatti, Mohammad Ashraf, Farukh Khan, and Arif Bangash.

62 See the statements of Nawaz Sharif: *Frontier Post*, 26 January 1993; *Dawn*, 10 February 1993.

63 See, Roedad Khan, *op. cit.*, pp. 121–2.

64 Aamer Ahmed Khan, 'Walking the Tightrope', *Herald*, June 1993, pp. 37–8; see the report of the News Intelligence Unit by Kamran Khan: *News*, 23 April 1993. In an address to the troops, General Abdul Waheed said that the Army had maintained 'absolute neutrality' in the political crisis which had been dealt with within the confines of the constitution. That the sole concern of the Army during this period was to safeguard the integrity and security from 'undue' pressures. *Nation*, 26 April 1993.

65 For the text of the judgement, see *PLD, 1993, Supreme Court*, vol. XLV, pp. 473–894 (see p. 570).

66 On 30 May (one day after the dissolution of the Punjab Assembly), NWFP Assembly was also dissolved by the Governor on the recommendation of the Chief Minister. The opposition approached the Peshawar High Court for revocation of the dissolution order. The High Court held the dissolution in order. See *Nation*, 31 May 1993; *News*, 15 July 1993.

67 For the text of the resolution, see *Nation*, and *News*, 30 June 1993.

68 See the interview of Mian Muhammad Azhar: *Weekly Zindigi* (Lahore), 27 January–2 February 1995, pp. 19–24.

69 See, Altaf Hassan Qureshi, *'Faislay ki Ghareehi'* (Urdu), *Nawa-i-Waqt*, 15 July 1993.

70 For an informed discussion of the political developments during January–July 1993, see Maleeha Lodhi, 'Why Nawaz Sharif Fell', *News*, 19 April 1993; Najam Sethi, '101 Days that Shook Pakistan', *The Friday Times*, 22–28 April 1993, p. 3; See by the same author, 'Countdown to D-Day', *ibid.*, 15–21 July 1993, pp. 6–7; Jagnu Mohsin, 'Five Days that Shook Islamabad', *ibid.*, 22–28 July 1993, p. 5; Hasan Askari Rizvi, 'The Year of Dramatic Changes', *Nation*, 31 December 1993.

71 They were Lt.-General Raja Muhammad Saroop Khan (Punjab), Lt.-General Imranullah Khan (Balochistan), and Major General Khurshid Ali Khan (NWFP).

72 Nawaz Sharif said in a public meeting, 'I confirm Pakistan possesses [an] atomic bomb.' *Nation*, 24 August 1994.

73 *News*, 13 September 1994; for the text of the *Washington Post* story, see *Friday Times*, 22–28 September 1994.

74 *Nation*, 14 September 1994; *Daily Pakistan*, 14 September 1994; *News*, 15 September 1994.

75 The problem started during Nawaz Sharif's tenure (1990–3) when a number of cooperatives collapsed, most of which were linked with, or had given huge loans to, politically powerful people. The Benazir government provided some relief to the investors of small amounts. A large number of people, mostly belonging to the middle and lower middle strata of society lost their investment. The cooperatives had enticed these people by offering interest at rates higher than what the regular banks offered. For the background of the scandal, see the cover story entitled 'The Great Loan Scandal', *Newsline*, September 1991, pp. 20–37; see special report on the same subject by Nasir Malick, Tariq Hussain and Zafar Abbas in *Herald*, September 1991, 37–48.

76 *Pakistan Times*, 27 and 28 June 1996.

77 In July 1995, the government initiated a dialogue with the MQM which broke down after a couple of sessions.

78 See, for details, Zahid Hussain, 'The Government vs the Judiciary', *Newsline*, January 1996, pp. 16–27. In a resolution the Law Reforms Committee of Pakistan Bar Council expressed concern on the harassment of the Chief Justice and termed it 'a brazen attack on the independence of judiciary'. *Muslim*, 7 January 1996.

79 For the text of the short order of the Chief Justice on the appointment of judges, see: *Muslim*, 21 March 1996; *Dawn*, 21 March 1996; Nasim Hasan Shah, 'Judiciary in Pakistan: A Quest for Independence', in Craig Baxter and Charles Kennedy (eds.), *Pakistan: 1997* (Boulder: Westview, 1998), pp. 61–78.

80 Other judgments which embarrassed the government were: acquittal of Sheikh Rashid (an opposition leader convicted by a lower court for illegal possession of a kalashnikov. He was released in March 1996 after spending about 19 months in prison); restoration of local bodies in the Punjab (June); and restoration of the Wattoo government in the Punjab. (November).

81 *Muslim*, 15 July 1996.

82 Within a week of the murder of Murtaza Bhutto, wall chalking in Lahore accused Leghari of involvement in the incident. The local administration removed the wall chalking quickly but the damage was done. Benazir Bhutto and some of her cabinet members made statements playing up the conspiracy theme. On 27 September, Leghari expressed concern at such statements and advised them to 'refrain from making statements and insinuations that cast doubts on the integrity of important institutions'. *Dawn*, 28 September 1996. The widow of Murtaza Bhutto and some opposition leaders talked of the involvement of Asif Ali Zardari and Syed Abdullah Shah (Chief Minister of Sindh) in the murder. A judicial tribunal headed by Justice Nasir Aslam Zahid of the Supreme Court investigated the murder. Its report submitted in June 1997 described the murder as 'an extra-judicial act by the police, acting on the orders of some higher authority', but it did not hold any particular individual or institution responsible for the incident. For the text of the report, see *Dawn*, 11 June 1997. In July 1997, Asif Ali Zardari and 18

others were formally indicted for involvement in the murder of Murtaza Bhutto. They denied the charges.

83 Leghari made this charge in his speech on the dismissal of the Benazir government. For Benazir Bhutto's complaint about the role of intelligence agencies against her government, see her statement: *Muslim*, 30 June 1997; see also *Herald*, October 1996, p. 48. See the statement of the former IB Chief, Masood Sharif, in the Supreme Court: *Dawn*, 5 February 1997. He informed the Supreme Court in a subsequent statement that 12 state agencies were involved in phone tapping and monitoring of the phone calls of the officials and citizens. The government agencies were: IB; ISI; MI; Anti-Narcotics Task Force; Special Branch of the Punjab Police; Sindh Police; Frontier Police; Inspector General Frontier Corps, Balochistan; Director General Rangers, Karachi; and all telephone exchanges. See *Muslim*, 10 October 1997.

The Supreme Court obtained from the IB 5,727 audio-cassettes of phone conversations of important leaders and officials recorded secretly during 1995–6. Ninety people were targeted for phone tapping and eavesdropping which included, among others, Nawaz Sharif, Chief Justice Sajjad Ali Shah, Chairman Senate Wasim Sajjad, Speaker and Deputy Speaker of the National Assembly Syed Yousaf Raza Gilani and Zafar Ali Shah respectively, and a large number of other political leaders including Ghulam Mustafa Jatoi, Chaudhry Shujaat Hussain, Gohar Ayub and Aslam Khattak. *Dawn*, 6 November 1997.

84 For Nawaz Sharif's demand for the dismissal of the government, see *Muslim*, 12 and 25 July 1996.

85 In June, the Chief Minister of the Punjab, Arif Nakai, was summoned to the Army headquarters in Rawalpindi for discussion on the law and order situation in the province with the Army Chief. See, *Pakistan Times*, 7 June 1996.

86 Ahmed Rashid, 'The Final Countdown', *Herald*, September 1996, pp. 88–90.

87 See *Nation*, 6 November 1996; *New York Times*, 5 November 1996; *Independent*, 6 November 1996. On 29 January 1997, the Supreme Court in a six to one judgement upheld the removal of the Benazir government, maintaining that the President had submitted substantial evidence to the court in support of the dismissal order.

88 *Muslim*, 19 November 1996.

89 See the editorials 'Infusion of the Military' in *Muslim*, 11 December 1996, and 'Militarizing Bureaucracy' in *ibid.*, 18 December 1996. See a news item on this matter in *Dawn*, 11 and 16 December 1996.

90 See *Dawn*, 1 February 1997; *Pakistan Link* (Los Angeles), 21 March 1997.

91 See Ahmed Rashid's report entitled 'Power Grab', *Far Eastern Economic Review*, 23 January 1997, p. 20; see also by the same writer, 'Council of Contention,' *Herald*, January 1997, pp. 49–50; Zahid Hussain, 'Democracy on a String,' *Newsline*, January 1997, pp. 27–32.

92 For the functions and composition of the CDNS, see *Dawn*, 7 January 1997.

93 For an evaluation of the accountability process adopted by the Nawaz government, see Zafar Abbas, 'Improper Channels', *Herald*, July 1997, pp. 43–5; Aamar Ahmed Khan, 'Moving the Goalpost', *ibid.*, pp. 46–8; see the cover story entitled 'Ehtesab or Farce?' by Zahid Hussain, Kamal Siddiqi, Amir Zia and I.A. Rehman. *Newsline*, June 1997, pp. 19–31.

94 See, Ihtshamul Haq, 'Factors behind the Change', *Dawn*, 3 April 1997; Ahmed Rashid, 'Clipped Wings', *Far Eastern Economic Review*, 10 April 1997, p. 18.

95 *Dawn*, 3 and 20 May 1997; *Muslim*, 1 July 1997.

96 See the reports on meetings of General Jehangir Karamat with Farooq Leghari and Nawaz Sharif: *Muslim*, 24 and 30 April 1997; see also the first page comments entitled 'Brass Baiting, Bashing?' by S.A.I. Tirmizi in *Muslim*, 29 April 1997.
97 *Muslim*, 30 October 1997. Some of Nawaz Sharif's colleagues also made derogatory remarks about the orders of the Supreme Court.
98 Five judges of the Supreme Court addressed a letter to the President taking exception to the conduct of the Chief Justice. They were Saeed-uz-Zaman Siddiqui, Nasir Aslam Zahid, Irshad Hassan Khan, Munawar Ahmad Mirza, and Fazal Ellahi Khan. For the text of the letter, see *Herald*, November 1997, pp. 37–8.
99 For the government's efforts to split the Supreme Court, see, Zafar Abbas, 'How the Judiciary was Won', *Herald*, December 1997, pp. 33–5. For the government's involvement in the mob attack on the Supreme Court, see Idrees Bakhtiar, 'The End of Civility', *ibid.*, pp. 42–42a; Zahid Hussain, 'Winner Takes All', *Newsline*, December 1997, pp. 22–7; *Muslim*, 29 and 30 November 1997; see also Zahid Hussain, 'A Year of Living Dangerously', *Newsline*, March 1998, pp. 19–24; see also Mohammad Shan Gul, 'Who is Right and Who is Wrong?' *The Friday Times*, 12–18 December 1997.
100 The Army Chief forwarded the letter of the Chief Justice to Defence Ministry for necessary action without taking any position. This showed that the Army Chief did not want to be involved in the controversy either by endorsing the demand of the Chief Justice or by sending the troops as proposed by the Chief Justice.
101 The President sent the Chief Justice's letter to the Prime Minister, condemning the attack on the Supreme Court by the Prime Minister's supporters and endorsing the Chief Justice's demand for deployment of the Army for the security of the Supreme Court. The government released to the press the letter of the President and the Prime Minister's response which amply manifested the deep cleavage that had developed between them. For the text of these letters, see *Dawn*, 30 November 1997. The text of the Chief Justice's letter was withheld by the government. In May 1998, the Chief Justice (now retired) released the text of his letter. See *Nation*, 16 May 1998.
102 The Lahore High Court restored the nomination papers of the government's candidate who was later elected President with an overwhelming majority.
103 General Jehangir Karamat said that 'Pakistan currently faces a threat from within and not from outside', and that stringent measures should be taken to counter the threat to the national economy. *Dawn*, 5 May 1998. For a couple of other statements, see *Pakistan Times*, 28 July 1998, *Dawn*, 23 September 1998. For reports on the discussion of economic and political problems during the meetings between the Army Chief and the Prime Minister, see *Muslim*, 12 July 1998 and *Dawn*, 4 October 1998.
104 *Muslim*, 6 October 1998; *Wall Street Journal*, 7 October 1998; Ejaz Haider, 'Cautiously with the NSC', *The Friday Times*, 9–15 October 1998.
105 See, the Pakistan Armed Forces (Acting in Aid of the Civil Powers) Ordinance, 1998. *Dawn*, 21 November 1998.
106 About 35,000 in-service JCOs and Officers were inducted into WAPDA in December 1998. The posts of Chairman and Vice Chairman were given to a Lt.-General and a Major-General respectively. Eight Brigadiers took over WAPDA's eight transmission companies. Army personnel were given all sort of assignments, i.e. controlling electricity theft and transmission losses, checking of electricity meters at consumers' premises, distribution of bills and dealing with public complaints. They could register criminal cases for power theft and related

irregularities. The Army was also assigned the management role in Karachi Water and Sewerage Board, and National Data Base Organization. They were also given key positions in several other civilian organizations including the police and civilian intelligence agencies, Karachi Electricity Supply Company, and Cholistan Development Authority.

Chapter 11: The Changing Parameters

1 S.E. Finer, 'The Military and Politics in the Third World', in W. Scott Thompson (ed.), *The Third World: Premises of U.S. Policy* (San Francisco: Institute of Contemporary Studies, 1978), p. 84.

2 In the case of the lowest and lower middle level jobs (Service Grades 1 to 15), the government has periodically increased quota for ex-servicemen, see *Muslim*, 19 March 1984.

3 For information on some such cases, see Abdullah, 'Marshalling of the Civil Service', *Pulse* (Islamabad), 2 April 1993, pp. 6–7; see also the news item in *Jang*, 3 September 1991.

4 The University of Balochistan was headed by a Brigadier in the 1980s. A Major General served as Vice Chancellor of Peshawar University for a brief period in 1993. A Lt.-General worked as Vice Chancellor of the Punjab University in 1993–7. Another Lt.-General was appointed Vice Chancellor of Punjab University in September 1999, despite strong protest by the faculty.

5 *Muslim*, 1 July 1997; *Dawn*, 20 May 1997.

6 See the statement of the Interior Minister in the National Assembly: *Dawn*, 27 December 1998.

7 Fazal Muqeem Khan, *The Story of the Pakistan Army* (Karachi: Oxford University Press, 1963), pp. 232–3.

8 See Ayaz Ahmed Khan, 'Decorating the Military', *Nation*, 2 June 1993. As late as 1992, the Punjab government admitted that some land was being given under the gallantry scheme. In Khanawal district alone, 19,342 *kanal* land was allotted to 150 retired and in-service army personnel. *Frontier Post* (Lahore), 1 June 1992.

9 The following officers imported duty-free luxury cars during 1977–97. The Army – Generals: Mohammad Shariff, Mohammad Iqbal Khan, Mohammad Musa, Tikka Khan, Zia-ul-Haq, Rahimuddin Khan, Sawar Khan, Akhtar Abdul Rahman, K.M. Arif, Mirza Aslam Beg, widow of Asif Nawaz Janjua, Abdul Waheed Kaker, and Jehangir Karamat. Lt.-Generals: Fazle Haq, Ghulam Jilani Khan, S.M. Abbasi, Gul Hassan Khan, Jahandad Khan, Abdul Hamid Khan, K.K. Afridi, Muhammad Iqbal, Imranullah Khan, and Raja Saroop Khan. Major Generals: Khurshid Ali Khan, and Abdur Rahman Khan (President Azad Kashmir). Brigadiers: Amir Gulistan Janjua, and Sardar A. Rahim Durani. The Navy – Admirals: Karamat Rahman Niazi, Mohammad Sharif, Tariq Kamal Khan, Iftikhar Ahmed Sirohi, Yastural Haq Malik, Saeed Mohammad Khan, and Mansoorul Haq. Vice Admirals: A.R. Khan, H.M.S. Choudri, and Muzaffar Hassan. Air Force – Air Chief Marshals: Jamal Ahmed Khan, Hakimullah, Farooq Feroze Khan, and Muhammad Abbas Khattak. Air Marshals: Nur Khan and Rahim Khan. They invariably imported different models of Mercedes Benz; custom duty and other taxes on such cars at the 1997 rates ranged from six to ten million Rupees. In the post-martial law period, some civilians also imported duty-free luxury cars. In September 1997, the National Assembly revoked this facility.

10 M.A. Niazi, 'COAS as CEO: Pakistan's Military-Industrial Complex', *Nation*, 22 June 1991.

11 Fazal Muqeem Khan, *op. cit.*, pp. 232–6.

12 *Ibid.*, p. 235; Raymond A. Moore, 'Military Nation Building in Pakistan and India', *World Affairs* (Vol. 132, No. 3, December 1969), pp. 219–34.

13 See the statements of the Director Finance and the Secretary of the *Fauji* Foundation: *Dawn*, 1 May 1997.

14 The fully owned projects include three sugar mills at Tando Muhammad Khan, Khoshki, and Sangla Hill; Experimental and Seed Multiplication Farm, Nukerji; *Fauji* Cereals, Rawalpindi; Corn Complex, Jehangira; Polypropylene Products, Hub Chowki; and *Fauji* Gas, Rawalpindi. The shareholding projects include *Fauji* Fertilizer; Oil Terminal and Distribution Company; Mari Gas Company; and Lifeline Company dealing with liquefied petroleum gas. Two projects were closed down: *Fauji* Metals and Fauji Autos. Another project, *Fauji* Electric Power Company was dropped.

15 The joint ventures include a cement project at Fateh Jang, near Taxila, initiated in 1993 in collaboration with a Danish company; a power generation project at Kabirwala in cooperation with an American firm; and a Di-ammonia Phosphate (DAP) and Urea fertilizer plant (FCC-Jordan Fertilizer Company) at Port Qasim as a joint venture with a Jordanian company.

16 *Fauji* Foundation advertisements: *Nation*, 27 December 1994, and *Defence Journal* (Vol. 20, Nos. 5–6, July 1994), p. 12; and *Dawn*, 1 May 1997.

17 These data have been collected from various advertisements put out by the Army Welfare Trust in newspapers. See advertisements in *Jang*, 29 June 1991; *Nation*, 14 April 1992 and 1 May 1994; *Dawn*, 31 October 1996, 27 July 1997 and 13 July 1998 (Special Supplement). Two housing schemes were launched in Lahore and Peshawar. Commercial market projects were launched in Rawalpindi and Faisalabad.

18 See the interview of the Managing Director of the *Shaheen* Foundation: *Defence Journal* (Vol. 2, No. 2, February 1998), pp. 12–17.

19 The *Shaheen* Foundation had signed an agreement with a Canadian firm in May 1996, but that firm withdrew later on. In 1998, it began negotiations with three foreign companies.

20 *Dawn*, 24 January 1997.

21 See the NUST advertisement in the special supplement on educational institutions in *Dawn*, 30 December 1998.

22 See the admission advertisements of the NUST: *Nawa-i-Waqt*, 14 April 1993; *Jang*, 28 September 1994, *Dawn*, 5 April 1998; see also the press statement of the Rector of the University: *Nation*, 27 June 1991.

23 For details, see Zahid Hussain and Amir Mir, 'Army to the Rescue', *Newsline*, May 1998, pp. 18–23; and Sardar F.S. Lodi, 'Army's New Role', *Dawn*, 1 May 1998.

24 *Dawn*, 23, 24 December 1998; *Pakistan Times*, 25 December 1998.

25 The government and the Army do not release data on the ethnic composition of the armed forces. The author has arrived at these figures after discussing the issue with a good number of Pakistani political analysts and those who have a good understanding of the Army.

26 Talat Aslam, 'The Changing Face of the Army', *Herald*, July 1989, pp. 64–73.

27 Cited from Henry F. Goodnow, *The Civil Service of Pakistan* (New Haven: Yale University Press, 1964), p. 107; Hasan-Askari Rizvi, *The Military and Politics in Pakistan* (Lahore: Progressive Publishers, 1986), pp. 135–45.

28 Asaf Hussain, 'Ethnicity, National Identity and Praetorianism: The Case of Pakistan', *Asian Survey* (Vol. 16, No. 10, October 1976), pp. 918–30.

29 See Samina Ahmed, 'Centralization, Authoritarianism, and the Mismanagement of Ethnic Relations in Pakistan', in Michael E. Brown and Sumit Ganguly (eds), *Government Policies and Ethnic Relations in Asia and the Pacific* (Cambridge, Mass: The MIT Press, 1997), pp. 83–127.

30 For a discussion of the role of the Army as an employer and how it has contributed to improving the material conditions of the people and the areas, see Clive Dewey, 'The Rural Roots of Pakistani Militarism', in D.A. Low (ed.), *The Political Inheritance of Pakistan* (New York: St. Martin's Press, 1991), pp. 255–83.

31 See *Nawa-i-Waqt*, 25 February 1984; *Dawn*, 1 April 1984; *Muslim*, 25 April 1984.

32 *Jang*, 22 March 1991.

33 See the official statement in the National Assembly: *Dawn*, 2 January 1999.

34 Stephen P. Cohen, *The Pakistan Army* (Berkeley: University of California Press, 1984), pp. 55–75.

35 For a discussion of continuity and change in the Army, see Ayaz Amir, 'The Khaki Clan', *Herald*, February 1986, pp. 40–2; A.R. Siddiqi, *The Military in Pakistan: Image and Reality* (Lahore: Vanguard, 1996), pp. 64–5.

36 The press periodically reports on altercations between young officers and the police. Such incidents are also reported in letters to the editor, see, for example. a letter, entitled 'Upstarts', in *Nation*, 22 July 1991. In Peshawar, the entire staff of a local girls' college were taken hostage by a group of young officers after the daughter of the Corps Commander was reprimanded by the Principal for cheating in an examination. *Newsline*, June 1996, p. 83.

37 Khalid Rauf Khan, 'Officers but Gentlemen?', *Nation* (Friday Review), 7 May 1993.

38 Muhammad Yahya Effendi, 'Pakistan Army Officer Corps: Values in Transition or the Erosion of a Value System?', *Pakistan Army Journal* (Vol. 34, No. 1, March 1993), pp. 45–58.

39 M. Attiqur Rahman, *Our Defence Cause* (London: White Lion Publishers, 1976), p. 258.

40 Gerald A. Heeger, 'Politics in the Post-military State: Some Reflections on the Pakistani Experience', *World Politics* (Vol. 29, No. 2, January 1977), pp. 242–62.

41 *Star* (Karachi), 1 October 1987. See a critical statement by the ANP leader, Wali Khan, on the activities of generals: *Frontier Post*, 30 June 1991; see two letters to the editor entitled 'Perks for Generals', in *Dawn*, 7 April 1996, and 27 April 1996.

42 The three Air Force chiefs were Air Marshal Asghar Khan (1957–65), Air Chief Marshal Zulfikar Ali Khan (1974–8), and Air Chief Marshal Jamal Ahmed Khan (1985–8). They sent a draft legislation for controlling kickbacks to the Prime Minister. See *Dawn*, 10 August 1997.

43 See the statement of the Defence Minister: *Nation*, 15 November 1995; *Frontier Post*, 15 November 1995; *Dawn*, 12 November 1995. For details of the coup plan and excerpts from the statement that was to be issued after the plotters had assumed power, see, Zafar Abbas, 'Day of Reckoning', *Herald*, January 1996, pp. 89–95; *New York Times*, 12 April 1996. The two officers who led the group had been passed over for promotion.

44 *Dawn*, 31 October 1996. In November 1997, the Army's Court of Appeal reduced the sentence of Brigadier Billah from 14 to 7 years.
45 Talat Masood, 'Lessons for the Military', *News*, 19 October 1995.
46 A.R. Siddiqi, 'Army: Chickens are Coming Home to Roost', *Nation*, 23 October 1995.

Bibliography

The bibliography includes the books and articles focusing directly on the Pakistan mlitary: its heritage, the changing role and character over time, and civil–military relations. Consult the endnotes for theoretical literature on civil–military relations, official publications/public documents, politics and society, security and foreign policy. The articles published in newspapers and news magazines are also not included in the bibliography.

The Military Heritage

Books

Alavi, Seema, *The Sepoys and the Company: Tradition and Transition in Northern India 1770–1830*. Delhi: Oxford University Press, 1995.

Ali, Chaudhri Muhammad, *The Emergence of Pakistan*. New York: Columbia University Press, 1967.

Ali, Imran, *The Punjab Under Imperialism 1885–1947*. Princeton: Princeton University Press, 1988.

Beaumont, Roger, *Sword of the Raj: The British Army in India, 1747–1947*. New York: The Bobbs-Merrill Co., 1977.

Callahan, Raymond A., *The East India Company and Army Reforms, 1783–1798*. Cambridge, Mass: Harvard University Press, 1972.

Connell, John, *Auchinleck*. London: Cassell, 1959.

Das, S.T., *Indian Military: Its History and Development*. New Delhi: Sagar, 1969.

Farewell, Byron, *Armies of the Raj: From the Mutiny to Independence, 1858–1947*. New York: W.W. Norton, 1989.

Heathcote, T.A., *The Indian Army: The Garrison of British Imperial India, 1822–1922*. New York: Hippocrene Books, 1974.

MacMunn, George F., *The Armies of India*. London: Adam & Charles Black, 1911.

——, *The Martial Races of India*. London: Sampson Low, Morston, 1933.

Magnus, Philip, *Kitchener: Portrait of an Imperialist*. London: John Murray, 1958.

Menezes, S.L., *Fidelity and Honour: The Indian Army from the Seventeenth to Twenty-first Century*. New Delhi: Viking, 1993.

Omissi, David, *The Sepoy and the Raj: The Indian Army, 1860–1940*. London: Macmillan, 1994.

Pasha, Mustafa Kamal, *Colonial Political Economy: Recruitment and Under-development in the Punjab*. forthcoming.

Peers, Douglas M., *Between Mars and Mammon: Colonial Armies and the Garrison State in India, 1819–1835*. London: I.B. Tauris, 1995.

Robert, Andrew, *Eminent Churchillians*. London: Weidenfeld & Nicolson, 1994.

Rosen, Stephen P., *Societies and Military Power: India and its Armies*. Ithaca: Cornell University Press, 1996.

Saxena, K.M.L., *The Military System of India, 1850–1900*. New Delhi: Sterling, 1974.

Singh, Madan Paul, *Indian Army under the East India Company*. New Delhi: Sterling Publishers, 1976.

Sinha, N.C. and Khera, P.N., *India's War Economy: Supply, Industry and Finance* (Official history of the Indian Armed Forces in the Second World War). New Delhi: Orient Longmans, 1962

Venkateswaran, A.L., *Defence Organisation in India*. New Delhi: Publication Division, Ministry of Information and Broadcasting, Government of India, 1967.

Articles

Ahmad, Riaz, 'Quaid-i-Azam Jinnah and Indianisation of Officer Ranks of Army', *Pakistan Army Journal* (Vol. 35, No. 3, Autumn 1994), pp. 3–21.

Cohen, Stephen P., 'Issue, Role and Personality: The Kitchener–Curzon Dispute', *Comparative Studies in Society and History* (Vol. X, No. 3, April 1968), pp. 337–55.

——, 'Subhas Chandra Bose and the Indian National Army', *Pacific Affairs* (Vol. 36, No. 4, Winter 1963–4), pp. 411–29.

Dewey, Clive, 'Some Consequences of Military Expenditure in British India: The Case of the Upper Sind Sagar Doab, 1849–1947', in Dewey, Clive (ed.), *Arrested Development in India: The Historical Dimension*. New Delhi: Manohar, 1988, pp. 93–169.

Gutteridge, W., 'The Indianisation of the Indian Army, 1918–1945', *Race* (Vol. IV, No. 2, May 1963), pp. 39–48.

Jacob, Sir Claud W., 'The Indian Army and its Future', *English Review* (February 1931), pp. 169–74.

Jahanzeb (Major General), 'Role of Armed Forces in the Independence of the Subcontinent', *Defence Journal* (Vol. 10, No. 9, September 1984), pp. 20–6.

Jalal, Ayesha, 'India's Partition and the Defence of Pakistan: An Historical Perspective', *Journal of Imperial and Commonwealth History* (Vol. XV, No. 3, May 1987), pp. 289–310.

Jefrey, Robin, 'The Punjab Boundary Force and the Problem of Order, August 1947', *Modern Asian Studies* (Vol. 8, No. 4, October 1974), pp. 491–520.

Sundaram, Chandar S., 'Preventing Idealness: The Maharaja of Cooch Behar's Proposal for Officer Commission in the British Army for the Sons of Indian Princes and Gentlemen, 1897–1898', *South Asia* (Vol. XVIII, No. 1, June 1995), pp. 115–30.

Wainwright, Mary, 'Keeping Peace in India, 1946–47: The Role of Lt.-General Sir Francis Tuker in Eastern Command', in Philips, C.H. & Wainwright, Mary D. (eds), *The Partition of India: Policies and Perspectives, 1935–47*. London: George Allen & Unwin, 1970.

The Pakistan Military

Books

Ahmad, Mohammad (Colonel), *My Chief*. Lahore: Longmans, 1960.

Amin, Mohammed, et al., *Defenders of Pakistan*. Lahore: Ferozsons, 1988.

Arif, Khalid Mahmud (General), *Working with Zia: Pakistan's Power Politics 1977–1988*. Karachi: Oxford University Press, 1995.

Asghar Khan, Mohammad (Air Marshal), *Generals in Politics: Pakistan: 1958–1982*. New Delhi: Vikas Publishing House, 1983.

Ayub Khan, Mohammad (Field Marshal), *Friends Not Masters: A Political Biography*. London: Oxford University Press, 1967.

Chishti, Faiz Ali (Lt.-General), *Betrayals of Another Kind: Islam, Democracy and the Army in Pakistan*. London: Asia Publishing House, 1989.

Cloughley, Brian, *A History of the Pakistan Army: Wars and Insurrections* (Karachi: Oxford University Press, 1999).

Cohen, Stephen P., *The Pakistan Army*. New Delhi: Oxford University Press, 1998. (First edition, 1984, by University of California Press, Berkeley.)

——, *The Indian Army*. Delhi: Oxford University Press, 1990. (1st edition, 1971, by University of California Press, Berkeley.)

Gauhar, Altaf, *Ayub Khan: Pakistan's First Military Ruler*. Lahore: Sang-e-Meel, 1994.

Jalal, Ayesha, *The State of Martial Rule: The Origins of Pakistan's Political Economy of Defence*. Cambridge: Cambridge University Press, 1990.

Gill, Azam, *Army Reforms*. Lahore: People's Publishing House, 1979.

Hamid, S. Shahid (Major General), *Early Years of Pakistan*. Lahore: Ferozsons, 1993.

——, *Autobiography of a General*. Lahore: Ferozsons, 1988.

——, *Courage is a Weapon*. Karachi: Sani Communications, 1980.

Haq, Inam-ul (Air Commodore), *Islamic Motivation and National Defence*. Lahore: Vanguard Books, 1991.

Haq, Noor-ul, *Making of Pakistan: The Military Perspective*. Islamabad: National Institute of Historical and Cultural Research, 1993.

Hussain, Syed Shabbir and Qureshi, M. Tariq, *Story of the Pakistan Air Force, 1947–82*. Karachi: PAF Press, 1982.

Khan, Fazal Muqeem (Major General), *The Story of the Pakistan Army*. Karachi: Oxford University Press, 1963.

——, *Pakistan's Crisis in Leadership*. Islamabad: National Book Foundation, 1973.

——, *History of the 2nd Battalion (Guides) Frontier Force Regiment, 1947–1994*. Rawalpindi: The Army Press, n.d. (1998?).

Khan, Gul Hasan, *Memoirs of Lt.-General Gul Hasan Khan*. Karachi: Oxford University Press, 1993.

Khan, Mohammad Nawaz, *The Guardians of the Frontier: The Frontier Corps*. Peshawar: Frontier Corps, 1994.

Kukreja, Veena, *Civil-Military Relations in South Asia*. New Delhi: SAGE, 1991.

——, *Military Intervention in Politics: A Case Study of Pakistan*. New Delhi: NBO Publishers, 1985.

Latif, Rahat (Major General), *...Plus Bhutto's Episode: An Autobiography*. Lahore: Jang Publishers, 1993.

Malik, Iftikhar Haider, *State and Civil Society in Pakistan*. New York: St Martin's, 1997.

Malik, S.K. (Brigadier), *The Quranic Concept of War*. Lahore: Wajidalis, 1979.

Malik, Tajammal Hussain (Major General), *The Story of My Struggle*. Lahore: Jang Publishers, 1991.

Moore, Raymond A., *Nation Building and the Pakistan Army, 1947–69*. Lahore: Aziz Publishers, 1979.

Musa, Mohammad (General), *Jawan to General*. Karachi: East & West Publishing Co., 1984.

Pataudi, Nawabzada Sher Ali Khan (Major General), *The Story of Soldiering and Politics in India and Pakistan*. Lahore: Wajidalis, 1978.

Poshni, Z. (Captain), *Zindigi Zinda Dili Ka Nam Hai* (Urdu), Karachi: the author, 1976).

Qureshi, M. I. (Major), *The First Punjab Regiment*. Aldershot: Gale & Polden, 1958.

Rahman, M. Attiqur (Lt.-General), *The Wardens of the Marches: A History of the Piffers, 1947–71*. Lahore: Wajidalis, 1980.

——, *Our Defence Cause*. London: White Lion Publishers, 1976.

——, *Leadership: Senior Commanders*. Lahore: Ferozsons, 1973.

Rizvi, Hasan-Askari, *The Military and Politics in Pakistan*. Lahore: Progressive Publishers, 1st edition: 1974, latest edition: 1986.

Rizvi, S. Haider Abbas (Brigadier), *Veteran Campaigners: A History of the Punjab Regiment, 1759–1981*. Lahore: Wajidalis, 1984.

Salik, Siddiq (Brigadier), *Witness to Surrender*. Karachi: Oxford University Press, 1979.

Shafqat, Saeed, *Civil–Military Relations in Pakistan: From Zulfikar Ali Bhutto to Benazir Bhutto*. Boulder: Westview, 1997.

Siddiqi, A.R. (Brigadier), *The Military in Pakistan: Image and Reality*. Lahore: Vanguard Books, 1996.

——, *Fauj aur Siaysat* (Urdu). Karachi: South Asian Printers & Publishers, 1984.

Tirmazi, S.A.I. (Brigadier), *Profiles of Intelligence*. Lahore: Room 30, Faletti Hotel & Fiction House, 1995.

Zaheer, Hasan, *The Times and Trial of the Rawalpindi Conspiracy, 1951: The First Coup Attempt in Pakistan*. Karachi: Oxford University Press, 1998.

Ziring, Lawrence, *The Ayub Khan Era: Politics in Pakistan, 1958–69*. Syracuse: Syracuse University Press, 1971.

Articles

Ahmed, Samina, 'The Military and Ethnic Politics', in Kennedy, Charles and Rais, Rasul (eds), *Pakistan 1995*. Boulder: Westview, 1995, pp. 103–31.

Alavi, Hamza, 'The Army and the Bureaucracy in Pakistan', *International Socialist Journal* (Vol. 3, No. 14, March–April 1966), pp. 149–88.

Bordewich, Fergus M., 'The Pakistan Army: Sword of Islam', *Asia* (New York), September-October 1982, pp. 16–23, 48–53.

Chang, D.W., 'The Military and Nation-building in Korea, Burma and Pakistan', *Asian Survey* (Vol. 9, No. 11, November 1969), pp. 818–30.

Cohen, Stephen P., 'State Building in Pakistan', in Banuazizi, A., and Weiner, Myron (eds), *The State, Relgiion and Ethnic Politics*. Lahore: Vanguard Books, 1987, pp. 299–332.

——, 'The Role of the Military in Contemporary Pakistan', in Olsen, Edward A. and Jurika, Stephen (eds), *The Armed Forces in Contemporary Asian Societies*. Boulder: Westview, 1986.

——, 'Pakistan: Army, Society and Security', *Asian Affairs: An American Review* (Vol. 10, No. 2, Summer 1983), pp. 1–26.

Dar, E.H. (Major General), 'The Pakistan Army in the Eighties', *The Army Quarterly and Defence Journal* (Vol. 114, No. 3, July 1984), pp. 287–94; and (Vol. 114, No. 4, October 1984), pp. 412–15.

Dewey, Clive, 'The Rural Roots of Pakistani Militarism', in Low, D.A. (ed.), *The Political Inheritance of Pakistan*. New York: St. Martin's, 1991.

Effendi, Muhammad Yahya, 'Pakistan Army Officer Corps: Values in Transition or the Erosion of a Value System', *Pakistan Army Journal* (Vol. 34, No. 1, March 1993), pp. 45–58.

Hashmi, Bilal, 'Dragon Seed: Military in the State', in Gardezi, H. and Rashid, J. (eds), *Pakistan: The Roots of Dictatorship: The Political Economy of Praetorian State*. London: Zed Press, 1983.

Heeger, Gerald A., 'Politics in the Post-military State: Some Reflections on the Pakistani Experience', *World Politics* (Vol. 29, No. 2, January 1977), pp. 242–62.

Husain, Noor A. (Brigadier), 'Pakistan's Growing Defence Industries', *Strategic Studies* (Vol. VII, No. 1, Autumn 1983), pp. 38–53.

Hussain, Asaf, 'Ethnicity, National Identity and Praetorianism: The Case of Pakistan', *Asian Survey* (Vol. 16, No. 10, October 1976), pp. 918–30.

Khan, Mohammad Akbar (Major General), '*Phali Jang-i-Kashmir ki Fire-bandi aur Pindi Sazish Case*, (Urdu), *Hikayat* (Lahore) (Vol. 5 No. 1, September 1972).

Looney, Robert E., 'Budgetary Dilemmas in Pakistan: Costs and Benefits of Sustained Defense Expenditures', *Asian Survey* (Vol. 34, No. 5, May 1994), pp. 417–29.

Malik, Zafar Mehmood, 'Pakistan Ordnance Factories: A Force Behind the Forces', *Asian Defence Journal* (July 1998), pp. 40–1.

Mazari, Shireen M., 'Militarism and Militarization of Pakistan', in Rupesinghe, K., and Mumtaz, Khawar (eds), *Internal Conflicts in South Asia*. London: SAGE, 1996.

Moore, Raymond A., 'The Army as a Vehicle for Social Change in Pakistan', *The Journal of Developing Areas* (Vol. 2, No. 1, October 1967), pp. 57–74.

——, 'The Use of the Army in Nation-building: The Case of Pakistan', *Asian Survey* (Vol. 9, No. 6, June 1969), pp. 447–56.

——, 'Military Nation Building in Pakistan and India', *World Affairs* (Vol. 132, No. 3, December 1969), pp. 219–34.

Parimoo, J.N., 'Night of the Generals', *The Illustrated Weekly of India*, 23 October 1988, pp. 20–3.

Richter, William L., 'Persistent Praetorianism: Pakistan's Third Military Regime', *Pacific Affairs* (Vol. 51, No. 3, Fall 1978), pp. 406–26.

Rizvi, Gowhar, 'Riding the Tiger: Institutionalizing the Military Regimes in Pakistan and Bangladesh', in Clapham, Christopher and Philip, George (eds), *The Political Dilemmas of Military Regimes*. London: Croom Helm, 1985.

Rizvi, Hasan-Askari, 'Civil–Military Relations in Contemporary Pakistan', *Survival* (Vol. 40, No. 2, Summer 1998), pp. 96–113.

——, 'Civil–Military Relations under General Beg', *Defence Journal* (Vol. 17, Nos. 6 & 7, August 1991), pp. 17–21.

——, 'The Legacy of Military Rule in Pakistan', *Survival* (Vol. 31, No. 3, May-June 1989), pp. 255–68.

——, 'Civil–Military Relations and National Stability in South Asia', *Pakistan Horizon* (Vol. XLll, No. 2, April 1989), pp. 47–78.

——, 'The Military in Pakistan: National Security and Domestic Politics', in Ziring, L. and Dickason, David (eds), *Asian Security Issues: National Systems and International Relations*. Kalamazoo: Institute of Government and Politics, Western Michigan University, 1988, pp. 85–97.

——, 'The Civilianization of Military Rule in Pakistan', *Asian Survey* (Vol. 26, No. 10, October 1986), pp. 1067–81.

——, 'Pakistan: Military and the Political Process', *Defence Journal* (Vol. 12, No. 7, July 1986), pp. 27–37.

——, 'Civilianization: A Transition from Rule to Role', *Defence Journal* (Vol. 11, No. 12, December 1985), pp. 3–8.

——, 'The Paradox of Military Rule in Pakistan', *Asian Survey* (Vol. 24, No. 5, May 1984), pp. 534–55.

——, 'Pakistan', in Katz, James E. (ed.), *Arms Production in Developing Countries*. Lexington, Mass: D.C. Heath, 1984.

Sayeed, Khalid B., 'The Role of the Military in Pakistan', in Doorn, J.V. (ed.), *Armed Forces and Society*. The Hague: Mouton, 1968, pp. 274–9.

Siddiqi, A.R. (Brigadier), 'Of Pakistan's First War and Coup', (The Rawalpindi Conspiracy including an interview with Major General Akbar Khan), *Defence Journal* (Vol. 11, Nos. 6 & 7, June–July 1985), pp. 1–32.

Sieveking, O., 'Pakistan and Her Armed Forces', *Military Review* (Vol. 43, No. 6, June 1963), pp. 91–7.

Singh, Jasjit, 'The Army in the Power Structure of Pakistan', *Strategic Analysis* (New Delhi), (Vol. 18, No. 7, October 1995), pp. 855–80.

Tahir-Kheli, Shirin, 'The Military in Contemporary Pakistan', *Armed Forces and Society* (Vol. 6, No. 4, Summer 1980), pp. 639–53.

Wilcox, Wayne A., 'The Pakistan Coup d'État of 1958', *Pacific Affairs* (Vol. 38, No. 2, Summer 1965), pp. 142–63.

Index